THE PROGRESSIVE CHURCH IN LATIN AMERICA

DATE DUE

AUG 10 1992			

KELLOGG INSTITUTE TITLES FROM
THE UNIVERSITY OF NOTRE DAME PRESS

Debt and Development in Latin America
edited by Kwan S. Kim and David F. Ruccio

Profits, Progress and Poverty:
Case Studies of International Industries in Latin America
edited by Richard Newfarmer

Development, Democracy, and the Art of Trespassing:
Essays in Honor of Albert O. Hirschman
edited by Alejandro Foxley, Michael S. McPherson, and
Guillermo O'Donnell

Development and External Debt in Latin America:
Bases for a New Consensus
edited by Richard Feinberg and Ricardo Ffrench-Davis

The Progressive Church in Latin America
edited by Scott Mainwaring and Alexander Wilde

The Moral Nation:
Humanitarianism and U.S. Foreign Policy Today
edited by Bruce Nichols and Gil Loescher

The Progressive Church in Latin America

Scott Mainwaring and
Alexander Wilde, editors

UNIVERSITY OF NOTRE DAME PRESS
NOTRE DAME, INDIANA

Library of Congress Cataloging-in-Publication Data

The Progressive church in Latin America.

Includes four papers presented at an international
conference on the New Church in Latin America, held
at the Helen Kellogg Institute for International
Studies, 1983.
1. Catholic Church—Latin America—History—20th
century. 2. Latin America—Church history—20th
century. I. Mainwaring, Scott. II. Wilde, Alexander.
BX1426.2.P697 1988   306'.6   88-40324
ISBN 0-268-01573-2

Manufactured in the United States of America

CONTENTS

PREFACE

The Helen Kellogg Institute for International Studies has included the Catholic Church in Latin America, and the social role of religion more generally, among its principal themes of research. Since beginning its activities in 1982, the Institute has regularly invited specialists as fellows to work on their individual research and also to participate in Institute seminars, workshops, and conferences. As members of the Institute, each of the editors of this volume brought an established professional interest and research experience in the subject to developing these activities. In 1983 the Institute held an international conference at Notre Dame on "The New Church in Latin America" which was organized by one of the editors and for which the rapporteur's report was written by the other. Four of the chapters of this book were written by Institute fellows, in addition to the Introduction by the editors. The other four chapters were chosen from some dozen manuscripts submitted for consideration by specialists in the United States, Europe, Australia, and Latin America.

This is a book about the progressive Church in Latin America, seen in four of its most important national cases. It is also, more implicitly, a book about how the social sciences fruitfully study the Church and its relationship to politics. Beyond the professional diversity among the authors, their research has several characteristics in common. It is, of course, analytical within the frameworks of the authors' academic disciplines. In addition, however, it is also empathetic—in the sense that it enters the world of religious ideas, motivations, and conflicts. All of the authors have substantial direct experience of what they are interpreting. They all possess a strong sense of the Church as an institution, and of the ways that different groups operate within it. Their personal sympathies with the subject vary, but all the authors take the religious dimension of social life seriously. They do not, for example, reduce the Church's social mission to politics but aim to understand it first in religious terms. As scholars they believe that such empathy is not only compatible with critical judgments but indeed necessary to a full interpretation of the progressive Church and its development.

A third common characteristic of the analyses in this book is their historical approach. What that means for the authors is that the progressive Church in Latin America must be understood in its historical context. It is legitimate, of course, to interpret this Church in terms of foundational religious beliefs and doctrines, orthodox or not, that are implicitly timeless. That has been the character of much of the discussion of liberation theology—particularly by its critics. However, by itself such an approach can easily overlook the dynamic character of the progressive Church—its interaction with particular social and political settings, and the changes it experiences from that interaction over time. It is thus important for scholars to analyze how the choices of believing Catholics have been influenced, even structured, by their societies and—given the emphasis in the progressive Church on politics—by their polities at different points in time. The contributors to this volume therefore have a perspective of the Church as a living reality, made up of human beings interpreting their faith in response to their own social and political experiences. We hope that this focus on the Church in a dynamic human context will contribute to a fuller understanding of the progressive Church in Latin America as it continues its historical journey.

Ernest Bartell, C. S. C.
Executive Director
Helen Kellogg Institute
    for International Studies

Acknowledgments

The Kellogg Institute was a stimulating and supportive environment in which to work on this book—not least for the countless discussions it afforded us over the four years we were colleagues there together. The Institute's intellectual agenda, particularly its work around the themes of democratization and the popular sectors, certainly enriched our work on the Church. The Executive Director of the Institute, Ernest Bartell, C. S. C., was vitally interested throughout and provided funds for the translations. We are also grateful to our other colleagues in Kellogg's early years, Guillermo O'Donnell and Alejandro Foxley, for their leadership and encouragement.

The authors of the various chapters were singularly responsive and responsible, greatly aiding our efforts to produce what we hope is a cohesive and distinctive book. Paulo Krischke's encouragement was indispensable in our decision to undertake the project, and Daniel Levine offered helpful criticisms of our introductory chapter and warm support for the whole project. David Hathaway translated the chapters by Cáceres, Doimo, Pásara, and Romero. James Langford, Andrea Midgett, and Carole Roos of the University of Notre Dame Press provided many useful suggestions. Louis Brenner, Jr., provided research assistance, and Caroline Domingo helped edit several chapters. Dolores Fairley, Sandy Krizmanich, Rosario Bell, and Daphne Shutts processed the many words of the manuscript through various incarnations: our thanks for their capabilities and kindnesses.

Contributors

Jorge Cáceres Prendes, a Salvadoran political scientist and lawyer, is a member of the sociology of religion group at the Higher Council of the Central American Universities (CSUCA) in San José, Costa Rica. Cáceres received his M.A. from Essex University and is co-author of *Iglesia, política, y profecía* (1983) among other books on the Church in Central America.

Margaret Crahan has published widely on church-state relations and on twentieth-century Cuba. Her most recent book is *Human Rights and Basic Needs in the Americas* (1982). She is Luce Professor of Religion, Power, and Political Processes at Occidental College. She has been a fellow at Georgetown University's Woodstock Theological Center, at the Woodrow Wilson Center of the Smithsonian Institution, and at Columbia University, from which she received her Ph.D. in history. Since 1986 she has been a member of the Kellogg Institute Advisory Council.

Ana Maria Doimo is a professor of anthropology in the department of social science at the Federal University of Espíritu Santo, Brazil, and is currently working on her Ph.D. at the University of São Paulo. She is the author of *Movimento social urbano, igreja y participação popular* (1984) and has published more generally on the Brazilian grass-roots Church, most recently in *A Igreja nas bases em tempo de transição (1974-1985)* (1986), edited by Paulo Krischke and Scott Mainwaring.

Rowen Ireland is a member of the department of sociology, La Trobe University, Australia. He has published on popular and folk religions in Brazil and has a forthcoming book, *The Challenge of Secularisation.* He received his Ph.D. from Harvard University and has been a fellow at the Woodrow Wilson Center of the Smithsonian Institution.

SCOTT MAINWARING, the co-editor, is a senior associate of the Kellogg Institute at the University of Notre Dame, where he is also a member of the department of government. He has published extensively on social movements, democratization, and religion in Latin America. His most recent book is *The Catholic Church and Politics in Brazil, 1916–1985* (1986). He received his Ph.D. in political science from Stanford after taking B.A. and M.A. degrees at Yale.

LUIS PÁSARA, a lawyer, journalist, and researcher, is a graduate of the Catholic University, Lima, Peru, where he was a member of the National Union of Catholic Students. He has been a research fellow at the Woodrow Wilson Center of the Smithsonian Institution, and at the Kellogg Institute, the University of Notre Dame. At present he heads the Latin American regional office of InterPress, in San José, Costa Rica.

CATALINA ROMERO is the director of the Instituto Bartolomé de Las Casas, Lima, Peru. She is a sociologist, trained at Iowa State, at the New School for Social Research and at the Catholic University in Lima, where she is now on the faculty. She has published on the Church in Peru and in Latin America more generally.

ALEXANDER WILDE, the co-editor, directs the Washington Office on Latin America. He was previously senior fellow and Associate Academic Director of the Kellogg Institute, University of Notre Dame, and research associate and acting secretary of the Latin American Program at the Woodrow Wilson Center of the Smithsonian Institution. He is the author of *Conversaciones de caballeros: la quiebra de la democracia en Colombia* (1982) and has published widely on the Latin American Church. He received his Ph.D. from Columbia University.

PHILIP WILLIAMS is an assistant professor of political science at Northeastern Missouri State University, Kirksville. His research on the Nicaraguan Church draws upon a year's fieldwork in that country. He
received M.Phil. and D.Phil. degrees from Oxford University and
took his B.A. from the University of California, Los Angeles.

THE PROGRESSIVE CHURCH IN LATIN AMERICA: AN INTERPRETATION

Scott Mainwaring and Alexander Wilde

In the period just after the Second World War, the Catholic Church in Latin America seemed an antiquated ornament of a social order that was passing away. The trends of the twentieth century appeared unalterably against it. The traditional institutional interests that composed the Church's agenda had ceased to be important political issues. The Church was a marginal factor in the play of politics, particularly in the populist regimes emerging in many countries in that time. As such, the Church was relatively content to exist in a modus vivendi with the state in most countries.[1] This political relationship implied, in turn, an alliance with dominant elites, a broader identification with the existing distribution of power that increasingly faced fundamental challenges. The Church had almost wholly lost contact with the masses in rapidly urbanizing and increasingly secularized societies. The majority lived beyond the limited reach of its institutions and, as the Church itself recognized in the 1950s, beyond its social influence as well.

All this changed dramatically in the following generation. The Church became more prominent in politics in many countries—both as actor and as acted-upon—than it had been since the nineteenth century. In its relationship with governments, the Church asserted a new autonomy. Conflict and confrontation became increasingly common. Moreover, the Church considerably broadened its agenda and alliances. Both in its declarations and its institutions, it expressed a new pastoral commitment to the poor. To the masses marginalized from the processes and benefits of modernizing society, it became, in its own description, "the voice of the voiceless." It sought their welfare through enlarged activism, much beyond traditional charity, which aimed at transforming society's basic structures. This was not a painless choice for the Church. As it identified more closely with suffering in society, it took more of that suffering into itself and became

1

more sharply divided internally. Reactionary forces and repressive regimes retaliated against it, creating a new generation of martyrs. Yet although the process was complex and often painful, the Church emerged in the 1960s and 1970s with a vitality unparalleled in modern Latin American history. As it distanced itself from established power, it gained both political visibility and social authority.

In its short existence, the progressive Church has had a substantial impact both in Latin American politics and the international Church. An institution that had long been allied with established elites, it began to work for social change. In several South American countries (most conspicuously, Brazil and Chile), the Church led the fight to defend human rights and was a leading force in opposing military rule. In Nicaragua, El Salvador, and even Guatemala, committed Christians took up arms to fight for revolution. In the religious sphere, the Latin American Church became for the first time a major source of innovation in the Church Universal, with liberation theology, ecclesial base communities, and the whole range of efforts to link Christianity to radical (and even revolutionary) political action. For those committed to the progressive Church, what is taking place in Latin America is a beacon of hope and source of renewal. For those opposed, it is a grave threat to unity and a betrayal of the ancient purposes of the institution.

This book analyzes the political role of the progressive Latin American Church, focusing on Brazil, Peru, Nicaragua, and El Salvador. The book addresses primarily two sets of issues:

(1) The nature and causes of change within the Church, focusing particularly on the progressive sectors. How, and why, did this Church emerge and evolve? What are the scope and staying power of the changes that occurred? How are they affected by the neo-conservative ecclesiastical challenge? How do the progressive sectors relate to the institution as a whole?

(2) The relationship of religious changes to politics. How do groups within the Church relate to political struggles in these societies? In what ways do they strengthen or weaken popular movements? How are the options of religious progressives conditioned by changing political contexts?

The four national Churches considered in this volume are among the most important and controversial in Latin America. They are apt precisely because grass-roots innovation went further there than elsewhere and had a greater impact both on the national Church and on national politics. Ecclesiastical innovations can be found almost everywhere in Latin America during the 1960s and 1970s, but in most countries their broader impact was limited because they were isolated by the hierarchy and/or repressed by authoritarian political regimes. Most analyses have under-

stated the considerable differences that exist among the Churches throughout Latin America. Despite the radical theological and political positions
taken by some individuals, the Churches of Argentina, Mexico, Colombia, and Venezuela—to mention four of the continent's most important
countries—were much less changed overall than those we study here. In
this sense, our cases are exceptional because change went further than
the norm: a significant part of the Church opted for progressive pastoral
positions.

The Nicaraguan Church has a symbolic significance which belies
its diminutive size, largely because of the controversy regarding the Church's
role in the revolution. While supportive of the broad national movement
that overthrew the Somoza dictatorship in 1979, the Church is profoundly
divided, as Crahan and Williams both make apparent, by its continuing
involvement in the process. Radical Catholics ardently defend and participate in the revolution, while criticizing more conservative Catholics
for failing to understand the nature of their religious commitment and
for undermining the revolution. Conservative Catholics condemn the
Sandinistas for betraying the pluralistic character of the revolution, and
they blame radical Catholics for destroying religious unity. Papal criticisms
of the popular church in Nicaragua have bolstered the conservative position while drawing international attention to this young revolution.

The Brazilian Church also has great symbolic weight, matched in
its case by size. There are more Catholics in Brazil than anywhere else
in the world, and the country has the second largest episcopate in the
world (after Italy), numbering over 350 bishops. During the lengthy authoritarian regime (1964–1985), the Brazilian Church became one of the
most dynamic and progressive in all Catholicism. It led the struggle for
human rights during the harshest years of authoritarian rule (1968–1976).
It was also a leader in implementing pastoral practices shaped by liberation theology, and in all Latin America was easily the pathbreaker in creating base ecclesial communities, the CEBs. Its pastoral innovations influenced progressive Church leaders throughout the continent.

El Salvador is another important case of the complex interaction
between radical Catholics, the institutional Church, and revolutionary
political movements. As was the case in Nicaragua, radical Catholics have
been actively involved in the revolutionary movements, and here, too,
the Church has been deeply divided. The political context in which the
Church has acted—a pattern of coups and corrupt elections, with society
immersed in civil war—has posed complex and ever-changing dilemmas
for the Church. The Church has found itself caught between revolution
and reaction, an indeterminate, stalemated situation in which naked force
has repeatedly driven out other currencies of politics. As Cáceres' analysis

makes clear, "making a political option" is fiendishly difficult when the regime itself is constantly at stake.

Like the Brazilian Church, the Peruvian has been among the most progressive national Churches and has also established an important presence in national politics. As in the other cases, the issue of the relative importance of internal and contextual factors in determining the Church's direction arises in Peru. In 1968, a progressive military government came to power as the Church was promoting internal reforms. The period until 1975 raised interesting questions about the Church's role under a self-proclaimed progressive government (which makes for interesting comparisons to Nicaragua). Subsequent years have posed questions about its response to a more conservative military government (1975–1979) and to centrist elected governments (1979–present).

By focusing on these four national Churches in the post-Medellín period, we have two main objectives. One is to illustrate the striking diversity found even within the progressive Church. Inspired by many common ideas about religion, grass-roots experiences have nevertheless taken a variety of forms between countries and even within a single national setting. Our other objective is to provide the basis for tighter comparative reflection on a number of key themes.

This introductory chapter has two fundamental purposes. First, we provide a theoretical overview of some of the central issues found in the book. We are particularly interested in calling attention to the complex interactions between religion and politics and between the grass roots and the hierarchy. Second, we explicitly bring out some of the comparative issues that would otherwise only be implicit in the book. One of our key themes, already adumbrated, is the great diversity found within the Latin American Church—even among the progressive sectors. We focus here above all on the interactions between Church and politics and the relationship between progressive sectors and the institution as a whole. We will begin by making more explicit what we mean by "the progressive Church."

CHARACTERISTICS OF THE PROGRESSIVE CHURCH

Within the Churches of Brazil, Peru, El Salvador, and Nicaragua, we focus particularly on "the progressive Church." We mean by this a sector within the national Churches, roughly synonymous with other designations used by social scientists and theologians: the popular Church, the radical Church, the grass-roots Church, the Church of the poor, etc. However, the progressive Church is not a distinct entity, separate from the Church as a whole (the "institutional" Church). This is precisely one of the grave fears and accusations of conservatives,[2] and of Pope John Paul II as well, but it simplifies what are complex Latin American realities. Whatever initial impulses existed among progressives toward confrontation with the ecclesiastical structure have generally given way with time to a greater appreciation of institutional strengths. With few exceptions, the progressive Church does not eschew the institutionality of the Church as a whole but rather has attempted to develop an alternative conception of that institutionality. The national Churches analyzed here—in Brazil, Peru, Nicaragua, and El Salvador—are all "progressive," in that institutionally they all exhibit characteristics associated with the progressive sector. This implies more than the presence of a progressive pressure group. It means that the center of gravity in these Churches is now more progressive. These Churches have been moved qualitatively toward a new institutionality and sense of mission in society.

Although there are many differences within the progressive Church, it shares three characteristics throughout Latin America: an emphasis on the small, local religious groups known as ecclesial base communities (CEBs), an adherence to liberation theology, and the belief that the Church must assume a political responsibility to promote social justice. These three main distinguishing marks of the progressive Church are, of course, closely linked to one another. For example, the base communities are the foundation of the Church's struggle for social justice. Similarly, these communities of poor people remain privileged objects of attention by liberation theologians.

There is considerable conflict and controversy as to what CEBs are and should be, but a common working definition focuses on the three constituent elements of the term.[3] The ecclesial character of these groups stems from the fact that they are almost always created by "pastoral agents" —bishops, priests, nuns, and lay people trained and commissioned by the Church. Base communities have enduring ties to the ecclesiastical institution, ties that the poor people who participate in CEBs value greatly. Theologians and social scientists commissioned by the Church produce the written materials that CEBs use; CEB leaders take training courses; pastoral agents regularly (though not necessarily frequently) visit CEBs; and the Church sponsors intra-CEB, diocesan, regional, and even national meetings of base communities.

Base has a double meaning as used here, to refer both to the base of the Church and the base of society. The first meaning suggests the Church—the People of God, in the Conciliar formulation—at the local level; the second refers to the poor stratum of society. This latter meaning is particularly important for us here, as much of the controversy about

CEBs focuses around it. Conservatives argue that the Church must be above social classes, that the "preferential option for the poor" refers to the spiritually poor, or that it is a spiritual but not a political option. Therefore, they eschew the second meaning that progressives impute to the notion of base. For the progressives, the base communities, and specifically the poor people who participate in them, are the foundation of a new Church. The progressives have clearly taken the lead in creating CEBs, even though in recent years some conservatives have attempted to form more politically conservative, clerically controlled CEBs. In any case, the overwhelming majority of CEB participants are poor people.

"Community" also has a double meaning. In the first place, it refers to the geographic basis and size of the CEBs, typically groups of fifteen to twenty-five people. In urban areas, CEB members live in the same neighborhood and generally even one part of it. In rural areas, they are peasants living in the same region and at times living and/or working on the same farm. In both settings members meet regularly, usually each week or two, to discuss the Bible and its social and political relevance. In the second place, "community" refers to one of the fundamental goals of CEBs: to foster a sense of community, of sharing affective and sometimes also sociopolitical concerns. Although CEBs may vary considerably in their political involvements, this concern with community is ubiquitous.

Base communities are generally more religious in a conventional sense and less political than most analysts have suggested.[4] Throughout Latin America, base communities spend most of their time praying and reading the Bible. Affective concerns such as developing a sense of community and solidarity, discussing one's daily life, and developing friendship are also central. Political activities are generally less prominent. People participate in base communities not out of some desire to change the society at large, but rather because of their religious faith. Participation in the CEB may lead them to awareness of the broader implications of their faith. The ways that people translate that into action, however, are strongly conditioned by political context. In general, outside Central America, the political initiatives of CEBs are limited to activities such as creating cooperatives, doing self-help projects, or signing petitions for rudimentary material needs. These limited political aims of the CEBs are apparent in several chapters in this book, particularly the three on Brazil.

A second characteristic we find in the progressive Church throughout Latin America is adherence to some variant of what is commonly known as "liberation theology."[5] Liberation theology has evolved considerably over time and is generally more focused on spiritual matters and less explicitly political than many North Americans, sympathizers as well as critics, have suggested. Despite the heterogeneity within this broad school, several common themes run through it. Perhaps most important is a view that Christian faith requires a commitment to social justice and human rights, which in turn requires working to change the world. God works not only in the human heart but also realizes His purposes through history. Salvation can be understood both individually and collectively. It is a process that, even though completed only within the afterlife, begins with the construction of a better temporal reality. Christians learn the full meaning of their faith only through acting upon it.

Latin America's liberation theologians have addressed a great range of concerns: spirituality, biblical interpretation, ecclesiology (the study of the nature of the Church), popular religiosity, and the role of the laity. This outpouring has no precedent in Latin America, which was not historically a region of theological creativity. Liberation theologians share a strong commitment to the poor, both in terms of pastoral options and of political views. Their theology is often a product of contact and interaction with the people of the CEBs, as well as of scholarship and study. Indeed, the method of liberation theology and much of its content are an effort to interpret what these new Christian communities are actually doing. In this book, we address liberation theology only tangentially, but it is important to note that it underpins the pastoral practices and political orientations of the progressive Church.

The third characteristic one finds in the progressive Church throughout Latin America is the belief that, in the pursuit of social justice, political commitment and participation are a legitimate – indeed, necessary – expression of religious faith. As the eight country studies indicate, however, the politics of the progressive Church are quite varied across Latin America. While the protagonists of the progressive Church share important perceptions of what faith is about, their specific political actions depend to a great extent on the options open in a particular political context. Nevertheless, we can detect some common threads.

Without exception, progressive Church leaders believe that Latin American societies need radical transformation. Otherwise, they argue, even a minimum level of social justice is impossible. Existing social structures are highly inegalitarian and therefore unjust; piecemeal reform is not sufficient to bring about the needed changes. Both in theological and political terms, progressive Church leaders are particularly concerned with the plight of the poor. This particular progressive concern has greatly affected the Latin American Church as a whole. The "preferential option for the poor," the hallmark of the 1979 meeting of the Latin American Bishops Council at Puebla, Mexico, captures the essence of this concern. At Puebla, the Latin American bishops affirmed "the need for conversion on the part of the whole Church to a preferential option for the poor, an option aimed at their integral liberation. . . . Committed to the poor, we condemn as anti-evangelical the extreme poverty that affects an extremely large part of the population on our continent. We will make every effort to understand and denounce the mechanisms that generate this poverty."[6]

Accompanying this predilection for radical restructuring of society to help meet the needs of the poor is an emphasis on participation. Participation is seen as both a means that ensures that needs of different segments of society are expressed and as an end in itself, a way that individuals and groups achieve fuller humanity. Throughout Latin America, progressive Church leaders encourage participation in an amalgam of social movements: labor unions, peasant leagues, neighborhood associations. This does not mean that all or even most of the poor people in CEBs participate in progressive social movements, but simply that they are generally encouraged to do so. Where revolutionary movements are strong, as in El Salvador and Nicaragua, many in the progressive Church have gravitated toward them, believing that in their societies more conventional channels for change are exhausted. Their involvement does not mean that the progressive Church is uniformly, or even generally, revolutionary.

The progressive Church supports many different forms of political action in the name of "participation." Behind these variations—strongly related to differences of political context—there is a common predisposition in favor of participation in social movements, as distinguished from more conventional political organizations. This preference is rooted in distrust of the established political class, and is widely diffused throughout all four national Churches. It may also reflect, as suggested from quite different perspectives by both Pásara and Mainwaring, a certain antipathy to the liberal conception of politics as an arena of inevitable incrementalism and compromise. In any case, the progressive Church has only begun to consider the significance of the more formal forms of broad-based political action, such as electoral participation, that have been the cornerstone of liberal Western democracies.

While there is a consensus about the need for radical change, there is no similar consensus about how it should be achieved. Indeed, on this point progressives have argued that the Church has no specific solutions for society. It should be a moral critic, while Christians participate with others working to overcome through means that will vary in different times and places. The issue of whether Church progressives are socialists or Marxists gains inordinate space in many writings,[7] but in reality most progressive Church leaders hold inchoate views. Generally, there is a diffuse anti-capitalist ideology—but even conservative Church documents have expressed criticisms of capitalism over a long period of time. Most progressive Church leaders are sympathetic toward socialist ideals; relatively few, however, embrace Marxism, notwithstanding the controversy about Marxian influences in liberation theology.

The progressive Church does accept that conflict is a part of society and is shaped in certain characteristic ways by Latin America's predominantly capitalist economies. It also believes that the mobilization and organization of social conflict is an inevitable concomitant of change. Indeed, this is what "participation" implies if the poor and the excluded are to become the subjects of their own destinies. These positions represent a break from older Catholic teaching, which held a more static view of society and emphasized the natural harmony of its different parts. This change has been heavily criticized by neo-conservatives, who argue that the Church should conciliate social conflict, not exacerbate it. The debate between the two sides takes its sharpest form over the issue of violence. It was the Medellín documents that denounced "institutionalized violence" in Latin American life and recognized that the violence of some groups in society was a response and defense against that practiced against them. This kind of understanding has led the Church to condemn both the violence of the state and of revolutionaries, although in a few rare instances (such as Nicaragua in 1979) even the hierarchy has legitimated revolutionary violence as a lesser evil. In practice, progressives have expressed their commitment to radical transformation in a variety of different political choices.

Progressive Church perceptions of liberal democracy vary considerably according to context. In the two Central American cases, liberal democratic institutions have never functioned, and there is pervasive skepticism about them. In this context, progressive Church leaders tend to see liberal democracy as a sham and argue for "popular democracy," a system responsive to the majority if not formally accountable to it. Even between our two Central American cases, however, perceptions differ. In Nicaragua, most progressive Church leaders perceive demands for liberal democracy as a means of strengthening the "bourgeois" opposition to the revolution. In contrast, as Cáceres' postscript makes evident, the Salvadoran hierarchy, and in particular Archbishop Rivera y Damas, have since 1980 attempted to promote conciliation and generally see liberal democracy as a political system consistent with these efforts. Some progressives who formerly endorsed the revolutionary movement have become more skeptical of its viability and are more willing to consider participation in liberal democratic politics.

Both Peru and Brazil, in contrast, have some past experience with liberal democratic institutions. In both countries, progressive Church leaders have been critical of the processes and policies of those systems in practice. Nevertheless, in both countries the progressive Church supported and fought for the return to democracy after protracted military rule (1968 to 1980 in Peru, and 1964 to 1985 in Brazil).

In response to the hardships endured under dictatorships, in the 1980s the Church in most countries has identified itself with democracy as never before. At the same time, however, it remains uncomfortable with the open conflict and institutionalized partisanship of this political regime, not to mention the common temptations to corruption and demagogy.[8] Progressives are drawn more to "popular" democracy, to a new social order for the benefit rather than the exploitation of the people. They are frequently divided today between those who believe that political democracy is the precondition for such social transformation and those who fear that liberal democratic regimes are inimical to the realization of democracy in its full social sense.

Much of the criticism of Church conservatives revolves around the linkages between religion and politics as practiced by the progressive Church. Church conservatives believe that progressives reduce religious faith to political options.[9] Paradoxically, the progressives generally view conservatives in much the same way; they believe that the conservatives' criticisms are politically, and not religiously, motivated. In our opinion, religious faith must be taken as a powerful motivating force in Latin America, and one that is generally not used in a manipulative fashion. Far from employing religion for political purposes, both conservatives and progressives generally undertake political action as part of their understanding of Christian faith.

THE EMERGENCE OF THE PROGRESSIVE CHURCH

The progressive Church in Latin America emerged in a particular historical context and evolved throughout the period that defined it. The context conditioning this process had both religious and political dimensions. The initial impetus to change from within the Church itself, particularly from European reform movements and the Vatican, is now a story well-told.[10] The Second Vatican Council (1962–1965), convoked by Pope John XXIII to address the challenges of the modern world, reinterpreted the Church's mission in fundamental ways. New theology insisted that the Church stand in defense of human rights; that authority lines within the Church be redrawn to give greater responsibility to the laity; that the Church actively promote social justice as an integral part of its mission.

Even before the Council the Vatican had encouraged the Latin American Church to modernize its organization by subdividing old dioceses grown too large, creating new urban parishes, initiating new forms of pastoral ministry, and transferring thousands of priests, nuns, and lay activists from the richer Churches of Europe and North America. Beyond all this was another institutional change that, marking a break from long tradition, slightly antedated the Council's emphasis on collegiality. This was the construction of the national bishops' conferences as effective organizations, with permanent staff and a capacity for concerted response. Before the 1950s, the bishops of a given nation had no institutionalized vehicles for speaking as a collegial body. Collective episcopal gatherings and decisions were uncommon, and intra-diocesan pastoral efforts were not well coordinated. Antiquated and ineffectual ecclesiastical structures limited the Church's presence in society. The construction of national bishops' conferences allowed for coordinated pastoral action, notwithstanding the marked diversity of viewpoints found in most hierarchies. The Brazilian Conference of National Bishops, established in 1952, was the first such entity in Latin America. Equally important was the linking of the national conferences into a regional body without precedent, the Latin American Bishops' Conference, CELAM, created in 1955.

Vatican II was primarily a European event, dominated by European theologians and prelates and addressing the Church's mission particularly in the context of the developed Western world. Nevertheless, it promoted broader reforms in Latin America than elsewhere. In part this occurred because the ecclesiastical reforms suggested by Vatican II required greater change in Latin America than in Europe. Serious commitment to social justice implied the need for radical change in a continent plagued by widespread poverty and repression. Similarly, the goal of giving lay people greater voice and dignity entailed greater ecclesiastical innovation in societies in which most of them lacked even rudimentary knowledge of basic doctrines.

In 1968, CELAM held a general assembly at Medellín, Colombia, to discuss the applicability of Vatican II to Latin America. This meeting was a watershed in the history of the Latin American Church. The bishops denounced "structural sin," called for social justice, criticized past failures of the Church, encouraged broad participation in politics, and demanded reshaping of ecclesiastical structures so that the laity would be more effectively evangelized. Medellín was made possible by a host of earlier innovations, and in turn provided support for further reform.

The broad institutional changes set in motion by Vatican II and Medellín were crucial to the emergence of radical Catholicism in Latin America. These changes in the international Church, however, do not constitute a comprehensive explanation for the emergence of radical Catholicism in Latin America. If changes in the international Church were an adequate explanation for the character of ecclesiastical change, then we would not expect sharp differences across national borders. The Church is an international institution, but it is one in which considerable diversity and crossnational differences exist.

These crossnational differences are explained in part by the differing contexts the Church faces. Like that of any social institution, the Church's vision of its mission responds to diverse aspects of the society in which it exists, including the political context. In the emergence of the progressive Church in Latin America, the political dimension was particularly important. The political factors shaping the emergence of the progressive Church did not have exclusive primacy nor were their effects simple. We do believe, however, that the Church's efforts at religious reform in the period were given concrete content by the political context of the region as a whole and of the different national settings.

The broad context of the period was established initially by the triumph of the Cuban revolution and the perceived failures of the Alliance for Progress. The Cuban revolution catalyzed profound changes in Latin America, inspiring the emergence of guerrilla insurgencies in many countries. At the time, the counterreaction, including the formulation of the national security doctrine by the armed forces, drew less attention, but it ultimately proved to have a greater impact. Concerned with the events in Cuba, Pope John XXIII called on the Latin American Church to encourage social reform, lest other revolutions take place. The Alliance for Progress, President Kennedy's formula for development, democracy, and anticommunism, generated new hope about Latin America's future. At the time, democracy seemed to be taking root in many Latin American countries, but with the exceptions of Colombia and Venezuela, the civilian governments inaugurated in the late 1950s and early 1960s all proved ephemeral. The shortcomings and then breakdown of most of these governments led many to believe that liberal democracy was incapable of resolving crucial social and economic problems. In the intellectual sphere, dependency theory became a leading influence on social analysis, offering a framework linking internal and international forms of exploitation. All these elements, in different ways, suggested that radical change was necessary, desirable, and possible. The predominant political reality defining the decade following Vatican II, however, came to be military dictatorship. From the late 1960s through the 1970s, the progressive Church was formed in the particular conditions imposed by harsh and arbitrary regimes, from Central America to the Southern Cone.

In all four national cases considered in this book, the primary expansion of the radical sectors of the Church occurred under conditions of political dictatorship. In two countries, Brazil and Peru, radical Catholic sectors appeared before dictatorship. Although the early radical cadre was important in later developments, it was only a small, relatively uninfluential sector within the Church until the military periods. The other two countries, Nicaragua and El Salvador, had almost no experience of liberal democracy, even of the limited variety found in Brazil before 1964 and Peru before 1968. The progressive Church grew up within traditions of dictatorship.

Why was the experience of authoritarianism important in the formation of the progressive Church? In contrast to the more open regimes, the dictatorships attempted to repress the political expression of the different voices of society. In most countries, authoritarian rule led to conflicts between a minority sector of radical Catholics and the state. Church-state conflict is hardly new in Latin America, but in the past it characteristically took place between a liberal, secular, or radical state and a Church tied to the established order. In the 1960s and 1970s, conflict in most cases involved conservative authoritarian regimes that repressed priests and lay leaders pursuing radical or liberal political ideals. When committed Catholics were imprisoned, tortured, and even killed, bishops in a significant number of cases then denounced the state, setting off a spiral of greater repression against the Church, followed by new Church denunciations of authoritarianism. This dynamic was a key element in the transformation of several national Churches, including Brazil, El Salvador, and Nicaragua. Peru offers an interesting variant of this pattern, with the Church moving from some support for the military government in its early progressive phase to opposition as it became more repressive in the mid-1970s.

Historically the hierarchy had entered the realm of public politics in defense of the rights of the Church. Now bishops did so in the name of their pastoral responsibilities in society more generally. They acted on behalf of their own, but the context of dictatorship and repression gave some ecclesiastical leaders a far broader sense of their responsibility. All those without voice—and many times they were not only the poor but virtually the whole society—were "their own." The Church, they believed, must become the voice of the voiceless. Where the Church accepted that responsibility, it took on representing civil society itself. The Church did not become the voice of the voiceless out of some easy self-interest. It paid a high price for doing so, and to make such a choice required qualities of clarity, leadership, and courage.

Several other Latin American countries—Mexico, Colombia, Costa Rica, Venezuela—retained more open civilian political regimes during the

1960s and 1970s. However distant from some democratic ideal, all of them offered channels for responsiveness absent in military dictatorships, whether traditional (as in Central America) or bureaucratic-authoritarian (as in South America). It is significant that the churches in all four countries have been relatively conservative,[11] notwithstanding the presence of small, occasionally vocal radical groups. The Church has sought to integrate itself in stable political orders, and in recent decades there has been no major experience of repression by conservative authoritarian leaders against the Church. These political circumstances have fostered continuity and conservatism in the Churches.

Dictatorship was a necessary but not sufficient condition to bring the progressive Church into being.[12] The Church's option for the voiceless did not occur by some automatic process of displacement, a social logic by which—other institutions repressed—the Church had to assume the defense of the repressed. Argentina is only the most dramatic example among many countries where, in the face of dictatorship and violence, the Church did not assume such a political role; the Churches of Guatemala, Paraguay, and Uruguay also supported, more than they denounced, military rule. In these countries, progressive Church sectors criticized authoritarian rule, but they failed to move the ecclesiastical institution as a whole. Far from catalyzing a protective response by the hierarchy, state repression annihilated the radical Catholics. If dictatorship was not a sufficient condition, however, it seems to have been a necessary one for a given national Church to accept the broad responsibility of political representation and the transformation of its own social mission.

Note that dictatorship is a specifically political rather than social factor conditioning the emergence of the progressive Church. Of course the Church is aware of the broader social context of Latin America— widespread poverty, egregious income inequalities in all but a few countries, ethnic discrimination in many. Confronting social injustices has been central to the mission of the progressive Church since Medellín. In trying to explain the emergence of the progressive Church, however, those injustices in themselves are of limited utility. Recent increases in poverty were not so dramatic as to move the Church from its historical conservatism. Moreover, social inequalities and injustice were not notably greater in the countries where Church progressives have exercised great sway and those where they have been relatively marginal to the overall ecclesiastical enterprise.

The interaction between Church change and political repression was crucial in the four countries we analyze in this book. As Vatican II and Medellín called for social justice, political events in our four countries undermined opportunities for it. As Medellín denounced "structural sin," governments in our four countries embodied it. Alone, neither the broader institutional reforms nor political dictatorship explain the strength of radical Catholic sectors in these four countries; together, they had a catalytic effect upon the ecclesiastical institution.

THE PROGRESSIVE CHURCH, THE HIERARCHY, AND CHURCH STRUCTURES

The progressive sectors of the Latin American Church do not exist in isolation from the rest of the institution. The broader institution sets the framework within which the progressives must define themselves. The Church, after all, is a global institution, and despite the change it has undergone during the past three decades, it remains very hierarchical. The extensive innovations in grass-roots ecclesiastical practices did little to erode formal papal and episcopal authority. Indeed, under the leadership of John Paul II, the Church has reasserted the importance of maintaining clear lines of authority.

The Church's hierarchical nature means that change at the grass roots in single dioceses, or in national churches as a whole, ultimately requires at least the acquiescence of institutional authority. A bishop has the authority to reverse any change in his diocese that does not meet his approval, just as the pope has the authority to impose sanctions against individuals, movements, or theologies that he opposes. Even local redefinitions of authority lines within the Church ultimately depend upon higher official sanctions. This fact has been apparent when newly appointed conservative bishops have dismantled the grass-roots structures created by progressive predecessors. Of course, the exigencies of collegiality dictate that bishops and the pope attempt to avoid radical confrontation most of the time. Nevertheless, hierarchical structure imposes constraints on democratization within the Church.

Bishops need not actually sponsor progressive grass-roots activities, since all over Latin America pastoral agents are anxious to do so. But where the bishops are hostile to autonomous grass-roots groups, their dissemination is next to impossible. In this context, progressive Church sectors are easily isolated; in isolation, progressives readily become more radical and engage in activities opposed by the hierarchy.

In light of the hierarchy's central importance in the Church, its relationship to the progressives fundamentally shapes the overall impact the progressives have in the national Church. All over Latin America, progressive innovators have emerged, but in many countries they have been consistently isolated by conservative prelates. The Colombian Church serves as the paradigmatic example: a cohesive conservative group of bishops has sponsored the formation of grass-roots groups, but the bishops have tightly controlled the way such groups are run.[13]

No matter how conflictual their relationship with the institution as a whole may be, progressive Church people generally want to remain part of the institution. To do so, however, they must recognize the authority of Rome. Nowhere in Latin America have progressive Church leaders seriously considered creating a splinter church. They may have sharp criticisms of institutional leaders, but they define their own lives in terms of this institution. Progressive Church leaders almost never go beyond asserting a claim to having rediscovered the true nature of the Church's mission, which illustrates how much they value the institution. If they did not they could break from the Catholic Church to enter other religious or secular organizations.

Beyond a belief in the institution's legitimacy, being part of the Church means that a pastoral agent has access to resources and contacts that would otherwise be difficult to obtain. Above all, where popular religiosity is strong, the Church can help a pastoral agent establish initial trust with the popular sectors. Church ties may also offer some protection from repressive states, though as the roll of martyred clergy and lay people shows, such affiliation is no guarantee of personal security.

Progressive pastoral agents have discovered time after time that the poor people with whom they work have great respect for bishops and the pope. With the exception of Nicaragua, where ecclesiastical conflicts have reached extremes, the poor people who participate in base communities have little patience with pastoral agents who constantly attack the institution. Beyond religious sentiment, the poor people who participate in base communities may also derive status and access to resources and people from their ties to the institution.

The progressive sectors have confronted ongoing dilemmas from being part of the institution. These involve essentially the difficult balance between pushing for change and accepting some limits to avoid being marginalized. The way the progressives have responded to their situation has changed over time; there has been a process of learning and adaptation. In the early phases of the progressive Church (1965–1973), the progressives were more hostile and confrontational in their relationship with the institution. What was important was the people and their liberation; the Church's purpose should be to further this process of liberation, which was largely seen in political terms.[14] Over time, these more critical attitudes toward the institution gave rise to a more sympathetic and nuanced understanding of the Church.

Although this change was partly tactical, in a more fundamental way it reflected a process of religious and political maturation. The progressives came to a keener awareness of the difficulties of acting out religious ideas in the political sphere. Just as the hierarchy came to understand that its authority is empty when it is not based in society, so the progressives came to realize that they had failed to appreciate certain positive aspects of the Church's tradition, including its tradition of spirituality.

Few changes in the progressive sector are so notable or important as the changing evaluation of spirituality. When these sectors emerged in the mid-1960s, they had a marked orientation toward social activism. Liberation was seen primarily as a political process, and spirituality received relatively little attention. In fact, it was seen as a negative part of the Church's heritage, as a kind of escape from the exigencies of political reality. By the mid-1980s, spirituality was a major concern of the progressives. Several leading theologians addressed it at length.[15] This change was not simply or even primarily "strategic." The progressives, through extensive contact with the poor and learning through the institution, came to value spirituality as an integral part of their own mission.

Of course the dilemmas of the Church are not faced by only one side. All institutions, regardless of how hierarchical, must prove responsive to their cadres if they are to thrive. For this reason, sharp confrontation with the Latin American progressives would be counterproductive to the Vatican. The progressive Church in Latin America has demonstrated vitality and has had considerable success in engaging millions of people in the Church in more active ways. Furthermore, it would be misleading to suggest that the progressives are pitted against the rest of the institution. At times, this characterization is apt, but on balance the reality is more complex. While it is analytically neat to distinguish between the progressives and the Church as a whole, progressives hold key leadership positions at all levels of the Church, including the Vatican. Moreover, the progressive theological agenda has become very prominent in Latin America.

In speaking of the institutional Church, we should not assume the existence of uniformly conservative Church leaders who oppose innovation, and grudgingly cede minor spaces to the progressives simply to appease them. Were this the case, the extensive grass-roots and theological innovations that progressives have promoted during the past two decades would be far less significant. It has been precisely the willingness of the peak leaders of the international Church to accept and encourage an amalgam of innovations and reforms that has made the progressives' initiatives so important. Just as there was a learning process on the progressive side, so, too, has the hierarchy come to appreciate some innovations of the progressives.

Among those progressive innovations that have affected the entire Church is the creation of a new range of Church structures that link the grass roots and the institutional. These new structures are as important as the new ideas of liberation theology. New grass-roots structures that feed back and affect processes within the entire institution have emerged and flourished. Various chapters illustrate how, in very different settings, the Church has been transformed by new kinds of interchange between the base and the highest levels of the Church. Among the most important of these new structures are the CEBs, but as Mainwaring's chapter suggests, an entire panoply of new structures has emerged at both the grass-roots and intermediate levels. These new structures simultaneously express the kinds of issues raised by Church progressives and make possible a new, more intense communication between the hierarchy, the clergy, and the grass roots. Traditionally, the clergy imparted its teachings to the faithful with little exchange from below; today, although the formal authority of the clergy remains largely intact, these new grass-roots and intermediate structures have made possible a communication that was unknown in the past. Moreover, relations within the Church have changed, as the clergy and pastoral agents have more autonomy than they did in the past. In her chapter, Romero captures this new communication and exchange with the suggestive term, "moments of collective reflection." Conservatives often voice concern about the nature of these new Church structures, but they question neither the importance of established structures, nor the vitality of the structures created by progressives.

Having outlined some general issues in the relationship between the progressive Church and the hierarchy, we now compare this relationship in the four countries. A minority sector throughout Latin America, the progressives nevertheless managed to attain considerable sway in several national churches, including the four which are the focus of this volume. But the chapters that follow make apparent that there are significant differences in the relationship between the progressives and the bishops in our four cases.

Progressives have had the strongest position in Brazil. This situation is nothing new. During the 1950s, the Brazilian Church promoted an extensive series of reforms that anticipated Vatican II. While the Church in many Latin American countries was still predominantly allied to very conservative sectors of society, the Brazilian bishops generally supported the democratic, populist-reformist governments of Juscelino Kubitschek (1959–1960), Jânio Quadros (1960–1961), and João Goulart (1961–1964), until the last year before the March 1964 coup. By 1963, ecclesiastical hegemony shifted to the prelates who opposed Goulart because they feared that the left was becoming too powerful. The bishops' conference (CNBB) partially endorsed the 1964 coup, and until 1968 more conservative bishops dominated it. But in the meantime, the number of bishops committed to radical change in religious and political structures increased.

These bishops began to promote the creation of CEBs (even though they were not generally called that at the time) and other grass-roots innovations in the years immediately following the coup. They also became increasingly critical of the military regime, censuring its human rights violations and inegalitarian development model. The CNBB itself began to speak out about human rights violations by the end of the 1960s; at the same time, reformist bishops sympathetic to many positions of the progressives assumed the top leadership positions in the CNBB. By 1973, the Brazilian episcopacy had arguably become the most progressive in the world. A growing number of bishops supported widespread Church reform, with the expansion of CEBs, the promotion of new understandings of the Church's mission that draw upon liberation theology, and the attention to the Church's role in social and political questions being the most important. From 1973 until the inauguration of a democratic government in March 1985, the CNBB continued to criticize—often in very sharp terms—the military government.

The critical point here is that there was no cleavage between the progressive Church and the bishops. In contrast to some other cases (including Nicaragua and El Salvador), the bishops themselves were responsible for introducing and promoting most of the grass-roots innovations. With few exceptions, base communities in Brazil emerged in dioceses where the bishop directly encouraged them. By the early 1980s, when Vatican pressures and internal political changes started to push the Brazilian Church to move in a more cautious direction, there were approximately sixty bishops who supported base communities. This is a distinct minority in a country that has 350 bishops, but the progressive bishops exercised an influence greater than their numerical strength would suggest.

Among the four countries we analyze here, progressives in Brazil have been the most disposed to make concessions to the institution as a whole. A clearly defined movement of radical clergy who opposed the hierarchy never emerged, and by the early 1970s, progressive attitudes toward the institution as a whole were remarkably conciliatory. This disposition was fostered by the receptivity of the Brazilian hierarchy to promote grass-roots innovations. It was also encouraged by the political situation during the formative years of the progressive Church in Brazil. Given the stability and strength of the authoritarian regime between 1968 and the end of the 1970s, progressives were disinclined to opt for revolutionary politics that have proven divisive to the Church elsewhere, while at the same time they were driven to seek institutional protection since the Church was the most effective opposition voice.

As the chapters by Crahan and Williams indicate, Nicaragua is at the opposite end of the spectrum. Here, the progressive Church was always more autonomous vis-à-vis the hierarchy and enjoyed less episcopal support. CEBs in Nicaragua often emerged with little support from the hierarchy and in some cases may have been created by lay people who were not authorized by the Church. This is a sharp contrast to Brazil, where CEBs were virtually without exception created by pastoral agents.

While Church progressives in Nicaragua always enjoyed less episcopal support than in Brazil, only after the Sandinistas took power in 1979 did the conflicts between the progressives and the bishops assume their current virulence. In 1978 and the first semester of 1979, there was an apparent convergence between Church progressives and the bishops, based largely on mutual opposition to the Somoza dynasty. Moreover, as both chapters on Nicaragua show, in the months immediately following the FSLN victory, relations between the progressives and the bishops remained cordial. Subsequently, the bishops have become extremely critical both of the government and of the "popular Church." In their criticisms, they are fully supported by CELAM and John Paul II.

In Latin America as a whole, the Church of Nicaragua is the most divided. Here, without renouncing their ties to the Church or their faith, progressives have defied Church leaders. The most famous example is the steadfast refusal of several priests to resign cabinet positions in the Nicaraguan government. These individuals feel called by their faith to serve in government; they see their governmental positions as an expression of, rather than contradictory to, their religious belief. Most of the Nicaraguan bishops, the Vatican, and the Secretariat of the Latin American Bishops Council (CELAM), conversely, see the actions of the progressive Church in Nicaragua as threatening the Church's unity and integrity.[16]

The relationship between the hierarchy and the progressives in El Salvador and Peru rests somewhere in between the Brazilian and Nicaraguan situations. As Cáceres makes apparent, since the 1960s the archdiocese of San Salvador has given support to a wide range of grass-roots innovations, with Oscar Romero's tenure as archbishop (1977–1980) particularly notable. As in Nicaragua, the archbishop of the capital city has an inordinate weight in the Salvadoran Church, so the support of Archbishops Luis Chávez, Romero, and Rivera y Damas has offset conservative predilections of the other Salvadoran bishops. Since 1980, because of the more cautious orientation of Rivera y Damas, the extraordinary repression unleashed against CEBs in El Salvador, and the revolutionary involvement of most Church progressives, the hierarchy has offered less support for the progressives, and the progressives, conversely, have had less influence within the Church.

In Peru, progressive Catholic initiatives have had a good measure of support from the hierarchy, which is one of the more progressive in Latin America. As Romero notes, Peruvian CEBs have close ties to parishes and to the hierarchy and have received strong support from the latter. Moreover, a majority of dioceses issued denunciations of the military government during its most repressive and regressive phase (1976–1978). Since that period, however, a substantial majority of episcopal appointments have been conservative, with a significant representation among them of *Opus Dei*, as mentioned by Pásara. With the retirement in late 1988 of Lima Cardinal Juan Landázuri Ricketts—a crucial figure in shaping the whole progressive Peruvian Church—many expect conservative bishops to take control of key episcopal commissions heretofore held by progressives. Peruvian bishops rallied behind liberation theologian Gustavo Gutiérrez when he was under Vatican scrutiny in the mid-1980s, but his position in an increasingly polarized Church is more problematical. Nevertheless, grass-roots communities and movements appear to remain a vibrant presence and foundation for the progressive sector.

THE POLITICS OF THE PROGRESSIVE CHURCH

What is the proper relationship of the Church to politics? The question is as old as the Church itself. It is central to present debate within the international Church, and it is one of the fundamental issues throughout the chapters of this book.

Three general comments are in order. First, the question is not whether the Church is linked to politics, but rather how it is. Whether or not religious practitioners want their faith to have a political dimension, it inevitably does; even the way people pray is political, as liberation theologians and grass-roots pastoral agents have observed. The content and practice of religion affect conceptions of social hierarchy, justice, and legitimacy. Catholicism, moreover, is a religion explicitly concerned with the public order. While it mediates the individual relationship between the believer and God, the Church also desires that Christian values be expressed in the structures of state and society. In this sense, there is nothing distinctive about the progressive viewpoint that politics is an important part of Christian faith. What distinguishes the progressive position is rather the understanding of what constitutes a good social order and of what the Church should do to help realize it.

Second, analysis of the Church's proper role in politics must take into account the interaction between ideas and political practice. Too often analysis is limited to theological or political exegeses of texts that, depending on the perspective, are sacrosanct or anathema. This kind of analysis fails to assess adequately political and religious practice, which cannot simply be inferred from ecclesiastical documents. What Church leaders and theologians say about politics and religion in formal documents is important, but it provides only the broadest parameters that shape political behavior. Grass-roots groups on the whole care little about academic debates about religion. Their understanding of doctrine reflected in their actions is significantly shaped by their immediate political context. What takes place at the grass roots is, of course, affected by elite debates, but it also affects them in turn. Since it is at the grass roots that these debates are most directly carried out in political action, our discussion of differences in political activities necessarily looks not only at elite ideas, but also at popular processes.

Our perspective stands in contrast to the kind of "essentialism" found in many analyses of the Church, by which the Church's orientations in practice can be extrapolated from presumably authoritative ecclesiastical doctrine. Doctrine is important: it sets the parameters within which competing claims for legitimacy in the Church take place and establishes limits to acceptable orientations and behavior. Nevertheless, in the contemporary Church, different political activities are justified by the same doctrine. The same injunctions are interpreted in quite different ways, not only according to individual idiosyncracies but also according to the context in which doctrines are lived out.

Third, because the concrete significance of religious doctrines is worked out in specific contexts, it should not be surprising that there is considerable heterogeneity in the political activities of progressive Catholics. The Church is the repository of certain timeless truths, but it is also, inescapably, a social institution. It consciously addresses a wide range of social and political issues. In doing so, it affects other actors interested in such issues but is in turn affected by them. Church leaders may consciously react for or against the agenda of other actors in society, or they may unconsciously be swayed by societal debates at large.

In this book such differences in context are manifest particularly between the two countries where revolution is an issue (Nicaragua and El Salvador) and the two new democracies (Brazil and Peru). That the Church faces very different issues in these two broad contexts is apparent in every chapter in this book. Revolution profoundly changes a society and even presents new challenges to the world order. Under revolutionary conditions, politics becomes polarized and political passions run high. The stakes are apparent in the way the world and the Church have focused attention on this small region.

These differing contexts help shape the identity of the churches in the four countries. For this reason, it would be misleading to treat the context simply as an environmental factor which, if changed, would push the Church to respond in new ways while maintaining a fundamentally similar understanding of its mission. The Brazilian Church did not simply respond to the authoritarian government and then revert back to its old self under democratic rule. The experience of repression and of becoming the "voice of the voiceless" led many Catholics to a new understanding of the Church's mission. The return to liberal democracy in March 1985 altered the political context, but it did not mean that the Church would give up its preferential option for the poor. What it did mean, however, is that progressive Catholics faced new questions about how to realize that commitment in practice. Such questions arose in even more dramatic form in the passions and polarization of revolutionary politics. The dilemmas of living under a revolutionary regime in Nicaragua were different from those of coping with the massive violence of an unresolved revolutionary situation in El Salvador, but in both countries the regime itself was at stake. Political context raised fundamental questions within each Church about its mission and identity.

In its official pronouncements, the Church Universal has taken a critical stance to capitalism since publication of the papal encyclical *Rerum Novarum* in 1891. In Latin America, however, the Church long remained in practice clearly on the side of an established capitalist order, even as it harbored a vaguely ancien-régime anticapitalist mentality. This posture began to change in the period following World War II, when in a number of countries the Church supported a variety of reformist initiatives in the political realm as it also moved to modernize ecclesiastical structures. For example, in the 1950s and early 1960s, the Brazilian Church organized educational efforts in urban slums, called for agrarian reform, and collaborated with populist governments in educational programs for the poor. The Churches in Brazil and Chile were the continental leaders in supporting reform, but change was widespread. In the first half of the 1960s Christian Democracy became a major political force in Chile, El Salvador, and Venezuela.[17] In broad terms, the Church was most inclined to support political reform where the state was interested in the same objective; it was still little inclined to do so when such support entailed confronting dictatorships. In El Salvador, however, the archdiocese of San Salvador spearheaded efforts for political reform, even in a thoroughly inimical context. Among the Churches studied in this book, that of Nicaragua lagged longest in the traditional pattern under the Somoza family dictatorship.

Disillusion with reformist efforts set in rather quickly. The Catholic left in Brazil, already eschewing reform by the early 1960s, anticipated the pattern later followed by radical Catholics in other countries. Influenced by new conceptions of faith that emphasized social justice and by widespread admiration for the Cuban revolution, the Catholic radicals came to believe that reform would never meet the pressing social problems of Latin America, rooted as they were in capitalist development. Already by 1963 Brazil's Catholic radicals were denouncing "the failure of the so-called nationalist struggle" and calling for "a revolutionary strategy based on the concrete conditions of Brazil."[18] Their structural critique of the capitalist system went beyond earlier, more theoretical Church pronouncements. It was to receive powerful legitimation in the epochal Medellín document of the Latin American bishops in 1968. Also new in the nascent years of the progressive Church was the positive espousal of socialism expressed by many Catholics, even though others continued to speak of a third path between socialism and capitalism. And whereas during the 1950s progressive Catholic efforts for social change usually took place within the bounds of state-sponsored initiatives, this was no longer true by the end of the 1960s.

By the late 1960s, the radical political options of middle-class laity were accompanied by innovations at the grass roots. Lay people, priests, and some bishops began to support popular organization and mobilization of a new kind. Previous popular Church groups had generally been in the mold of Catholic Action; they were under close hierarchical supervision and were markedly anticommunist.[19] The late 1960s and the early 1970s witnessed the formation of new groups in which pastoral agents encouraged greater lay autonomy, and in which capitalism, rather than communism, was seen as the primary cause of social misery. Pastoral agents encouraged peasants and workers to mobilize in their own interests, even against their governments. The attempt to help poor people become more autonomous actors was reflected in the widely used term, conscientização/concientización (consciousness raising). In the past, poor Catholics had occasionally rebelled out of religious conviction, [20] but their mobilization by Church leaders to work for radical change and social justice was something new in Latin American history.

Catholic radicals argued in the 1960s that the Church was inevitably political, and that it had always been so. Whether or not it wanted to, the Church supported some classes and was part of a system of domination that exploited others. They wanted the Church to recognize this fact and to take a stance—for justice, for socialism, for human rights, and above all for the poor. To realize its identity, to be true to Christ's message, they argued, the Church needed to take a "political option" (in the direct translation of the Latin phrase). Significant numbers of Christians—bishops, clergy, lay people—associated themselves with popularly based movements as a way of living their religious faith.

But the confidence of the late 1960s, when the clamor for a political option was common among radical Catholics, gave rise to new and difficult questions in the following decade. Which option should be taken? In many contexts, the question proved divisive: the "correct" political practice (to use an irritating but characteristic phrase) did not flow directly from a concern for the poor, and moral commitment was no guarantee of political judgment. Granted, for example, that revolution was desirable, and that violence might be justified to bring it about. But is a successful revolution likely, or even possible, and how soon? To what extent, and in what situations, should radical Catholics use violence against what the Medellín documents called the "institutionalized violence" of existing arrangements? These thorny issues are still far from resolved.

If we view the evolution of the progressive Church over the past two decades, we can see a process of collective learning. Progressives opted to become political in new ways but over time reinterpreted what that should mean. In different national settings, they did so responding both to shifts in secular politics and to their own evolving understanding of the political implications of faith. In general terms, the political maturation of the radical Catholics has been similar to the evolution in the relationship between them and the hierarchy. Over time, they have become more accepting of compromise, more willing to work within the system (while working for different outcomes within it), less confrontational, and less certain that revolutionary socialism holds the answers.

In part, the retrenchment of progressive Catholicism reflects the fact that it has been under fire by the Vatican and CELAM for some time. Of equal importance is the fact that the political situations in all four countries have changed significantly. As we noted above, the progressive Church emerged under conditions of political dictatorship. Church progressives were united—among themselves and with moderates—against the governments. The same conditions no longer obtain, and lines about the relationship between the Church and politics have blurred. Despite obtrusive military interference, the governments of Brazil and Peru are democratic by most criteria. Most progressive Catholics are in the opposition— but many are not. Under the FSLN government the Church has divided badly and even those committed to socialism are uncertain about the Church's role in revolutionary Nicaragua. In El Salvador, an elected government presides over a stalemated civil war, with diminished but continuing violations of basic human rights. Here, too, the apparent clarity of political options during earlier years has eroded.

In all four countries, the macropolitical changes have created new dilemmas for progressive Church people. Opposition to oppressive dictatorships united Church progressives and moderates in Brazil, El Salvador, Nicaragua, and Peru. Under dictatorial rule, the viewpoint that the Church should be the voice of the voiceless won widespread sympathy in the Church. Even the Nicaraguan bishops, today often dismissed as conservative or reactionary, eventually spoke out strongly against the Somoza dictatorship.

Under less repressive situations, this unity between progressives and moderates has eroded—a great deal in Nicaragua, but visibly even in Brazil. Moderates are less likely than the progressives to criticize democratic governments that fail to fulfill their promises—or even to live up to the rules of democratic politics as generally understood. Moderates may support the same episcopal documents and voice support for base communities, but they are less likely directly to encourage lay people to act in the political world. They tend to be more fearful of the divisive consequences of strong Church stances about what measures should be taken to transform unjust social structures.

But civil society became more capable of voicing its own interests in all four countries, posing new questions for the Church about what it meant to act as voice of the voiceless. Should the Church attempt to represent civil society under the new conditions? If so, what groups within civil society? More important—and more divisive—if it continued to act as a voice for oppressed groups, how should it relate to social movements and political parties that were also attempting, in different ways, to act as voice for the poor? Should the Church, in Levine's suggestive terms, function as activist or as activator?[21] If earlier the Church needed to choose between voice and silence, now it had to address a second set of questions: What kind of voice, for whom, how expressed? Now that opportunities for meaningful participation are greater, to what extent should the Church continue to articulate popular needs? Should it still have popular organizations that are "its own," linked to the Church's ecclesiastical structures? How broadly should it extend its umbrella of protection and patronage in new political conditions? Should it welcome or resist the "membership drain" (as Williams labels it in his chapter on Nicaragua) from Church groups to popular movements? Who legitimately represents the "voice" of those previously "voiceless"?

In general terms, the progressive Church no longer has the centrality it once had within the broader forces of political opposition. Conditions of dictatorship in the 1960s and 1970s gave progressives greater influence within their national Churches and, in our four cases, moved those Churches into an oppositional role. With ordinary forms of political expression disrupted or proscribed, the progressive Church could fill the gap in the name of its pastoral responsibilities and social leadership. As political opposition coalesced around the issue of changing the regime, an oppositional role united national Churches both within themselves and with civil society.

An evolution toward more cautious political positions is visible among Church progressives in all four countries, especially in the Central American cases. Cáceres' postscript, written in early 1986 with a tone that differs visibly from the rest of the chapter, which was written four years earlier, provides a fascinating account of Church change in El Salvador. The protracted and violent character of the civil war, which the guerrillas expected to win years ago, has led some Catholics to back away from their commitment to revolution and toward a renewed search for conciliation. The death of Archbishop Romero and the proclivities of his replacement, Archbishop Rivera y Damas, have clearly pushed the Salvadoran Church in this more cautious direction. The fact that the Christian Democrats are in power has led to some divisions among progressive Catholics. Most are in the opposition, but they are divided among those who support the guerrillas, those who argue for conciliation, and a small minority who have supported the government. The easing of repression in a country that continues to be plagued by considerable violence has allowed for the inchoate reemergence of popular movements, giving grass-roots Catholic groups a chance to resurface.

As Williams' chapter so clearly illustrates, there has also been a move toward more cautious political positions among radical Catholics in Nicaragua. Some of those who were most committed to the revolution have left the Church, usually because of pressing commitments in government and defense activities, in some cases because of disgruntlement with the hierarchy. In addition, Williams describes the questioning of the relationship between Church and revolution that has taken place in recent years among some progressive Catholics. Although they are still supportive of the revolution, these individuals have articulated the argument that the Church needs to maintain some autonomy with respect to the government.

As important as the change over time of the progressives' political viewpoints are differences among countries. While there are important similarities in the political ideals of the progressive Church across borders, political activities differ notably. The sharpest differences are those between Brazil, on the one hand, and El Salvador and Nicaragua, on the other.

In comparative terms, Brazil stands out as the case in which grass-roots Catholic groups have been the most cautious about political activities. Mainwaring's chapter argues this point at length, and in their case studies, Doimo and Ireland come to similar conclusions. Doimo argues that at a critical conjuncture (the end of the 1970s), when there existed a possibility of establishing more dynamic social movements, the Church backed away from direct support of these movements, leading to their enervation. Ireland, while more sanguine about the positive effects of Catholic groups on democratization, nevertheless notes that their impact would result not from the Church's deep involvement in political life, but rather from changes that might be effected at the level of consciousness. There are interesting variations from diocese to diocese and in some cases the Church is more directly involved in political life than in others. But even where its involvement is most direct and pronounced, the generally cautious and limited character of the political activities of grass-roots groups in Brazil is a contrast to what one finds in Central America.

More so than has been the case in the two Central American countries, the leading progressive bishops and theologians in Brazil have consistently argued for the importance of defending the specifically religious character of the Church institution. Frei Betto, a leading progressive theologian, has clearly articulated this viewpoint, specifically with reference to the CEBs:

> The specificity of the base communities lies in their religious character. This is the center of their existence. The people who participate in these communities are not motivated by professional, educational, or political interests. They are there because of their faith. This faith in Jesus Christ, lived and made explicit in communion with the Church, impels the simple people to participate in the base communities.[22]

Betto is far from alone in making this argument; it is widespread among progressive bishops, social scientists, theologians, and think tanks.

The sharpest contrast to Brazil is found in Central America. Whereas the chapters dealing with Brazil note the difficulty in encouraging CEB participants to engage in political life, in El Salvador and Nicaragua, grass-roots groups were at times overrun by politics. This was not necessarily the direction initially sought by members, but they found themselves in the midst of revolutionary upheaval. As Cáceres notes, in El Salvador the vicious repression that was unleashed after October 1979 made it virtually impossible for CEBs to function. The options were seemingly twofold: silence and submergence or commitment to the revolutionary struggle. In a similar way, Crahan and Williams note the deep commitment of a significant minority of Catholics to the revolutionary process in Nicaragua. In the period of approximately eighteen months before the Sandinistas took power, this struggle was all consuming for many grass-roots Catholics.

THE NEO-CONSERVATIVE CHALLENGE

The historical period in which the progressive Church was born is now over. Its beginnings are best dated to the mid-1960s, since the Medellín meeting of CELAM in 1968 affirmed and legitimated a movement already underway. For the end of the period, 1979 marks a persuasive line of division. Since then it has become clearer with each passing year that the context in which the progressive Church continues is quite different from that in which it was formed.

Politically as well as religiously, 1979 marked the inception of a new period. On one hand, it saw the triumph of the Sandinistas in Nicaragua, the first success for revolutionary forces since Cuba twenty years earlier. Although in South America it lacked the earlier impact of Cuba, the Nicaraguan revolution has had a central place in the policy both of the United States and of the Vatican toward the region as a whole. On the other hand, after 1979 Latin America seemed to be swept by a wave of democracy, as it had been earlier by dictatorship. Brazil, Argentina, and Peru were the largest of a whole group of countries that opened up their politics again after prolonged periods of authoritarian rule. The return to democracy in South America, a social revolution in the Isthmus: together they establish a political setting very different from that of the predominant military regimes of the 1970s.

In the new context, politics is far more divisive—between Church and society, between progressives and conservatives within the Church, and indeed among progressives themselves. Obviously the political situations in our four cases differ considerably among themselves. In none of them, however, does the progressive Church lead widespread opposition to the regime. Where the repression and arbitrary action of the state have decreased, civil society lacks its former focus on achieving a new political order (whether democratic or revolutionary). Where politics has become more democratic, those formerly voiceless now have many organizations claiming to represent them. In both ways a new political context narrows the needs and opportunities for Church political action. This situation has been welcomed by many in the Church. While continuing to express support for "the people," hierarchies have tended to pull back from direct identification with popular organizations. The leadership and involvement given by progressives are seen as a temporary stage, important in an earlier setting but now no longer necessary or appropriate.

In the religious sphere, the pontificate of Karol Woytila has in countless ways brought the conciliar era to a close. One of his earliest acts as Pope John Paul II was opening the 1979 CELAM meeting at Puebla, Mexico, at which the Latin American bishops gathered to consider what had happened in their Church since Medellín. As an event, Puebla marked a kind of tie between the progressives and neo-conservatives that had been engaged in an intramural struggle over the preceding years.[23] Since that time, however, the neo-conservatives have continued their ascent, begun earlier in the decade, and have turned the CELAM secretariat away from its former activism. Rome has called liberation theologians such as Leonardo Boff and Gustavo Gutiérrez to account, if not to recant, and has leaned toward conservative choices in filling vacant episcopal appointments. None of these events and actions represents a simple rejection of the progressive Church. Taken together, they attempt to retain some elements of what has happened since Medellín while restricting others. However, they clearly provide a very different religious context for the progressive Church in Latin America.[24]

The progressive Church has been profoundly affected by the conservative direction in the institutional Church. Following the Second Vatican Council, progressives in Latin America raised fundamental questions about the basic nature of the Church. They found a response from conservatives within the different national Churches, who from the early 1970s have counted on increasing support from the Vatican. The conservatives have reasserted traditional aspects of both the Church's internal character and external mission. Without attempting to summarize what has been a complex, multifaceted debate, let us consider briefly one of the key differences between the conservatives and progressives, the question of authority.

For conservatives the issue of authority is fundamentally linked to doctrinal orthodoxy. The Church is seen primarily in terms of the ecclesiastical institution. The hierarchical structure of this institution, in their view, is divinely ordained to preserve and transmit timeless truths of salvation. They recognize that the Church may need to adapt its teaching to new social circumstances, but this should never, they would insist, change the basic content of its doctrines or of the Church itself. The judge of any adaptation must always be those given hierarchical authority, the bishops and ultimately the pope, the successors to St. Peter and the other apostles. In the view of the conservatives none of the new, more horizontal structures within the Church—such as the collegial episcopal conferences or the basic Christian communities—affects the essentially vertical character of Church authority. Democracy may be a desirable form for political society, but the Church cannot and should not be democratic. The question of authority concerns essentially who speaks for the Church, and that is determined by those who hold the highest positions in its structure.

The progressive Church emerged from concern with the Church's authority in a different sense — its moral reach and significance in society. In the period after the Second World War, the Church's authority in this sense had become very marginal in Latin America. Rapid change was sweeping the area, and what the Church said or did made little difference. In the eyes of those who created the progressive Church, this lack of authority stemmed from the Church's dependence on established power and its distance from the great masses. It had to involve itself in their problems and to share their suffering, and it had to learn not merely to order but also to listen. The growth and vitality of the progressive Church seems to bear out their conception. The major role it played in the life of its societies in recent decades was based on the moral authority it had reestablished through its renewal. At an individual level, the immense authority of an Archbishop Oscar Romero in El Salvador or a Dom Helder Câmara in Brazil stemmed far less from a formal ecclesiastical position than from a relationship to the faithful. The progressive Church pointed back toward authority based, in the Conciliar metaphor, on the People of God.

This concern with the Church's social authority is a continuing legacy of the progressive Church in Latin America. There is no question that conservatives have successfully reasserted the issue of doctrinal authority, but it has not brought the Church back to the status quo ante. The two conceptions of authority — doctrinal within the institution, moral within society — have become fundamental to the Church. They will continue to be disputed between progressives and conservatives, but even very conservative leaders have accepted the legitimacy of some new Church structures.

While radical Catholicism has come under fire throughout Latin America, the progressive Church has experienced widely varying fates under the papacy of John Paul II. As the chapters by Crahan and Williams make evident, the pontiff has been deeply troubled by the "popular Church" in Nicaragua. The Brazilian case is entirely different. The pope has approved a series of conservative episcopal nominations, but he still manifested sympathy for the Brazilian Church. In April 1986 he sent a widely publicized and highly supportive letter to the Brazilian bishops, affirming that "we are convinced, we and you, that the theology of liberation is not only timely, but useful and necessary. . . . In this field, the Church in Brazil can play an important and at the same time delicate role — that of creating the space and conditions for the development of a theological reflection that fully adheres to the Church's constant teaching on social matters and, at the same time, is suitable for inspiring and effective pastoral praxis in favor of social justice, equity, the observance of human rights, the construction of a human society based in brotherhood, harmony, truth, and charity."[25]

Notwithstanding an amalgam of measures that indicate a real strength of conservative forces within the Church, we believe that the progressive Church has left an indelible mark. The chapters in this book indicate the extent to which radical Catholics have influenced politics in their countries. Their impact on the international Church is perhaps best suggested by an unlikely source: conservative Church leaders, because of their acceptance of many progressive themes. A leading example was the Congregation for the Doctrine of the Faith's second document on liberation theology, the "Instruction on Christian Freedom and Liberation."

> The evil inequities and oppression of every kind which afflict millions of men and women today openly contradict Christ's gospel and cannot leave the conscience of any Christian indifferent. . . . The love which impels the Church to communicate to all people a sharing in the grace of divine life also causes her . . . to pursue people's true temporal good. . . . Therefore, when the Church speaks about the promotion of justice in human societies or when she urges the faithful laity to work in this sphere according to their own vocation, she is not going beyond her own mission. . . . Situations of grave injustice require the courage to make far-reaching reforms and to suppress unjustifiable privileges.[26]

DEBATES ABOUT THE PROGRESSIVE CHURCH

Written around common themes and a defined historical period, the chapters in this book nevertheless provide a considerable range of viewpoints. The book includes contributions by an Australian, a Brazilian, four North Americans, two Peruvians, and a Salvadoran. The contributions come from scholars of different disciplines: history (Crahan), law (Pásara), political science (Mainwaring, Wilde, Williams), anthropology (Doimo, Ireland), and sociology (Cáceres, Romero).

This common interest of scholars in several different disciplines is revealing of the object of study. Typically, anthropologists have been more sensitive to popular processes; sociologists and political scientists to the importance of institutions. Here, regardless of discipline, the authors attempt to locate their studies historically, by providing an overview of the institutional and political contexts in which progressive Catholics act.

Most important, there is a wide range of evaluations of the progressive Church, from Pásara and Doimo, who are critical (though express different reasons for their criticisms), to Cáceres and Romero, who are openly supportive of it; the others are somewhere in between, though generally sympathetic. But the differences are not simply subjective or political; there are also implicit debates about the nature and impact of the progressive Church. Part of the interest of the volume, we believe, stems from having diverse viewpoints on a set of common themes. Here we wish to briefly signal some of the more important debates found in the chapters that follow.

(1) How important is the progressive Church within the Church as a whole? There is a generalized agreement that the progressives are in a minority everywhere, and also that they are under attack everywhere, but there is considerable contrast even in the analysis of the same case: Pásara argues that Catholic radicals in Peru are relatively marginal, while Romero argues that they have influenced the institution's central orientations. In assessing the Brazilian case, Mainwaring comes close to Romero's position; in analyzing Nicaragua, Crahan and Williams point to the profound rift between a conservative hierarchy and a fairly broad segment of the clergy and laity committed to progressive viewpoints. Cáceres argues that in El Salvador, the progressives had considerable impact, but that this impact has diminished markedly since 1980, both because of Archbishop Romero's death and because of the turmoil of the civil war.

(2) What is the impact of the progressive Church on democratization? Romero offers the most favorable assessment of the democratic character and contributions of the progressive Church. Cáceres, Ireland, and Mainwaring cautiously argue that the Church has contributed to democratization, but with some caveats. Cáceres underscores the intense difficulties of a true process of democratization in the midst of the internecine war in El Salvador. Ireland argues that CEBs have the potential to become "intermediate groups" that encourage deeper democratization in Brazil, but also notes obstacles to realizing this potential. Mainwaring suggests that grass-roots groups were important in the opposition to the military government, but that their sectarian political viewpoints and practices may limit their ability to intervene effectively in democratic politics. Doimo argues that the Church helped stimulate the formation of democratizing social movements, but later inhibited their autonomy and vigor. In contrast, Pásara points to utopian and authoritarian strains in radical Catholicism in Peru, while Crahan and Williams implicitly raise doubts about the Church's potential to contribute to democratization in Nicaragua.

(3) To what extent do the changes of the past two decades indicate democratization within the Church? Some authors (Cáceres, Mainwaring, Ireland, and Romero) maintain that CEBs represent a real shift in authority lines, even while recognizing their linkages to the hierarchy. Doimo, however, emphasizes more the authoritarian ecclesiastical con-

trols over CEBs, and Pásara disagrees radically, arguing that clericalism, a vertical hierarchical structure, and authoritarianism are as strong as ever inside the Church. From a different perspective, Crahan and Williams both note that the Nicaraguan case indicates important limits in this process of internal democratization.

While the authors have different views on some issues, all of them attempt to bring new scholarly perspectives to the questions at hand. All of the essays in this sense transcend the facile characterizations found in many writings on the Latin American Church. All of the authors treat seriously the nature of religious motivations; none of them sees religion as epiphenomenal. Moreover the chapters, without exception, attempt to understand the Church's institutionality without treating it simply as another institution, and thereby exorcising the religious element out of social scientific analysis. In doing so, these chapters contribute to pushing the state of the art in directions we find salutary and encouraging. We hope the book will make a modest contribution to some of the most interesting issues found in the contemporary world in the relationship between religion and politics.

NOTES

1. There are, of course, exceptions to this generalization. During the 1950s, Perón clashed with the Argentine Church, and Rojas Pinilla did likewise with the Church in Colombia. Generally speaking, however, relations between the Church and state were amicable during the populist period. Although many contemporary radicals stress the Church's historical association with the established regime, there were numerous conflicts between Church and state in prior periods of Latin American history. For extensive documentation on this point, see Lloyd J. Mecham's classic *Church and State in Latin America* (Chapel Hill, N.C.: University of North Carolina Press, 1934).

2. For example, see Paul Johnson, *Pope John Paul II and the Catholic Restoration* (New York: St. Martin's Press, 1981), pp. 124–145.

3. A considerable part of the extensive literature on CEBs is of an apologetic character. In recent years, however, a solid theological and social science literature has emerged. A good starting point is Marcello Azevedo, *Basic Ecclesial Communities in Brazil* (Washington, D.C.: Georgetown University Press, 1987). See Mainwaring's chapter for an extensive list of works on CEBs in Brazil.

4. For an elaboration of this point, see Daniel H. Levine, "Religion and Politics: Dimensions of Renewal," *Thought* 59 (June 1984); and Daniel H. Levine and Scott Mainwaring, "Religion and Popular Protest in Latin America: Contrasting Experiences," in Susan Eckstein, ed., *Protest and Resistance: Latin American Experiences* (Berkeley, Calif.: University of California Press, forthcoming).

5. The bibliography on liberation theology is vast. Good starting points in-

clude Phillip Berryman, *Liberation Theology* (Philadelphia: Temple University Press, 1987); Phillip Berryman, "Latin American Liberation Theology," in Sergio Torres and John Eagleson, eds., *Theology in the Americas* (Maryknoll, N.Y.: Orbis, 1976), pp. 20–83. Good histories of the emergence and early development of liberation theology are Roberto Oliveros, *Liberación y teología: Génesis y crecimiento de una reflexión* (Lima: Centro de Estudios y Publicaciones, 1977); and Alfonso García Rubio, *Teologia da Libertação: Política ou Profetismo?* (São Paulo: Loyola, 1977).

6. Third General Conference of Latin American Bishops, *Puebla: Evangelization at Present and in the Future of Latin America* (Washington, D.C.: National Conference of Catholic Bishops, 1979), Para. 1134, 1159, 1160.

7. For example, Vatican Congregation for the Doctrine of the Faith, "Instruction on Certain Aspects of the 'Theology of Liberation'," *Origins* (September 13, 1984); Alfonso López Trujillo, *Liberation or Revolution?* (Huntington, Ind.: Our Sunday Visitor, 1977); Michael Novak, *Will it Liberate?* (New York: Paulist Press, 1986); Heráclito Sobral Pinto, *Teologia da Libertação: O Materialismo Marxista na Teologia Espiritualista* (Rio de Janeiro: Lidador, 1984).

8. Catholic social thought has never paid much attention to political parties. Parties are a distinctly modern (post-1790) form of political organization, but since 1900 they have been at the center of a good part of democratic theory. Catholic social thought has generally continued to conceive of politics in terms of a common good and has usually questioned the legitimacy of conflict, which is seen as resulting from egotism.

9. For a scurrilous variant, see Boaventura Kloppenburg, *Igreja Popular* (Rio de Janeiro: Agir, 1983), who writes, "It is not because of their love for or identification with the Church that they [the radicals] demand their place in the Church; it is to realize within the Church – like a Trojan horse – an ideological struggle" (p. 84).

10. On the significance of Vatican II, see Thomas O'Dea, *The Catholic Crisis* (Boston: Beacon, 1968); and Peter Hebblethwaite, *The Runaway Church: Postconciliar Growth or Decline?* (London: Collins, 1975).

11. On Costa Rica, see Andrés Opazo Bernales, *Costa Rica: La Iglesia Católica y el orden social* (San José: DEI/CSUCA, 1987). On Venezuela and Colombia, see Daniel H. Levine, *Religion and Politics in Latin America: The Catholic Church in Venezuela and Colombia* (Princeton, N.J.: Princeton University Press, 1981). On Colombia, see Daniel H. Levine, "Continuities in Colombia," *Journal of Latin American Studies* 17, no. 2 (1985): 295–317; Alexander Wilde, "Creating Neo-Christendom in Colombia," in Donald L. Herman, ed., *Democracy in Latin America* (New York: Praeger, 1988).

12. We are critical of interpretations, usually written by intellectuals of the progressive Church, that explain change in the Church largely on the basis of changing social and/or political conditions. For an interpretation of this nature, see Pablo Richard, *Morte das Cristandades e Nascimento da Igreja* (São Paulo: Paulinas, 1982). As we note, in many countries dictatorship and inequalities did not lead to the emergence of a strong radical sector in the Church. The internal process of Church change is crucial; without it, dictatorship would not have had such a radicalizing effect on the Church.

13. See Daniel Levine, "Colombia: The Institutional Church and the Popular," in *Religion and Political Conflict in Latin America* (Chapel Hill, N.C.: University of North Carolina Press, 1986), pp. 187–217.

14. This position characterized the Christians for Socialism group, among other examples. See John Eagleson, ed., *Christians and Socialism: Documentation of the Christians for Socialism Movement in Latin America* (Maryknoll, N.Y.: Orbis, 1975).

15. For example, see Gustavo Gutiérrez, *We Drink from Our Own Wells* (Maryknoll, N.Y.: Orbis, 1984); Segundo Galilea, *The Future of Our Past* (Notre Dame, Ind.: Ave Maria Press, 1985); Jon Sobrino, *La oración de Jesus y del Cristiano* (Mexico: Centro de Reflexión Teológica, 1981).

16. For analysis of the Nicaraguan situation, see, in addition to the chapters in this book, Phillip Berryman, *The Religious Roots of Rebellion: Christians in Central American Revolutions* (Maryknoll, N.Y.: Orbis, 1984).

17. On Christian Democracy, see Michael Fleet, *The Rise and Fall of Chilean Christian Democracy* (Princeton, N.J.: Princeton University Press, 1985); Stephen Webre, *José Napoléon Duarte and the Christian Democratic Party in Salvadoran Politics, 1960–1972* (Baton Rouge, La.: Louisiana State University Press, 1979); Edward Williams, *Latin American Christian Democratic Parties* (Knoxville, Tenn.: University of Tennessee Press, 1967).

18. Ação Popular, "Documento-Base," in Luiz Gonzaga de Souza Lima, *Evolução Política dos Católicos e da Igreja no Brasil* (Petrópolis: Vozes, 1979), p. 141. Ação Popular was not formally connected to the Church, but it was created by Catholic radicals who had become disgruntled with the Church's limitations as a vehicle for promoting political change.

19. See Gianfranco Poggi's classic book, *Catholic Action in Italy: The Sociology of a Sponsored Organization* (Stanford, Calif.: Stanford University Press, 1967); Jean-Guy Vaillancourt, *Papal Power: A Study of Vatican Control over Catholic Lay Groups* (Berkeley, Calif.: University of California Press, 1980); and the chapter by Luis Pásara in this book.

20. The Cristeros' rebellion in Mexico (1926–1929) is one of the most famous examples. See Alicia Olivera Sedano, *Aspectos del conflicto religioso de 1926 a 1929: Sus antecedentes y consecuencias* (Mexico City: Instituto Nacional de Antropología, 1966). Another famous example was the uprising in Canudos, Brazil, led by Antonio Conselheiro. See Euclides da Cunha's famous account, *Rebellion in the Backlands* (Chicago: University of Chicago Press, 1944).

21. Levine, *Religion and Politics in Latin America.*

22. Frei Betto, "Da Prática da Pastoral Popular," *Encontros com a Civilização Brasileira* 2 (1978): 95.

23. For interpretations of Puebla, see Phillip Berryman, "What Happened at Puebla," in Daniel H. Levine, ed., *Churches and Politics in Latin America* (Beverly Hills, Calif.: Sage, 1979), pp. 55–86; Alexander Wilde, "Ten Years of Change in the Church: Puebla and the Future" in Levine, *Churches and Politics in Latin America,* pp. 267–280.

24. On the neo-conservative movement, see Scott Mainwaring, *The Catholic Church and Politics in Brazil 1916–1985* (Stanford, Calif.: Stanford University Press, 1986), pp. 237–253; Ralph Della Cava, "The Church and the 'Abertura', 1974–1985," in Alfred Stepan, ed., *Democratizing Brazil* (New York: Oxford University Press, forthcoming); Joseph Comblin, "A América Latina e o Presente Debate Teológico entre Neo-Conservadores e Liberais," *Revista Eclesiástica Brasileira* 41 (1981): 790–816; Joseph

Comblin, "Os Movimentos e a Pastoral Latinoamericana," *Revista Eclesiástica Brasileira* 43 (1983): 227–262.

25. "Pope's Letter to Brazil's Bishops," *Origins* 16 (May 22, 1986): 14.

26. The Congregation for the Doctrine of the Faith, "Instruction on Christian Freedom and Liberation," *Origins* 15 (April 17, 1986): 721–722, 724.

PART I

Central America

Religion and Politics in Revolutionary Nicaragua

Margaret E. Crahan

The ideological and political struggle currently underway in Nicaragua is largely focused on and in the Catholic Church. This is the result of the relative strength of the Catholic Church as an institution in a society that until recently did not have very high organizational levels. It is also due to the historical role of Christianity as a key element of Nicaraguan cultural identity and to the rapid expansion of grass-roots activities on the part of the Catholic Church beginning in the 1960s. The latter involved churchpeople not only with the Sandinista movement during the struggle to overthrow Somoza, but also with popular sectors of society considered the potential backbone of the revolutionary process by the Government of National Reconstruction which took power in July 1979. Competition, however, for the ultimate loyalty of the masses in Nicaragua is not strictly between the government and the Church, but rather between pro and antigovernment coalitions, both of which incorporate Church personnel. Hence the current ferment within Nicaraguan society has exacerbated differences within the Catholic Church over how best to fulfill the Church's repeatedly expressed preferential option for the poor. This debate has its roots in ecclesial responses to pressures for change dating back to the 1920s and 1930s and the consequent redefinition and refinement of the Catholic Church's mission emanating from Vatican II (1962–1965) and the meetings of the Latin American Bishops' Conference at Medellín, Colombia (1968) and Puebla, Mexico (1979).

It is a serious miscalculation to ascribe to Marxist penetration the openness to socialism and the Sandinista movement by substantial minorities within the Nicaraguan Catholic Church. There are few churchpeople who are uncritical of Marxism, although some use aspects of Marxist analysis in their evaluations of contemporary socioeconomic conditions. For most, the Marxist materialist interpretation of life remains antitheti-

41

cal to Christian beliefs. What has happened is that a good proportion
of churchpeople, including moderates and conservatives, have lost faith
in the ability of capitalist development to substantially improve the lot
of the poor in Latin America. In addition, among churchpeople throughout Latin America in the 1960s and 1970s there was a diminution of confidence in traditional governing elites, particularly when repression was
used to limit change or defend certain models of development. This led
the Church to modify its traditional alliances.

In the past the strategy of the Church leadership in Latin America
was to cultivate and maintain good relations with political and economic
elites in order to benefit from their resources and control over society.
This identification with dominant elites became more and more questioned
on moral and strategic grounds in the context of popular pressures for
structural change in the post–World War II period. With the increase of
repression and violations of human rights by the state, particularly in the
1960s and 1970s, and as new generations of professionals entered the Church
bureaucracy, the argument began to be made more frequently that to maintain legitimacy, fulfill its universal salvific mission, and survive as an institution, the Church should identify itself with the masses. This reflected
an acceptance of the necessity of substantial changes in societal structures, as well as those of the Church.

The Church's most public acknowledgment of the relegation to a
secondary position of its traditional strategy of cultivating political and
economic elites in favor of identification with the masses is contained in
the preface to the Puebla documents. There the bishops criticize themselves for sins of omission for not having spoken out more forcefully against
socioeconomic injustice or committed themselves – progressives, liberals,
moderates, conservatives alike – to a preferential option for the poor. This
new position was the result not only of the long process of adaptation
to generalized pressures for change, but also to actual and potential losses
to secular and religious competitors for the ultimate loyalty of the people.

Having embarked on a strategy of cultivation and expansion of the
grass-roots Church, the Catholic Church has become deeply involved in
the debate over how best to effect socioeconomic change. It has also witnessed the development within the Church of new theologies, pastoral
practices, and definitions of the Church that challenge traditional forms
and authority.

The ferment generated by such changes had particular impact on
Nicaragua in the aftermath of the 1972 earthquake. That disaster prompted
greater involvement of churchpeople with the poor and the homeless, as
well as increasing awareness of corruption within the Somoza government.
It also led to greater knowledge of violations of basic socioeconomic rights,

as well as civil and political rights, which were a prime reason for the Nicaraguan hierarchy's June 2, 1979 pastoral letter in support of the insurrection to overthrow Somoza.[1] Such approval did not, however, mean a carte blanche for whatever government succeeded Somoza. Rather the bishops from the outset indicated a preference for a multiparty political system committed to reformist rather than radical change. The presence of some Marxist-Leninists in the Sandinista leadership also conflicted with the Catholic Church's deeply rooted anti-Marxism. Not all churchpeople were, however, opposed to the ideological orientation of the Government of National Reconstruction. Differing definitions of the obligations of Christians in situations such as Nicaragua have resulted in considerable internal debate and conflict within the Church.

Involvement in the ideological debate and political struggle currently underway in Nicaragua presents real threats to the Catholic Church as an institution. In such circumstances, while the institutional Church remained strongly anti-Marxist, the desire of the Nicaraguan hierarchy to identify with the broad-based popular insurrection against Somoza and subsequently to avoid exacerbating internal divisions led initially to pragmatic policies of compromise with prorevolutionary sectors both within and outside the Church. Since 1982 the bishops have attempted to reassert episcopal authority and doctrinal and political orthodoxy, becoming increasingly critical of the "popular" Church and the Sandinista government. In this the bishops are supported by Rome and the leadership of CELAM (Conferencia Episcopal Latino-Americana), the permanent coordinating body of the national bishops' conferences in Latin America.

Such attempts are extremely difficult in the face of the politicization of the Nicaraguan Church that occurred in the 1960s and 1970s, largely as a result of the introduction of such innovations as grass-roots Christian communities (CEBs), lay preachers, and of social action programs. The presence of such groups and programs in rural and urban areas previously devoid of organizational bases provided such communities with mechanisms for political and economic demand making that resulted in the mid-1970s in their increasing repression by Somoza's National Guard.

The Church defended its institutions and members against such attacks, while the bishops remained somewhat uneasy about grass-roots progressivism and autonomy. The bishops were increasingly critical of Somoza and some, like the Archbishop, now Cardinal of Managua, Miguel Obando y Bravo, took no pains to hide their distaste for Somoza and his government. In fact, in August 1978 the prelate publicly called upon him to resign. By 1979 it is estimated that 85 percent of the approximately 120 priests in the country, plus the majority of nuns were strongly opposed to Somoza.[2] The Jesuits, Maryknollers, and Capuchins were in the forefront of clerical opposition to the regime, but it was not until the late 1970s that a substantial number began cooperating with the Frente Sandinista de Liberación Nacional (FSLN). During the final stages of the struggle in 1978–1979 Church groups not only provided humanitarian and other assistance, but served to publicize outside Nicaragua the issues involved in the struggle and mobilize international support for the opposition.

In June of 1979 shortly before the final toppling of Somoza, the Nicaraguan bishops held the insurrection to be moral and legitimate in the face of a system and structures that resulted in grave inequalities between classes and citizens. Failure of the government to guarantee civil and political rights, as well as to promote the fulfillment of basic socioeconomic rights undercut, in the bishops' minds, its legitimacy. The existence of prolonged denial of the fundamental rights of the individual justified the insurrection, as witnessed by its broad popular base. The bishops cautioned, however, that care must be taken in any process of reconstruction to overcome political partisanship, ideological differences, and special interests. Furthermore, the bishops warned that the maintenance of political pluralism was indispensable and that socioeconomic improvements must be linked to popular participation.[3]

On July 31, 1979 the bishops issued another pastoral letter urging that Nicaraguans beware of all "imperialisms" and freely mold their own political and social structures. These should incorporate those human values that implied authentic liberation and were free from the domination of state idolatries. In raising the political consciousness of the people the government should be careful not to encourage massification. Furthermore, belief in God must not be excluded from the task of national reconstruction, for this "would newly enslave the people, not liberate them."[4]

During the summer and fall of 1979 as the bishops were expressing their preoccupations with the possible direction of the new government, several priests were incorporating themselves into it., The Maryknoller, Miguel D'Escoto, was named Foreign Minister, a Trappist-trained diocesan priest, Ernesto Cardenal, became Minister of Culture, while the Jesuit Xabier Gorostiaga was head of national planning. Cardenal's brother Fernando, a Jesuit, was made director of the national literacy campaign, then director of the Sandinista Youth, and is currently Minister of Education. Father Edgard Parrales served as Minister of Social Welfare and is presently Nicaraguan Ambassador to the Organization of American States. A number of other priests also accepted official positions. Their actions pointed up the fact that among the clergy there was less caution in supporting the Sandinista government than among the hierarchy.[5]

On November 19, 1979 episcopal disquiet over possible Marxist inroads was expressed in a pastoral letter entitled "Christian Commitment for a New Nicaragua" that continued to affirm support for the Government of National Reconstruction. The bishops were, however, clearly worried that the creation and expansion of Sandinista organizations and other mechanisms such as the literacy campaign would be used to inculcate atheism and lead to the ultimate abandonment of the Church by the people. They placed a premium on maintaining unity within the Church, which encouraged the maintenance of somewhat ambiguous positions in order to incorporate a fairly wide spectrum of opinion. Nevertheless, in November 1979, the Episcopal Conference urged recognition of the "risks, the dangers, the errors of this revolutionary process while being conscious of the fact that in history there are no absolutely pure human processes. Therefore, we must give importance to freedom of expression and criticism as the only way of indicating and correcting errors in order to perfect the achievements of the revolutionary process."[6] The bishops further asserted that their commitment to the revolutionary process should not be interpreted as signifying "naive or blind enthusiasm." Moreover, "dignity, respect, and Christian liberty are irrenounceable rights within an active participation in the revolutionary process."[7]

Coming as it did at a time of increasing criticism of the government by conservative Nicaraguan political sectors, the cautionary words of the bishops were interpreted by some as support for the latter. The episcopacy wanted to establish the legitimacy of the Church as a critic of the revolutionary process and as a non-partisan actor whose actions stemmed from concern for individuals of all political persuasions. The bishops did praise the revolutionary government for its accomplishments and urged it to continue in its attempts to satisfy basic needs and reduce injustice. This, the prelates asserted, could only be accomplished through the transfer of power to the common people thereby encouraging them to assume responsibility for the realization of the Christian obligation to perfect the world.[8]

Motivated in part by the November 1979 pastoral letter, the Sandinistas prepared a position paper on religion that was intended to reassure the Catholic leadership that they would respect religious liberty and recognize the role of the Church within Nicaraguan society. It recognized the extent of Christian collaboration in the insurrection and the revolutionary process and expressed the belief that there was no contradiction in being both a Christian and a revolutionary. In addition, the statement confirmed that membership in the FSLN was open to all irrespective of their religious beliefs. However attempts to proselytize within the FSLN on behalf of specific religions was to be discouraged on the grounds that such activities were inappropriate and divisive. The Sandinista Directorate expressed its respect for Nicaraguan religious traditions and celebrations and offered assistance to ensure that they were not used for political or commercial purposes. Specifically it stated that if "political parties or individual persons tried to convert popular religious fiestas or activities into political acts contrary to the Revolution (as had occurred on occasion in the past) the FSLN declared its right to defend the people and the Revolution. . . ."⁹

The FSLN also denied accusations that it had attempted to divide the Catholic Church, arguing that if divisions existed they resulted from factors completely independent of the Sandinistas. It noted that different and sometimes contradictory positions concerning political issues historically existed within the Church. The FSLN Directorate also felt that most Nicaraguan Christians actively supported the revolution, with only a minority opposing it.

With respect to the participation of priests in the Government of National Reconstruction, the Directorate took the position that all Nicaraguan citizens had a right to participate in the political management of the country irrespective of their civil status. They attributed the participation of priests in government largely to the fact that they were among the few Nicaraguans with higher educations. Furthermore, the FSLN held that the decision to participate in government was a matter of individual conscience. The declaration concluded with the statement that the revolution and the state had different origins, ends, and spheres of action than religion did. Furthermore, the state was secular and should not establish an official religion, since it represented both believers and non-believers. The bishops reacted by preparing in late 1980 a detailed commentary on the Sandinista statement. It reflected fear of the emergence of a single party state that propounded an atheistic ideology and the massification of society. It also denied the government the authority, which the Sandinistas had asserted, to decide if political parties or individuals were trying to convert religious activities into political events. The bishops also insisted that the government should not make a show of atheism or proselytize ideologically at the expense of religious beliefs. In addition, no particular ideology should be preferred by the state.

The hierarchy warned against accepting international assistance from sources they regarded as contrary to the religious beliefs of the Nicaraguan people. This apparently referred to the Soviet Union and its allies. The bishops insisted that religious and socioeconomic matters were not separate, but rather converged to promote the common good. Furthermore religious motives were not individual or personalistic, but rather a reflection of the action of the Holy Spirit within society. Hence, the Church had a legitimate role to play as a promoter and critic of socioeconomic policies. The Sandinista position allowing priests to hold political office was criticized on the grounds that it was not in accord with the priestly ministry and could be interpreted as providing legitimacy to a particular political system. Finally the bishops insisted that it was not the Catholic Church, nor Christians, who were against the revolution, but those who deviated ideologically from the religious sentiments of the Nicaraguan people.[10] The bishops' commentary drew some criticism on the grounds that it was harmful to the process of national reconstruction. These were expressed by a number of CEBs, youth and student organizations, the Jesuits, the national conference of religious (CONFER), and some social action and study groups.[11]

The latter had previously promoted efforts to increase Marxist-Christian dialogue and Christian participation in the revolution. In September 1979 a seminar was held at the Universidad Centroamericana in Managua to explore ways the Church could contribute to the revolution. Participants included junta members, priests, Protestant ministers, and CEB leaders. It resulted in the mobilization of the University's Instituto Histórico, under the direction of the Jesuit Álvaro Argüello, to assist in the analysis of the role of the Church in national reconstruction. The Instituto represented some of the most progressive elements in the Church, and as a result of criticism from within the University tended to seek a somewhat independent identity. In August 1979 the Centro Antonio Valdivieso was created to help promote support for the revolution among Christians and assist ecclesiastical leaders to understand the process. It had the further objective of countering rightist influences on the churches. Headed up by an ecumenical team of a Franciscan and a Baptist minister, it aimed to work with Church leaders, as well as the CEBs.

There is some evidence that the strength of the CEBs is somewhat reduced in areas where Sandinista organizations expanded.[12] In communities such as Estelí in northern Nicaragua and Ciudad Sandino on the outskirts of Managua there was some loss of CEB members as they became heavily involved in Sandinista organizations. This was especially true of young people who were strongly attracted to the mass organizations because of the opportunity they provided to participate directly in the revolutionary process. Involvement in such organizations was enormously time consuming and left little energy for other activities. Commitment to the revolution led some to give it their first loyalty, placing religious loyalties in a secondary place. In addition, as the government began increasing social services there was less need for certain Church programs. The loss of some Church activists tended to feed the fears of those who believed consolidation of the revolution would undercut Church strength.

As ideological and political debate sharpened within Nicaragua, particularly after 1980, so did divisions within the Catholic Church. In addition, there were increased attempts by all sides to utilize Church person-

nel and institutions to legitimate particular stances. Given the varieties
of opinion within the Church, it was possible for both pro and antigovernment forces to adduce support. The "battle of the quotations" from
Church leaders and papal documents in the pages of *La Prensa* and *El
Nuevo Diario* testifies to this. Increasingly the episcopacy, and particularly
Cardinal Obando y Bravo, identified with antigovernment elements. For
its part the government generally tried not to alienate the prelates, although
it was increasingly preoccupied and angered by critical statements of the
hierarchy and their identification with antigovernment elements. The rapid
reversal of the expulsion of two priests and three nuns from the Atlantic
Coast area in early 1982 for allegedly counterrevolutionary activities indicated a continued commitment to avoid an open break. In the summer
of 1984, however, ten foreign priests who were expelled by the government from Nicaragua in the wake of allegations that they supported the
counterrevolutionaries were not readmitted. Some of them returned to
Nicaragua in 1986 and 1987.

     Tensions between Church leaders and the Sandinistas tended to ex-
acerbate differences among conservative, reformist, and pro-Sandinista sectors in the Catholic and Protestant churches. Catholic progressives have
been highly critical of the episcopacy, particularly of Cardinal Miguel
Obando y Bravo who emerged as the most influential critic of the government. The prelate's public distaste for Somoza in the 1970s had garnered
him considerable popularity in Nicaragua, a fact which was not lost on
the Sandinistas, who sought initially to use him to legitimate the Government of National Reconstruction. The presence of clerics in very visible
positions in the government reinforced this and was accepted originally
by the episcopacy as a means of influencing the course of the new government. However, as antigovernment attitudes among the bishops hardened,
the prelates increasingly appeared to be supporting opposition forces. The
frequency with which the episcopacy's and especially Obando y Bravo's
activities and statements appeared on the front page of *La Prensa* testifies
to this. While this contributed to the government limiting Obando y Bravo
to one televised mass a month, instead of the usual four, not all the
episcopacy reportedly were unhappy about this, some having resented the
Cardinal's monopoly. Well before Obando y Bravo's upsurge of national
popularity during the insurrection, there existed some criticism of him
within the episcopacy. However, as the bishops became more unified in
their criticism of the government, internal divisions were reduced, as well
as collegial competition. This has allowed them to present a stronger front
to the government, as well as appeal to the people with more unity. Hence,
the impact of their positions and statements has been increased.

     As the episcopacy became more critical of the government, it also began to attempt to rein in the more progressive sectors of the Church. Obando y Bravo or his assistants reportedly sought the removal of some progressive priests or religious from working-class parishes or base communities, precipitating sit-ins in a number of churches in 1982.[13] While the Cardinal has on a number of occasions denied involvement, there is conflicting evidence from some religious superiors. Obando agreed to enter into discussions with representatives of the protestors, but this did not defuse the situation. In fact, by July 1982 dissension had reached such a point that when the auxiliary bishop of Managua, Monsignor Bosco Vivas Robelo, went to the Church of Santa Rosa to retrieve the blessed sacrament during a sit-in, a scuffle ensued. Obando y Bravo responded by placing the parish under interdict and excommunicating those who were alleged to have roughed up the bishop.[14] This incident marked the beginning of a serious deterioration of relations between the hierarchy and progressive elements within the Church.

The latter argues that there are no grounds for charges that they are intent on establishing a separate Church and progressive clergy and religious as a parallel magisterium. The national conference of religious (CONFER), student and youth groups, the Instituto Histórico, and Centro Antonio Valdivieso have all been intent on combating such charges, arguing that they believe in one Church, led by the episcopacy, but with greater dialogue to resolve differences and misunderstandings. Progressive elements within the Church have repeatedly asserted their respect for the hierarchy and rejected charges that they were intent on flouting established Church authorities. As early as October 1981 the base Christian communities in Managua issued a public statement countering all of the allegations against them:

> What grieves us most is that we are accused of not being in communion with the hierarchy that represents Jesus Christ here on earth, insinuating that we are separated from Christ himself. The Lord is aware of the pain that these falsehoods cause us, because we truly recognize the bishops as His representatives. The Lord knows that we have always been in communion with our parish priests and that we always wish to be in communion with our bishops. It grieves us that we have not understood how to express this communion in a more visible manner, but we will continue trying to do so by means of intraecclesial dialogue with our archbishop and with all of the bishops.[15]

Such efforts do not, however, appear to have had much impact on diminishing the growing distance between progressives and the hierarchy.

Criticism of progressive elements within the Church was stimulated by *La Prensa*, the businessmen's organization COSEP, and the allied Centro de Estudios Religiosos. In November 1981 the Centro published a survey that suggested that most Nicaraguans opposed the continued participation of priests in politics, objected to the cancellation of Obando y Bravo's televised masses, and strongly supported religious education in all schools, public and private.[16] It did not, however, offer data that demonstrated broad-based opposition within or without the Church to the government.

In July 1982 the Nicaraguan government decided that it would no longer allow U.S. foreign aid to private business, educational, and Church groups. Of the several million dollars involved, $115,000 went to the archbishopric of Managua for overhead or existing programs, the creation of small ecclesial communities, and leadership training. The latter two were regarded as means to compete with progressive grass-roots communities and lay leaders. In testimony before Congress, Assistant Secretary of State for Inter-American Affairs, Thomas O. Enders, and AID official Otto Reich confirmed that the funds were intended to support groups in opposition to the government of Nicaragua.[17]

Although 80 to 90 percent of Nicaraguans are Catholics, there has been considerable growth over the past twenty years of Protestant groups, particularly Pentecostals.[18] These groups have also become involved in the political struggle within Nicaragua. The Mormons, Jehovah's Witnesses, and Seventh Day Adventists have increasingly come into conflict with the government, in large measure due to their opposition to military training and public education. They are strongly anti-Marxist and have identified with the opposition to the present government. As a result, the government has restricted the activities of these churches and their ministers, expelling some of the latter from the country. These problems are akin to those encountered by these denominations in other countries, both under leftist governments (e.g., Cuba) and under rightist ones (e.g., Brazil).

The Moravian Church which is centered on the Atlantic Coast is a special case. Established in the nineteenth century by German and U.S. missionaries, the church is closely identified with the Miskitos (population ca. 120,000) and Creoles (population ca. 80,000). These peoples, together with the Sumo and Rama Indians, long enjoyed considerable autonomy from the central government and maintained a strong cultural, ethnic, and linguistic identity different from Nicaraguans on the Pacific Coast. Efforts by the Government of National Reconstruction beginning in 1979 to incorporate this area more firmly into centralized administrative structures, insensitivity to local organizations and customs, and preoccupation with escalating counterrevolutionary military attacks in the region led to a series of confrontations. The arrest of Steadman Fagoth, and other leaders of MISURASATA (a coalition of indigenous groups) led to a 1981 shoot-out in which four Miskitos and four soldiers were shot. The subsequent incorporation of Fagoth, and allegedly some Moravian ministers, into armed counterrevolutionary forces in Honduras increased tensions.

Hostilities along the border with Honduras resulted in the removal of several Indian communities into the interior of Zelaya Province in early 1982. This action was highly controversial within and without Nicaragua and was strongly criticized by the Catholic hierarchy for violating human rights. The bishops alleged that there had been insufficient consideration of the weak, elderly, women, and children, as well as unjust destruction of homes, goods, and livestock, and some deaths. The latter was not substantiated. They called upon the inhabitants of the area to conserve, cultivate, and defend their Christian faith. For their part, the bishops promised to intensify efforts to evangelize the region and called upon the government to assist them in relief efforts.[19]

The government reacted strongly to what it regarded as unjust accusations and lack of appreciation of the military situation in an area where there had been increased fighting with anti-Sandinista elements based in Honduras. Beyond this the government criticized the bishops for not having accepted its invitation to inspect the new settlements and for failure to use the means of communication established to maintain dialogue between the leadership of Church and state. The government categorized the episcopal document as political rather than pastoral, and a calculated effort to undermine national unity in line with U.S. objectives. The government asserted that the bishops' failure to condemn the climate of terror created in the region by the actions of counterrevolutionaries, including some ex-National Guardsmen from the Somoza period, impugned the bishops' motives. Finally the government pointed out that the bishops had said nothing about the fact that some Moravian pastors and Catholic deacons had been providing support for the counterrevolutionaries. The gulf between the government and the bishops was confirmed by the former's call for a special Vatican mission to discuss Nicaraguan Church-state relations.[20] The Vatican did not accept this suggestion and gave indications of supporting the Nicaraguan episcopacy's increasingly negative view of the government.

The leadership of the Moravian Church assumed a more temperate view of the removal of the inhabitants of thirty-nine villages along the Honduran border. The local Moravian Bishop, John Wilson, asserted in early 1982 that while the move was painful, it was necessary.[21] Moreover, he viewed the situation as a challenge to the churches to help deal with a conflict of cultures in the face of considerable turmoil precipitated by rapid and substantial change.[22]

In early August 1982 the U.S.-based Executive Director of the Board of World Mission of the Moravian Church, Graham H. Rights, expressed the opinion that the dialogue initiated to resolve differences between the government and his church was jeopardized most by "outside threats to Nicaraguan national security. The Miskito people and the Moravian church are hostages in an international situation not of their making, which severely hinders their efforts to defend ethnic and religious freedom in their own country." With respect to U.S. policy, he argued that "attempts to destabilize Nicaragua are mischievous, and probably self-defeating: more likely to hasten than to halt the erosion of economic pluralism and political freedom in the country as a whole. From the viewpoint of the Miskito, the result has been catastrophic; it has wrought terror and destruction, divided families and left homeless, and brought down on all of them the hostility and suspicion of the authorities."[23] He then called upon U.S. Christians to urge their government to end support for Nicaraguan counter-revolutionaries as a means to stabilize the region in order to pursue dialogue and reconciliation.

Since mid-1982 internal divisions within the Catholic Church in Nicaragua have become more acute, as has the generalized polarization of society. U.S. political, military, and economic pressure has aggravated the situation with the hierarchy being widely regarded as a focus for counterrevolutionary and pro-U.S. sentiment. The bishops have the support of the bulk of the native-born diocesan clergy, with progressive sentiment being strongest among the foreign-born religious, particularly Jesuits and Maryknollers. Lay support of the hierarchy cuts across classes, with some coming from elements of the rural proletariat. It is difficult to establish the actual strength of the pro and antigovernment sectors, but it does appear that a good number are inclined to accept the bishops' lead.

On June 29, 1982 Pope John Paul II, in a letter to the Nicaraguan bishops, reinforced their antigovernment and anti-"popular" Church stance. The pope urged the Nicaraguan laity to beware of systems, movements, parties, or organizations that promoted the divisiveness of class hatred. The letter also denounced churches characterized as non-institutional, non-traditional, or alternative. These themes the pope reiterated in his March 4, 1983 homily during a public Mass in Managua. The pope's criticism of the "popular" Church rests on the belief that it undercuts the authority of the bishops and their role as interpreters of the Church's official positions on doctrine and morals. John Paul also criticized the "popular" Church on the grounds that it was heavily ideological and radical. The pope inveighed particularly strongly against those who would accept violence to achieve certain ends as contrary to the will and salvific plan of Jesus Christ. Therein, he warned, resides great potential for the disruption of Church and society.[24] This position was reinforced by the Vatican's August 1984 condemnation of the use of Marxist analysis by some theologians of liberation.[25]

Progressives within the Church by and large responded mildly to the pope's 1982 letter, arguing that discord within the Church was the result of disagreements over politics, not over the faith, and insisted that their ecclesial communities were striving to be truly Christian and supportive of Catholic and Nicaraguan unity.[26] Progovernment forces continued to attempt to avoid an open breach and to insist upon their legitimacy as an integral part of the institutional Church. In recent years, however, many Churches feel that their continued support of the government puts them in opposition to Church leadership.

Tension has also been generated by the government's attempts to revamp the elementary and secondary school curriculums of both public and private schools. Twenty-five to thirty percent of Nicaraguan students attend Church schools which are partially funded by the government.[27] In a December 8, 1982 pastoral letter, the bishops expressed concern that under the new curriculum schools would promote a single conflictual interpretation of life that would inflame existing tensions between classes. It was also criticized for potentially undermining Christian values. The government's response was that under the new system religious schools would have more class time than ever to incorporate their own materials and that government subsidies made it possible for Catholic schools to accept more students.[28]

It is notable that Catholic school students and their parents have increasingly identified themselves with the opposition to the government, with a serious outbreak of violence occurring in Masaya.[29] Government control of education has become an extremely volatile issue, prompting John Paul II to devote one of his major addresses in Nicaragua in 1983 to the right of parents to choose the type of education they desire for their children and of confessional schools and teachers to freedom in discharging their responsibilities.[30] Some bishops currently allege that education in Nicaragua today is being used to inculcate Marxism. The August 1984 appointment by the Sandinista government of a Jesuit, Fernando Cardenal, as Minister of Education, was obviously a response to such criticism. Cardenal's acceptance of the post demonstrates the gulf between the Vatican-supported episcopacy and some of the clergy.

The pope's visit to Nicaragua was itself fraught with controversy from the outset, in part as a result of Cardinal Obando y Bravo having announced it before the Papal Nuncio had officially informed the government. Well aware that the pope's presence could be used to promote the cardinal and other critics of the government, both Church and state treated the visit as an opportunity for a major propaganda offensive. Extraor-

dinary amounts of government time, energies, and monies were spent
organizing the visit in the hopes of diminishing its negative impact. Special efforts were undertaken by both the government and the Church to
disseminate their respective views of the import of the visit. The hard line
that John Paul took during his one-day visit appeared to disconcert the
Sandinista leadership, as well as progressive elements within the Church.
The latter were critical of the language and tone of the pope's speeches
on the grounds that they "seemed admonishing and negative, lacking any
connection with the people he addressed. In its religious aspect this language was political. The theological subjects dealt with were beyond the
comprehension . . . of the great majority of the people."[31] In addition,
the pope's

> admonitions about unbelief and atheistic education sounded strange to us,
> as we experienced the presence of Christian motivation in the revolution-
> ary process. The Sandinista Revolution, for the first time in the recent his-
> tory of revolutions, has proclaimed the right to religious liberty and the
> freedom of apostolic action by the churches. We feel the same way about
> his allusions to a division in the church due to theological reasons, because
> frictions that occur in the Christian community are rooted in socio-political
> options. There is a constant effort not to break the Church's unity of faith.
> Perhaps some of us Christians committed to the revolutionary process have
> not always known how to safeguard the complete identity of the faith in
> our temporal commitments, but we regret that the Pope has never referred
> to the brazen use that groups opposed to the Revolution in Nicaragua have
> made of the faith. Tensions will continue.[32]

Antigovernment forces were reportedly overjoyed by the pope's statements. As the *Washington Post* reported:

> "The Pope has helped us a hell of a lot," said a wealthy business opponent
> of the government. "That's the best thing that could have happened to us."
> His comment reflected a widely held assessment that the church hierarchy
> increasingly could become the focus of political opposition in this over-
> whelming Catholic country. Under Obando y Bravo's uncompromising
> leadership, it is considered more able to attract mass following than the
> alliance of conservative parties and business groups that constitutes the San-
> dinistas' tolerated political opposition.[33]

Coming as it did after an upsurge in attacks across the Honduran
border by anti-Sandinista forces, the visit and the pope's statements appear to have bolstered conservative elements within the Catholic Church,
as well as the country. The visit increased rather than decreased polarization. The hierarchy followed the pope's lead and became not only more

critical of the government, but also more active in attempting to impose episcopal authority on progressive clergy and laity, including the priests serving in government.

Without doubt the visit weakened attempts by progressive elements to insert the Church into the revolutionary process. The sense that the Church and the Sandinista revolution were antithetical was heightened and competition between the government's mass organizations and episcopal-sponsored groups increased. Local conflicts between such groups have occurred pitting Sandinista youth against Catholic school students such as those at the Don Bosco Center in Managua. An expanded religious offensive calling into question the political legitimacy of the government was undertaken in 1983. The bishops had already initiated a series of social welfare programs, aimed at diminishing the impact of similar government efforts.[34]

On August 29, 1983, the bishops directly challenged the legitimacy of the Sandinista government in a communique criticizing the implementation of a military draft. Calling the Sandinista army an extension of a specific political party rather than of the nation, the episcopacy deemed the call to universal military service illegal.[35] Since that time individual prelates have challenged the legitimacy of the government on other bases, particularly in terms of respect for civil, political, and religious rights. Progressive Church sectors have criticized such attacks. Hence Church-state polarization is reflected in splits within the Catholic Church.

By 1984 relations between the leadership of the Catholic Church in Nicaragua and the Sandinista government were very difficult. At the root was fear that the Sandinistas would consolidate a one-party state that would be ideologically inimical to the Catholic Church. The Church hierarchy felt this would seriously undercut the influence of the institutional Church within Nicaragua. Churchpeople supportive of the government were accused of having "abandoned ecclesial unity and submitted to the orders of a materialistic ideology."[36]

Government relations with the episcopacy were so difficult by mid-1984 that a delegation of Sandinista officials went to Rome in September of that year in an attempt to ameliorate the tensions. This effort had virtually no positive effect. To have done so would probably have required the government to abandon its ideological orientation, as well as make concessions on some specific items such as the national educational curriculum. Pope John Paul II and the Nicaraguan bishops clearly indicated that they would not accept anything less than a major modification in Sandinista control of the government. This was reconfirmed in late 1985 when Cardinal Obando y Bravo undertook a series of trips throughout Nicaragua during which he repeatedly challenged the legitimacy of the Sandinista government and universal military service. In an article in the *Washington Post* in May 1986 the Cardinal bluntly stated his opinion that the leadership of the revolution had "betrayed the hopes of the Nicaraguan people and even its own promises."[37]

During the autumn of 1985 a number of youths claiming to be seminarians were detained by the government as draft evaders. It was the government's practice to exempt from military service youths registered in Catholic or Protestant seminaries. Since the implementation of the draft in the fall of 1984, there had been a sharp increase in the number of youths claiming to be seminarians. The Catholic hierarchy has defended these individuals and denounced their detention in communications with the government, in sermons, and in church publications.[38]

In the aftermath of the reimposition of a state of emergency in October of 1985, a number of religious workers from fundamentalist Protestant groups were also detained. According to the Ministry of Interior, this was done because all these Protestants had preached against universal military service and encouraged draft evasion. As a consequence, the churchpeople were called in by the Ministry of the Interior to be apprised of the fact that they were publicly counseling unlawful acts.[39] According to the Washington-based Institute on Religion and Democracy, the churchpeople involved included the national director of the Nicaraguan Campus Crusade for Christ, the president of the Nicaraguan Bible Society, the pastor of the First Central American Church in Managua, the president and vice-president of the Assemblies of God Youth Organization, and the leader of the Alliance for Evangelization of Children. The Institute charged that these churchpeople, while released within twenty-four hours, were forced to "endure several hours of humiliation," some having been strip searched.[40]

Such actions point up the degree to which relations between the government and some sectors of the Catholic and Protestant churches have deteriorated since 1979. They also indicate the degree to which the Sandinista government is preoccupied with criticism of the draft by churchpeople. According to the *New York Times*, the President of Nicaragua, Daniel Ortega, deemed the imposition in October 1985 of a state of emergency as necessary, in part, in order to prevent "'propaganda' against the draft at a time when many Nicaraguan soldiers are winding up their two-year hitches and new recruits are preparing to enlist."[41] As the war with the U.S.–backed counterrevolutionaries continued, the government became more inclined to move against domestic critics, including churchpeople, who had been in the forefront of the domestic opposition.

This was essentially the situation until August 7, 1987 when the presidents of Nicaragua, Costa Rica, El Salvador, Guatemala, and Honduras signed the Esquipulas accord aimed at achieving peace and stability in Central America. This agreement mandated cease-fire talks, national dialogues with the opposition within each country, and clear efforts toward democratization. As a consequence, the Nicaraguan government took several steps to improve their relations with the Catholic and other churches. These included allowing clerics who had been exiled from Nicaragua to return, the most senior of whom were Bishop Pablo Vega of Juigalpa and Monsignor Bismarck Carballo, Vicar of the Archdiocese of Managua. In addition, Radio Católica, which had been highly critical of the government and resisted prior censorship, was allowed to reopen. The most important move was the naming of Cardinal Obando y Bravo to the National Reconciliation Commission and his subsequent selection as mediator between the government and the civilian opposition, as well as the contras. As such Obando in late 1987 and early 1988 took an aggressive role proposing his own peace plans and publicly pressuring for their acceptance. This was in strong contrast to the more neutral role played by the Archbishop of San Salvador in his mediation between the government of El Salvador and the civilian, as well as the armed opposition. Whether Obando's more interventionist tactics will facilitate agreement is unclear. Given the level of polarization among Nicaraguans, it is highly problematic.

The Nicaraguan case raises some important questions concerning the nature and depths of the transformation of the Catholic Church since the 1960s. Frequently styled in recent years as the prime institutional support of political and economic change in Latin America, the Nicaraguan case suggests that when faced with a Marxist revolutionary situation the episcopacy, as well as a good portion of the clergy and laity, will oppose it. Support for a revolutionary option continues to be a minority position. The unity forged within the Catholic Church during periods of rightwing repression tends to disintegrate when it is ended, with old ideological and political divisions reemerging in the context of the generalized societal conflict and tensions generated by the revolutionary process. This confirms the hypothesis that the frequently expressed preferential option for the poor on the part of the Church is not rooted in any agreement over how best to achieve greater socioeconomic justice. In fact, the commitment has not caused the institutional Church to abandon its historic acceptance of traditional Western political and economic structures. In the struggle between Marxist-Leninist socialism and capitalist-based liberal democracy, the Catholic Church has not yet established its political neutrality. Rather, in situations of direct ideological confrontation, such as Nicaragua, the Catholic Church is one of the prime actors in the struggle. In fact, the response of the Catholic Church in the Nicaraguan situa-

tion bears some similarities to its response to the Cuban revolution.[42] This
suggests that the post–Vatican II Church may not have been as profoundly
changed at its institutional core as has been thought.

The Catholic Church in Cuba in 1959 was institutionally, pasto-
rally, and numerically weaker than the Nicaraguan Church in 1979. Of
the 70-75 percent of the population who identified themselves as Catholics in Cuba in the mid-1950s, only 3-4 percent were active in the church,
with 85 percent of Church personnel and activities being concentrated
in Havana. Rural Cuba was virtually unevangelized and the image of the
Church was that of a foreign (Spanish) institution servicing the bourgeoisie
and allied to the Batista regime. Concern over social issues was limited
and the Church was largely uninvolved in the struggle to overthrow Batista. The deep-rooted conservatism of the Cuban Church was such that
by mid-1959 it had become the institutional base for counterrevolutionary forces.

In Nicaragua the Catholic Church in 1979 had penetrated all sectors of society to a much greater extent with between 85-90 percent of
the population identifying themselves as Catholics. More importantly, the
level of participation in Church activities was much higher, particularly
as a result of post–Vatican II efforts of the Church to involve itself in the
daily life and concerns of the people. The contribution of churchpeople
to the insurrection against Somoza, as well as to the Government of National Reconstruction reflected greater political and ideological diversity
within the post–Vatican II Church. While the majority of priests in
Nicaragua in 1979 were foreign, their attitudes were eminently more progressive and open to cooperation with a radical revolutionary process than
in Cuba. However, anti-Marxism continued to be a generalized sentiment,
not just among the episcopacy. In Cuba in 1959 nothing comparable to
a "popular" Church nor CEBs existed and, hence, there was no base for
progovernment support from within the Church. As a consequence, the
Castro government confronted a united rather than a divided Church,
as was the case in Nicaragua.

The consolidation of the revolution in Cuba, after an initial period
of turmoil, prompted a mass exodus of the Spanish clergy and religious,
reinforced the conservatism of those who remained, and caused the Church
to withdraw into itself, refusing to respond to the revolutionary process.
This situation lasted until the late 1960s, when the Church in an effort
to deal with its existential situation began to seek a limited rapproche-
ment with the government. While in recent years the Catholic Church
in Cuba has begun to reinsert itself into the mainstream of Cuban society, to date it remains a relatively marginal institution.

As in Cuba, the institutional Church in Nicaragua under the direction of the episcopacy[43] has become a focus of counterrevolutionary sentiment. This development appears to be rooted in the continuing strong belief among the Church hierarchy that Marxism and Catholicism are ultimately antithetical. This belief persists in spite of some dialogue and occasional cooperation between Marxists and Catholics, particularly during periods of rightist repression, as in Brazil and Chile. The fragility of such initiatives on the part of the institutional Church and their potential for dividing it have been amply demonstrated by the Nicaraguan situation. The Catholic leadership, in general, continues to be opposed to Marxism and remains profoundly ill-disposed to Marxist governments.

In Cuba the involvement of the Church in the counterrevolution ultimately contributed to its marginalization in the face of the consolidation of Castro's government. The consolidation of the Sandinistas in Nicaragua in the face of strong external and internal threats may have like consequences for the institutional Church there. If that occurs, there is a possibility that progressive sectors currently within the Church will pursue an independent course of integration into an ongoing revolutionary process without formally leaving the Church. Thus Nicaragua would be weakened by division, in contrast to Cuba's united but weak Church.

The challenge posed to the legitimacy of the Sandinista government by its ecclesial opponents appears to be greater than that posed by Church opposition to the Castro government. Cuba in 1959 was a more secular society than Nicaragua in 1979. The Cuban rural and urban poor did not expect much from the Catholic Church. In image and in fact, the Church was a support of the status quo, rather than a champion of human rights and social justice. Hence the moral impact of the Cuban Church's challenge to the Castro government was more limited than that of the Nicaraguan episcopacy to the Sandinista government. The greater preoccupation of the Sandinistas with such a challenge appears well founded. There is potential for sharper conflict than in Cuba, for the Nicaraguan hierarchy has more capacity to mold attitudes and mobilize the populace as is suggested by the crowds attracted during Obando y Bravo's 1985 tours of the Nicaraguan countryside. In Cuba a full-scale confrontation was avoided in part because the Church did not have the ultimate loyalty of a good proportion of the people and those who were active in the Church tended to migrate abroad.

The reforms stimulated by Vatican II as well as those Latin American developments signaled by Medellín in 1968 and Puebla in 1979 do not appear to have necessarily better equipped the institutional Church to deal with Marxist revolution. Dialogue with Marxists and the utilization of some aspects of Marxist critiques of capitalism have not meant acceptance by the institutional Church of Marxist governments. In fact, anti-Marxism continued to strongly influence official policy. New theological developments, particularly liberation theology, while influential have also contributed to a reassertion of hierarchical authority and attempts to reimpose doctrinal orthodoxy, thereby heightening divisions with the Church. The presence of the Church among the rural and urban poor, while resulting in their greater formal religious involvement, has also radicalized grass-roots clergy and religious, frequently placing them in opposition to the hierarchy.

Clearly the Catholic Church is much more present in the modern world than it was prior to Vatican II. As a result, it is much more divided by the current worldwide ideological and political struggle spearheaded by the U.S. and USSR. Insertion into the world poses, therefore, a substantial threat to the institutional survival of the Church as presently constituted. It appears that the Church leadership in Nicaragua and elsewhere may, as a result, lessen its strong commitment to change, thereby departing from the course initiated at Vatican II. Whether the bulk of the faithful in areas such as Latin America will follow remains to be seen.

NOTES

Earlier versions of this essay appeared in *Igreja e Sociedade* (Spring 1984) and as a working paper for the Kellogg Institute, University of Notre Dame and for the Latin American Studies Centre, La Trobe University, Melbourne, Australia.

1. Conferencia Episcopal de Nicaragua, *Presencia Cristiana en la Revolución: Dos mensajes—momento insurreccional 2 de junio 1979; Iniciando la reconstrucción, 30 de julio 1979* (Managua: Cristianos en el Mundo, Comisión Justicia y Paz, Documentos, 1979), pp. 4–8.

2. Sergio Méndez Arceo, Bishop of Cuernavaca, Mexico, "Introduction to Pastoral Letter of the Episcopal Conference of Nicaragua," November 17, 1979, Managua, p. 2.

3. *Presencia Cristiana en la Revolución, 2 de junio 1979*, pp. 4–8.

4. *Presencia Cristiana en la Revolución, 30 de julio de 1979*, p. 14.

5. The 1980 Vatican directive that priests should not hold political office was not insisted upon by the Nicaraguan bishops until June 1981. In resisting pressure from Rome, as well as from the local episcopacy, a number of priests holding high office claimed in June 1981 that their obligation to the Nicaraguan people overrode their responsibility to accept episcopal authority. At a two-day meeting in mid-July 1981 a compromise was reached between the Nicaraguan Episcopal Conference and the priests. The latter would retain their political offices, but would not in any way use their clerical status to support the government. The priests also committed themselves to remain obedient to and in close communication with the hierarchy. Acceptance on the part of the episcopacy of the continuance in office of the priests reflected the bishops' desire to avoid a breach not only with the lower clergy but also with the

government. By 1984 both the Nicaraguan bishops and the Vatican were increasingly expressing their displeasure with the priests who continued to hold political appointments. Such criticism came to a head in July 1984 when the Jesuit Fernando Cardenal was nominated for the post of Minister of Education. Reports circulated widely that Rome had directed Cardenal not to accept the office. Cardenal did and in an August 24, 1984 interview with this author insisted that he had not received any official communiques from Rome ordering him not to. In the fall of 1984 Miguel D'Escoto, Fernando Cardenal, Ernesto Cardenal, and Edgard Parrales were all subjected to canonical censure by Rome. As a result none can exercise their priestly functions even in private. (Christopher Dickey, "Nicaraguan Priests to Stay in Office under Compromise," *Washington Post*, July 17, 1981, p. A24.)

6. Pastoral Letter, November 17, 1979, Managua, p. 2.

7. Ibid., p. 3.

8. Ibid., p. 4.

9. Dirección Nacional del Frente Sandinista de Liberación Nacional, *Comunicado oficial de la dirección nacional del F.S.L.N. sobre la religión* (San José, Costa Rica: Departamento Ecuménico de Investigaciones, n.d.), p. 10.

10. Conferencia Episcopal de Nicaragua, "Respuesta al comunicado del Frente Sandinista de Liberación Nacional," *CELAM* XIX, 158 (January 1981): pp. 11–21.

11. National Catholic News Service, November 7, 1980, p. 1.

12. Michael Dodson and Tommie Sue Montgomery, "The Churches in the Nicaraguan Revolution," paper presented at the Latin American Studies Association National Meeting, Bloomington, Indiana, October 16–19, 1980, pp. 29–32. Published in Thomas Walker, ed., *Nicaragua in Revolution* (New York: Praeger Publishers, 1982), pp. 161–180.

13. Shirley Christian, *Nicaragua: Revolution in the Family* (New York: Random House, 1985), pp. 206–211.

14. Interview with an official of the United States Catholic Conference, August 4, 1982.

15. Comunidades Eclesiasticales [sic] de Base, Managua, Nicaragua. "Managuan BECs Defend Their Church Identity," *LADOC* XII, 5 (May-June 1982): pp. 5–6.

16. Centro de Estudios Religiosos, *Encuesta de opinión, agosto 1981: Análisis de métodos, resultados y conclusiones* (Managua: La Prensa, November 1981). The Centro de Estudios Religiosos was formed by individuals linked to the antigovernment newspaper *La Prensa* to combat the impact of progressive individuals within the Catholic Church who supported the Sandinista revolution, as well as such institutions as the Centro Antonio Valdivieso and Instituto Histórico Centroamericano. The results of this survey reflect chiefly the attitudes of urban middle-class elements.

17. Interview with an official of the United States Catholic Conference, August 4, 1982.

18. *The World Christian Encyclopedia* estimates that approximately 87.8 percent of Nicaraguans are affiliated with the Catholic Church and 8.4 percent with Protestant churches as of 1985. Volume 24 of the Statistical Abstract for Latin America estimates that 85 percent of the population was Christian in 1980. Calculations based on the Vatican's *Anuario Pontíficio* for 1985 tend to support the *World Christian Encyclopedia* estimates.

19. Conferencia Episcopal de Nicaragua, "Documento de la Conferencia Episcopal, 17 de febrero de 1982," *Informes CAV*, 11–12 (March 1982): p. 2.

20. Secretaría General de la Junta de Gobierno de Reconstrucción Nacional, "Respuesta del Gobierno a los obispos, 22 de febrero de 1982," *Informes del CAV*, 11–12 (March 1982), p. 3.

21. John Wilson as quoted in Junta de Gobierno de Reconstrucción Nacional *Verdad vivida y no mensaje político* (Managua: JGRN, 1982), p. 9.

22. John Wilson, "Apreciaciones de Iglesia Morava," in Junta de Gobierno de Reconstrucción Nacional, *Verdad vivida y no mensaje político*, p. 9.

23. Graham H. Rights, Executive Director, The Board of World Mission of the Moravian Church, "Memorandum to Moravian Ministers of the Northern and Southern Provinces, Other Christian Clergy and Lay People in North America, U.S. Government Officials and Congressional Representatives re: New Fighting in Nicaragua; Reprisals Against the Miskito Indians and the Nicaraguan Moravian Church," Bethlehem, Pennsylvania, August 3, 1982, pp. 1–4.

24. John Paul II, "Letter to the Nicaraguan Bishops," June 29, 1982 (Rome) and "Threats to the Church's Unity," *Origins: NC Documentary Service* 12, 40 (March 17, 1983), pp. 633, 635–636.

25. The Congregation for the Doctrine of the Faith, "Instruction on Certain Aspects of the 'Theology of Liberation'," *Origins: NC Documentary Service* 14 (1984), pp. 193 ff.

26. Católicos de Nicaragua, "Carta a Juan Pablo II," August 15, 1982, Managua, Nicaragua, *Informes CAV* 15–16 (September 1982): p. 7.

27. In 1986 there were 247 private schools in Nicaragua of which 173 were religious. Approximately ten percent of primary school students attend private schools, while about twenty-five percent of secondary students do. Government financial assistance is received by 188 private schools of which 152 are Catholic and 21 are Protestant. The remainder (15) are non-confessional. Universities are free and largely supported by the government. (Statement of Ambassador Carlos Tunnerman, Nicaraguan Minister of Education, 1979–1985, New York University Law School, April 19, 1986.)

28. Central American Historical Institute, "Greater Resources for Education in Nicaragua: The New Curriculum Stirs Public Response," *Update* 2, 3 (March 3, 1983): p. 2.

29. Christian, *Nicaragua: Revolution in the Family*, pp. 228–229.

30. John Paul II, "Laicado y educación," March 4, 1983, León, Nicaragua.

31. "Christian Reflection on the Pope's March 4 Visit to Nicaragua by a Theological Reflection Group," translated from "Imperialismo, enemigo del pueblo y la paz dicen intelectuales cristianos," *El Nuevo Diario*, March 6, 1983, pp. 1–2.

32. Ibid., p. 2.

33. Edward Cody, "Tension Grows in Nicaragua: Sandinistas Take Harder Line," *Washington Post*, March 5, 1983, pp. A1; A10.

34. Ana María Ezcurra, "La jerarquía católica nicaragüense y EU contra la revolución sandinista," *Testimonios y Documentos* (February 21, 1983), pp. 8–10.

35. Conferencia Episcopal de Nicaragua, "Communicado" (August 29, 1983), Managua, Nicaragua, pp. 1–3.

36. Episcopal Conference of Nicaragua, "Pastoral letter on Reconciliation," April 22, 1984, Managua, Nicaragua, p. 4.

37. Miguel Obando y Bravo, "Nicaragua: The Sandinistas have 'Gagged and Bound' Us," *Washington Post*, May 12, 1986, p. A15.

38. "Obispos denuncian acoso a la Iglesia," "Capturan seminaristas de Río San Juan," "Clero granadino protesta," "Otros seminaristas reclutados," *Iglesia*, año 1, no. 1 (October 12, 1985), pp. 1; 6–8. The publication of *Iglesia* occasioned another confrontation between the archdiocese of Managua and the government when in October 1985 it was printed without being registered with the government as required by law, nor was it submitted to prior censorship. As a consequence, the first (and only) number was confiscated by the government. Nevertheless, copies of it have circulated widely within and without Nicaragua.

39. Foreign Broadcast Information Service, "Interior Ministry Official on Religious Activities," *Daily Report: Latin America* VI, 235 (December 6, 1985), pp. P9–14.

40. The Institute on Religion and Democracy, *Action Alert* (November 22, 1985); Roy Howard Beck, "Church Officials in Nicaragua Said Arrested, Harassed," *United Methodist Reporter*, November 15, 1985; National Association of Evangelicals, "Nicaraguan Evangelicals Subject to Harassment," November 8, 1985.

41. Margot Hornblower, "Ortega, in N.Y., Defends State of Emergency," *Washington Post*, October 21, 1985, p. A17.

42. For a detailed analysis of the impact of the Cuban revolution on Catholic and Protestant churches, see Margaret E. Crahan, "Salvation Through Christ or Marx: Religion in Revolutionary Cuba," in Daniel H. Levine, ed., *Churches and Politics in Latin America* (Beverly Hills, Calif.: Sage Publications, 1980), pp. 238–266.

43. In contrast to Pope John Paul II's support of the Nicaraguan bishops in the current struggle, in the early 1960s John XXIII repeatedly urged the Cuban hierarchy to seek dialogue and to avoid exacerbating tensions. By and large the Cuban Church leadership ignored Rome.

The Catholic Church in the Nicaraguan Revolution: Differing Responses and New Challenges

Philip J. Williams

The Catholic Church in Nicaragua is far from united in its response to the revolutionary process. Whereas on the eve of Somoza's fall, the Church appeared in a rare moment of almost total unity, since then consensus has given way to division. The conflict within the Church, which is closely linked to the hierarchy's ongoing struggle with the Sandinista government, has undermined the efforts of progressive clergy and religious to construct a grass-roots Church in Nicaragua. Their alternative pastoral strategies are now interpreted by the Church hierarchy as an attempt to form a breakaway Church, and their collaboration with the government is viewed as an excessive involvement in partisan politics. Clearly, the outcome of the conflict will have important implications for the Latin American Church as a whole.

The main body of this chapter will focus on the Church in the period after July 1979. The first section will provide a typology of five different responses to the revolutionary process within the Church. Such an approach, as opposed to a simple "for or against" dichotomy, proves more useful in understanding the internal Church dynamic. In the second section, I analyze the development of the FSLN's position toward the Catholic Church and religion, demonstrating how its practical collaboration with Catholics contributed to its currently pragmatic view of religion. Also, I look at the FSLN's ongoing conflict with the Catholic hierarchy, especially its impact on the search for a constructive relationship between the Sandinista government and the Catholic Church. Finally, the last section will focus on the progressive sector of the Church and the challenges it faces in constructing a grass-roots Church in Nicaragua.

Before going on to our discussion of the Catholic Church in the

Nicaraguan revolution, however, it is useful to look briefly at the evolution of the Church before 1979. It was not until after 1970 that the Catholic hierarchy began to alter its traditional alliance with the Somoza dictatorship. Its gradual distancing from the regime was rooted in a number of factors. First of all, the development model initiated in the early 1960s under the auspices of the Central American Common Market and the Alliance for Progress had, by 1970, proven incapable of fulfilling the expectations it had generated — namely, that "development" would benefit the large majority of Nicaraguans. Rather than opening up channels for political participation to vent social frustrations arising from the unequal distribution of economic growth, the regime continued to resort to repressive measures to quell political opposition. To these factors must be added the process of change within the Nicaraguan Church. During the late 1960s, a small group of vocal young priests, inspired by the new currents of renovation within the Latin American Church, challenged the Church hierarchy to alter its stand vis-à-vis Somoza. They pointed out that the bishops' silence in the face of increasing injustices, human rights abuses, and government corruption would be interpreted by the majority of Nicaraguans as complicity. It was these factors — the inability of the development model to improve the miserable social conditions, the absence of channels of political participation, and the growing commitment of progressive clergy to social change — which opened the way for the hierarchy's disassociation from the Somoza regime.[1]

The hierarchy's gradual distancing from Somoza developed into an open break after 1973. In the wake of the devastating Managua earthquake in December 1972 it soon became clear that the dictator was enriching himself from the disaster. The final straw was Somoza's fraudulent "re-election" in 1974. The major opposition parties boycotted the elections and the bishops indirectly endorsed their position in a pastoral letter published on the eve of the elections, which recognized the voters' right to abstain. In January 1977, after a two-year period of silence (partly the result of the State of Emergency), the bishops issued a harshly worded pastoral letter denouncing the torture, "disappearances," and murder of hundreds of peasants, victims of the National Guard's counter-insurgency campaign in the countryside. By the end of 1977, they began to openly collaborate with moderate opposition groups in an attempt to force Somoza from power. And on June 2, 1979, after a series of failed attempts to shore up a negotiated settlement, the bishops justified armed resistance against the Somoza regime.[2]

Although during this period there were tensions within the Church, especially concerning the political activities of progressive clergy and religious who supported the armed struggle against Somoza, these never constituted a serious threat to the Church's internal unity. In fact, those priests accused by the government of collaborating with the guerrillas were publicly defended by their bishops. It would not be until after Somoza's fall that these underlying tensions burst forth into the open. It is important to remember that the situation before July 1979 was very different from that which was to follow. Within the context of a repressive and corrupt dictatorship, the majority of clergy agreed as to the Church's opposition to the regime. Indeed, its opposition to Somoza provided a focus for unity between moderates and progressives within the Church. Consequently, while the bishops warned progressive clergy about the implications of their collaboration with the FSLN, they tolerated such activities since any show of disunity within the Church might be easily exploited by the regime.

Paralleling the Church's growing opposition to the Somoza regime was the development of alternative pastoral strategies aimed at creating a grass-roots Church in Nicaragua. Initial efforts were made between 1966 and 1968 by the Spanish priest José de la Jara and the Nicaraguan poet-priest Ernesto Cardenal. The former organized "Family of God" courses along the lines of the San Miguelito experiment in Panama, which served as the basis for the first ecclesial base communities (CEBs) in Nicaragua. Cardenal founded a contemplative community, Nuestra Señora de Solentiname, on a small island in Lake Nicaragua, where local peasants met to reflect on and discuss the Bible, thereby relating the Gospel message to their own lives. These early pastoral experiments received impetus from the First Pastoral Conference in January 1969.[3] Out of the conference came a call for a national pastoral plan which would incorporate the principles set forth at Medellín. Although the hierarchy never implemented such a plan, a series of meetings, held at the diocesan and parish levels in the early 1970s, generated enthusiasm among progressive Catholics.

The greatest progress toward creating a grass-roots Church was the development of CEBs, especially in poor neighborhoods of Managua, and the program for Delegates of the Word (DPs), implemented in a number of rural parishes. The earliest CEBs arose from the Family of God courses initiated by Father de la Jara in the San Pablo Apóstol parish of Managua. While the Family of God courses had been effective in breaking the individualism characteristic to traditional Catholicism—i.e., faith was now practiced collectively rather than individually—participants began to see the need to place more emphasis on the social dimension of pastoral activities. After 1970, this resulted in the organization of courses which incorporated a variety of themes concerning the social, economic, and political reality. Out of these courses emerged the first CEBs. During the early 1970s, CEBs underwent a process of growing sociopolitical commitment, which was reflected in their organization of popular protests against rises in bus fares and milk prices. However, as a result of their increasing political activities, some members withdrew from active participation, fearing government repression. Those who remained adopted an even more radical political commitment. Between 1975 and 1977, and coinciding with the worst period of repression, a shift in emphasis occurred, from an analysis of national reality toward a discussion of alternatives to the situation of injustice and oppression. This led the CEBs to focus on the biblical theme of liberation.[4] The ensuing radicalization of the CEBs was manifested in the participation of many of their members in the insurrections of 1978 and 1979.

In the countryside, the training of Delegates of the Word (DPs) was spearheaded by the Capuchin Fathers in Zelaya and Nueva Segovia, and by the Center for Agrarian Education and Promotion (CEPA) in the Pacific region. The Capuchins began training DPs in 1971, and it was through their efforts and those of the CEPA after 1974, that the program spread to a number of parishes.[5] Like CEB members, DPs participated in courses which analyzed "social reality," and, in turn, organized similar courses in their own communities. Besides analyzing the national reality, peasants were also encouraged to organize themselves to defend their rights. These efforts bore fruit with the creation of the Association of Rural Workers (ATC) in March 1978. In fact, several of its leaders, including the Secretary General, were themselves DPs and had participated in CEPA courses.[6]

Although the hierarchy blocked the attempts by progressive Catholics to formulate a national pastoral plan in the early 1970s, generally speaking, its position toward these alternative pastoral strategies was one of toleration. Of course, some bishops were more open to the new pastoral orientations than others. The Bishops of Zelaya and Estelí, for example, supported the efforts to train rural lay leaders in their dioceses. Other bishops, while cautioning priests about the political repercussions of the new strategies, were at least willing to give them a chance. As long as they remained pilot projects, these pastoral experiments did not constitute a threat to the bishops' authority. Obviously, the relatively high degree of unity within the Church during this period and the fact that many of the bishops were more concerned with political considerations (i.e., the Church's opposition to Somoza) contributed to the toleration of the hierarchy. After 1979, when serious divisions surfaced within the Church, the bishops would no longer remain tolerant of the attempts to create a grass-roots Church. Instead, they would view such efforts as a direct challenge to their authority and as constituting a parallel magisterium.

DIFFERING RESPONSES TO THE REVOLUTIONARY PROCESS

The arrival to power of a revolutionary regime on July 19, 1979 presented the Church with a radically different situation. It seemed that after years of denouncing government abuses and injustices, the Church could begin to "announce the Kingdom of God." Amid the heady euphoria in the wake of the triumph, even the most skeptical clergy had a kind word for the new Governing Junta of National Reconstruction (JGRN). Progressive clergy were especially elated by what they saw as a historic opportunity to join together both believers and non-believers in a national project of reconstruction. Their optimism was given added impetus by the bishops' November 17, 1979 pastoral letter, "Christian Commitment for a New Nicaragua," which, on the balance, was favorable toward the revolutionary process.

It was not long, however, before the first doubts arose concerning the future direction of the revolution. As the euphoria began to wear thin, the Church was faced with some difficult questions. First, what role would the Church play within the revolutionary process? Whereas progressive clergy considered the participation of Catholics in popular organizations and government projects essential to ensure the Church an active presence in the revolution, conservative clergy warned that the Church's identification with the new regime would jeopardize its autonomy. Instead, they advocated a critical role for the Church—the Church as the moral conscience of the revolution. Another important question was the composition of the new regime, especially the weight that each of the different political configurations would be allotted within the new government. By April 1980, it became clear that, although the new regime welcomed the political participation of private sector interests, these would not be given a dominant role within the government. Rather, the FSLN and the mass organizations, representing popular interests, would assume a dominant position.

Since 1980, the growing political polarization and increasing U.S. economic and military aggressions have placed serious strains on the regime. With the revolution under threat from external forces, most internal political opposition has been viewed as counterrevolutionary. While political opposition groups point to the restrictions on political liberties (under the State of Emergency Law) as proof of the absence of political pluralism, the Sandinista government maintains that these are necessary to protect the revolution. As could be expected, the Catholic Church has been drawn into the current political-ideological debate, and this has clearly affected its responses to the revolutionary process.

Although initial responses from the Catholic Church were quite supportive of the revolution, they were in no way uniform, and the extent of participation and collaboration among clergy and religious varied greatly. Today, we can point to five ideal-type postures adopted by Catholic clergy and religious regarding the revolutionary process: (1) direct participation; (2) active collaboration; (3) passive collaboration; (4) passive opposition; (5) active opposition.[7] This typology is more useful than lumping clergy into two broad categories (i.e., those favoring the revolutionary process and those opposed) since such a breakdown does not adequately describe what is a more complex phenomenon.

(1) *Direct Participation.* The first group includes those priests and religious serving in government offices and ministries. Immediately after the triumph, two priests, Ernesto Cardenal and Miguel D'Escoto, became Minister of Culture and Foreign Minister respectively. Fernando Cardenal, S.J., who was called on to direct the literacy campaign, later became director of the Sandinista Youth, and then Minister of Education. Edgard Parrales was appointed Minister of Social Health, later to become Nicaragua's representative to the Organization of American States (OAS). Álvaro Argüello, S.J., became ACLEN's (Association of Nicaraguan Clergy) delegate to the Council of State, and a number of priests and religious took up technical and advisory positions within government ministries and institutions.[8]

The priests in government point to their positions as a manifestation of their obedience to God, since they view the project of the revolution as consistent with the Gospel message. As Ernesto Cardenal states: "My obedience to the revolution is my obedience to God. And this does not imply any disobedience to the Church."[9] Moreover, as long as the revolution is under threat, they consider their presence in the government as a necessary sacrifice to defend the revolution. While these priests themselves find no contradiction between their obedience to God and to the revolution, their permanence in the government leaves them open to charges of disobedience to the Church hierarchy. Their refusal to comply with ultimatums calling on them to leave the government has been interpreted by Church officials as proof that their loyalty to the Sandinista revolution overrides their loyalty to the Church. In response to these charges, the priests point to the political nature of the ultimatums and stress the exceptional nature of their positions in the government; the country is still undergoing a period of reconstruction and is threatened by U.S. economic and military aggressions. Equating the Church with the people, they cannot understand why they should be forced to choose between the two. Consequently, they adopt a position of "conscientious objection," insisting upon their loyalty to the Church hierarchy, but affirming that their duty to serve the poor is more important than retaining their ecclesiastical status. In response to criticisms that their presence in the government represents a blind commitment to the FSLN, they point out that this presence ensures the Church an active role within the revolutionary process, which can prevent it from becoming antireligious. They reject the notion that their identification with the revolution precludes them making an objective questioning of the process and consider themselves in a better position to judge the merits and to criticize abuses of the revolution than most of its detractors. If they are forced to step down, their valuable Christian presence would be lost.[10]

The priests in government recognize that theirs is a special case, and they distinguish themselves from other priests supportive of the revolution, who choose to manifest their commitment to the poor through pastoral work. This does not, however, imply any contradiction, since militancy in the FSLN is simply another way to manifest one's option for the poor.[11] In response to accusations that their presence in the government represents an excessive involvement in partisan politics, these priests contend that their political activities are based upon purely religious motivations. They consider any interpretation of the Gospel message as necessarily having political implications. They consider the hierarchy's criticisms of their activities hypocritical, pointing to the bishops' identification with opposition political groups.

If anything, the priests in government are more determined than ever to continue in their posts. This remains true in spite of the fact that the bishops have repeatedly called on them to step down. In July 1981, a temporary agreement was worked out (with the mediation of the Apostolic Nuncio) which allowed for the priests to remain in office as long as they refrained from their priestly functions. The bishops renewed their calls, however, in the wake of the new canon law which went into effect November 27, 1983. The new law concerning clergy in positions of civil power was much more explicit than in the past and did not allow for exceptions. Consequently, Fernando Cardenal, S.J., was removed from the Jesuit Order in December 1984, and Ernesto Cardenal and Miguel D'Escoto were sanctioned in January 1985. Edgard Parrales asked to leave the priesthood about the same time. The terms of the sanctions are exactly the same as those of the agreement—the only difference being that whereas the terms were according to an agreement, today they are the result of a sanction. Whenever the priests decide to leave the government they can once again assume their priestly functions.

Although the priests lamented the hierarchy's decision to impose the sanctions, their determination to continue in the government remained unshaken. According to Ernesto Cardenal, as long as the revolution is under attack, he cannot return to the contemplative life of Solentiname, something which he considers tantamount to surrender.[12] Likewise, his brother Fernando states that "to leave the revolution precisely in these moments would be interpreted as a desertion of my commitment to the poor" and, moreover, "an act of treason against my country."[13]

(2) *Active Collaboration.* The second group, of which the majority are foreign religious, corresponds to priests and religious actively collaborating in the tasks of the revolution. One significant example was the massive participation of Christians in the literacy campaign. More than three hundred religious took part, as did thousands of Catholic youths who made up the bulk of the brigades that traveled to the countryside to teach peasants to read and write. CONFER (the National Conference of Religious) provided moral and financial support, helping in organization, transportation, and teaching materials.[14] Another instance of active collaboration is the Center for Multiple Services (CSM), which coordinates the social pastoral work of many religious in Nicaragua. Programs of adult education, preventive medicine, community development, emergency assistance, and production cooperatives are carried out in collaboration with government ministries and institutions. This is to avoid possible overlap and to concentrate on those areas normally outside of the government's reach.[15] While this type of collaboration may be commonplace in many Latin American countries, in Nicaragua it cannot be ignored, since other organizations for social pastoral work are known to refuse collaboration with the government. An example is the Archdiocesan Commission of Social Promotion (COPROSA), which is the Archdiocese branch of Cáritas de Nicaragua, a Church-run social assistance organism. Working in those areas not yet reached by government agencies and ministries, COPROSA has attempted to counterpose itself as an alternative to the government. Community leaders who participate in COPROSA's training programs are discouraged from participating in any government-sponsored organizations and are subjected to an overtly political discourse which is critical of the revolutionary process.[16] Such activities contrast sharply with those of the CSM.

The Maryknoll sisters have been especially supportive of the revolutionary process. Besides carrying out pastoral work in a number of parishes (Ciudad Sandino, León, Ocotal, and San Juan de Limay) they also assist in various government programs, especially health and education. For example, in Ciudad Sandino, the sisters trained and coordinated health *promotores* (promoters) for local Sandinista Defense Committees (CDSs).[17] The health *promotores* in turn organized brigades to participate in vaccination and malaria eradication campaigns. The sisters also served as a liaison between the local CDSs and health clinics in the neighborhood, and between health *promotores* and the Ministry of Health.[18] In addition to these activities, the Maryknollers play a key role in the international solidarity campaign for Nicaragua. They regularly meet with delegations from North America and Western Europe, who come to Nicaragua on fact-finding trips, and provide progressive Christian groups abroad with fact sheets and informative bulletins documenting contra atrocities and the effects of the U.S.–sponsored aggressions.[19]

All of these examples of active collaboration are rooted in a particular interpretation of the Gospel message which equates serving the poor with the organization of the people for their own benefit. Accordingly, it is natural to support those government programs which advance the cooperation and organization of the people, and to encourage Christians to participate in them. Priests and religious within this group view the Church's role as one of awakening the people to the revolution—helping them to understand its significance and pointing to its positive aspects. In these ways the Church can help to build among the people a sense of community, which is necessary for the revolution to succeed. These priests and religious also stress the need for constructive criticism of the revolutionary process, criticism whose aim is to better the revolution and not to destroy it. Some of the errors and abuses they would point to are: (1) the excessive bureaucratization of the government; (2) the inadequate distribution of certain products; (3) the imperfect liberty of political debate; (4) the antireligious rhetoric on the part of some government officials; and (5) the government's deficient understanding of the ethnic problem of the Atlantic Coast region.[20] Despite the need to criticize such abuses, however, Catholics should not lose sight of their first and foremost duty, which is to serve the poor.

Although their activities are accused of being overly politicized, these priests and religious maintain that the Church cannot and should not separate itself from politics. They argue that Christ had a general political project, which was his option for the poor, and that the Church, as follower of Christ, should carry out his project. In this sense, it is logical to support the revolution, since its basic objectives are in agreement with the Gospel message.

Since about 1982, this second group has undergone a reevaluation of its objectives and strategies, which has resulted in a change of attitude regarding certain issues. An example has been its relations with the Church hierarchy. Recognizing the futility of the conflict within the Church (which has led to the removal of a number of priests and religious from their parishes), some within this group have become more prudent in their criticisms of the bishops so as to avoid unnecessary confrontations. Instead of responding carelessly to the hierarchy's criticisms of their activities, they consider these criticisms of a strictly political nature and therefore not binding. The second group no longer refers to itself as the "Popular Church." The term has been exploited by conservative sectors of the Church to accuse progressive clergy of attempting to form a break-away Church. In response to such charges, this group is emphatic about its loyalty to the Church hierarchy and denies that it seeks to create a Church outside the bishops' authority. Rather, its intentions are simply to change the Church, to make it a grass-roots Church.

(3) *Passive Collaboration.* A third group is characterized by a posture of passive collaboration. Priests and religious within this group are open to and fairly supportive of government programs without participating directly in them. Although generally in agreement with the revolution's objectives, they tend to be more critical of what they consider unnecessary government abuses. Their criticisms are similar to those of the second group, but they warn against using the external aggressions to excuse the errors and abuses of the revolutionary process. Within this group, in addition to a handful of Nicaraguan secular priests, we can find several foreign religious who initially assumed a posture of active collaboration but, because they serve as parish priests, have had to curtail their public identification with the revolution. For example, a Franciscan priest in the Diocese of Juigalpa told me that since 1982 he has had to discontinue his relations with the Antonio Valdivieso Center (CAV), an ecumenical center for theological reflection that is closely identified with the revolutionary process, because his bishop has publicly denounced its activities.[21] Unlike other religious, who teach at universities, technical colleges, and schools (and who are not engaged in pastoral work), these priests are responsible to both their local bishops and their religious superiors. With the hierarchy's growing opposition to the revolutionary process, many found it impossible to sustain a position of active collaboration. Those who did were either transferred to other parishes or were removed from their pastoral duties. Consequently, a position of passive collaboration enables them to avoid serious conflict with their bishops.

While respecting those who choose to collaborate actively in the tasks of the revolution, these priests and religious prefer to avoid such political identification. They recognize the danger of over-identification with the revolution, but consider an active Christian presence essential to prevent it from becoming too radical. They view their own pastoral work as necessarily having political implications, but distinguish between pastoral work which is based on political motivations and that which is based on purely religious ones. They also draw the distinction between politics in the general sense of the word and partisan politics. While the Church can never divorce itself from the former, it should not involve itself in the latter. A typical position during the elections was to encourage people to vote, emphasizing that it was their duty as Christians and Nicaraguans. Parishioners were also urged to vote for that party which they thought would improve the country's well-being. Finally, this group considers hypocritical the position of conservative clergy, who claim political neutrality while openly identifying with political parties of the right.

(4) *Passive opposition.* The fourth group would include clergy and religious who reject collaboration with the government. This is based upon their fundamental questioning of the revolutionary process which they regard as Marxist-oriented. Although these priests and religious do not support the Sandinistas, on the other hand, they do not *actively* seek to undermine the government. Dialogue, as opposed to confrontation, is seen as a more effective way to criticize government abuses. They are generally supportive of the hierarchy, although some are critical of the political activities of the more hardline bishops. They fear that the hierarchy's continuing silence concerning U.S. aggressions will be interpreted as insensitivity. Others within this group (especially Nicaraguan secular priests in the Archdiocese), try to downplay the bishops' criticisms of the government, suggesting that the bishops do not oppose the revolutionary process, but are only critical of certain aspects of it. They contend that pastoral letters which denounce specific government abuses have been misinterpreted by pro-government newspapers as signaling the hierarchy's fundamental opposition to the revolution.

Within this group we can find some of the more moderate bishops including the Bishops of León, Matagalpa, and Estelí, and the Auxiliary Bishop of Zelaya. Recognizing that the Sandinistas have a legitimate claim to power, especially in the wake of the elections, they prefer a relationship of coexistence with the government. Their disposition to seek dialogue with the government is based on the belief that private channels are a more effective means of working out points of contention. They view public denunciations of the government as many times counterproductive since they usually result in smear campaigns against the bishops. While aware that the government might consider the Church an obstacle, these bishops do not support the notion that the Sandinistas intend to stamp out religion in Nicaragua. On the contrary, they point out that the government recognizes the Church's strength among the faithful and the religiosity of Nicaraguans, and, moreover, that the Church should use this to its advantage in its negotiations with the government.[22] Also included in this group are a number of foreign priests, who, if not for their nationality, might otherwise adopt a more openly critical posture toward the revolutionary process. As foreigners, however, they do not consider themselves entitled to publicly voice their political opinions.

This fourth group stresses the importance of greater autonomy for the Church—not tied to any particular political party or government. While whatever the Church says or does will have political implications, it should limit itself to making pronouncements on moral and ethical issues. Pastoral work should be directed toward all people, regardless of class, and should emphasize religious rather than political themes.[23] This group criticizes the political activities of both progressive clergy and of the more hardline bishops, maintaining that clergy should keep their political opinions to themselves. While the fourth group likes to think of itself as politically neutral, it tends to focus most of its criticisms on priests and religious who support the revolution. Similarly, it makes little mention of the positive attributes of the revolutionary process, focusing instead on its negative aspects. Nevertheless, this group prefers to keep a low public profile with regard to political issues.

After initially adopting a position of conditional support vis-à-vis the new government, the fourth group became increasingly critical of the Sandinistas. It viewed the participation of Cubans in the literacy campaign, the resignations of moderate leaders from the governing junta, and the government's heavy-handed treatment of some clerics as proof that the FSLN had changed its original position regarding such issues as education, political pluralism, and religion. Although its disillusionment with the revolutionary process paralleled that of the hardliners within the Church, in the wake of the most serious period of conflict with the government (1983–84), its position began to diverge somewhat from that of the hardliners. Viewing the hierarchy's confrontation with the government as futile (especially after the government's expulsion of ten priests in July 1984), this group now favors a more diplomatic approach. An example of this is the continuing efforts by the moderate bishops, with the help of the Apostolic Nuncio, to create conditions for dialogue between the government and the hierarchy. These efforts, in fact, bore fruit in December 1984, with the renewal of talks between the Episcopal Conference and the government, which have continued intermittently. On an individual level, Msgr. Pablo Schmitz's decision to invite Daniel Ortega to his consecration as bishop in September 1984 was a clear sign of this more conciliatory approach toward the government. Schmitz's attitude contrasted with that of the other newly appointed bishop, Msgr. Pedro Vílchez, who used his consecration to criticize the Sandinista government, referring to the fact that "it is difficult to be a bishop in a dechristianized country like Nicaragua." Despite this group's disposition to achieve a more constructive relationship with the government, it points to the intransigence of the FSLN leadership and to the political activities of the more hardline bishops as constant frustrations to its efforts.

(5) *Active Opposition.* The last group is largely made up of Nicara-

guan secular clergy and includes some of the bishops. It not only rejects any collaboration with the government, but also actively seeks confrontation with the government. It refuses to acknowledge the positive aspects of the revolution, only pointing to what it considers abuses and injustices. Its criticisms of the government challenge the very legitimacy of the revolution. This group's strategy of confrontation vis-à-vis the government is based on the assumption that the Sandinistas can eventually be overthrown and that in a serious confrontation with the government the people will side with the Church hierarchy. One bishop told me that such a confrontation was inevitable. Moreover, as it intensified, the true Marxist face of the government would show through. Even Catholics supportive of the revolution would come to realize the government's fundamental opposition to religion. This confrontation and eventual rupture, then, would result in greater unity for the Church. According to the bishop, "That's dialectics."[24] This group dismisses dialogue with the government as a useless enterprise, pointing out that the Episcopal Conference has repeatedly engaged in dialogue with the government, yet to no avail.[25] Consequently, it prefers to publicly denounce government actions and policies it disagrees with. This is viewed as a more effective way to pressure the government than through the use of private channels.

Underlying the fifth group's fundamental opposition to the revolutionary process is a very narrow view of Marxism, especially in regard to religion. According to this view, Marxism is equated to totalitarianism and seen as an all encompassing ideology which cannot be used exclusively as a scientific tool for analysis; its acceptance as an analytical tool presupposes an acceptance of the whole ideology. Marxism is also considered to be fundamentally antireligious and as seeking to do away with religion entirely. In this sense, the government's current position toward religion is viewed as tactical, one which will change as soon as the Sandinistas have consolidated their power. This group often points to the example of Cuba as proof that the government's position will change. As was mentioned above, dialogue is dismissed as futile. In fact, one bishop told me that it was impossible to sustain fruitful dialogue with Marxists since, according to him, their Logos was totalitarian and closed. Promises are made but never kept.[26]

Regarding the Church's involvement in politics, this last group is by far the most vocal in its call for a politically neutral Church. Accordingly, the Church should denounce human rights abuses and social injustices without aligning itself to any particular government or political party. Those priests and religious who actively collaborate with the government are considered a liability to the Church since they undermine its efforts to create a politically neutral Church. Their identification with the revolution is seen as a blind commitment to the FSLN and as giving the government badly needed legitimacy. Unlike groups 1 and 2, which freely admit to the political nature of their activities, this last group is emphatic about its political "disengagement." Its criticisms are of a purely moral and ethical nature, and any similarity between them and those of political opposition groups is simply a matter of coincidence.

Despite its claims to the contrary, it is quite clear that the last group openly identifies with political opposition groups of the right. Immediately after Somoza's fall, this group adopted a wait-and-see attitude, conditioning its support for the government on the direction the revolution would take in the following months. Of greatest importance was the role that the Church, under the guidance of the bishops, would play in the revolutionary process. The incorporation of progressive Catholics in popular organizations and the identification of Catholic clergy and religious with the revolution was interpreted as a challenge to the authority of the Church hierarchy. Moreover, the participation of hundreds of Cubans in the literacy campaign and the U.S. administration's cool reception of the new government triggered off the anticommunist sentiments of many within this group. Also of importance was the participation of moderate opposition figures in the government. Their presence might serve to temper the government's more radical policies. With the resignations of Violetta Chamorro and Alfonso Robelo from the governing junta in April 1980, however, it became clear that the influence of the moderate opposition groups on the government would be minimal.[27] From this point on, the fifth group's growing opposition to the government would parallel that of political opposition groups.

The coincidence between the last group and the political opposition could be seen in the timing and content of a number of pastoral letters.[28] The clearest example was the April 22, 1984 pastoral which called on the government to enter into talks with the contras. This demand was identical to that put forward by the Nicaraguan Democratic Coordinating Committee (CDN)[29] in December 1983 as a condition for its participation in the upcoming elections. In an individual capacity, some of the hardline bishops have been even more explicit in their opposition to the government and in their sympathy for political opposition groups. An example of this was the position of skepticism adopted by Msgr. Obando y Bravo and Msgr. Vega during the run-up to the 1984 elections. Their public questioning of the electoral process was identical to that of right-wing political opposition parties and of U.S. administration officials. During the campaign, Obando met with CDN leaders on a few occasions, pointing to the lack of necessary conditions and lamenting the CDN's decision to abstain. Vega made his criticisms quite clear in a press conference on the eve of the elections, in which he questioned the validity of the elections.[30] As a consequence of their activities, the hardline bishops have come to be identified with the political opposition. In fact, the figure of Obando is regularly used by *La Prensa*, the CDN, and other political opposition groups as a symbol of resistance against the government. It is this last group which is at the center of the conflict with the Sandinista government.

Although it would be difficult to determine accurately the percentage for each group, it is possible to make some rough estimates. The only attempt so far at a comprehensive survey was that of the Central American Historical Institute (IHCA) during 1982–83. Of 220 priests interviewed (which represents 69 percent of the country's total—See table 1), 46 percent supported the revolutionary process in varying degrees and 54 percent opposed the process in varying degrees.[31] Unfortunately, no other details of the survey have been made available. While there is no reason to doubt the reliability of the survey, I would estimate that during the period in which I conducted my own interviews (1983–1985), the percentages would be closer to 35–40 percent for the first group and 60–65 percent for the second. The first group would correspond to groups 1, 2, and 3 of my typology, and the second to groups 4 and 5. A further breakdown would be as follows:

Groups 1 and 2:	15–20%
Group 3:	20%
Group 4:	40–45%
Group 5:	20%

Clearly, the large majority of clergy and religious belong to the third and fourth groups. While it would be speculative to estimate changes over time, it is possible to point to some general trends. For example, during 1981–82, as a result of the hierarchy's removal of a number of clergy and religious from their parishes (see last section of this chapter), there was some shift from groups 2 to 3 by several foreign religious who served as parish priests. Other shifts were from groups 3 to 4 and from groups 4 to 5, both of which reflected a growing disillusionment with the revolutionary process (especially after 1982–83) on the part of some clergy.

The divisions within the Church clearly arise from the conflict between group 5 and groups 1 and 2. Nowhere is this so pronounced as in the Archdiocese, where the percentages for groups 2 and 5 are much higher than the national average. Both the Archbishop, Cardinal Obando y Bravo, and his auxiliary bishop, Msgr. Bosco Vivas, pursue a position of active opposition to the government, and they are supported by the majority of secular clergy. This is exacerbated by the fact that in the Arch-

TABLE 1

Distribution of Clergy and Religious by Diocese, 1983

			PRIESTS			
DIOCESES	INHABITANTS	PARISHES	Total No.	Secular	Religious	Non-ordained Religious
Bluefields	229,945	12	18	4	14	35
Estelí	311,162	17	31	14	17	35
Granada	333,027	20	38	16	22	112
Jinotega	141,289	5	6	4	2	–
Juigalpa	136,342	14	13	6	7	2
León	517,226	27	39	22	17	59
Managua	1,215,969	66	152	50	102	372
Matagalpa	229,779	17	25	12	13	60
Totals	3,114,779	178	320	128	192	675

SOURCE: Seminario Nacional (Vice-Rector), Managua, 1983.

diocese foreign religious outnumber Nicaraguan secular clergy by a two to one ratio, and the former tend to be much more supportive of the revolutionary process than the latter.[32] The importance of this is confirmed by the fact that in other dioceses, where the ratio of religious to secular clergy is more balanced, and where the bishops tend to pursue a more moderate line vis-à-vis the government, the conflict within the Church is nowhere near as serious. While this may be partly the result of the peripheral nature of these dioceses (i.e., they are less likely to be affected by events in Managua), it is still significant that only in the Archdiocese has the conflict reached explosive proportions. Clearly the much higher degree of polarization in the Archdiocese would also seem to be rooted in the hierarchy's conflict with the government, which regularly spills over into the conflict within the Church. The conflict, in fact, has taken on all the appearances of a personal struggle between the Archbishop and the FSLN leadership, and has had a negative impact on the search for constructive dialogue within the Church. Later I discuss the challenges which the conflict presents for the progressive sector of the Church; next, however, I analyze the FSLN's position regarding the Catholic Church and its ongoing conflict with the Catholic hierarchy.

THE FSLN AND THE CATHOLIC CHURCH

The *Frente Sandinista de Liberación Nacional* (FSLN) was founded in July 1961 by Carlos Fonseca, Tomás Borge, and Silvio Mayorga. In-

spired by the life and thought of the nationalist hero Augusto C. Sandino, the FSLN was dedicated to a program of social revolution. After
limited success during the 1960s, the FSLN's strength began to grow after
1970. Contacts with workers and student groups were improved as were
support networks in the countryside. Initially, the FSLN had little reason
to collaborate with the Catholic Church which had supported the U.S.
intervention against Sandino and allied itself with the Somoza regime.
In the early 1960s, there were few signs of the Church's adopting a more
favorable position toward social change as urged in the Vatican II Council. With rare exceptions, the Church continued to grant the regime its
unconditional blessing and to remain silent in the face of socioeconomic
injustice and government repression. The hierarchy's cozy relationship with
the dictatorship convinced the FSLN of the Church's inherently reactionary nature, reinforcing the Sandinistas' originally dogmatic Marxist conception of religion. According to this conception, religion was viewed as
an obstacle to change and as an instrument used by the dominant classes
to oppress the people.

In the late 1960s, the efforts by a group of young priests to promote
social change and to denounce human rights abuses influenced the FSLN's
thinking somewhat. Their example of commitment to social change ran
counter to the FSLN's traditional view of the Church and religion. It was
not long before the Sandinistas began to contemplate the possibility of
forming a strategic alliance with progressive Catholics. Carlos Fonseca had
hinted at it when he insisted on the "compatibility between Marxism and
Christianity, the unity of revolutionary believers and non-believers in the
liberation of the people."[33]

The earliest formal contact aimed at inducing progressive clergy to
collaborate with the FSLN was with Ernesto Cardenal in 1968. The meetings with Cardenal (usually with both Borge and Fonseca present) continued sporadically through the 1970s.[34] It was not until 1976, however,
that Cardenal appeared as a spokesman for the FSLN. Uriel Molina, a
Franciscan priest working in a poor barrio of Managua, was contacted
soon after Cardenal. He and a group of fellow priests refused to make common cause with the FSLN. According to Tomás Borge, these early contacts were "confrontations in which personal cordiality and political and
ideological distrust prevailed."[35] The tactical nature of these initial encounters led priests like Cardenal and Molina to reject direct collaboration with the FSLN. While agreeing with many of the FSLN's objectives,
they were not so convinced that armed struggle was the only way to ac-
complish a radical transformation of society. Moreover, they feared that
the FSLN would manipulate their faith to benefit its political project.
Only through practical collaboration did these fears eventually disappear.

The FSLN had good reason to seek collaboration with certain sectors of the Church. In the countryside, for example, the FSLN needed to cultivate peasant links to build a rural support system. In many isolated areas the only organizational presence was the Church, in the person of the local priest. One way to gain the confidence of the peasants was to build a relationship with the local priest. This the FSLN began to do partly out of necessity and partly out of respect for the work of some individual priests. Indeed, many priests and their faithful proved to be the FSLN's most trustworthy allies in the countryside.[36]

In urban areas, CEBs were viewed by the FSLN as potential points of contact with poor working-class neighborhoods. In such neighborhoods, where other forms of organization were lacking, the CEBs served an array of functions (e.g., education, organization, and mobilization). Because of mutual distrust, however, initial collaboration was carried out through intermediate organizations such as the Movement of Revolutionary Christians (MCR). The MCR, which was founded in early 1973 by a group of university students, was initially involved in pastoral work in poor neighborhoods of Managua. By the mid-1970s, the MCR began to collaborate with the FSLN, providing militants with safe houses and recruiting people for the guerrillas. In fact, during the insurrections of 1978 and 1979, a significant number of young FSLN militants passed through its ranks.[37]

Of greatest importance to the increasing collaboration between the FSLN and progressive Catholics was the participation of significant sectors of the Church in the political opposition to Somoza. One example was the active role played by CEBs (especially after 1974) in denouncing human rights abuses and in demonstrating their solidarity with political prisoners and the victims of repression. Another was the work of the Capuchin Fathers in northern Nicaragua, where they documented the brutal repression unleashed by the National Guard in the countryside. They brought to the public's attention the torture and disappearance of thousands of peasants between 1975 and 1977. Also significant was the Catholic make-up of many of the young combatants who participated in the final stages of the insurrection, not to mention the presence of a number of Catholic priests in the very ranks of the FSLN. Fernando Cardenal, S.J., his brother Ernesto, and Miguel D'Escoto were all active in the FSLN by 1976, and two Spanish priests, Gaspar García Laviana, M.S.C., and José Antonio Sanjinés, S.J., served as combatants in the guerrillas.

The incorporation of Catholics into the armed struggle clearly must have contributed to the FSLN's rethinking of its originally dogmatic Marxist view of religion. The practical collaboration enhanced the potential for theoretical convergences. Statements by various FSLN leaders suggest

that the Sandinistas came to consider Christianity an important element
in the revolutionary process. In February 1984, for example, Daniel Ortega Saavedra, member of the FSLN's National Directorate and President
of the Republic, declared that "Christianity and Marxism are part of Sandinista democracy."[38] The year before, another member of the National
Directorate, Victor Tirado, affirmed: "In Nicaragua, the Gospel, Sandinismo,
and Marxism found that they coincided in their central objectives; they
agreed as to the necessity of improving the situation of the poor."[39] While
such declarations might be shrugged off as rhetorical, one can at least point
to some coincidence of objectives between progressive Catholics and the
FSLN. An example would be the FSLN's political program which is based
on the "logic of the majorities." For many progressive Catholics the government's efforts to expand health services, eradicate illiteracy, redistrib-
ute land, and subsidize public transportation and basic food products are
proof of its "option for the poor." They also point to the government's
program of penal reform, including the abolition of the death penalty (the
maximum prison sentence is thirty years) and the introduction of *granjas
abiertas* (open farms),[40] as a clear manifestation of its adherence to the
Christian principle of forgiveness. While such a "coincidence of objectives"
may not prove the degree of Christian inspiration behind the revolutionary
project, it would at least suggest a fundamental agreement between the
FSLN and progressive Catholics as to the basic objectives of the revolution. Moreover, this is confirmed by the fact that a significant number
of Catholics did participate in the insurrection and continue to participate in the tasks of reconstruction.

The FSLN's position toward religion is revealed in its October 1980
"Document on Religion." The document represents the most detailed and
comprehensive statement on religion ever issued by the FSLN. In it, the
FSLN recognizes the participation of Christians and of the institutional
Church in the popular struggle to overthrow Somoza: "Christians have
been an integral part of our revolutionary history, to a degree unprecedented in any other revolutionary movement in Latin America and possibly the world."[41] The document lists nine points which define the FSLN's
position on religion, the most important of which are:

(1) Freedom of religious practice is an inalienable right.
(2) All Nicaraguans have the right to become members of the FSLN,
    regardless of their religious beliefs.
(3) The FSLN will respect religious celebrations and traditions. How-
    ever, it will not allow them to be manipulated by political parties
    or individuals (including FSLN militants) for political purposes.
(4) No FSLN militant should express his opinion on religious ques-
    tions in an official capacity.

(5) All Nicaraguans have the right to participate in the country's
political decision making (including clergy and religious).

The document's uniqueness and historical significance is worth noting.
As one author points out:

> It is the first declaration of a Marxist-inspired political movement *in power*
> that states not only that religion is a right of conscience for every citizen
> of the state, but also that in recent Nicaraguan history Christian faith has
> shown itself to be an active force for justice even at the level of the insti-
> tutional churches. In this historic judgement the document expressly con-
> tradicts those theoretical statements of traditional Marxism which dismiss
> all religious beliefs as always delusory and reactionary.[42]

The FSLN's official position on religion has been publicly reaffirmed on
at least three occasions—the first being in February 1982, in response to
the Episcopal Conference's criticism of the government's relocation of
Miskito Indians in Zelaya; the second in August 1982, following the government's intervention of the Salesian School in Masaya; and the third
in March 1983, shortly after the pope's visit.

Despite its historical transcendence, some sectors of the FSLN have
not entirely overcome their distrust of religion. This continuing distrust
has been fueled by the opposition political activities of some conservative
clergy, making the FSLN's official position on religion increasingly difficult to sustain in practice.[43]

Although the dogmatic Marxist position does not hold much weight
within the FSLN leadership, recent young cadres, who have learned their
Marxist theory by memory from Soviet manuals, may be somewhat confused by the government's relatively flexible attitude toward the institutional Church. These texts "introduce theoretical confusion" which consequently "affects the practical unity between believers and Marxists."[44]
While such a trend could have a negative impact on the future collaboration of progressive Catholics and the FSLN, it must be remembered that
the present Minister of Education, Fernando Cardenal, S.J., is a Catholic
priest. The decision to put a Catholic priest in charge of the country's
educational system demonstrates, at least on the surface, the Sandinista
leadership's adherence to a pragmatic view of religion.

The ongoing conflict between the government and the Catholic
hierarchy, which potentially threatens the position of the pragmatists within
the FSLN, has enabled the hardliners in the government to assert their
influence on a number of occasions. A well-known example was the confused incident concerning Msgr. Bismark Carballo, spokesman for the
Archbishop, in August 1982. According to the official police version of
the incident, shots were heard near a house where Carballo was allegedly

"lunching with a parishioner." When the police arrived, a naked man was seen running out of the house pursued by another man hitting him. While pro-government newspapers suggested that Carballo had been "caught in the act" by a jealous boyfriend, Carballo claimed he had been the victim of a government plot to discredit him. More significant than the incident itself was the fact that the government lifted a ban on the publication of photographs of Carballo naked, although many people were offended by the printing of such material. Whatever the government's intention may have been, it backfired, since the overall impact was negative. For many, it symbolized the government's disrespect toward the Church, and for others, a direct attack upon the Church. Archbishop Obando y Bravo publicly defended Carballo, denouncing the incident as another attempt to damage the Church's image, and even government officials later admitted that the photographs should not have been released.[45]

Although the government's heavy-handedness serves as ammunition for opposition groups' charges of Sandinista persecution of the Church, it is necessary to look below the surface of such incidents to obtain a clearer picture. Initially, the government prohibited any news coverage regarding the Carballo incident.[46] Nevertheless, the day after the ban, Carballo held a press conference giving his version of the story. It was only after the news conference that the government decided to lift the ban on the publication of the photographs. Here was a clear example of the FSLN hardliners asserting their influence. The government felt compelled to respond forcefully to what it considered Carballo's provocations. Failure to respond would be interpreted as weakness, inviting similar incidents in the future.

Another occasion when force prevailed over moderation was in the wake of the bishops' controversial pastoral letter of April 22, 1984.[47] In it, the bishops called on the government to begin a dialogue that would involve all sectors of Nicaraguan society, including those who had taken up arms against the government. Despite the fact that the pastoral came in the wake of the CIA's mining of Nicaraguan ports, the bishops made no mention of the incident. In fact, in their discussion of the "national reality," the bishops omitted any specific references to U.S. military and economic aggressions, only vaguely referring to economic and ideological exploitation by "foreign powers." Moreover, they characterized the war as a civil war, "between Nicaraguans." The government's response to the bishops' call for a dialogue with counterrevolutionary forces was predictable. Denouncing the pastoral letter in harsh terms, the government pointed to it as proof of the hierarchy's links with reactionary forces. The official newspaper *Barricada* began a smear campaign against the bishops, running past photographs of Somoza with various bishops. Never in the five years since the triumph had the government's criticisms of the hierarchy reached such a high pitch. Clearly the government's hypersensitivity was a result of the critical conjuncture of U.S. aggressions against Nicaragua and of the overtly political message of the pastoral. Nonetheless, the media's tasteless smear campaign against the hierarchy only added to an already explosive situation and, as a result, Church-state relations plunged to an all-time low.

The crisis reached a head in July 1984 with the expulsion of ten priests accused of counterrevolutionary activities. While internationally the expulsions were depicted as further proof of religious persecution in Nicaragua, the events leading up to the expulsions reveal a more balanced story. In June 1984, Father Amado Peña was arrested by government agents for his involvement in counterrevolutionary activities, including the trafficking of arms and explosives. Tomás Borge, Minister of Interior, presented the President of the Episcopal Conference, Msgr. Vega, and the Secretary of the Nuncio, Msgr. Goebels, with the incriminating evidence during a private meeting. In return for the Church's public denunciation of such actions, the government offered to treat the incident as an isolated case. While Vega refrained from commenting on Peña's guilt or innocence, the Archbishop immediately "absolved" Peña of any guilt, charging that Peña had been the "victim of a government frame-up against the Church."[48] Despite the government's repeated insistence that Peña's case did not necessarily represent the attitude of the Church, Obando interpreted it as a direct attack on the Church.[49]

On July 9, Obando organized a march in solidarity with Father Peña. The march had been announced a few days earlier by *Radio 15 de Septiembre* (a contra radio station), the Voice of America, and UPI, as the first anti-Sandinista demonstration in the five years since the Somoza fall. Borge tried to dissuade Obando from holding the march, but it went ahead anyway with the participation of about 200 people, including some 20 priests and 100 journalists.[50] The day before, the Ministry of Interior had issued a communique pointing to the political nature of the march and placing all responsibility upon Obando.[51] Under the State of Emergency Law, unauthorized demonstrations were prohibited; thus, the government considered the march an illegal act. Its response was swift. Within hours of the march, the government cancelled the residence permits of ten foreign priests whom it charged with "carrying out intensive political activities against the government" and of "provoking confrontation between the Catholic Church and the revolution."[52]

Although the expulsion of the priests was a drastic measure, it obviously reflected the attitude within the government that Obando's provocations could no longer be tolerated, especially so soon after the bishops' pastoral calling on the government to begin talks with the contras. In this sense, the decision was not so much an attack on the Church as it was a direct response to the political activities of the Archbishop. Even progressive Catholics lamented the government's decision but saw it as a consequence of the confrontational strategy pursued by Obando and the conservative sector of the Church. Internationally, the expulsions had a very negative impact since they were portrayed as a general government policy toward the Church. It is interesting that in the wake of the expulsions, there was little polemic in the Nicaraguan media. Even more surprising was the fact that none of the other bishops made public statements in support of Obando. The more moderate bishops, favoring a relationship of coexistence with the government, viewed Obando's political machinations as counterproductive for the Church.

An even more serious incident was the expulsion of Msgr. Pablo Vega in July 1986. Vega, the Bishop of Juigalpa, had been deeply involved in opposition activities. In June 1986, Vega was invited to Washington by PRODEMCA, a conservative political action group active in the opposition to the Sandinista government. The visit came at a time when the U.S. Congress was debating whether to approve an additional $100 million in aid to the contras. While in Washington, Vega denounced the Sandinista government in particularly harsh language, going so far as to defend the contras' right to armed struggle. Upon his return to Nicaragua, Vega reiterated his belief in the justification of armed struggle and of the United States' right to support the contras. Never before had a high Church official been so explicit in his opposition to the regime, and the government wasted no time in expressing its outrage at what it considered a blatant provocation. On July 4, less than forty-eight hours after Vega had made public his statements, the government suspended "indefinitely" the bishop's right to reside in the country, noting that the bishop did not "deserve to be Nicaraguan."

One last source of friction between the FSLN and the Church hierarchy concerns Sandinista efforts to interpret Christian symbols and celebrations.[53] An example was the FSLN's August 1980 decree prohibiting any advertising which sought to utilize Christmas for commercial purposes. Although the FSLN justified the decree as an attempt to recover the "true popular and Christian meaning" of Christmas, the bishops were not persuaded.[54] In their October 1980 response to the FSLN's "Document on Religion," they pointed to the decree as a reflection of the government's tendency to interfere in religious matters—"to substitute the religious content of our traditional celebrations with a political one."[55]

Another example is the government's participation in *La Purísima* celebrations. The nine-day event, which celebrates the Immaculate Conception of the Virgin Mary, culminates on the ninth day with the *Gritería*, a popular event, during which candy and toys are traditionally distributed to the children. Since 1982, the *Casa de Gobierno* has made it a custom to sponsor the festivities in Managua. During the 1984 celebrations, for example, the *Casa de Gobierno*, in conjunction with other government institutions and Sandinista organizations, constructed altars along the Avenida Bolívar and provided candy and toys for thousands of children. Daniel Ortega, along with other members of the National Directorate, was among the participants in the festivities.[56] The government's official interpretation of *La Purísima* was that it should symbolize a call for peace. Daniel Ortega pointed out that the celebration of *La Purísima* was a right which the revolution guaranteed to all Nicaraguans, and Tomás Borge declared that "no one is going to snatch the celebration away from revolutionary Nicaraguans."[57]

While the FSLN may have considered its promotion of *La Purísima* a demonstration of its good intentions regarding religion, some of the bishops viewed its activities as an unwelcome interference in religious matters. For these bishops, the papal visit in March 1983 was final proof of the government's disrespect for religious celebrations.

Underlying the FSLN's desire that the pope's visit be a boost for the revolution was the fear that the visit would be manipulated by its political enemies. Its fears were confirmed by the highly polarized situation prior to the pope's arrival. Catholics supportive of the revolution expected the pope to respond positively to the accomplishments of the revolution and to condemn the U.S. aggressions against Nicaragua. Conservative Catholics, on the other hand, stressed the religious and pastoral nature of the trip: the pope was coming to bless Nicaragua and to bring unity to the Church.[58] This climate of expectation and mistrust (both sides feared the other would manipulate the visit in a political manner) convinced the FSLN to do all in its power to make the visit a success.

The government devoted scarce resources to the visit, including one month's supply of gasoline. Tomás Borge pointed to the government's efforts as proof of its "profound respect for religion."[59] Nevertheless, public statements by government officials, suggesting that the Pope would condemn the aggressions, did little to reduce the tensions. These were probably made worse by the government's naïveté regarding religious celebrations. One priest in the diocese of León, who advised government officials on the celebrations in León, told me that the government had planned to fill the Campus Médico in León with posters of Msgr. Romero and Gaspar García Laviana (the guerrilla-priest who died fighting during the insurrection).[60] Although he succeeded in convincing officials that the idea was too provocative, still the most prominent poster in the Campus was one of the pope with Msgr. Romero. Another example of this naïveté was the FSLN's instructions to Sandinista organizations concerning the visit. While stressing the importance of respecting the pope and Msgr. Obando, the FSLN deemed it appropriate to chant "Queremos la Paz" (We want peace) during the passing of the Peace.[61] It was this chanting, in fact, which ignited the disruption of the Mass in Managua. In short, rather than turning out a success for the FSLN, the visit was a disaster. Most foreign newspapers painted a negative picture of events, suggesting that the government had orchestrated the disruptions. Within Nicaragua, the visit added to the political polarization and, as a result, Church-state relations plunged to their lowest point ever.

Although within the FSLN leadership the overwhelming consensus appears to favor a conciliatory approach to Church-state relations, as we have seen, a number of factors have made this position difficult to sustain. The FSLN's attempts to interpret religious celebrations and symbols have been invariably viewed as government interference in religious matters. Hardliners within the Church point to these as proof of the government's tactical position on religion. Moreover, the tension between the dogmatic Marxists and the pragmatists within the FSLN has had a negative impact on the search for meaningful dialogue between the government and the Church. The political activities of the conservative sectors of the Church lend increasing weight to the dogmatic position. The fact that Obando allows himself to be used by political opposition groups (including counterrevolutionary forces and the Reagan administration) serves as additional proof of the Church's links with reactionary forces. Within a context of increasing political polarization and U.S. military and economic aggressions, even the moderates within the FSLN feel compelled to respond forcefully to Obando's provocations. The problem is, however, that with so many eyes scrutinizing every move of the Sandinistas, it is impossible to respond in such a way without being accused of religious persecution. While the FSLN may have equated the expulsion of the ten priests with "cutting off the fingers of Obando," it was not interpreted as such internationally. Finally, the spillover from the conflict within the Church seriously undermines the attempts to achieve reconciliation between the FSLN and the Catholic Church. Although the FSLN regards the conflict as an internal Church matter, it is undoubtedly related to the FSLN's conflict with the hierarchy. Surely there can be no solution to the one without there being a solution to the other.

NEW CHALLENGES

Since Somoza's fall, the progressive sector of the Church has been confronted with many new challenges. One of the most serious is the problem of "membership drain." After the triumph, many of the best lay leaders who were involved in the armed struggle gave up their work as Delegates of the Word and catechists to become local leaders in the FSLN or to take up positions in the government. Because of their leadership capabilities and prestige within their communities, the FSLN considered them desirable candidates for political positions. Their new responsibilities, however, no longer leave them time to devote to pastoral work. In fact, there has been a much diminished participation in pastoral activities in general, as many Catholics are involved full-time in other activities (e.g., popular organizations, adult education programs, militia duties, and production brigades). This has been especially true in the case of CEBs, which have lost many of their most dynamic members. A priest in Rivas, for example, complained to me about the difficulty in organizing Bible reflection groups in the evenings, since most of the people who expressed an interest either had classes or other meetings.[62] Catholic youth groups have been especially hard hit, since many of the most capable student leaders are involved in Sandinista youth organizations and are constantly being mobilized for militia training or crop harvesting. Another large number (young males) have been called up for their two-year military service. Consequently, today, there is an urgency to attract new people to participate in pastoral activities. Nevertheless, despite the membership drain, most priests interviewed pointed to the positive side of the phenomenon — that is, through these Catholics the Church is guaranteed a very active presence within the revolutionary process.[63]

The membership drain has been seriously complicated by the war. In northern departments, many lay leaders have been kidnapped or assassinated by the contras, and those still working in conflictive zones are in constant danger.[64] They have been targeted by the contras because of their participation in the struggle to overthrow Somoza and their continuing support for the revolution. Few are able to remain in their communities, and those who do must keep their political sympathies to themselves. Most have chosen to move to larger towns to avoid falling victims to the contras. Although on the one hand this has resulted in the decline in pastoral activities in the countryside, on the other hand, the arrival of lay leaders has instilled new life in the towns which were traditionally weak links in parish life.[65] The work of priests and religious has also been made more difficult by the war. Those working in war zones and who are sympathetic to the revolution are themselves targets. The Capuchin Fathers in El Jícaro, not far from the Honduran border, are a good example. Since the end of 1982, they have been unable to visit communities where the contras are known to be active and must first check with the military before leaving the town. As a result, they have lost contact with lay leaders in some communities, and a few, in fact, have gone over to the contras—some, because of intimidation, and others, because they are persuaded to join. In other cases, fundamentalist sects have penetrated communities cut off by the contras. These sects try to persuade peasants to reject civil defense schemes and any other involvement in Sandinista-sponsored programs. For example, in one small community in the extreme north of the country, a pastor from a fundamentalist sect succeeded in convincing the entire community to follow him across the border to Honduras.[66]

Clearly, carrying out pastoral work in such conditions is no small task. Sometimes families are split down the middle, some sympathizing with the contras and others with the government. In other cases, lay leaders are pressured to act as informers (by both the contras and government troops), since they know where the people's sympathies lie. This can be especially problematic for progressive clergy working with traditional peasant communities. One such priest told me of an incident where three catechists were compelled by government troops to act as their informers. Because the priest's sympathies for the revolution were well known, he lost the confidence of many in the community where the incident took place. It was especially bothersome since he had spent much time and energy building up the community's trust in him.[67]

Another challenge to the progressive sector is that of overcoming the traditional Catholicism and superstition of many peasants. An excellent example is in the Ocotal and Totogalpa parishes in the Diocese of Estelí. Until the arrival of four new priests in 1980 (a French Canadian to Totogalpa and three Spanish Jesuits to Ocotal), lay leaders had been virtually unknown in the two parishes. The previous parish priest, Father Madrigal (who served some forty years), had adopted a sacramentalist pastoral approach, visiting communities once or twice a year to say Mass and give baptisms. Many of the local peasants, who are quite superstitious, had considered Madrigal a prophet of sorts. One of his prophecies was that after his death, communists, posing as priests, would replace him. Unfortunately for the actual priests, all of whom are supportive of the revolution, many peasants still remember Madrigal's prophecies. The parish priest of Totogalpa (Father Enrique), for example, took me to a community where he had been initially rejected by the campesinos. Because on his first visit to the community, Father Enrique arrived on foot and without a cassock—Father Madrigal, the previous priest, had always arrived on horseback wearing a cassock—the peasants refused to believe that Father Enrique was their new priest. Only after two years have the peasants allowed him to celebrate Mass.[68]

In such rural communities, the peasants have no experience with CEBs or Delegates of the Word. In fact, for many, the extent of their lay participation has been simply attending Mass, and this only a few times a year. While more progressive pastoral approaches were implemented in a number of parishes before the revolution, these were never adopted by the hierarchy on a nationwide scale. Consequently, many parishes remained "frozen" in a pre-Vatican mold. This situation, however, was overlooked by many progressive priests and religious who arrived in Nicaragua soon after the triumph. They saw in Nicaragua a historic opportunity to achieve a greater synthesis between religious faith and political commitment, something which they thought had been accelerated by the insurrection.[69] Those who took over the administration of rural parishes where peasants had not participated in Bible reflection groups or courses for lay leaders found that their efforts to introduce new pastoral programs met with little success. Some peasants viewed with skepticism training courses which focused primarily on political themes. As a result, many priests and religious have learned to temper their enthusiasm for the revolution with a patient understanding of the campesinos' inherent wariness of change.

Closely related to this problem is the "identity crisis" within the progressive sector of the Church, which can be seen at two levels. On a group level, CEBs and Christian communities in the countryside have sought to redefine their evangelizing role. Before the triumph, they served as the only channels for political expression and grass-roots organization. Today, however, within the new revolutionary context of Nicaragua, this is no longer the case. The possibilities for political participation have greatly expanded, as people can now take part in popular organizations, trade unions, and political parties. In some neighborhoods, CEBs have become almost redundant, as their composition and activities differ very little from that of CDSs. To avoid becoming merely rival organizations, CEBs must find a new identity within the revolutionary process. Unfortunately, before the revolution CEBs did not focus on their future role within a revolutionary Nicaragua. Instead, the emphasis was on more immediate concerns such as human rights abuses, political repression, and the political alternatives available to change the situation of injustice. After Somoza's fall, new questions arose, such as what form the revolution would take and what role the Christian communities would have within the revolutionary process.

Another dimension of the "identity crisis" within the CEBs concerns their relationship with the institutional Church. CEBs have been attacked by some of the bishops for being overly politicized. In some parishes, CEBs have occupied churches to protest the hierarchy's removal of priests and religious supportive of the revolution. They have publicly expressed their solidarity with the priests serving in the government and have criticized the bishops' more controversial pastoral letters. Because of their activities, some of the bishops no longer consider them to be "in communion" with the Church hierarchy. Although CEBs insist on their loyalty to the bishops, some have found it difficult, if not impossible, to maintain their "ecclesial" identity. On an individual level, this has led to a feeling of isolation and confusion on the part of some members. An example of this is in the San Pablo Apóstol parish, where, in 1983, the Archbishop took advantage of the departure of the parish priest to install four priests more to his liking. Whereas the previous priest had been instrumental in developing the CEB movement in San Pablo, his replacements have refused to lend their support. As a result, many CEB members no longer feel themselves accepted as part of the Church.[70]

The "identity crisis" has also manifested itself in the efforts of many CEB members to "rediscover" the spiritual dimension of their faith, much of which was lost during the insurrection period. The urgent tasks of the armed struggle permitted very little time for any serious theological reflection and, as a result, CEBs came to function more like political action groups rather than Bible reflection groups.[71] Today, however, people need not attend their CEB to discuss political problems since they can do this in other groups. Consequently, many CEB members have turned to such movements as the *catecumenado* which emphasizes a complete conversion to Christianity. Within these groups, some find the spiritual element which seems to be lacking in many CEBs, where the focus is on sociopolitical issues.[72] An example is in the parish of Juigalpa, where *catecumenados* have replaced the CEBs as the most dynamic groups in the parish. Many of the members, in fact, come from the original CEBs. The *catecumenado* is a long process (sometimes up to seven years) of personal conversion. Emphasis is placed on Bible study and members are required to make significant sacrifices. For instance, in some communities members share their food and money. Because the *catecumenados* tend to be quite insular, however, they can alienate other groups in the parish.[73] Those which do not have their origins in the CEBs place little emphasis on social commitment and generally express a negative view of the revolutionary process. The dilemma, then, is how to reintroduce the spiritual element without losing the social dimension of pastoral activities.

The most serious challenge for the progressive sector is the counteroffensive which has been launched by the Nicaraguan hierarchy, CELAM, and the Vatican, who blame progressive priests and religious for the divisions within the Church and for attempting to create a "Popular Church" outside the authority of the bishops. According to Church hierarchy, internal unity and stability are threatened by the political activities of priests and religious in support of the revolution. The clearest statement of this view is contained in the bishops' October 22, 1980 pastoral letter entitled,

"Jesus Christ and the Unity of his Church in Nicaragua." In it, the bishops point to the doctrinal confusion among some sectors of the Church and to the divisions within the Church. These are viewed as arising from differences between the bishops and those priests who deviate from the "doctrine of the Pope." If priests and religious are to remain "in communion" with their bishops, they must remember their duty "to accept the doctrine of the Pope and the Bishops on questions of faith and custom."[74] To oppose the doctrinal or pastoral plan of the bishops, or to turn the faithful away from the bishops, constitutes "Parallel Magisterium," an attempt at juridical and doctrinal self-sufficiency by a sector of the Church. In other words, unity is threatened by the disobedience of some priests and religious. The bishops do not mention dialogue or a healthy diversity of views as facilitating unity. Rather, they see any efforts by priests and religious to introduce pastoral initiatives without the consent of their bishops as acts of "grave disobedience." In short, according to the bishops, uniformity is the best guarantor of unity.

One example of the hierarchy's efforts to undermine the progressive sector is the removal of several priests and religious from their parishes. Between 1980 and 1982, fourteen priests and twenty-two sisters were either removed from their parishes or had their official pastoral authorization suspended.[75] The series of removals, which fueled tensions within the Church, reached a peak in the summer of 1982, when CEBs in several parishes occupied churches to protest the removals. Although the bishops claimed that the removals were routine, part of normal rotation procedures, the fact that all of those removed or transferred were sympathetic to the revolutionary process suggests otherwise. The bishop's refusal to engage in dialogue with priests and religious concerning their removals was interpreted by the progressive sector as proof of persecution *within* the Church. It seems that Obando has pursued a strategy aimed at purging his diocese of progressive clergy. A clear illustration of this is Obando's ongoing conflict with the Dominicans. In September 1981, two Dominicans, Manolo Battalla and Rafael Aragón, were removed from their parishes in Managua. Both had actively encouraged parishioners to participate in popular organizations. Besides calling for the removals of Batalla and Aragón, Obando also tried to pressure the Dominican superiors to withdraw the entire Order from Nicaragua.[76] Although his request was rejected, Obando is reported to have persisted in his efforts to expel the Dominicans.[77]

Although a large number of progressive priests and religious still remain in the Archdiocese, only a handful are authorized to engage in pastoral work. The replacements have tended to be priests loyal to Obando, who have attempted to undo the pastoral strategies of their predecessors.

This has created tensions in a number of parishes. In the Managua parishes of San Judas and Colonia Centroamérica, for example, CEBs have openly clashed with Father Silvio Fonseca and Antonio Vacarro, who replaced priests removed by Obando. In October 1983, CEBs staged demonstrations in both parishes to protest against the priests' public opposition to the military service law. In Colonia Centroamérica, CEBs even succeeded in preventing Father Vacarro from saying Mass.[78] The effect of the removals has been to worsen already serious divisions within the Church.

Those progressive priests and religious who have been fortunate enough to survive the removals live in constant fear that their day will soon come. Several such priests told me of the strained relations they have with their bishops. Because of their collaboration with the government, their bishops have attempted to undermine their pastoral work which is considered "politicized." For example, one priest related to me an incident where lay leaders in his parish (in the Diocese of Juigalpa) attended a course given by the bishop. The bishop contradicted most of what they had been taught by the priest, and even suggested that their priest was "confused."[79] Another example was in the Diocese of Estelí, where the bishop, during a visit to one of the parishes in the summer of 1984, announced that a new catechism course would be introduced in the parish. The announcement was made without prior consultation with the parish priest or the catechists, in spite of the fact that the new catechism course represented a substantial change from the old one.[80] In the same diocese, the bishop sent out a circular in September 1984, informing priests that any Delegates of the Word not trained in courses expressly authorized by the bishop had no authority to carry out pastoral work.[81] The bottom line was that hundreds of Delegates of the Word were no longer recognized by the bishop as legitimate lay leaders. Such strategies can only be aimed at undermining the pastoral work of priests no longer considered "in communion" with their bishops.

CELAM has also played a significant role in the counteroffensive against the progressive sector. It is interesting that only *after* Somoza's fall and the subsequent rise to power of the FSLN did CELAM begin to take an active interest in Nicaragua. In fact, during the Puebla Conference in 1979, Msgr. López Trujillo (then general secretary of CELAM) and other conservative bishops refused to sign a letter of solidarity with the Nicaraguan Episcopate.[82] In January 1980, however, CELAM held an assembly in San José, Costa Rica, at which it met with the Nicaraguan bishops and proposed a Plan of Assistance.[83] In May of 1980, a course on the Puebla documents was organized for the bishops, followed by similar courses for priests, religious, and laity throughout August and September. A team of theologians from CELAM conducted the courses, among which were few progressive theologians. CELAM also set up a program to train cate- chists and lay leaders, and distributed 10,000 New Testaments (an old ver- sion not written in the vernacular) and various CELAM publications. In addition, it provided priests and religious to fill empty posts at the Na- tional Seminary in Managua, and declared August 15 a day of solidarity with the Nicaraguan Church, to collect donations throughout Latin America.[84] Although the alleged reason for CELAM's arrival in Nicara- gua was that the Church did not have adequate time to study the Puebla documents in light of the past insurrection, the scope of CELAM's Plan of Assistance penetrated much further. CELAM's efforts have been directed toward the consolidation of the bishops' authority within the Church and the development of pastoral strategies which pose an alternative to those of the progressive sector.

The Vatican has also publicly expressed its support for the bishops and its distaste for the progressive sector of the Church. In its offensive against priests and religious who identify with the Sandinista revolution, the Vatican has adopted a more subtle but effective strategy, which is to modify the statutes of clergy associations and religious conferences. This, it says, is being done throughout Latin America with the aim of mak- ing such associations more uniform. For example, ACLEN (Association of Nicaraguan Clergy), which had been known to take an independent line from the bishops with regard to the revolution, had its statutes re- viewed by the Sacred Congregation for Clergy in 1982. One of ACLEN's members, Álvaro Argüello, S.J., had served as the Association's represen- tative to the Council of State since May 1980. In a pastoral letter dated May 13, 1980, the bishops made sure to point out that Argüello only rep- resented ACLEN and not the Church as such.[85] In a letter to one of the bishops, dated July 14, 1982, the Sacred Congregation called on the hier- archy to impose substantial modifications on ACLEN's statutes, with the objective of putting it "under complete control of the local Ecclesiastical Authority."[86] Although the bishops claimed that the aim of the modifi- cations was to create greater "communion" between them and the clergy, a closer look at the modifications suggests otherwise. The Sacred Con- gregation recommended that ACLEN should only include diocesan priests (secular and religious priests in charge of a parish) and not religious priests without a parish. As was pointed out in the first section, religious priests, especially those without a parish, tend to be more supportive of the revolutionary process than diocesan priests. Clearly, then, the aim was to change the political configuration of ACLEN, making it much more to the liking of the bishops. The Sacred Congregation also recommended that ACLEN not permit its representatives to take part in any government institutions. This was intended to prevent Álvaro Argüello, S.J., from continuing as ACLEN's representative in the Council of State. Furthermore, the modifications clearly sought to augment the hierarchy's control over ACLEN. One article stated flatly that, "ACLEN is under the authority of the Episcopal Conference," and another made the election of ACLEN's directorate subject to the bishops' approval.[87] Not surprisingly, the modifications were deemed unacceptable by ACLEN's directorate and, after unsuccessful attempts to negotiate with the bishops, it made the decision to dissolve ACLEN.[88]

Likewise, CONFER's (National Conference of Religious) statutes were reviewed by the Sacred Congregation for Religious in 1983. CONFER was composed entirely of religious (both ordained and non-ordained), and its directorate was decidedly in favor of the revolutionary process. CONFER had collaborated in a number of government projects, such as the literacy campaign and the training of health *promotores*, and had publicly voiced its support for the revolution on several occasions. At the end of 1983, CONFER's statutes were revised. The most significant changes regarded the composition of CONFER. Whereas before, CONFER was composed of superiors from all religious communities, under the new statutes only regional and provincial superiors were to be members of CONFER. Member status included the right to vote in the General Assembly and to serve on CONFER's directorate.[89] The immediate result was that during subsequent elections in March 1984, the conservatives took control of the directorate, winning four of the seven seats, including president and vice-president.[90] Conservatives argue that before the new statutes were implemented, CONFER's directorate, which was controlled by the progressives, only represented the interests of one group within CONFER. Moreover, most were not in agreement with CONFER's openly pro-Sandinista posture, and some even discouraged their religious from participating in CONFER. Now, they say, CONFER is representative of a diversity of views and more accurately resembles the actual relationship between religious and superiors outside of CONFER.[91] Conservatives also argue that the revised statutes were aimed at improving relations with the hierarchy, which had deteriorated under the previous directorate.[92] Indeed, because of the new political configuration of CONFER's directorate, relations have improved. However, the difference is that whereas before, CONFER encouraged the participation of the great majority of religious, today, it is a hierarchical organization dominated by the regional and provincial superiors.

The challenges facing the progressive sector of the Church in Nicaragua are great. Besides trying to find its new identity within the revolutionary process, it is under constant attack from the Nicaraguan hierarchy, CELAM, and the Vatican. Its efforts to promote a grass-roots Church are interpreted by the bishops as an attempt to form a "Popular Church" outside of the hierarchy's authority. While the progressive sector contends that it only seeks to change the model of the Church by providing an alternative grass-roots model, its pastoral strategies are no longer tolerated by the bishops, who consider them "politicized" and "out of communion" with the institutional Church. Likewise, the participation of priests and religious in the revolutionary process is viewed as undermining the hierarchy's attempts to create a politically neutral Church. The dilemma, then, is how to keep alternative strategies alive without provoking a confrontation with the bishops and without having to split off from the institutional Church. For some, such a split may be inevitable, yet for others the continuing participation of Catholics in the revolution is a sign for hope.

CONCLUSION

Clearly, the tensions within the Church are closely related to the conflict between the Catholic hierarchy and the Sandinista government. As has been shown, the political activities of hardliners within the Church, combined with the FSLN's resolve to respond forcefully to what it considers political provocations, tend to undermine the efforts of the moderate bishops who pursue a relationship of coexistence with the government. Their more conciliatory approach is supported by the new Apostolic Nuncio to Nicaragua, Msgr. Paolo Giglio, who arrived in July 1986. For example, the reactivation of the Church-state dialogue in September 1986 was largely the result of Giglio's overtures. Although the two sides came very close to reaching a general agreement on Church-state relations, the talks were broken off by the bishops in May 1987.

Recently, though, a number of events give some cause for hope. The most significant was the government's appointment of Obando y Bravo to head up the National Reconciliation Commission—as called for by the Central American Peace Accords—and to serve as mediator in the cease-fire negotiations with the contras. Such a move by the government can only have a beneficial impact on Church-state relations and on divisions within the Church. Moreover, the decision to allow *Radio Católica* back on the air and to permit the return of Msgr. Vega has cleared away the major obstacles to an agreement on Church-state relations. Ultimately, however, the success of the Church-state dialogue will largely depend on the outcome of the fragile peace process now under way in Central America.

NOTES

1. A reflection of this position was the bishops' March 1972 pastoral letter, in which they affirmed that "the political structures do not respond to the demands of our time." See Conferencia Episcopal de Nicaragua, "Sobre los principios que rigen la actividad política de toda la Iglesia como tal" (Managua, March 19, 1972, p. 11.

2. For an analysis of the development of the hierarchy's position during this period, see Philip Williams, "The Catholic Hierarchy in the Nicaraguan Revolution," *Journal of Latin American Studies* 17:341–369.

3. The conference was the first of its kind. Approximately 100 of Nicaragua's 277 priests, plus 110 nuns, and 3 of the 9 bishops attended the conference at which a highly controversial discourse was given by Noel García, S.J. García analyzed the current situation of the Church in Nicaragua, criticizing the majority of clergy for openly identifying with landowners and businessmen and for seeking after their own economic benefit. He also pointed to the absence of commitment to the promotion of social change and to the principles set forth at the Vatican II Council and Medellín. As a result of the conference, the bishops officially accepted the Medellín conclusions.

4. Rosa María Pochet and Abelino Martínez, "Nicaragua. Iglesia: Manipulación política o profecía?" unpublished mimeo (CSUCA, February 1985), chap. 2, pp. 18–44.

5. It was estimated that in 1979 there were approximately 5,000 DPs in Nicaragua. See Luis Serra, "Ideología, religión y lucha de clases en la revolución," in Richard Harris and Carlos M. Vilas, eds., *La Revolución en Nicaragua* (Mexico, D.F., 1985), p. 260.

6. On the Capuchins, see Gregorio Smutko, "Cristianos de la costa atlántica en la revolución," in *Nicarauac*, no. 5 (April–June 1981); and on CEPA, see Manuel Rodríguez García, *Gaspar Vive* (San José, 1981), pp. 120–126.

7. The typology is based on information collected during over fifty interviews with bishops, priests, and religious in Nicaragua (all dioceses were represented). The interviews were conducted during three visits to Nicaragua: July–August 1983; October 1984–February 1985; and May 1985. While the typology is an attempt to describe a particular historical conjuncture, it may also be of a more general use.

8. Examples are Xabier Gorostiaga, S.J., who served in the Ministry of Planning until 1982, and Peter Marchetti, S.J., who works for the Centro de Investigaciones y Estudios de la Reforma Agraria (CIERA).

9. Teófilo Cabestrero, *Ministros de Dios, ministros del pueblo* (Bilbao, 1983), p. 36.

10. Interview with Ernesto Cardenal (Minister of Culture), January 15, 1985.

11. Interview with Fernando Cardenal, S.J. (Minister of Education), Feburary 8, 1985, Managua.

12. Interview with Ernesto Cardenal, January 15, 1985.

13. Fernando Cardenal, S.J., "Carta a mis amigos," in *Barricada*, December 11, 1984.

14. Anabel Torres, et al., "Lucha ideológica en el campo religioso y su significado político," unpublished mimeo (Managua, 1981), p. II–3.

15. The CSM was originally affiliated with CONFER. It became an independent organization in 1984, when a group of conservative religious took control of CON-

FER's directorate. Conversations with Ani Wihbey of the Central de Servicios Múltiples, November-December 1984, Managua.

16. Interview with Roberto Rivas (Director of COPROSA), January 31, 1985, Managua; also see Ana María Ezcurra, *Agresión ideológica contra la revolución sandinista* (Mexico, D.F., 1983), pp. 51–70.

17. CDS's are organized at the urban block level and function as political decision-making bodies concerned with production, distribution, health, education, and militia organization.

18. Maryknoll Sisters, "Ciudad Sandino Evaluation," unpublished, undated mimeo, Managua.

19. Interviews with Maryknoll sisters in Ciudad Sandino (November 26, 1984), Ocotal (December 2, 1984), and León (January 1, 1985).

20. The clearest statement of this group's criticisms of the revolutionary process is contained in the Jesuits' response to the bishops' April 22, 1984 pastoral letter. See "Declaración del delegado de los Jesuitas con su consulta," in *Barricada*, May 9, 1984.

21. Confidential interview.

22. Interview with Msgr. Julian Barni, O.F.M. (Bishop of León), August 23, 1983, León; interview with Msgr. Carlos Santi, O.F.M. (Bishop of Matagalpa), July 21, 1983, Matagalpa.

23. Priests and religious within group 4 carry out a pastoral strategy which is based on apostolic movements, such as the Charismatics and *Catecumenado*, rather than CEBs. The former tend to concentrate on personal conversion as opposed to sociopolitical commitment.

24. Interview with Msgr. Pablo Antonio Vega (Bishop of Juigalpa), December 18, 1984, Managua.

25. Interview with Msgr. Miguel Obando y Bravo (Archbishop of Managua), August 16, 1983, Managua.

26. Interview with Msgr. Vega, December 18, 1984.

27. Both Robelo and Chamorro represented groups from the moderate opposition to Somoza. The former resigned because of political differences with the FSLN, and the latter, for reasons of health.

28. On this point, see Philip Williams, "Catholic Hierarchy in the Nicaraguan Revolution," pp. 365–367.

29. The CDN is a right-wing umbrella group made up of the Social Christian Party (PSC), the Social Democratic Party (PSD), the Constitutionalist Liberal Party (PLC), the Conservative Party of Nicaragua (PCN), labor groupings (CTN and CUS), and the private sector association COSEP.

30. Msgr. Pablo Antonio Vega, "Nuestro aporte de Iglesia a la humanización de la historia: Una invitación a la reflexión cristiana ante el momento nicaraguense" (Managua, October 24, 1984).

31. *Envío*, no. 30 (December 1983): 9b.

32. Because of the scarcity of native-born clergy, the Nicaraguan Church has always relied heavily on foreign religious, who make up 60 percent of the total number of priests in the country. The percentage is even higher in the Archdiocese because of the existence of several Catholic schools and the Jesuit-run university.

33. Luis Serra, "Ideología, religión y lucha de clases," p. 276.

34. Margaret Randall, *Cristianos en la revolución* (Managua, 1983), p. 57.

35. Tomás Borge, *El Axioma de la esperanza* (Bilbao, 1984), p. 101.

36. Interview with Teodoro Niehaus, O.F.M. Cap., (former parish priest in Siuna), July 26, 1983, Managua; interview with Alfredo Gundrum, O.F.M. Cap., (parish priest in El Jícaro), December 7, 1984, El Jícaro; also see Gregorio Smutko, "Cristianos de la costa atlántica."

37. See Margaret Randall, *Cristianos en la revolución*, pp. 150–154, 159.

38. Quoted in Luis Serra, "Ideología, religión, y lucha de clases," p. 277.

39. Ibid.

40. Instead of being confined to jails, some prisoners are assigned to farms where they live and work. Although a government *responsable* assists them during the day, they are left unguarded at night.

41. *Barricada*, October 7, 1980.

42. César Jerez, S.J., *The Church and the Nicaraguan Revolution* (London, 1984), pp. 15–16.

43. For a useful typology of the various attitudes toward religion within the FSLN, see Jerez, *Church and the Nicaraguan Revolution*, pp. 16–17.

44. Luis Serra, "Ideología, religión y lucha de clases," p. 279.

45. For a full account of the Carballo incident, see Pat Hynds, "The Catholic Church in Nicaragua," in *Central America Update* (November 1982): 4.

46. *Barricada*, August 12, 1982.

47. CEN, "Carta Pastoral del Episcopado Nicaragüense Sobre la Reconciliación" (Managua, April 22, 1984).

48. *La Prensa*, June 22, 1984.

49. *Amanecer*, no. 28–29:9–10.

50. *Barricada*, July 10, 1984; *El Nuevo Diario*, July 10, 1984; *La Prensa*, July 10, 1984.

51. *Barricada*, July 9, 1984.

52. *Barricada*, July 10, 1984.

53. One can also point to the manipulation of religious symbols by political opposition groups. A good example was *La Prensa's* stories on the "Virgen de Cuapa." *La Prensa* interpreted the Virgin's appearances before a poor peasant in Cuapa as signaling the Virgin's desire to save Nicaragua from its present suffering—implicitly suggesting that the revolution was responsible for the suffering. See *La Prensa*, March 30, 1981, April 21 and 28, 1981.

54. "Decreto de la JGRN sobre la Navidad," in CEP, *Nicaragua: La hora de los desafíos* (Lima, 1981), pp. 101–102.

55. CEN, "Respuesta de la Conferencia Episcopal de Nicaragua" (Managua, October 17, 1980), p. 17.

56. This author was in El Jícaro (near the Honduran border) during the 1984 *La Purísima* celebrations. There, members of the army distributed small toys, candy, and fruit to hundreds of young children.

57. *Barricada*, December 8, 1984.

58. For a discussion of the pope's visit to Nicaragua, see IEPALA, *El Papa en Nicaragua: Análisis de su visita* (Madrid, 1983), and *Envío*, no. 21 (March 1983).

59. *El Nuevo Diario*, March 3, 1983.

60. Confidential interview.

61. IEPALA, *El Papa in Nicaragua*, pp. 86–87.

62. Interview with Gregorio Barriales, O.P. (parish priest in Rivas), January 7, 1985, Rivas.

63. Interview with Bernard Wagner, O.F.M. Cap. (parish priest in Wiwilí and Quilalí), November 20, 1984, Managua; interview with Ramón Pardina, M.S.C. (parish priest in San Juan del Sur). January 10, 1985, San Juan del Sur; interview with Enrique Coursol (parish priest in Totogalpa), December 2, 1984, Totogalpa.

64. In the El Jícaro parish (Nueva Segovia), for example, nine Delegates of the Word have been assassinated by the contras. This represents about a third of the total number working in the parish. Interview with Alfredo Gundrum, O.F.M. Cap. December 7, 1984; for a collection of first-hand accounts of contra atrocities against Catholic lay leaders, see Teófilo Cabestrero, *Blood of the Innocent* (London, 1985).

65. Interview with Bernard Wagner, O.F.M. Cap., November 20, 1984.

66. Interview with Alfredo Gundrum, O.F.M. Cap., December 7, 1984.

67. Confidential interview.

68. Interview with Enrique Coursol, December 2, 1984; interviews with José Luís Ortega, S.J. and Augustín Torranza, S.J., December 1, 1984, Ocotal.

69. *Envio*, no. 30 (December 1983): 6b.

70. Pochet and Martinez, "Nicaragua. Iglesia: Manipulación política o profecía?" p. 60.

71. *Amanecer*, nos. 7–8 (March–April 1982), p. 13.

72. Pochet and Martínez, "Nicaragua. Iglesia: Manipulación política o profecía?" chapter two, pp. 63–64.

73. Interview with Domingo Gatti, O.F.M., May 17–18, 1985, Juigalpa.

74. CEN, "Jesucristo y la Unidad de su Iglesia en Nicaragua" (Managua, October 22, 1980), p. 11.

75. It is not surprising that the majority of the removals were carried out in the Archdiocese. *El Nuevo Diario*, November 4, 1983.

76. The Dominicans are particularly united in their support for the revolutionary process. Interview with Juan Merino, O.P. (Former Regional Superior of Dominicans in Central America), April 24, 1985, San José, Costa Rica.

77. In October 1985 Obando met with Vatican Secretary of State, Cardinal Casaroli, asking his intervention in the matter. See *Update*, no. 84a (January 21, 1986).

78. *Envío*, no. 30 (December 1983): 22b–23b; *El Nuevo Diario*, November 1, 1983.

79. Confidential interview.

80. Confidential interview.

81. Msgr. Rubén López Ardón, "Instrucción Diocesana 'Eminente Vocación' sobre los Delegados de la Palabra" (Estelí, September 24, 1984). Although the Bishop of Estelí is one of the moderate bishops, as the only Nicaraguan among this group he is under constant pressure from the hardline bishops (most of whom are Nicaraguan) to adopt a tougher stance. Consequently, he has assumed a highly ambiguous position. While on the one hand he has sought to consolidate his authority within the Diocese of Estelí, on the other hand he was the only bishop to greet Miguel D'Escoto during the February 1986 March for Peace.

82. Miguel Ernesto Vigil, "Sospechoso interés del CELAM sobre la Iglesia en Nicaragua," *El Nuevo Diario*, September 21–22, 1980.

83. The total budget for the Plan was $320,000. CELAM, "Proyecto de programa de ayuda a la Iglesia de Nicaragua," undated memo.

84. CELAM, no. 159 (February 1981): 16–18.

85. CEN, "Comunicado pastoral de la Conferencia Episcopal de Nicaragua" (Managua, May 13, 1980).

86. "Sagrada Congregación para el Clero" (Rome), letter dated July 14, 1982.

87. Ibid.

88. *Barricada,* July 23, 1983.

89. Archivo de CONFER, "Observaciones de la Sagrada Congregación de Religiosos e Institutos Seculares (SCRIS) al Proyecto de Estatutos de CONFER," undated memo; also see CONFER, "Estatutos de la Conferencia Nacional de Superiores Mayores de Nicaragua," November 21, 1983.

90. Interview with Sister Rosalia Cereda, M.S.C. (Former Secretary of CONFER), November 27, 1984, Managua.

91. Interview with José Manuel Guijo, S.D.B. (President of CONFER), January 18, 1985, Managua.

92. Article 34, in fact, provides for a *comisión mixta* to be composed of bishops and religious, who will meet periodically to discuss differences. See CONFER, "Estatutos," November 21, 1983.

Political Radicalization and Popular Pastoral Practices in El Salvador, 1969–1985

Jorge Cáceres Prendes

This chapter analyzes the emergence and development of radical Catholicism in El Salvador. In recent years, this small Central American nation has drawn considerable international attention because of the prolonged civil war. As is well known, Christian groups have played an important role in the revolutionary struggle. This chapter addresses why radical Catholicism emerged, linking this emergence to structural phenomena in Salvadoran society. It then discusses the evolution and impact of radical Catholicism, again seeking to explain these processes as part of the overall political developments in the society.

This work comes out of a concern with comprehending the relationship between the appearance of new forms of consciousness (and their corresponding forms of practice) among Christian social sectors in El Salvador and the country's overall sociopolitical process. We propose to offer a general frame of reference for interpreting that sociopolitical process, with particular emphasis on the role played by these Christian sectors throughout the period under consideration. We work with a conception of politics and, by extension of power, as essentially structural phenomena, or, in other words, as class relations.

The corpus of this paper was written in July 1982 and appeared in a somewhat expanded version in *Estudios Centroamericanos* (ECA) 33 (1982): 93–153. Parts of the paper were also previously published in *Social Compass* 30, no. 43 (1983): 261–298. The final section on the Church's role in Salvadoran politics since the assassination of Archbishop Romero in March 1980 was written in early 1986, specifically for this volume. The protracted stalemate in the Salvadoran civil war explains the change of tone in this last section. – Ed.

The underlying assumption of analysis is that the development of radical Catholicism must be understood in relation to developments in the society at large, and especially the evolution of the Salvadoran left. We therefore have picked three different arenas for our analysis. The first is the state itself, with all its established means and procedures for participation, and its progressive crumbling under the weight of social protests that it has been unable to contain. Secondly, we look at the surfacing of contending political alternatives which demand a radical form of democracy counterposing "the people" to the system of domination. It is in this context that we speak of the emergence of a new type of "popular-revolutionary organization,"* which puts into practice alternative and revolutionary forms of participation. It is their development that characterizes the general radicalization of the country's political process. Finally, we will focus attention on the development of a core of conceptions and practices within the Catholic Church. The inclusion within its pastoral practice of a similar radical demand for democracy has also been an important stimulus to the process of radicalization. The institutional Church, a powerful apparatus traditionally dedicated to legitimizing "law and order," was shaken by the present political crisis. This led to the appearance of a sector identified (albeit in varying degrees and forms) with radical understandings of the Church's mission. Through its "option for the poor," this sector came to openly confront the system of domination as the political crisis deepened.

Precursors to Social Christianity in El Salvador

A few recent studies have dealt with the Salvadoran Church's "social action" during the tenure of Msgr. Luis Chávez y González (1938–1977).[1] These studies emphasize the process of pastoral renewal initiated very early by this minister, who was quite attentive to similar changes underway in other parts of the world. As a result of Chávez's attitude, by the 1960s the Salvadoran Church, and particularly the archdiocese of San Salvador, had already gained infrastructure, personnel, and valuable experience in the fields of pastoral and social work. Rather than going further into this point here, we should mention other aspects of what we call "social Christianity": a type of social action inspired by explicitly Christian ethics, but lacking the mediation of a scientific analysis of social rela-

---

*We have translated "organizaciones populares" as popular-revolutionary organizations. Cáceres' usage of "organizaciones populares" embraces guerrilla groups that, in the usage common to North and South American readers, would not be considered "popular organizations."–Ed.

tions and the concept of *praxis* that would later come to characterize the revolutionary tendency of Christian ethics.

We will focus on specifically political movements: the Christian Democratic Party (PDC) and the University Social Christian Movement. The PDC appeared in the late 1960s in the same mold as its counterparts in Latin America, attempting to unite ethical aspects and abstract postulates of the Church's social doctrine with the developmentalist and reformist programs so much in vogue at the time. In the case of El Salvador, the PDC soon became the main focus of opposition to the National Conciliation Party (PCN), organized in 1961 in the long-standing tradition of official parties. The PDC organized mainly around electoral campaigns, with a goal of acquiring progressively greater shares of power within the system of proportional representation established in 1963. The party was to develop little ideologically, tending to follow the technocratic banners of similar parties, like the Venezuelan COPEI, as well as displaying a technically oriented focus on vote-getting. With the novelty, frequency, and initial relative success of its electoral performance, relatively unencumbered by traditional official impositions, the party showed considerable growth despite functioning only during the electoral campaigns. It was able to cultivate effectively the antimilitary sentiments dominant in the country's urban sectors, as well as the ongoing frustration of demands for social reform. Only in the late 1960s, with the influx of new members into its ranks, did the PDC begin to develop concrete proposals for major reforms. It was unable, however, to move forward on these proposals due to the absence of any real social base in the party structure.[2]

In 1964, concurrent with the development of the PDC, another movement with a similar social Christian inspiration arose within the universities, and within a few years grew into the Revolutionary Federation of Social Christian University Students (FRUSC). While autonomous in relation to the PDC, the two did maintain relations at certain levels. The leadership of this movement had studied in social Christian Institutes abroad (especially in Chile, after 1963) and had also been influenced by the work of Catholic Action movements, whose outlook was more heterogeneous than that of the Christian Democrats. These factors, along with numerous personal contacts and the circulation of South American Catholic intellectuals' publications, made this sector more receptive than the PDC to the various progressive positions that from the mid-1960s on began to divide social Christian tendencies in Latin America. After 1967, these groups began to seriously question the nonscientific conceptions of social Christianity, and particularly the practices epitomized by the PDC.[3] Many young people rejected a purely electoral approach and advanced vague organizational initiatives ("popular power"), abandoning en masse the university movement, which disappeared by the end of 1969. At the same time, a growing frustration among social Christians with the unending and sterile infighting of student politics led to interest in the new experiences of "popular consciousness-raising" as enunciated by Paulo Freire. This new phenomenon did not necessarily imply a rupture with the PDC, since many still believed it possible to take initiatives that would complement and develop some of that party's programs. Such was the case, for example, of the "Community Action" projects carried out in several municipalities governed by the PDC. These projects attempted to promote popular participation and obtain material benefits for poor people in urban areas and in the countryside and raised expectations among many former social Christians.[4] Other sectors moved toward social programs sponsored by the Church, some of which—such as the cooperative movement organized in 1955—experienced significant development until encountering competition in the late 1960s from similar new governmental initiatives.[5] Along the same lines, the Center for Social Studies and Popular Promotion (CESPROP) was founded at the end of the decade to place technicians in supporting roles in the various projects of the Archdiocesan Social Secretariat.

We will see how the sociopolitical development of the 1970s unveiled the limits of these initiatives. Born out of a reformist social Christianity, they were incapable of becoming integrated into the mainstream of class struggle.

FROM THE HONDURAS–EL SALVADOR CONFLICT TO THE FORMATION OF THE NATIONAL UNION OF OPPOSITION (JULY 1969–MARCH 1972)

The first period we will be examining opened with an event that shook Salvadoran society to its very foundations. The 1969 war with Honduras had economic, political, and ideological consequences that profoundly affected the Church's development.

At the time the so-called soccer war between these two small Central American republics was regarded by world opinion as a conflict between two "banana republics." In El Salvador, however, the war crystallized the various elements of a profound crisis affecting all segments of the society. In this sense, it was an escape valve which, although unable to resolve the contradictions it revealed, set off a succession of processes that, ten years later, would head the country into a profound crisis that approximates a revolutionary situation.   ·

The war had economic, political, and ideological roots. On the economic side, the pattern of development that had been promoted since the 1950s was exhausted by the late 1960s, and the ruling classes were incapable of coming up with an alternative. The ECLA (Economic Commission on Latin America)–inspired prescription for sustained, balanced growth combined with regional integration of the five Central American countries had been vitally compromised by the absence of political evolution in any of these countries. ECLA's original program clearly demanded that the sociopolitical structures of these small, dependent underdeveloped countries be reformed. Also important was the fact that North American capital, initially indifferent or even hostile to regional integration, had launched a process of financial penetration by the late 1960s. This penetration was mainly directed toward the establishment of branch offices that could exploit the facilities of a wider market, but without concern for balanced regional growth. What was achieved, on the contrary, was a sharpening of competition among the local bourgeoisie avid for foreign sources of financing.[6]

The project for Central American regional integration had ground to a halt by the late 1960s and its agencies, particularly SIECA, were foundering. Honduras especially was affected, and saw itself as the "poor cousin" (in a poor family) in relation to more aggressive Salvadoran and Guatemalan capital. Honduras had also been a traditional escape valve for El Salvador's surplus population, and it is estimated that in the late 1960s there were more than 300,000 illegal Salvadoran immigrants living in Honduras. The Honduran government faced growing social unrest, notably in peasant areas, and had launched an agrarian reform project which excluded foreigners. In a climate of nationalistic chauvinism promoted by economic groups resentful of Salvadoran capital, and under the complacent eyes of the government, a series of attacks were perpetrated against Salvadoran residents. Many Salvadorans were forcibly repatriated with nothing but the clothes on their back, displaying clear physical signs of the aggression they had suffered. In El Salvador, anti-Honduran feelings had not been so generalized as their counterpart in the neighboring country, but the mistreatment of Salvadorans was exploited to provoke a "holy war" frenzy that swept the two countries into confrontation. Salvadoran troops invaded Honduran territory. The scale of engagements was kept from escalating by material shortages on the part of both contenders. As soon as the Salvadoran army had established positions along the other side of the border, it was obliged to retreat following intervention by the OAS, which set up a "demilitarized zone" along the common border. All this transpired in less than 100 hours, but it meant much more than the demise of hopes for regional integration.

For the Salvadorans, the war brought to light political and social contradictions that had been festering for years.[7] The war with Honduras allowed the military government, at the time presided over by General Fidel Sánchez Hernández, to pull together a "National Unity" movement with the enthusiastic participation of the most disparate, and even antagonistic, sectors of Salvadoran society. But wartime enthusiasm could not hide pressing structural realities. It soon became clear that the aim of national unity could not be achieved without decisively confronting the problems that had given rise to the war in the first place. On August 15, 1969, the Salvadoran clergy as a whole published a declaration which defined peace as "integral development" and urged reform in the system of land holding.[8] The ruling classes, confronting the spectre of social reform, maneuvered rapidly and efficiently to exorcise it. They alleged that nothing could be done without "adequate technical studies and analysis" (a delaying tactic used successfully since 1948). The reformist mood was manifest in a Congressional Agrarian Reform, sponsored by the Legislative Assembly in January 1970, but this quickly died. The March 8, 1970 elections once again played the role of mediating rather than resolving the conflicts of Salvadoran society. Yet the Agrarian Reform Congress did lead a number of important groups to take clear stands, among them the National and the Catholic universities (Universidad de El Salvador [UES] and Universidad Centroamericana "José Simeon Cañas" [UCA], respectively) and the Church itself. These Catholic groups showed that they had gone beyond the stage of generic demands in favor of social justice, and now presented technically based and workable proposals which put them on a direct collision course with the interests of the oligarchy.[9] It is indicative that during the Congress the first direct act of repression against the Church was carried out with the kidnapping of Father José Inocencio Alas, the representative of the Metropolitan Curia. On January 8, 1970, immediately after presenting the position of the Curia at the Agrarian Reform Congress, Father Alas was arrested just outside the Assembly entrance. He was found naked and drugged at the edge of a cliff; his abductors apparently hoped he would "accidentally" roll over the edge. It seems that his life was saved by the decisive intervention of Bishops Rivera and Urioste.

Elections and Frustrations

Following the electoral reforms of 1963, which established proportional representation for congressional elections within the limited political liberalization begun by President Rivera (1962–1967) and continued through most of General Fidel Sánchez Hernández's administration (1967–1972), the opposition gained increasing shares of power in the legislative body. Equally important were the opposition's gains in local governments. The PDC, for example, elected 24 mayors in 1964, 83 in 1966, and 78 in 1968, the latter decline made up for by victories in the country's main cities. Representation in the Legislative Assembly offered the opposition a contact with public opinion that was certainly a novelty in the country, as well as the occasional chance to apply pressure on the executive on specific issues. Local power, especially for the PDC, was seen as the big chance for establishing community development programs suggestive of the "participatory" model of society to be created by the Christian Democrats once they achieved national power; the municipalities were also seen as bases of support for political recruiting.

The results of the March 1970 congressional and city council elections in El Salvador dashed these hopes for political reform through the electoral arena. Even considering the habitual fraudulent methods employed by the government party, the elections were a resounding success for the government and a serious setback to the other electoral forces that had risen over the preceding six years. In the eyes of the rightist PCN, the people had finally seen through the Christian Democrats' "big fraud" and had once again come to trust their true leaders. The PDC, in turn, justified its defeat on the basis of the wartime atmosphere. It claimed the "moral victory" of at least having held onto the post of mayor of San Salvador, where the PDC defeated one of the "war heroes," Colonel Mario de Jesus Velázquez, nicknamed "El Diablo" (The Devil) for his well-known ferocity. Running for the PCN, he presented the first real challenge in years to PDC predominance in the capital. The PDC victory in San Salvador is also explained in part because the candidacy of Dr. Carlos Herrera Rebollo was seen by the younger sectors of the PDC as an alternative to the old-time leadership, and their active support was decisive for his victory. These same forces later became disillusioned with the new mayor, who ended up joining the PCN later in the decade and was killed in a 1979 guerrilla action. The outcome of the elections undoubtedly allowed the PCN to continue identifying itself as the bulwark of bourgeois political forces, when militarist appeals alone could not capitalize on the laurels won in the war. More significant, the elections had exposed the incapacity of the traditional electoral machinery to address the structural origins of the war, offering nothing but the hackneyed rhetoric of "officialism" versus "opposition."

The experience also had an impact on the political postures of both progressive Christians and Marxists. Among the Christians, the process of "reaching out to the people" predominant in the late 1960s had produced a strategy of "popular power." Many activists opted in favor of the PDC as the political vehicle for that strategy. This explains the significant presence of university social Christian cadre among the ranks of the PDC beginning with the 1967 elections, but even more so in 1970. The 1970 elections marked the beginning of a process of withdrawal of former social Christian activists from the political program of the Christian Democrats. Along with dissidents of the Salvadoran Communist Party (PCS) and members of the independent left, one small but very significant sector of the PDC left their party tasks to begin the formation of a political-military organization which later adopted the name ERP (People's Revolutionary Army).[10] Others remained in the PDC with the idea of intensifying work among the masses, promoting new leadership, and ultimately confronting the government party under an alliance with other opposition parties. This alliance was later to take form in the National Opposition Union (UNO) in 1972.

Among Marxist sectors, the aftermath of the 1969 war saw the emergence of revolutionary groups that espoused guerilla warfare. The political-military vanguards presented themselves as heirs to a broad-ranging Latin American revolutionary experience, with armed struggle at the core of their strategy but remaining very closely tied to extensive work among the masses. This revolutionary model is certainly not exclusive to El Salvador, but nowhere else in Latin America has it reached the dimensions achieved here.[11] However, this vision of how to lead the revolutionary process took time to crystallize. In the early years, the militaristic components predominated in organizations like the ERP.

In their organizational work, these first revolutionary groups had to concentrate on establishing the professional and underground capacities of their cadre, who were few in number and generally untrained. This explains why the military aspect and violent actions (such as the kidnapping of wealthy figures) were so prominent in this early period. Over time, however, the work of organizing the people acquired higher priority.[12] Contact with progressive Christian sectors—mainly at an individual level, but sometimes through their organizations—became a crucial element in building this new kind of vanguard. At the time, however, these organizations did not clearly foresee the role of Christians in the revolutionary process. The contacts were more proselytic in nature and necessarily very selective, often as attempts to channel the resources of existing Church groups into support for the incipient vanguards.[13]

The economic crisis intensified with the collapse of the Central American Common Market, which diminished the government's capacity to respond to the people's demands. This was clear in the slow passage through Congress of a new labor law and especially in the conflict between the government and the combative teachers' movement (ANDES) through the first semester in 1971. The teachers also became a point of convergence for broad sectors of the population. As repression, jailings, and torture intensified in the cities and countryside, popular violence also began to make itself felt in incipient and even improvised expressions, which stimulated the regime's repressive fury all the more.

The elections scheduled for 1972 soon became the focal point of all political attention. Despite discouragement after the 1970 experience, the 1972 elections generated major popular expectations and extraordinary mass mobilization for several reasons. The crisis within the government was increasingly apparent and was expressed in the growing belligerence of the extreme right parties (PPS and FUDI).[14] The growth of repression and the paralyzation of promised reforms had fed unrest within the army, which leaked information to opposition leaders indicating that its reformist or constitutionalist sectors would prevent outright fraud.[15] The traditional opposition parties, including the PDC, launched a coalition with the hope of exploiting the situation to the utmost and founded the National Opposition Union (UNO) in September 1971. Popular sectors still had the 1968 upsurge of opposition fresh in their minds and an interest in trying to unite the people in a manner that some compared to the wartime unity. In the countryside, the consciousness-raising and organization promoted by Christian sectors still left the door open to an acceptance of an electoral alternative. The message of the new revolutionary vanguards was still far from the ears of the masses, despite sympathies evident in certain sectors.

The electoral campaign was plagued with intrigues aimed at undermining the UNO coalition's chances and culminated in a colossal wave of fraud that robbed José Napoleón Duarte and the united opposition of the presidency. A military revolt broke out on March 25, 1972, to denounce the fraud but was soon quelled, due mainly to the rebel officers' improvisations and lack of determination. The revolt had been nothing more than a palace conspiracy, lacking any coordination with other social or political forces; the latter were only summoned when the movement was already waning, with counterproductive results.[16]

This fraud and the frustrated "progressive" military coup clearly exposed the weakness of the electoral road, which offered no chance of meeting people's needs. The 1972 electoral fraud was a decisive turning point in Salvadoran politics. In the future, very few would retain their faith in elections as instruments of popular decision making in the style of bourgeois democracies. The 1972 elections struck the final death knell for such hopes, as well as ending the process of political liberalization inaugurated with the proportional representation scheme in 1963. Many political activists broke all contact with the traditional parties and moved directly into the new popular-based revolutionary organizations. Others remained

in the traditional parties in the hope of pulling together the sectors critical of election-oriented work methods and pushing for more direct involvement in popular struggles. For a number of traditional opposition
leaders the attempted coup suggested an alternative to which they might
resort in the future: they might be able to maintain a presence in the political arena while weaving intricate alliances that could bring them into
power with military support and with the approval of imperialism.

The "Option for the Poor" in El Salvador

This period was also of great importance for Salvadoran Christians.
Vatican II and the currents of pastoral renewal expressed at Medellín had
a strong impact on several groups within the Salvadoran Church, including
some members of the hierarchy. The Church's social programs, which
through most of the decade had been mainly developmentalist in outlook, began to incorporate new pastoral initiatives. Launched as isolated
experiences, these initiatives rapidly spread in an increasingly homogeneous and coordinated fashion. Father José Inocencio Alas arrived in
Suchitoto in December 1968 and in April 1969 began weekly training
courses for "Delegates of the Word," soon to become community leaders.
This early initiative provoked a reaction by the army, which besieged the
city twice that year, as a means of applying pressure against the priest's
work. In late 1969 the Pastoral Reflection Group (GRP) was founded. It
became known by the name "*La Nacional*" and its founders were a group
of forty priests, mostly Salvadoran diocesan priests. This sector's influence would be fundamental in the future development of the Salvadoran
Church. What had been no more than "social promotion" had now begun
to produce real renovation of Church structures and pastoral practices.
The limits of the hierarchy's support were quick to appear as well, as could
be seen clearly in the First National Week of Pastoral Work in June 1970.
Participating in the events were priests, religious, and lay people from around
the country, but significant absences were noted among the hierarchy. Only
Archbishop Chávez and his close collaborator, Msgr. Rivera, participated
actively, and afterward the majority of bishops tried to play down the encounter's conclusions. Opposition among the bishops was led by Msgr.
Aparicio from San Vicente. The conservative bishops named a commission to correct the conclusions, with very negative results. It is interesting to note that one of the commission members was Msgr. Oscar Romero. Nonetheless, the Week was seen as a break with the prevalent idea
of neo-Christendom, and marked the appearance of a new model for the
Church.

These early, dynamic developments emanated from the San Salvador archdiocese,[17] but were soon followed in other areas of the country. One key factor in the process was the incorporation of the laity into new responsibilities in Church life. This new progressive perspective also affected nuns and brothers, with significant consequences for two sensitive sectors in Salvadoran society: private education and rural areas. The airs of renewal born at Vatican II were present in the traditionally elitist education in Catholic schools. In El Salvador, important changes were registered at the San José Day School (run by Jesuits, as is the Central American University [UCA]) and several girls' schools. Nuns, for their part, took on the work of invigorating Church work in many peasant parishes where the shortage of priests had meant the Church's presence was either nil or very precarious. The Church-controlled media were also significantly affected, in particular the newspaper *Justicia y Paz* and radio station YSAX. In the hands of exponents of these new pastoral lines, they communicated news about the experiences of communities around the country. Through them, the phenomenon soon to be known as the "Church of the Poor" began to gain organization, identity, and nationwide projection.

The activities of the first base communities were centered in the area of educating, "conscientizing," and training lay leaders (Delegates of the Word). Several CEBs came into being around cooperatives, but both the difficulties encountered (often in the form of direct repression) and the methods of pastoral reflection soon gave the process of consciousness-raising a political dimension in confrontation with the system of domination itself.

The combined experiences of the war, the refugees from Honduras, and the 1970 elections led these first CEBs to an increasingly coherent antisystem discourse, which centered on the theme of "popular power" and on organization as the means of achieving it. Only some time later, however, would the first visible fruits of their work appear in both urban and rural areas. The only operational peasant organization at the time was FECCAS, still closely tied to social Christianity and the PDC. After a tumultuous period beginning in 1970, it came under the direct influence of the new political-military revolutionary vanguards in 1974.

While there was no persecution of the Church as such during this period, there were indications of what the future held. The Alas activities in Suchitoto were insistently identified as communistic by the bourgeoisie, and the army began to harass them. We have already mentioned the kidnapping of Father Alas during the Agrarian Reform Congress. In December 1970 Father Nícolas Rodríguez was murdered in a far-off hamlet in Chalatenango, in what Msgr. Rivera termed "a political crime committed with the aim of intimidating the entire clergy . . . a warning to abandon our ministry."[18] Another event, also isolated but significant, was the deportation of Spanish priest José María Cabello, S.J., accused of "inducing" a group of the homeless displaced from Honduras to squat on a piece of land in the capital.[19] There were also attempts to involve the Church, through its institutions, clergy, and hierarchy, in the "Regalado case" scandal. The government, however, was still hesitant to respond to bourgeois demands for energetic measures against the new Church. The following period would bring clearer definitions.

"NATIONAL TRANSFORMATION IN THE NATIONAL SECURITY FRAMEWORK" AND THE EXHAUSTION OF ELECTORAL POLITICS (MARCH 1972–MARCH 1977)

The five years beginning in March 1972, which coincide with the administration of the "victor" of the 1972 elections, Colonel Armando Molina, were crucial in defining the revolutionary situation which crystallized at the end of the decade. During this period the primary contradictions and the nature of the system of domination were fully revealed with the failure of Molina's "Agrarian Transformation" program and the subsequent ratification of the hegemony of the most backward sectors of the Salvadoran bourgeoisie. This was also the period of the birth and rapid growth of the mass expressions of the new popular revolutionary organizations which would become leading actors in a political process that showed the bankruptcy of traditional and reformist positions. The regime came to rely increasingly on repression as its response to popular organization, carrying its violence to the level of indiscriminate massacre under the ideological banner of the "national security" doctrine. The Christians were to be pushed into increasingly radical positions within this context of intensifying social conflicts. They would suffer their own share of repression by the end of the period, with priests murdered or expelled en masse.

The Failure to Reform

The fraudulent elections in February and March 1972, combined with the frustrated coup on March 25, led to the virtual dismantling of the high command of the UNO, with most leaders forced into exile. Throughout his mandate, President Molina sought to live up to his image established in previous public offices as an efficient and energetic administrator. He surrounded himself with modernizing elements of the bourgeoisie in an attempt to push forward the National Transformation program proclaimed by the government at the turn of the decade. The

program achieved relative success in a few areas but fell on its face socially and politically over the same stumbling block of every reform effort
in recent Salvadoran history: the agrarian issue.

Colonel Molina initially sought to combine energetic action against
the left with conciliatory rhetoric toward the social work of the Church.
He even declared (in October 1972) that as a Christian he welcomed the
initiatives of Vatican II and of Medellín and applauded the "consciousness-
raising" carried out by the Christians—a stance for which he was severely
criticized in the bourgeois media. Molina invited the bishops to dialogue
in an attempt to generate a consensus around his program but in this he
was only occasionally successful.

Molina announced a series of reforms, including an agrarian reform,
but failed to implement most of them. The failure of the agarian reform,
notwithstanding some aborted steps toward realizing it, was particularly
noteworthy. All attempts at reform in the countryside were annulled by
the pressure of the entire bourgeoisie under the banners of its most reactionary sector.[20] Their opposition had been clear since the issue of agrarian
reform was first raised, but during the months of June to October 1976
this opposition waged an unprecedented publicity campaign accompanied
by all sorts of actions aimed at halting the agrarian reform. The government was incapable of containing the offensive launched by associations
of landowners, who were proficient at rallying the rest of the business organizations around their cause. The opposition pushed to the point of
virtually issuing an ultimatum to the government. The government was
devoid of any social base of support, having been undercut by those who
perceived the precarious character of the government's plan and by the
army which maintained its traditional mistrust of the popular organizations, even the ones it controlled.[21] The Catholic University, one of the
few sectors to support the program,[22] published in the November 1976
issue of *ECA* a bitter editorial entitled, "At Your Orders, Capital," which
virtually denounced the government and the army as traitors. In response,
the university's offices were bombed for what was neither the first nor
the last time.

This four-year drama of reformism was also a time of accelerated
growth of the popular organizations and struggles, which had moved into
the center of political activity by 1974. The 1972 electoral fraud had revealed the limits of the electoral approach of the 1960s, a model to which
one North American researcher imputed the "logical flaw" of stimulating
active opposition while, "by definition," forbidding it access to power.[23]
Many militants of the traditional opposition parties had joined the newly
organized political-military vanguards and their mass organizations. This
whole process, however, was a gradual movement and arose from a com-

bination of repeated frustrations at the polls, intensified repression, and the growth of the popular organizations themselves, which were seen by the great majority as the only alternative to traditional domination. The UNO, although weakened in the wake of the fraud in 1972, again ran candidates in the March 10, 1974 congressional and mayoral elections. While it did win a third of the seats in the National Assembly, it suffered new setbacks in terms of municipal power, losing almost all the city elections.[24] The reality of fraud was once more brought home to public opinion, and more sectors sought new forms of struggle.

Even the UNO found it impossible to participate in the following elections on March 14, 1976 (for mayors and congress), which were held in an atmosphere of unprecedented violence. Nevertheless, the UNO insisted on searching out a chance for legal political participation. The visible weakening of progovernment forces with the failure of the Agrarian Transformation, combined with promising overtures toward "progressive" sectors of capital and the military, convinced the UNO to participate in the presidential elections scheduled for February 20, 1977. It was thought that this time such a favorable combination of factors would allow the people's triumph to be respected. Contributing to this optimism was the election of Jimmy Carter as president of the U.S., given his international stance on respect for human rights. Despite the varying degrees of opposition to any electoral programs by the now well-organized popular organizations, there was still a massive turnout of voters for the UNO, to such an extent that the PCN had to resort to even more blatant fraud to be sure of its "victory."[25] Just as in 1972, the UNO leadership revealed its inability to lead the voters past the voting booth. There was an improvised attempt to generate pressure by holding a continuous vigil on Plaza Libertad in San Salvador, but the rally was bloodily dissolved by the army four days later, on February 28. The routine of exiling UNO leaders was once again performed, leaving the UNO practically dismantled. Its member parties tried to maintain some degree of public presence, but for all practical effects they dropped out of sight until mid-1978, when they resurged in a clearly conspiratorial perspective.

The political-military organizations during this period lifted their heads, achieved their own identity, and established themselves as protagonists in the national political scene. The participation of Christians in these new vanguards was initially the fruit more of individual rather than collective decisions. Only some time later did the vanguards draw up deliberate strategies in relation to Christian organizations and groups. This was the case of the CEBs of Suchitoto, which were the object of intense recruiting work by members of the RN (National Resistance, a break-off from the ERP), who tried to repeat these efforts with the FECCAS until they were displaced by the BPR (People's Revolutionary Bloc, tied to the Popular Liberation Forces [FPL]). This latter organization was also more successful in its contacts with many priests working in "La Nacional," including seminarians involved in grass-roots organizing. One example of this was the well-known "Letter from the FPL–Farabundo Marti to Progressive Christians" in 1975, which had a tremendous impact on the consciousness of many Christians, not only because of its content but because of the massive repression of Christians at the time.[26] The very founding of the BPR on July 30, 1975 was marked by the action of a number of Christians who occupied the San Salvador Cathedral on August 1 to protest the murder of several students the day before. This identification of the BPR with Catholic groups, though criticized as opportunistic by other organizations, was very beneficial in the subsequent development of the BPR. The RN and its mass organization FAPU (Unified People's Action Front) also worked constantly with Christian sectors, including establishing ties with an important Protestant group.[27]

Base Communities, Popular Evangelization,
and the Discovery of Structural Sin

These five years were crucial for the development of recent innovations within the Church. New pastoral styles were energetically carried forward despite increasing obstacles that culminated in a frenzy of repression and the outright persecution of all aspects of Church activities.

The first half of the decade saw the flourishing of Christian communities. Teams of priests in more than a dozen parishes established CEBs beginning in September 1972, and twenty communities of nuns throughout the San Salvador archdiocese did likewise.[28] There were also training centers for lay leaders around the country. Many members of these CEBs and trainees from the centers were among the first victims of the growing repression, due to the kind of work described by Msgr. Rivera:

> CEB leaders made themselves felt, not only because of their "full, conscious and active" participation in the liturgical celebrations and their new style of programming fiestas for patron saints and leading processions, but also because of their activities in favor of justice: strengthening of peasant organizations, dissemination and study of pertinent labor laws, and struggles for better wages and for a dignified relocation of those whose homes were flooded by the Cerrón Grande Dam reservoir.[29]

Repression grew in direct proportion to the growth of popular organization and to the radicalization of Christian sectors. On the eve of the February 1972 elections, the archdiocese, already clearly critical of the situation, broadcast an incisive program on YSAX entitled "Bearing Witness to the Events," which won the station fire bombs that blew it off the air for several months. A similar attack was made on the Catholic Cultural Bookstore, a long-standing meeting place for more committed Christian sectors. The wave of exiles, "disappearances," and deaths in the wake of the frustrated coup was denounced by the CEDES. The Jesuits' work in Aguilares, begun in September 1972, was censured as a new intervention by the clergy in politics, particularly after a major peasant strike on May 24, 1973, near Aguilares. The government was also uncomfortable with UCA publications that undermined the regime's credibility within the middle class and internationally.[30] In June 1973 the bourgeois media launched a campaign against the inclusion of texts of a "socialist nature" in the study plans at San José Day School, directed by the San José order. Individual intimidation and selective repression were soon complemented by mass actions against the Church's grass roots, reaching crisis proportions with the events of 1974. The Alas brothers, priests who in June had played an important role in founding the original FAPU (Unified Popular Broad Front, a short-lived coalition of vanguard and "legal" opposition parties), were the victims of a slander campaign launched on July 10, culminating in an arrest warrant issued against them on August 21 for "incitation to rebellion against the government, and for anarchical and anti-democratic activities."[31] They were freed once the Curia interceded, and remained in the same area of work until 1977, when they were the victims of that year's mass expulsions.

On November 29, 1974 a massacre took place in the village of La Calletana (San Vicente diocese). Hundreds of peasants who had sustained a long dispute with a local landholder were attacked by military patrols and by ORDEN, the right-wing paramilitary organization. The operation became a model for future such attacks: using the pretext of searching for arms, the village is terrorized, "prisoners" are taken and immediately disappear, and a sham confrontation with "armed groups" is mounted to justify the murder of others. In this case six peasants were murdered outright and thirteen "disappeared." The bourgeoisie united with the government in proclaiming priests Rafael Antonio Barahona and José David Rodríguez (both Salvadorans) as responsible for the communist indoctrination which, in their eyes, had led to the tragedy. The bishops were emphatic in denouncing the incident through the CEDES, in a declaration made December 20. They credited the violence to structural causes and pressured for the necessary reforms.

In March 1975 Archbishop Chávez published a pastoral letter along the same lines, entitled "Inflation in El Salvador in the Light of Christian Consciousness," which was a vibrant call for "preventive" changes and

for the long-promised agrarian reform. The same style was to be maintained consistently both by Church authorities and by the "*UCA intel-
ligenzia.*" In these declarations, a vote of confidence was given to the reform programs, on which "social peace" was held to depend; but at the
same time repression was denounced and its dynamic analyzed as symp-
tomatic of the confrontation between opposing forces, above and beyond
the reformist rhetoric. It was argued that if the repression did not end,
the reforms would have no meaning, and that, inversely, implementation
of the reforms was necessary in order to overcome the conditions that
generate violence, whether revolutionary or repressive. This style of discourse, with its involuted logic accompanying positive and courageous denunciations, would be abandoned only much later and by Msgr. Romero,
who clearly identified the real forces in confrontation behind the abstract
formulas of "social reformism."

The year 1975 brought new acts of repression with major repercussions. The army's absurd justifications convinced no one, and the new
involvement of agencies such as Amnesty International brought world
attention to El Salvador. The long list of repressive actions continued to
grow, but so did popular unrest and mass actions.

This was the context for the holding of the First Archdiocesan Pastoral Week in the archdiocese of San Salvador in January 1976, after
months of preparation. The archdiocese did not seek national scope, since
by now the work of the archdiocese was much farther advanced and the
organizers feared possible interference by the CEDES. The objective of
the Week was to unify pastoral standards, reflect on current experiences,
and plan future work, especially with base communities. Some three hundred pastoral agents selected from all the parishes, congregations, and lay
associations attended the meeting, which had the main theme of "Evangelization and Action for Justice, Beginning with the Poor." The following objectives were adopted for a joint work plan: priority on evangelization at all levels, expansion of existing base communities of the Church
and their extension into new areas, and training of pastoral agents.[32] According to a report written by some of the participants, the encounter
"ended with a message that was a commitment to struggle for human
rights. . . . An executive secretary was appointed so that conclusions
would not fall through the cracks and a very efficient Information Office
was soon established with a Pastoral Commission, expeditious publications, etc. Bureaucratism had become a thing of the past." The agreements
"meant a second real shake-up which would end up generalizing the spread
of the base communities."[33] The Church went beyond simply demanding reforms from the authorities and the oligarchy to create the conditions
—as could be seen in the Aguilares experience—for "recreating a Church

of living communities of 'new men', pastoral agents conscious of their human vocation who take charge of their own destiny and move on to change reality."[34] It was only natural therefore that, as Msgr. Rivera recognized, the repression "added to the group's awareness, and a good share of the best Delegates of the Word joined the FECCAS and UTC peasant organizations."[35]

The year of 1976 brought more repression, and attention was focused on the unfolding of the confrontation between the government and the landholders' associations which left the military reformists looking ridiculous and reinforced the most backward sectors of Salvadoran capital. This sector felt freer, from then on, to organize their own death squads, strengthening those already in existence and creating new ones in close collaboration with sectors of the army and ORDEN. The selection of the PCN's candidate for president reflected this further turn to the right: Colonel Carlos Humberto Romero (promoted to general in August 1976) was Minister of Defense and the man directly responsible for the repression.

On December 5, 1976 the owner of a mill in Aguilares was killed, at the same time that peasants displaced by the Cérron Grande dam demanded the right to adequate resettlement. Although the Curia proved the contrary, the oligarchy seized the opportunity to launch a huge propaganda campaign accusing the FECCAS and the UTC, and more specifically Fathers Rutilio Grande and David Rodríguez, of killing the owner. One example excerpted from a landowners' manifesto stated, "Murderous hordes organized by third-world priests and Marxist leaders, and protected by official tolerance, bloody our soil."[36]

The archdiocese's defense clarified its position of struggle against the injustices which it held responsible for such events. The elderly Archbishop had already announced his retirement for early 1977, and the problem of naming his successor loomed on the horizon. The impending transfer of leadership to a new archbishop was naturally a critical point of concern for the clergy, who feared that Chávez's replacement might be opposed to the pastoral style of ministry they had adopted.[37] January 5, 1977 brought the deportation of two ex-Jesuit students who had been working in peasant organizations. On the eleventh, a bomb was placed near the home of Father Alfonso Navarro, a parish priest in the capital (he would be murdered on May 11). On January 26, Father Mario Bernal, a Colombian priest, was kidnapped and, two days later, deported.

The month of February 1977 marks the end of this period because of a number of events that indicated the beginning of a new and different stage. The Molina government had eroded politically, and the inauguration of General Romero required only a new electoral farce on February 20. On January 27 the ERP kidnapped a well-known business leader and personal friend of President Molina. The guerrilla group's demands were met, despite opposition from General Romero's "hardline" sector of the army. But when the ERP revealed that the hostage had died from wounds suffered during the kidnapping itself, the hardliners demanded the use of a heavier hand against the opposition. The consequences were the March 28 massacre in downtown San Salvador, the deportation or exiling of eleven more priests,[38] and the second arrest and torture of Father Rafael Barahona.

The new archbishop, Msgr. Oscar Romero, was named on March 3 and hastily invested on March 22. Archbishop Romero held a meeting with other bishops and government representatives who presented him with a list of priests considered to be subversive. Yet the bishops did protest against the deportations and denounced governmental abuses in an open letter published on March 5. These and other facts began to reveal that the new archbishop would not retreat from the pastoral style set by his predecessor. The future, in fact, would show that under Msgr. Romero, a new stage in ministry was inaugurated during which the Gospel was to be preached with prophetic dimensions never before heard in the teachings of the Salvadoran Church.

The uncompromising attitude by the bishops was even more valiant in regard to the clergy working with base communities. The most illustrative event was the Mass on the occasion of the deportation of Father Bernal, celebrated on February 13, 1977, with the presence of hundreds of members of the local CEBs. At this Mass Father Rutilio Grande gave a renowned sermon: "Cain is a miscarriage of God's plan; and there are groups of Cains. He is also the negation of the Kingdom of God. Here, in this country, there are groups of Cains who—what is worse—invoke the name of God. . . . Even those who are Cains are not our enemies. They are our brothers Cain. We hate no one. . . ."[39] Father Rutilio was to be murdered on March 12, machine-gunned along with two lay people who were with him.

February 1977 closed the curtain on an entire period in Salvadoran political history as it became clear that "legal" political channels had been precluded by fraud and by the indiscriminate escalation of repression. Following the February 28 massacre the traditional opposition effected a total retreat and the arena of the people's struggle was occupied by the new vanguards. UNO leaders turned to conspiratorial activities aimed at pressuring for changes in the structure of the military, both through contacts with members of the army and through pressures exerted at an international level. These relationships allowed them to have some effect on the course of events we will be analyzing in the next section, which culminated in the military coup of October 15, 1979.

GENERALIZED RADICALIZATION AND RESOLUTION
VIA COUP D'ETAT (MARCH 1977–OCTOBER 1979)

During this period the repression continued to intensify as the extreme right and its military allies were virtually given free rein. Christians were significant targets, with the murder of six priests, more deportations, and all sorts of attacks. The new pastoral line, however, continued to grow and to gain even greater projection under the new archbishop. Although divisions within the clergy also sharpened, effective use of the media, along with the message delivered, made Archbishop Romero a true unifying force. This phenomenon affected primarily the Christians, yet Romero also acquired authentic national importance because of his expressed commitment to involvement in popular struggles. The revolutionary organizations, in the meantime, continued to grow in both urban and rural areas, but with deep-seated rivalries still dividing them, both in tactical and strategic terms. The international impact of human rights violations also intensified late in the decade, closely tied to the unfolding of the anti-Somoza struggle in Nicaragua. All of these factors weakened the regime, and culminated with the overthrow of the government in a coup d'etat led by the "Young Military" sector of the army on October 15, 1979. The new government that came to power in October 1979 called for broad social reforms, an end to repression and corruption, and a return to democracy through a broadly representative government. The movement gained power without major difficulties and promised to open a brand-new chapter in Salvadoran history. Such hopes, however, were soon unmasked as illusions.

State Terrorism Enthroned: The Romero Government

General Romero was a man with ideas which, though not brilliant, were more clearly defined than those of his predecessor. He took over with the aim of resolving the problems for the bourgeoisie caused by growing popular unrest. Throughout his two and a half years as president, he sought to fulfill his mission with the only tool he believed to be efficient: indiscriminate violence against the people and its leaders, representatives, and organizations. While under Molina repression had been dressed up in more refined terminology as a requisite for "National Security," the Romero government plunged straight into state terrorism.

We have already seen how the lame-duck Molina appeared to be cleaning the deck for Romero with the closing of the UES in November 1976, deportations of foreign priests in early 1977, the decreeing of a state of siege following the February 28 massacre, and the greater freedom of action conceded to right-wing death squads. The death squads had now begun murdering Salvadoran priests as well, and opened the new period with the killings of Father Rutilio Grande, S.J., on March 12, 1977 and Father Alfonso Navarro on May 11, 1977.[40] Government complicity in the murders, at the very least through the withholding of evidence crucial to their investigations, was forcefully denounced by the Church and other democratic sectors. The month of May brought a new wave of expulsions and attacks on priests, this time including the forced exile of many Salvadoran priests.[41] The army and the security forces continued to refine the organization of "operatives" for the systematic and immediate repression of all demonstrations, extending their range of action to "preventive" functions and intimidation. Of these latter activities, the most important events in the first semester of 1977 were the May Day massacres of peasants and trade unionists and the raids against the people of Aguilares on May 19 and 20. Aguilares was the center of operations for the program run by the Jesuits. Hundreds of peasants and village residents were attacked and their houses ransacked "in search of arms," while three priests from Rutilio Grande's team were captured and expelled to Guatemala. The Church's reaction was immediate, but the wave of repression had already been unleashed. In a June 21 declaration, a group of right-wing terrorists set a July 20 deadline for the forty-seven Jesuits residing in El Salvador to leave the country, with a threat that after that date "their execution will be immediate and systematic."[42] This once again drew world attention to the country and led to the holding of special hearings in the U.S. Congress on the persecution of the Salvadoran Church.[43]

The International Context and Destabilization of the Regime

In this atmosphere General Romero inaugurated his government, seeking, despite his own precedents, to appear conciliatory, conscious as he was of the effects of a poor international image. Throughout the twenty-six months of his administration the government faced a growing crossfire of pressures: pushed on the one hand to offer a less unpleasant facade to world public opinion, Romero also felt the need to resort to repression as a means of curbing growing popular unrest. Steps were taken to at least tone down the harsh reality in the eyes of the world. The problem with the Jesuits was partially resolved through the holding of bilateral talks between government representatives and the order, during which the latter received sufficient guarantees to avoid an unfavorable outcome for the government in the U.S. congressional hearings. Nevertheless, although the regime tried out several expedients to give its repression an aura of formal legitimacy, none were convincing and the opposition was generally able to turn them to their own favor.

International pressure grew in 1978, and in November the Inter-

American Human Rights Commission made its second visit of the year to El Salvador, this time to write up a detailed report on repressive actions and procedures that the security forces were unable to hide. The official presentation of the report to the OAS in late October 1979 threatened to open a Pandora's box for Romero, coming as it did on the heels of the OAS condemnation of the Somoza regime in July just before his fall. This was one of the decisive factors behind the coup d'etat which overthrew Romero on October 15.[44]

The downfall of the Somoza dictatorship on July 17, 1979, upset the entire balance of forces in the region and unloosed political transformations that are still underway. This event not only was a clear advance for revolutionary options in the region but also—in the case of El Salvador—contributed decisively to the fall of the Romero regime. Without downplaying the differences between the two situations, the chances that El Salvador would follow the same path as Nicaragua were much greater after July 1979. Yet the social characteristics of the struggle in El Salvador implied a much clearer and a more radical class confrontation. Alliances within the opposition would be much more difficult to achieve and the degree of social suffering might well be much greater than that faced by the Sandinista struggle. The common front which began to raise its head with the People's Forum (a grouping of the UNO and other political and social organizations which issued a Common Platform of demands late in September[45]) offered obvious parallels to the alliances that had led to the victory of the FSLN, but with the substantial difference that the hegemony of clearly revolutionary forces was much more visible in the Salvadoran case.[46]

This latter fact was the trait most characteristic of the evolution of El Salvador's sociopolitical process during the late 1970s. While from 1972–1977 the "traditional" forms of political participation open to the people—the elections—still played an important role in mobilization and even in consciousness-raising, as of February 20, 1977 the scales tipped once and for all to agitational forms of direct participation, led by the new political-military vanguards.

All these organizations continued to build on the pattern characterized by a duality of vanguard and mass organizations. Throughout the period under discussion these organizations would continue to develop their military activities and underground structures while at the same time broadening their field of action in rural and urban social sectors.

In the countryside from 1977–1979, the FECCAS-UTC and several other peasant organizations carried out a large number of strikes, demonstrations, land take-overs, and other initiatives such as sit-ins at government offices to pressure for their demands and to denounce the repression

they were suffering. All these actions were aimed at implementing the plat-
forms of demands directed at a number of government agencies. The rural
workers' struggle thus became a major channel for the questioning of the
Romero regime, both domestically and internationally.

It was in the cities, however, that the most important changes in
people's organizations took place during the period, most particularly among
the trade unions. Labor's struggles were another crucial element in destabilizing General Romero's regime and were one more reason for its overthrow.

Archbishop Romero and the Pastoral de Acompañamiento*

Although few could have imagined it at the time, Msgr. Romero's
tenure as archbishop would leave indelible marks on the history of the
Salvadoran Church and on the country itself, from his investiture until
his death on March 24, 1980, when he was murdered while saying Mass
by a sniper in the pay of oligarchical interests. A number of serious analyses have already been written on both the theological and political implications of the life and work of Msgr. Romero.[47] Here we will look
particularly at how he personified a whole new pastoral attitude, deeply
incarnate in the lives of a suffering people.

When Msgr. Romero became Archbishop of San Salvador, the Salvadoran Church was deeply divided by the radicalization of class struggle. The undeniable appearance, for the first time in the country's history, of an organized people as the main protagonist in national politics
demanded definitions which the Church had comfortably been able to
avoid in the past. Despite the political divisions, a program of the people was obviously emerging—an alternative to be led and guaranteed by
the people themselves. Certain sectors and individuals who in the past
had spoken reformist language discourse (such as Msgr. Aparicio) resolved
that continuing to do so might encourage further political radicalization. In the future, they would have no scruples about collaborating with
repressive efforts aimed at weakening or even annihilating this popular
program.

We have already discussed how the rivalry within the popular-
revolutionary bloc made it impossible, during this period, to carry out

---

*No English expression adequately renders the "Pastoral de Acompañamiento."
In its verb form, *acompañar* means to go along with, to follow. Cáceres suggests that
the essence of Romero's pastoral line was to accompany the poor people on their road
of struggle. "Pastoral de Acompañamiento" suggests a pastoral approach of solidarity
with the poor and of witness, but alone, neither of these terms would convey the
author's intent.—Ed.

joint actions, much less to achieve a common strategy for taking power. The same divisions also appeared among Christians who in one way or another had taken the side of the people's struggle. Intellectual sectors were divided among those who lined up with one of the revolutionary organizations and those who maintained critical independence, generally in an effort to promote the programmatic unification of the people's movement as an enduring alternative to existing politics.[48] Among the politically aligned sectors, it is interesting to note the position of the "left sector" of the PDC. This group shared the party's conspiratorial outlook, but also sought ties with the popular organizations to help coordinate efforts to destabilize the regime. In this way they aimed to shore up their position within the PDC while opening the door to popular participation in a transitional government. This was their objective in supporting the October 15, 1979 coup.

This same range of attitudes toward the people's movement was manifest within the Church itself. Many members of base communities and other Church groups had actually joined the popular-revolutionary organizations. Priests involved in the new pastoral line also had to face the conflicts which this complex political process presented. The "pastoral de acompañamiento" defined more clearly the "option for the poor" launched at Medellín. It meant no longer conceiving of Christians in general, and priests in particular, in isolation from the community of the poor, but rather fully embodying their suffering and their struggles. For some priests, fellowship with the people came to mean joining a political party or even the guerrillas. The majority stuck more strictly to pastoral work with obvious political consequences but no partisan commitments. Exemplifying the two options, respectively, were individuals like Father Ernesto Barrera, on the one hand, and Father Rutilio Grande and Archbishop Romero, on the other.

The death of Father Ernesto Barrera Motto on November 28, 1978, was celebrated by the pro-government media as the "definitive proof of communist infiltration in the Church." Father Barrera was killed in an obscure incident presented by the press as a confrontation between FPL guerrillas and army troops. Although the official version was later proven false, Father Barrera's membership was recognized publicly by the FPL, a revelation that sent shock waves through Church circles. Although two priests deeply identified with the people's struggles, Fathers Rutilio Grande and Alfonso Navarro, had already been murdered, this was the first case involving a priest's membership in an organization that used revolutionary violence as a fundamental method of struggle. Father Plácido Erdozaín has described how the crisis reached even the base communities and, of course, the Church hierarchy.[49] At the root of the problem was the question of bearing witness and of the identity of Christians in the specific conditions of El Salvador.

From his own perspective, Archbishop Romero had progressively become more involved in the complex dimensions of the new "pastoral de acompañamiento." In his own way, he also "accompanied" the sociopolitical process and, above all, those like Father Barrera who dared to be "men of their times."[50] In the course of his twenty-one months as archbishop, Msgr. Romero had developed both an intellectual-theological vision and a practical-pastoral vision which allowed him to transcend pressures from all sides in favor of immediate reactions to this difficult juncture. For him, his presence alongside the body of the murdered priest was as natural as that of the man's own mother. As he said in his important but little-known sermon on the occasion:

> And if someone were to criticize the presence of the Church together with those who die in mysterious situations like this, we can say, "Is he not a Christian?" The Church must be present where there are human values. ... We are the world's true liberators; we, with the doctrine that speaks to us of transcendency and of the beyond, are called by God also to accompany all who work to make this world more humane, to give humanity a more Christian and fraternal equality, to give them their true hope and their true strength.[51]

These words, dramatic in themselves and even more so in the circumstances in which they were spoken, were an implicit critique of the existing state of a Church which had strayed from its vocation of commitment and fidelity to what he saw as the essence of its mission.

Archbishop Romero had taken office in the context of a total breakdown of the country's bourgeois legality, with government authority openly contested from all sides. For many radicals, he had been named precisely in an attempt to undermine the new pastoral practices—given his rather conservative past—and no doubt with the objective of strengthening the regime.[52] However the new archbishop very soon imposed a style based on dialogue, with predominance of a hopeful attitude—probably inherited from his predecessor, Archbishop Chávez—in the face of the new practices. This style also soon revealed an unexpected firmness which would lead him into confrontation with the established powers. Archbishop Romero's biographers all agree that his reaction to the murder of Father Rutilio Grande on March 12, 1977, less than a month after his investiture, was the clearest proof of this attitude. As Father Plácido described it, through simple gestures imbued with a great transcendency, Msgr. Romero laid down the lines for his later conduct.[53] He broke off the dialogue with the authorities and demanded clarification of the crime before it could be resumed. (He would later impose other conditions, as the persecution intensified). He thereby officially renounced the role of an ideological buttress for the stability of the state. In addition, he challenged the country's entire legal apparatus through actions such as that of burying Father Grande without court authorization and publicly denouncing the state of siege in effect since February 28. Even the rites of liturgy became vehicles of protest against which the government could do nothing. Under the state of siege, with public assemblies prohibited, Archbishop Romero and twenty other priests celebrated Father Grande's funeral Mass on March 14 before an immense multitude. In addition, on March 20 he ordered the suspension of Sunday Mass in all the parishes of the archdiocese and replaced it with a "single Mass" in front of the Cathedral, to which all the faithful were invited. Despite the scandalized criticism of the bourgeois media and some Church leaders, the faithful heeded the call and demonstrated their outspoken repudiation of the regime. Catholic schools were also closed for three days, resulting in an uproar from conservative parents. Many other similar Masses would also be held, with the liturgy and the very setting of the churches turned into symbolic elements of support for the people's struggles. One example was the June 12, 1977 celebration of a Mass of atonement in the city of Aguilares, following the massacre perpetrated there on May 19 and 20. Others were the occupations of churches frequently carried out by the popular-revolutionary organizations (not without conflicts, at times, with Archbishop Romero himself).

Archbishop Romero's new style soon deepened the cleavage already dividing the Church hierarchy. On the one hand, contacts among the clergy intensified, while religious and lay people were organized at different levels to enhance new pastoral practices and to assist the archbishop. On the other hand, the majority of the bishops' conference (CEDES) distanced itself from him and his supporters, whom they viewed with mistrust and even denounced in international forums. Such was the case of Bishop Revelo, named as Archbishop Romero's auxillary bishop at the bishops' synod in Rome in October 1977, and later Msgr. Aparicio at Puebla in 1979; these actions led both of them into direct confrontation with the archbishop. CEDES itself ceased operations as a more or less homogeneous expression of the institutional Church, since the bishops alleged that they did not want to be "manipulated by the communists." Yet Msgr. Romero was able to impose his authority as head of the Salvadoran Church by means that went beyond institutional mechanisms. This he did not only with the distinctiveness of his message but also through novel usage of the mass media—the press and, most importantly, radio.

Rituals like his Sunday sermons, when broadcast throughout the country by Radio YSAX, drew unequalled audience ratings.[54] By using the Gospel as a setting for his denunciations of repression and all forms of domination, the archbishop's sermons became mechanisms for collective consciousness building. These sermons could not be silenced by the bourgeoisie despite several violent attacks against this "voice of the voiceless," as Archbishop Romero referred to *his* Church. This phenomenon, from a sociological standpoint, was more effective ideologically than the actions of any other private organization and generalized the identity of an "oppressed people" in direct confrontation with the system of dominations as a whole. This gave an undeniable charisma to Msgr. Romero individually, as the messenger of this vision. It made him a true national leader whose intercession—disputed by some and sought after by others— would always be of crucial importance at the most critical political moments.

The increasingly dynamic presence of FECCAS, now allied with the UTC, combined with pressures from all sides (including Rome) and demanded a definition of the Church's relationship with the popular-revolutionary organizations. The conservative bishops of Santa Ana, San Miguel, and San Vicente had already taken it on themselves to label these organizations as "atheistic and materialist." The archbishop's Pastoral Letter of August 1978 ("The Church and the People's Political Organizations") was also signed by Msgr. Rivera y Damas, bishop of Santiago de Maria, to give it more weight. It was the first time that such a document had been directed to such a clearly defined social sector. In it, Archbishop Romero sustained the inalienable right of the people to create their own organizations. He proposed dialogue with these organizations, a proposal which no doubt legitimized them—given the specific circumstances of the struggle underway—despite his criticism of some of their practices. Several of the conservative bishops responded immediately with a declaration on August 28 that repudiated the letter's content, an act unprecedented in the history of the Salvadoran Church.[55] The FECCAS-UTC, for their part, took up the call in September when they addressed the Christians of El Salvador and Central America in a declaration that disavowed the bishops who had opposed Romero's Pastoral Letter. This exchange of volleys, which defined more clearly the positions of the protagonists in the struggle, was part of the immediate background to the murder of Father Barrera Motto, discussed above.

Over the next year, up to October 15, 1979, the ruling classes shed any remaining doubts about the stance of progressive Christians: they had become class enemies to be fought by all means and at all costs. The year 1979 opened with the January 20 murder of Father Octavio Ortiz Luna and several young people at a retreat in the village of San Antonio Abad. The utter brutality of the event, presented as a military "operation" against armed subversives, was seen by public opinion as a new expression of vicious intimidation against totally defenseless people, many of whom were murdered in their pajamas. Archbishop Romero ordered all churches closed for three days in protest, and on January 30 hundreds of priests and religious marched through the streets of San Salvador in impressive silence, preceded by a single banner which eloquently proclaimed *Basta Ya*—"we've had enough." But repression did not stop. At Puebla, Msgr. Romero was received as an international personality despite attempts by other bishops, headed by Msgr. Aparicio, to play down his presence. External factors, as we have indicated, were already an important element in Salvadoran politics. When the participants in yet another sit-in at the Cathedral on May 2 were savagely machine-gunned by the army at the Church gates, the image was broadcast in bloody detail by the international media. Any remaining fetters on repressive violence had been undone. On June 20 a death squad murdered Father Rafael Palacios on a street in Santa Tecla. Once again there were massive and dramatic protests by the clergy and base communities at his funeral. The series of attacks reached an isolated village, San Esteban Catarina, on August 4, leaving the body of Father Alirio Napoleón Macías before the Church altar. Two days later Msgr. Romero's final Pastoral Letter ("The Church's Mission in the Midst of the Country's Crisis") was issued as a profession of faith in his Church's evangelical practice, with all the risks that it implied.

The Pastoral Letter broached the possibility of qualified, insurrectional violence, which it considered to be legitimate. It is interesting to recall that on July 17 the Somoza dynasty had fallen in Nicaragua, and that during its final stages the popular insurrection had been legitimized by that country's archbishop, Msgr. Obando.

For all these reasons, the Salvadoran Church—or more precisely the sector most committed to the new pastoral line—had undeniably become one of the country's political forces. The October 15, 1979 coup was preceded by a broad range of protest actions including strikes and church sit-ins. Even so, several of the participants in the coup maintained contact with sectors of the Church at various levels. Msgr. Romero himself appears to have had contact with civilians and military while the coup was being planned; his specific role, however, has not yet been clarified. His work as a mediator of all sorts of conflicts, in any case, was already a habit; his collaboration had been in demand by various sectors over the last few years.

These characteristics explain the significance of Msgr. Romero's reaction to the October 15 coup, in the wake of which he issued a hopeful call for "a chance" to be given to the new government, which included persons with democratic and progressive reputations. Yet his attitude could hardly be seen as one of direct support for the new Junta which, because it could not break with the past, soon revealed its eminently transitory nature. As indiscriminate and brutal repression once more became the government's order of the day, Msgr. Romero again confronted it as an incorrigible opponent.

A month after the coup came the most serious split within the "progressive Christians." In November, the CEBs' coordinating office issued a declaration condemning the Junta and practically accusing civilian members of the government of complicity with the repression. In doing so, they directly confronted the UCA and Msgr. Romero, giving rise to a serious crisis in the archdiocese. Only in January, when it was evident that repression continued, was dialogue resumed and actually deepened in terms of the relationship with the popular revolutionary organizations.

THE DESCENT INTO CIVIL WAR:
OCTOBER 1979–DECEMBER 1980

Throughout the three periods we have analyzed up to October 15, 1979, the popular unrest had fallen into step with the political-military organizations. The mixed civilian-military Junta that took power in October 1979 had a chance to change that tendency; its failure set the stage for a new situation that continues into the present. We would characterize this situation as one of an open people's war whose logic commands the country's entire political dynamic. The date that best captures this new reality is March 30, 1980, the day of Msgr. Romero's funeral. That was the last time that the people were able to hold an open, massive demonstration, and it is now common knowledge that thousands were indiscriminately bombed and machine-gunned with the smug complicity of rulers who called themselves Christians.

There is still no definitive analysis of what has come to be called the "First Junta," which took office on October 15, 1979, nor of the reasons for its breakdown a month and a half later. It gave way to the "Second Junta," which arose from an arrangement between the Christian Democratic Party and the military on January 9, 1980. Any careful analysis will certainly have to delineate and weigh the roles of the various individuals and social forces influential in the new administration mustered by the "Young Military," whose apparatus was instrumental in deposing General Romero. We nonetheless believe it possible to assert that the coup was basically a reaction of the military apparatus itself to a critically unstable situation.

Democratic civilians, some of them with ties to revolutionary organizations, participated in the first Junta itself and in cabinet posts. It soon became clear, however, that while agreement existed within the armed forces about social and economic reforms, it did not about the main problem—popular participation. From the outset, the so-called "progressive" sectors of the army were unable to neutralize members of the military who were implicated in killings during the Romero regime and bent on destroying the popular organizations. This more repressive sector took advantage of a few violent actions to unleash an unprecedented wave of repression.

The final crisis of the government erupted late in December 1979, and during the first week of 1980 the Junta disintegrated. All the ministers (except for the hardline Minister of Defense) resigned in protest against the army's lack of guarantees for reform and against the continuing repression. The new Junta, organized on January 9, grew out of a pact between the military and PDC leaders, as a result of which the PDC split and lost a good number of its most representative cadres. On this note began the new period of what has been called "reforms with repression," as opposed to the "reforms with popular support" proclaimed as the objective of the first Junta. A few months were enough to reveal that this reformism was simply a smoke screen for the government's actual policies, which centered on eliminating the popular opposition through a counterinsurgency strategy directly promoted and maintained by imperialist forces.

The course of events obliged the political-military oganizations to take steps to catch up with the new reality. A process of coordination was initiated, the results of which were already seen on April 18, 1980, with the creation of the Revolutionary Democratic Front (FDR), bringing together the LP–28, FAPU, BPR, and UDN as well as a broad range of political, trade union, and professional organizations and observers from the country's two universities.

Msgr. Romero responded to these first steps toward unity with the same optimistic attitude shared by broad social sectors. He declared in his January 20 Sunday sermon that there was now a "people's program," opposed to two others, which he termed "oligarchical" and "governmental," respectively. He expressed his hope that the "people's program" would lead to "a broad and powerful unity of revolutionary and democratic forces that can make the reign of democracy and social justice possible in our country."[56] With this affirmation, Archbishop Romero was stretching the limits of what an exasperated oligarchy would concede to anyone, much less to an archbishop. The most authoritative voice in the country had taken the side of a long-oppressed people and had pointed them toward a path to liberation which constituted the greatest threat ever faced by the Salvadoran ruling class. For its vicious servants, and most particularly for those who had succeeded in identifying their repressive vocations with the destiny of the country's military institutions, Msgr. Romero's insistent appeals to the army were unbearable broadsides. That same sermon contained one such appeal: "Many of you come from poor families, and the army should therefore be at the service of the people. Do not destroy the poor; do not be the agents of greater and more painful outbreaks of violence with which a repressed people in all justice might respond."[57] Two months later, in his sermon on the fifth Sunday of Lent (March 23) and in response to the regime's utter delirium of repression, he pronounced the following words:

> If what the new government wants is to behead the people's movement and block the process desired by the people, then no other process will advance. Without popular support, no government can be effective, and much less so when it seeks to impose its will at the cost of blood and suffering. . . . I want to issue a call especially to the men of the army, and specifically to the rank and file in the National Guard, in the Police, in the barracks. Brothers, you are part of our same people, you kill your own peasant brothers when, in response to an order to kill, the law of God must prevail: "Thou shalt not kill.". . . No soldier is bound to obey an order against the law of God. . . . No one need carry out an immoral law. . . . It is time for you to reclaim your own conscience and to obey your conscience rather than the order to sin. . . . In the name of God, therefore, in the name of this suffering people whose ever-more tumultuous lamentations rise to the heavens, I ask of you, I beg you, I order you in the name of God: Stop the repression![58]

We register these words at length as a faithful reflection of how radical Msgr. Romero's message had become. His message not only delegitimized the very grounds of the ruling order; it undermined the repressive institution on which the state's own power was dependent. The response came quickly. The very next day, March 24, 1980, at 6:30 in the evening the archbishop was assassinated at the altar while delivering his last sermon.

This murder demonstrated the degree of desperation of the Salvadoran ruling class. Many of the thousands who attended the funeral were probably not even surprised when it turned into yet another massacre before the horror-stricken eyes of observers from around the world. Open war had now been declared and there would be no more room for organized forms of popular expression; anyone remotely considered an opponent of the regime was fair game for murder.

Archbishop Romero has been followed by many other martyrs, among them four more priests murdered by the end of 1980: Fathers Cosme Spesotto (June), Manuel Antonio Reyes Monico (October 6), Ernesto Abrego

(November 23) and Marcial Serrano (November 28), as well as the seminarian José Othmaro Cáceres (July 25) and the North American sisters Ita Ford, Maura Clarke, Dorothy Kazel, and the missionary Jean Donovan (December 2). Most priests committed to the progressive pastoral efforts left the country, while others continued their work virtually underground. Hundreds of base community members — considered to be the most dangerous of subversives — have also been murdered.[59]

The building of unity among revolutionary forces continued with some steps forward and others back. The coalition suffered hard blows, most notably the murder of the FDR's entire leadership on November 27, 1980. The inauguration of a Republican government in the U.S. closed channels of dialogue that might have opened other paths toward real popular participation, or at least reduced the toll of the war. The difficult challenge before the FMLN as a nucleus of the revolutionary vanguard, in close alliance with the FDR, came to be that of complementing its undeniable military strength and international support with a workable domestic political front.

THE SALVADORAN CHURCH AFTER MONSIGNOR ROMERO: FROM PROPHECY TO MEDIATION

The five years following the murder of Msgr. Romero have brought considerable changes both in Salvadoran politics and in the country's Church. Two factors have been central: the prolongation of the conflict with its projection into the spheres of international ideological confrontation and the change of attitudes in the Church hierarchy toward the government, based on conceptions about the Church's social role fundamentally different from those that prevailed during Msgr. Romero's time.

The vacuum of leadership left by the disintegration of the "First Junta" demanded a new civilian-military pact, this time with Christian Democratic predominance. The arrangement stipulated the army's support for three major reforms — agrarian, foreign trade, and financial — be counterbalanced by continued repression against the people's movement, which would be discredited as a participant in any future political agreements. The civilian-military pact also implied blocking right-wing attempts to derail the reforms and trying to dismantle the treacherous right-wing "death squads." Repression singled out the popular-revolutionary organizations, and 1980 came to be remembered as the "bloody year," with the murder of thousands of peasants and workers in addition to those of Msgr. Romero, the Rector of the National University, Felix Ulloa (in October), almost the entire leadership of the FDR including its president, Enrique

Álvarez C. (on November 27) and other martyrs. While repression has decreased since 1980, it has nevertheless remained very intense.

In 1980 the Junta itself was also rearranged, with the addition of a de facto president, Napoleón Duarte, on December 13, chosen by the army and the PDC and strongly supported by the U.S. The failure of the FMLN's insurrection in January 1981 at first seemed to strengthen the Duarte Junta. However, a pro-left international political campaign (which produced the eloquent Franco-Mexican declaration in August 1981) allied with the FMLN's successful military retreat and subsequent new offensive[60] pushed the government—increasingly dependent on U.S. economic and military aid—to respond politically to defend its international legitimacy. The result was the "electoral solution," first attempted in the March 1982 Constituent Assembly elections, to be followed with presidential elections in March and May 1984 and congressional elections in March 1985.

The FMLN's surprising military capacity has been the crucial factor in the development of political events over the past five years. The unity of the FMLN's member political forces and the alliance with the FDR have been consolidated and expanded, despite serious internal disputes which on several occasions have reached critical proportions.[61] This prolongation of the Salvadoran conflict has been a complicating factor for U.S. strategies in the region, focused on eliminating the Sandinista government in Nicaragua. To attain its objectives, the Reagan administration has worked through military and political channels, the latter focused on "democratic elections" as a criterion for judging the government's legitimacy (to be applied only to elections held according to Reagan's criteria). Yet the elections themselves have been largely unsuccessful as political solutions, often adding to the complications.

The political objectives of elections in El Salvador, in addition to legitimizing the local government, also included strengthening the reform programs proclaimed by the military-PDC alliance. This concern with reform programs existed because of the weight of public opinion in the United States, which increasingly conditioned U.S. aid to addressing the social causes of the armed conflict. The reforms, however, stagnated throughout the Duarte Junta government, until March 1982. They became even less viable when the 1982 elections not only failed to consolidate the PDC but strengthened its adversaries both in the old official party (PCN) and in the new right-wing opposition (ARENA, led by Major Roberto D'Aubuissón), with whom the PDC was obliged to share strategic sectors of power. One of the main mistakes in the U.S. perception of Salvadoran politics was the idea that a pluralistic government could be effective even if only among pro–U.S. parties. To this end the U.S. pushed for "national unity" around a president (Magaña) named by the Assembly in 1982. That government (virtually controlled by the right) and the agreements which had brought it into being practically paralyzed public administration with continuous interparty disputes. It was only able to subsist due to the ongoing and open intervention of North American emissaries.

In the 1984 presidential elections, despite Duarte's victory over D'Aubuissón, the PDC did not recover its lost political hegemony, with the right maintaining its control in the Assembly and strategic sectors of the state apparatus. Since the PDC was at best stalemated in the military arena, political initiatives were imperative. The March 1985 mayoral and legislative elections would be key to the success of those initiatives, and all the steps taken by the PDC during that period—including the dialogue with the insurgents initiated at La Palma on October 15, 1984—should be interpreted in that light.

The outcome of the March 1985 elections went beyond even the Christian Democrats' expectations, giving them not only an absolute majority in the Assembly but also an overwhelming number of city governments, this despite countless irregularities perpetuated by the extreme right-wing opposition. In the wake of his victory, Duarte reshuffled his cabinet to rid himself of all the pacts (especially with the extreme right-wing parties) that had weighted him down since 1980. This at first produced an outcry from the outgoing parties, who saw themselves as victims of the same kind of imposition practiced by the traditional "official parties." By the end of the year, however, the government had gradually come to support the demands of the dominant economic forces in a tendency that seems to foreshadow broader agreements aimed at stabilizing the PDC administration, at the cost of shrinking away from promised reforms and turning back the ones already underway.[62]

The elections were successful in legitimizing the PDC government, especially in terms of President Duarte's image overseas. One indication of this was the naming of ambassadors to El Salvador in 1985 by the French and Mexican governments, although both governments continued their criticisms of Duarte's impotence in solving the internal conflict. The government's domestic problems have been much greater, however, given its inability to win the war militarily. Regionally it has suffered from its submission to U.S. policies against Nicaragua, thus undermining the international image Duarte would like to project.[63] Domestically, elections have emerged as the instrument for maintaining a "restricted democracy." Participation of even moderate left forces is still impossible and voter turnout diminished to 40 percent of registered voters in March 1985. More fundamental, elections have been of no use at all in confronting the country's real problems: above all, the war.

The need for a "political solution" to the Salvadoran conflict has been raised insistently in recent years. Several initiatives have been undertaken,[64] most of them by the left. The idea was concretized at the meetings at La Palma and Ayagualo (October and November 1984) between government and insurgent representatives. The specific initiative for these talks, with the invitation issued by Duarte during his October 8 address at the UN, was probably taken on behalf of PDC electoral interests rather than any real desire to launch a process of pacification. In any case, it was significant that the government took a clear stance on an issue of overwhelming importance for the great majority of the population. The issue of dialogue/negotiations is necessarily at the top of the Salvadoran political agenda, both for the government party and for the opposition, including the PCN.[65] No political organization interested in winning popular support has opposed a dialogue that could lead to a political solution to the crisis. This declared disposition rounds out the backdrop for an examination of the role of the Church.

The Institutional Involution of the Church: From Prophecy to Mediation

It has been said that the death of Msgr. Romero marks "the turning point in the history of the Salvadoran Church and the beginning of a new age."[66] At that moment the Church hierarchy faced a difficult option: whether to carry on the prophetic line of action—risking the lives of clergy and the faithful, but *acompañando* the popular movement in whose birth and development the Church had played a major role—or to regroup within its own ranks and to redefine the social and political function of the power it wields as an institution capable of influencing the balance of forces within the state. The extreme repression unleashed during 1980, combined with the predominant inclinations of the Church hierarchy, left little room for anything but the second alternative. The only real doubt was as to the terms in which the option would be taken, or in other words, which sectors would come out on top: the majority of conservative bishops who had so often locked horns with Msgr. Romero, or the others who—while having declined to take clear stances of commitment with the people's cause—wished to maintain the Church's institutional role as an agent of social criticism within the tradition of the Church's social doctrine and, in particular, its influence over the formulation and implementation of projects and mechanisms addressing the country's acute political-military conflict. This latter option has been personified by Archbishop Rivera y Damas, who managed to consolidate his position as the highest authority of the Salvadoran Church in a convoluted process which is still unfolding.

This "involution" of the Salvadoran Church has been most notable within the hierarchy. Among the Christian people the presence and the ideas of Msgr. Romero are still significant, expressed in organizational forms which have survived these years of repression, especially in the San Salvador archdiocese.[67] Equally important is the fact that this turnabout in the political arena brought a substantial shift away from the theological conceptions advanced by Msgr. Romero, in terms both of pastoral work and of the role of authority within the institution. For the purposes of this chapter, we shall restrict ourselves to the second aspect and its impact on the national political situation.[68]

One of the main concerns of the Vatican under Pope John Paul II has been to maintain the unity of the Church, particularly in relation to the priesthood and religious orders.[69] To rebuild that unity in El Salvador in the wake of the tensions which arose from Msgr. Romero's tenure as archbishop could not be an easy task. It has only been possible—to a certain extent—because of the leadership that Msgr. Rivera has exercised over the Episcopal Conference (CEDES). His appointment as Apostolic Administrator shortly after Msgr. Romero's death filled an administrative vacuum, but it did not resolve the hierarchical problem, which was a point of heated contention within the CEDES and the object of much lobbying at the Vatican. Only on the eve of John Paul II's visit to El Salvador in March 1983 did the Vatican finally appoint Msgr. Rivera as Archbishop of San Salvador. Although the post in itself does not guarantee its holder any privileges within the CEDES, it does offer a capacity for initiative beyond that of any other bishop, an advantage which Msgr. Rivera has used extensively. His sway has been evident ever since his appointment as Apostolic Administrator in his ability to come out on top in many situations where he faced the opposition of more conservative bishops. He has maintained firm positions against the prolongation of the war and its excesses of violence, and in favor of alternative solutions based on dialogue and negotiations. He has even been able to gather the support of many who utterly scorn the left and who would otherwise have preferred positions more in line with the pro-war strategy of the U.S.[70]

At the initiative of Msgr. Rivera, the CEDES started to publish a series of official policy statements calling for national reconciliation, thus differing from the Salvadoran government as well as from the United States. The first of the series, dated October 17, 1980, had little impact. This was due, in part, to the atmosphere created by the belief in imminent triumph which pervaded the left at that time and, more important, to the fact that the assassination of the FDR leaders a month later left the Church's mediation proposal without practical content. Later, during the 1982 election campaign, the bishops continued to speak of the need for dialogue and emphatically reiterated this call during the 1984 campaign (in the February 2 declaration, most likely influenced by stances taken by the pope). The pope had been supporting dialogue ever since his August 6, 1982 letter to the bishops. He repeated this appeal during his March 6, 1983, visit to El Salvador and in his address to the Salvadoran bishops in Rome, on February 24, 1984. The significance of these calls is all the more important because during that whole period the issue of dialogue with the left was a virtual taboo for both the Salvadoran and the U.S. governments. Dialogue was seen as a banner of the left.

After the meetings at La Palma and Ayagualo (October and November 1984) it was clear that to favor dialogue was no more than a first step. It would have meaning only if followed by other initiatives taken in a spirit of constructive realism, leading to visible progress along the road to peace and the fulfilling of those conditions (social and political, national and international) that make peace possible. Dialogue in fact is being promoted from very different perspectives, including some that manipulate it as a pretext for justifying policies that actually contradict it. This is the case, for example, of the Reagan government, which uses the issue of dialogue for the sole objective of establishing a questionable – opportunistic – parallel to the Nicaraguan situation. Nevertheless, the issue of dialogue has certainly contributed to strengthening existing tendencies and to legitimizing the proponents of nonmilitary alternatives. It has contributed in particular to consolidating the role of mediator that Msgr. Rivera has tried to play between the government and the insurgents, a function he has tried to fulfill with considerable acumen, although as yet with few substantial results.

To be effective in his mediator's role, Msgr. Rivera has had to build an image of impartiality, not an easy task for one who must play the role of denouncing the social realities of violence and injustice. Obviously most of the mistrust toward him comes from the right wing, the army, and the U.S. embassy. The government, especially under the PDC administration, has given him more room to maneuver, largely because Msgr. Rivera has kept up close ties of friendship for many years with top Christian Democrat leaders. The left has also recognized his role as mediator, although not without questioning his conduct on several occasions. Msgr. Rivera has thus been an important communicator at several levels between the contending parties in the Salvadoran conflict. His first significant gesture was to deliver to the Magaña government, in the name of the FDR-FMLN, the insurgency's first call for dialogue ("Letter to El Salvador," dated October 1982). As Msgr. Rivera said on November 7, 1982, "We can now see more clearly the political will to resolve the conflict through paths more humane and democratic than warfare. . . . Now is the time for dialogue."

Despite the failure of that initiative and of others that followed it, he remained unshaken in rejecting both violent alternatives and "false solutions" through elections.

Once the PDC consolidated power following the March 1985 elections, expectations were raised that dialogue might be renewed, but the Duarte government was incapable of formulating any new proposals to the left. In the meantime the FMLN has been successful in turning back repeated military offensives and often has taken the offensive. Their actions included attacks on U.S. military personnel in the cities and the so-called "political-military kidnappings" (twenty-three mayors, Duarte's daughter, and others). It is significant that some of these actions have not been claimed by the FDR, which would seem to indicate differences within the FDR more in terms of the different character and strategies of each constituent group, than as a result of actual internal contradictions. In any case, both the government's military offensives and the FMLN response point to a hardening of the general situation.

This was the setting for the call for dialogue issued by the CEDES on August 6, 1985, entitled "Reconciliation and Peace." Received with much interest, given the post-election situation, the bishops' declaration was heavily influenced by the opinions of the conservative prelates. The bishops reaffirmed their support for a dialogue that would exclude none of the interested parties as the principal means for putting an end to the conflict. Yet the bishops revealed their prejudices regarding the causes and responsibilities for the violence, as well as their bias against the insurgent forces and their manifest sympathy for the Christian Democrat government. The results of the CEDES letter were hardly positive in terms of its declared intention. The FDR-FMLN accused the bishops of a "lack of neutrality,"[71] a subject that has continued to compromise the Church's role as mediator since then. Archbishop Rivera again was able to operate as an intermediary during the kidnapping of Duarte's daughter (September-October 1985), but it is difficult to see that event—as some observers would have it—as the beginning of a new round of negotiations to follow the timid bargaining begun in late 1984.

The nearly absolute dependence of the PDC government and its army on U.S. policies makes it hard to foresee any fruits for Church-sponsored efforts toward a political solution to the Salvadoran conflict. This is especially so considering that the Reagan administration's overall strategy for the region shows no sign of change for the near future and that there have been substantial modifications in other countries' foreign policies toward the region. The only positive process currently in view has to do with pressures that might develop within the country, coming from a broad range of social forces, to demand visible and immediate solutions for a crisis that has become unbearable. So far the Church hier-archy does not appear to be willing to invest all the energy necessary to mobilize such forces, among them the grass-roots movement of Christians that still identifies itself as the "Church of the Poor," and whose roots were firmly laid by prophets like Msgr. Romero and watered by the blood of thousands of martyrs in the drama of the Passion of the Salvadoran people.[72]

NOTES

1. Of those with which we are acquainted, the best summary is to be found in Pablo Richard and Guillermo Meléndez, *La Iglesia de los pobres en América-Central* (San José: DEI Editores, 1982), pp. 52–61.

2. The most complete study to date on the Salvadoran PDC is Stephen Webre, *José Napoleón Duarte and the Christian Democratic Party in Salvadoran Politics 1960–1972* (Baton Rouge, La.: Louisiana State University Press, 1979). The book is rich in descrip-tions of the Salvadoran political process during the 1960–1972 period.

3. It was precisely in 1967 that the first serious conflicts appeared in the ad-ministration of Eduardo Frei Montalva, elected President of Chile by the PDC in 1964. For many, he was the flagbearer *par excellence* of the "third position" touted by Chris-tian Democrats for Latin America. The Chilean Experience was to have a major im-pact on the Salvadoran university social Christians tied to dissident sectors of the Chilean PDC who came to support Salvador Allende's UP in 1970.

4. The history of community development work is another area where future research is needed. Its importance stems not only from the reasons mentioned but from the fact that it has been a proving grounds for other sectors as well, such as the University (through its extension programs) and several government agencies. A seminal study on work in urban areas is M. Lungo, "Las revindaciones urbanas de El Salvador," *Desarrollo Urbano y Regional Series* 15 (1978) (San José: CSUCA/Programa Centroamericano de Ciencias Sociales). Due to such limitations, the present essay will make minimal reference to this field.

5. A fundamental book on this subject is Walter Guerra Calderón, *Las Asocia-ciones comunitarias en el área rural de El Salvador en la década 1960–1970* (Costa Rica: Tesis Sociología Universidad, 1977), which also presents the background to popular organizations such as FECCAS (Christian Federations of Salvadoran Peasants), born in 1965 at the height of social Christianism. As we shall see, FECCAS later assumed revolutionary positions. A similar organization among urban workers was the UNOC (National Union of Catholic Workers), affiliated with the CLASC. Founded in 1950 under the wing of the Catholic Church, it won greater autonomy in 1961 and often worked jointly with the FECCAS until its disappearance at the end of that decade.

6. On this point see: *La inversión extranjera en Centroamérica* (San José: EDUCA, 1974–1975), especially the article by S. Bodenheimer, "El Mercomún y la ayuda norte-americana"; Edelberto Torres-Rivas, *Interpretación del desarrollo social centroamericano* (San José: EDUCA, 1971), chap. 5; *El fracaso social de la integración centroamericana* (San José: EDUCA, 1979); Héctor Dada Hirezi, *La economía de El Salvador y la inte-*

gración centroamericana: 1945–1960 (El Salvador: UCA Editores, 1978); R. Mejivar, "Algunos aspectos de la economía y la lucha de clases en El Salvador (1880–1980)," in Rafael Menjivar and Vincente Serrano, *Formación social y proceso de liberación* (n.d., n.p., AGEUS).

7. See the collection, *La Guerra inútil* (San José: EDUCA, 1971) and *ECA* (San Salvador: Universidad Centroamericana "José Simeón Cañas"), November-December 1969, for abundant information on the war, its background and its consequences.

8. See *ECA* (November-December 1969): 530–532.

9. See Asamblea Legislativa: *Memoria del Primer Congreso Nacional de Reforma Agraria* (San Salvador: Publicaciones de la Asamblea Legislativa, 1970), which contains the studies and speeches presented by the delegates of the Metropolitan Curia, from CESPROP and others.

10. Official ERP documents reveal that the first cells of what would become this organization arose in a struggle against PCS "revisionism" in 1970. In February 1971, one of these cells carried out (along with a command group of the Guatemalan Rebel Armed Forces [FAR]) the kidnapping of a leading member of the oligarchy, Ernesto Regalado Duenas. With the failure of this operation and censured by the ERP as "adventurous, with absolutely no correspondence to the political situation of Salvadoran society," the cell was practically dismantled ("Balance Histórico," in *Prensa Comunista*, Órgano del PRS, Special publication, October 1977, p. 13). The kidnapping was used to mount an ostentatious trial in which the government tried to impute the involvement of PDC and progressive Christian sectors in violent actions. The trial lasted until 1975 and, as a result of the contradictions within the government, culminated surprisingly with the acquittal of the defendants. From then on, as one police representative declared, "We will no longer commit the folly of sending *guerrilleros* to court. . . ." (Ana Guadalupe Martínez, *Las cárceles clandestinas de El Salvador* [n.p.: 1978]).

11. In this chapter we use the term "popular-revolutionary organizations" for all groups using this strategy. [See editors' note.] We distinguish between the "political-military organizations" as the nuclei of political orientation (sometimes as a party) which generally contain a complex clandestine and military structure, and the "mass organizations" with open structures and dedicated to the tasks of agitation and demand-oriented struggles in various sectors. Over time, it has been possible to identify "military arms," "armies," etc., within each of the political-military organizations, but this article will ignore these differences. A report on the state of the popular revolutionary organizations in 1982 is found in Higinio Alas, *El Salvador ¿por qué la insurrección?* (San José: Secretariado Permanente de la Comisión para la Defensa de los Derechos Humanos en Centroamérica, 1982) pp. 105–106. The PCS is included here due to its adherence to a political-military strategy in 1979 (Alas, *El Salvador ¿por qué*, p. 111). The ties among the various political-military and popular organizations were not explicitly recognized by them, both for practical reasons and also in order to set limits and responsibilities to militants.

12. In the case of the ERP, this process was made more difficult not only for the reasons mentioned, but also due to infighting that led to a split in the organization in 1975.

13. Such is the case of the contacts initiated by ERP sectors (which would soon

split off to organize the National Resistance [RN]) with Christian groups in Suchitoto (Father Alas), from 1970 on. This instrumental approach, also applied in relation to other social sectors, has persisted in many cases despite the later refinement of the vanguards' discourse.

14. The Independent United Democratic Front (FUDI) was organized by the extreme rightist, General José Alberto Medrano, following his break with the government. Before becoming a "war hero" in the conflict with Honduras, Medrano had oranized the vicious ORDEN (Democratic Nationalist Organization) paramilitary gangs, had been Director of the National Guard, and was held to have worked for the CIA. The PPS (Salvadoran Popular Party) was founded in 1965 by rightist dissidents from the traditional opposition party, PAR (Renovating Action Party), after the PAR leaderhip was taken over by a leftist sector. Some split-off sectors from the PCN also participated in founding the PPS.

15. In Salvadoran politics frequent reference is made to the existence of "progressive" sectors within the traditionally pro-oligarchy armed forces. Their first precursors were found in the rebellion that overthrew dictator Hernández Martínez in 1944. Under the general denomination of "*Juventud Militar*" (Military Youth), they also participated in the coups d'etat of 1948, 1959, 1972 (frustrated), and 1979. Without exception, these sectors have always been neutralized (and at times repressed) by the ruling apparatus. In this particular case, the group seems to have been influenced by the reformist Panamanian and Peruvian military experiences of the 1970s.

16. This was the case of Napoleón Duarte, undisputably the winner of the elections, who irresponsibly compromised his followers at the last minute by supporting the plot, about which – in his own words – he knew nothing. See Webre, *José Napoleón Duarte and the Christian Democratic Party*, p. 179.

17. The 1965 data show that there were 106 priests in the archdiocese, versus 30 in the diocese of Santa Ana and San Vincent, and 29 in that of San Miguel. The 1125 religious (775 women and 350 men) were also concentrated in the archdiocese and mainly involved in teaching. This would change in the succeeding years as many religious women did very important work in the renewal of Church ministries. The clergy was predominantly of Salvadoran origin and most came from peasant families. The high quality of their education had been a special concern of Msgr. Chávez. Threequarters of the religious, on the other hand, were foreigners. Richard and Meléndez, *La Iglesia de los Pobres en América-Central*, pp. 58–59).

18. *ECA* (October-November 1977): 8.

19. Alas, *El Salvador ¿por qué*, p. 174. It is possible that the frustration of this first attempt at urban social work convinced the Jesuits to move into the countryside. They did this in September 1972, in Aguilares.

20. This is when FARO, a federation of land-owners from eastern El Salvador noted for its ferocious opposition to the reforms, was organized in common cause with the National Association for Private Enterprise (ANEP), the modernizing sectors of which were virtually shunted aside. For an analysis of this case of "historical blindness," see R. Zamora, "Seguro de vida o despojo? Análisis político de la transformación agraria," *ECA* (September-October 1976): 511.

21. ORDEN and the UCS even published a declaration supporting the reforms on July 1, accompanied by a giant demonstration in San Salvador. The reaction of

the oligarchy was to increase pressure within the government. No more such mobilizations took place.

22. See the declaration published in *ECA* (September-October 1976): 424.

23. Webre, *José Napoleón Duarte and the Christian Democratic Party*, p. 181.

24. For this election and the next, no official voting figures were published. Municipal power had in any case been significantly reduced due to budget restrictions imposed by the central government.

25. Although the occurrence of fraud always makes any "official" result questionable, under the new conditions it became truly impossible to make objective evaluations. More than ever, the numbers came to represent intensely polarized power relationships in which the votes themselves bore little weight even though the voters, as a mobilized mass, were active participants in those relationships.

26. The killings at La Calletana (November 29, 1974) and at Tres Calles (June 21, 1975) involved peasant Christian base communities.

27. In El Salvador, the Protestant churches have generally been very conservative, and have even collaborated with agencies of repression. The exception has been the Emmanuel (Baptist) Church, which made contact with progressive Catholic sectors to begin important ecumenical activities. See Plácido Erdozaín, *Monseñor Romero: Mártir de la Iglesia Popular* (San José: DEI-EDUCA), pp. 78–79. This Church in particular went through a process similar to that of the Catholic Church in organizing base communities, and it generated important leaders for the popular organizations. One of its long-time ministers, Augusto Cotto, who died in a plane crash in 1980, was one of the main leaders of the RN. In November 1978 an "Ecumenical Committee" was formed with the presence of Baptists, Episcopalians, Lutherans, and the Central American Church, as well as related organizations such as MEC, ULAJE, ASEL, who offered support to progressive Catholic sectors at the height of the campaign against them.

28. Msgr. Rivera, *ECA* (October-November 1977): 809; and in reference to Aguilares on p. 838.

29. Ibid.

30. Particularly the publication of the collective study *El Salvador, año político*, coordinated by the UCA, which had a major impact inside the country and abroad and discredited the government policy makers.

31. Alas, *El Salvador ¿por qué*, p. 175.

32. *ECA* (October-November 1977): 812.

33. In Richard and Meléndez, *La Iglesia de los pobres en América-Central*, pp. 80–81.

34. See the report by Father Nicolás Carranza in *ECA* (October-November 1977): 938.

35. In *ECA* (October-November 1977): 811.

36. *Diario de Hoy*, December 7, 1976.

37. See Erdozaín, *Monseñor Romero: Mártir de la Iglesia Popular*, pp. 23–29.

38. Secretariado Social Interdiocesano, *Persecución de la Iglesia en El Salvador* (San Salvador: Colección "Iglesia y Derechos Humanos," June 1977), p. 19.

39. See the full text of this sermon in *ECA* (October-November 1977): 858–862.

40. Also murdered was the brother of Father Rafael Barahona, in circumstances that indicated that the latter was the target of the attack.

41. Those deported on this occasion were Fathers Jorge Sarsanedas, Salvador Carranza, José Luís Ortega, Marcelino Pérez, Inocencio Alas, Higinio Alas, and Guillermo Rodríguez. Fathers Gonzalo López, Aleandro Bantín, Víctor Guevara, and Antonio Vides were arrested and mistreated. See *Persecución de la Iglesia en El Salvador*, pp. 19–20.

42. *Violence and Fraud in El Salvador* (London: Latin America Bureau, 1977), pp. 434–450.

43. Testimony given at the hearings was published in ECA (July 1977): 520–527. We will refer below to the impact of the hearings.

44. For comments on the reports of the U.S. State Department to the Commissions on Foreign Relations of the Senate and the House, of the English Parliamentary Commission which visited El Salvador in December 1978, and the Report and Recommendations of the IHRC, see *ECA* (July-August 1979): 589–606.

45. For information on the participants, see *ECA* (October-November 1979): 876; and *ECA* (September 1979): 843–845 for the Platform of the People's Forum.

46. This hegemony, nonetheless, in addition to being seriously limited at the time by divisions among the popular-revolutionary bloc, was also far from clear at the Forum, toward which the popular-revolutionary bloc maintained a reserved attitude. In Nicaragua, revolutionary hegemony arose from the form in which the anti-Somoza struggle was finally resolved and from the events which preceded it. What is at stake in El Salvador is much more than the removal of a regime, a fact which the bourgeoisie and imperialism are well aware of, as later events have shown.

47. See *ECA* (March 1981): 198–201, for a bibliography on Msgr. Romero. We would also add Arnoldo Mora, *Monseñor Romero* (San José: EDUCA, 1981) and the articles by Sobrino and Ellacuria published in the *ECA* issues of April–May (p. 194) and June (p. 529) of 1981, respectively.

48. Among the latter was the entire UCA staff.

49. See Erdozaín, *Monseñor Romero: Mártir de la Iglesia Popular*, pp. 83–92.

50. Sermon at the funeral of Father Ernesto Barrera, in *Justicia y Paz*, No. 79, January 1979, p. 21.

51. Ibid., pp. 21, 23.

52. See Erdozaín, *Monseñor Romero: Mártir de la Iglesia Popular*, pp. 23–29.

53. Sermon at the funeral of Father Barrera, in *Justicia y Paz*, No. 79, January 1979, p. 38.

54. Audience ratings were estimated at 73 percent in rural areas and 47 percent in urban areas (cited in Sermon at the funeral of Father Barrera, in *Justicia y Paz*, No. 79, January 1979).

55. See the text in *ECA* (September 1978): 774–775, signed by Msgrs. Aparicio, Barrea, Álvarez, Revelo (auxiliary bishop of San Salvador), and F. Delgado. The same issue contains the text of the Pastoral Letter, the pertinent FECCAS-UTC declaration and other important analyses.

56. *La Voz* (El Salvador: UCA Editores), p. 238.

57. Ibid., p. 240.

58. Ibid., p. 291.

59. See the article "Qué queda de la opción por los pobres," in Richard and Meléndez, *La Iglesia de los pobres en América-Central*, pp. 129–133, which exposes the conservative bishops' commitment to the official army in the midst of the revolutionary war. The same book (pp. 122–125) contains a synthesis of the situation of the base communities, which have had no choice under present conditions but to "adopt methods of the Church of the catacombs" and either "join the fronts of struggle or seek exile with their families," and a call issued to the Salvadoran Church to redeem its true commitment and "prepare to respond in a revolutionary manner to the near and imminent revolutionary triumph." It is possible that the complexities displayed by the subsequent revolutionary process and the particularities of changing situations may demand that the Christians' contributions to that process take on different forms depending on the needs of the moment.

60. FMLN leaders explain that a "stage of resistance" which lasted until June 1982, with the objective of winning the strategic initiative from the government army, gave way to a stage of "intensifying the offensive and the dispute for vital zones" (through June-July 1984) and then to a "strategic counteroffensive" which continues until today, with the objective of "destabilizing the strategic command." See "Entrevista Militar" with the General Command of the FMLN in *Proceso*, 195, 196, and 197–198 (San Salvador).

61. The most serious have been the splits within the FPL, which led to the murder of comandante Ana María and the suicide of the Secretary General Salvador Cayetano Carpio in April 1983. As a result of this and other splits, there are some revolutionary groups that are not members of the FMLN, but they have been of little importance to date.

62. A fairly complete analysis of the Duarte administration was published in *ECA* no. 439–440 (May–June 1985).

63. The most illustrative example has been the Duarte government's open support for the U.S. economic blockade of Nicaragua, which is opposed by the rest of the Central American countries and the international community in general. A similar stance has been taken in relation to U.S. support for the contras, with a servility not seen in the region since the days of the Somoza dynasty.

64. A chronology published by the University of El Salvador revealed no less than 64 specific initiatives on behalf of the opening of a political dialogue, from 1980 through the La Palma meeting. See working paper "Seguimiento del diálogo" (mimeo, first part) (San Salvador: Centro de Documentación, January 11, 1985).

65. One illustrative example of the PDC's loss of the initiative on the dialogue issue was the public forum on alternatives for peace organized by the PCN on September 26–28, 1985, with the presence of representative leaderships from trade unions, universities, the Church, and the professional and private sectors. Most surprising was the presence of the FMLN-FDR in the form of a letter which expressed support for this kind of encounter and the FMLN-FDR's point of view. This letter was read at the forum and attentively discussed. The document was published in *Proceso*, No. 206.

66. See Iván D. Paredes, "Evolución de la Iglesia Salvadoreña, 24 de marzo 80–

28 de marzo 82," in *ECA* no. 403–404 (May 1982). In this case and in others ("Ernesto Cruz Alfaro," "Tomás R. Campos," etc.) the names of certain authors are pseudonyms, often the work of several authors.

67. See in this regard the reports by Guillermo Meléndez: "Nuevos signos de esperanza en la Iglesia salvadoreña," in *Iglesias* no. 8 (August 1984); and by Pablo Richard: "Iglesia salvadoreña acompaña a su pueblo en proceso de liberación," in *Noticias Aliadas* (Peru), April 25, 1985. They contain important accounts on the Church of the Poor in present-day El Salvador.

68. The "involution" of the Church and its specific effects in the case of El Salvador is analyzed in the editorial "Hacia dónde va la Iglesia," in *ECA* no. 434 (December 1984). See also the Paredes article mentioned above, and *ECA* no. 437 (March 1985), commemorating the fifth anniversary of the assassination of Msgr. Romero.

69. See, in this regard: *Juan Pablo II en Centroamérica* (Madrid: IEPALA, 1983); Ana María Ezcurra, *Agresión Ideológica contra la Revolución Sandinista* (Mexico: Nuevomar, 1983); and our own collective publication on the Pope's visit to Central America, Jorge Cáceres, et al., *Iglesia, política y profecía* (San José: Educa, 1983).

70. Msgr. Aparicio, then still a member of CEDES, declared in 1982 that dialogue would be impossible with the left, which he qualified as "murderers." The archdiocesan weekly *Orientación*, which has been giving clear editorial support to the PDC, claims that the FDR-FMLN is made up of "perverts" who do not murder more Salvadorans, not because they don't want to but because they can't (February 19, 1984).

71. The FDR-FMLN declaration was published in *Proceso*, No. 201, pp. 8–10.

72. Upon reviewing the text for publication (January 1988) the author would like to add a few remarks about the latest outcomes of dialogue in El Salvador. After assuming the Guatemalan presidency on January 14, 1986, civilian Vinicio Cerezo called for a meeting of Central American presidents in Esquipulas (May 24–25, 1986), thus initiating a process of revitalization of peace initiatives on a regional basis. After that meeting, and with the newly elected Costa Rican President Oscar Arias playing a crucial role (for which he was later awarded the Nobel Peace Prize) other meetings have taken place: "Esquipulas II" (August 7, 1987) and III (January 15–16, 1988). The issue of peace through dialogue and national reconciliation has gathered an unexpected momentum. In El Salvador, though military and U.S. opposition frustrated a proposed meeting between Duarte and the FDR-FMLN (scheduled for September 1986), the economic crisis—aggravated by the October 1986 earthquake—and renewed popular mobilization added to the regional peace initiatives to make dialogue possible. To this we should also add important reformulations of FDR-FMLN strategies, especially a whole new set of statements toward "humanization of the conflict," formulated during May 1987. These new strategies allowed broader and more flexible grounds for negotiation.

Msgr. Rivera's mediation was crucial for bringing about the San Salvador meeting on October 4–5, 1987, after a long complicated negotiation process involving a wide range of actors, both from Central America and from outside the region. Although there were not many agreements on paper, the meeting was followed by bold initiatives from the FDR leadership. FDR leaders Guillermo Ungo and Ruben Zamora have started to visit El Salvador more frequently, to the outrage of the extreme right. Dialogue now seems to be taking more the form of day-to-day domestic political negotiation than that of spectacular meetings. The outcome, however, is still uncertain — as is the place the Salvadoran Church will occupy in future balances of forces.

PART II
Brazil

GRASS-ROOTS CATHOLIC GROUPS AND POLITICS IN BRAZIL

Scott Mainwaring

During most of its lengthy history, the Catholic Church in Latin America has been closely identified with dominant elites. In exceptional places, Church leaders supported the poor in their struggles to win a better place in society, but generally they allied themselves with the privileged. There were many cases of religiously inspired popular protests, but most often the Church lined up against, rather than with, such movements. This has changed in the past three decades, though with great differences in the extent and nature of change from one country to the next. At times with dramatic gestures, at times through silent, courageous, and unpublicized acts of solidarity, a significant number of Church leaders have taken stances alongside the poor, encouraging them to fight for social change. CEBs (Ecclesial Base Communities) and other grass-roots groups have become very controversial as they have threatened to change the religious and political landscapes of a number of countries. Politicians and grass-roots activists, theologians, and social scientists, conservatives and revolutionaries have all become embroiled in the debate about CEBs. Many analysts have overstated the magnitude of Church change, but in several countries (Brazil, Chile, El Salvador, Nicaragua, Peru) the Church has undergone a conspicuous transformation.

Nowhere in the Roman Church has change gone farther than in Brazil. Brazil has the most progressive Catholic episcopate in the world. Brazil probably had the first CEBs in Latin America, created around 1963, and it certainly has the most CEBs, estimated (though possibly overestimated) at 100,000, with over two million participants. The Brazilian Church has also been a pioneer in creating other kinds of organizations that link the institutional Church with the grass roots. The size of the Brazilian Church has helped give it considerable weight internationally. With over 350 bishops Brazil has the second largest Roman Catholic episcopate (behind only Italy), and the Church is the largest in the Western world.

Given its size, the importance it has assumed internationally, and the centrality of grass-roots groups within it, the Brazilian Church deserves particular attention. And within the Brazilian Church, the nature and the role of CEBs and other grass-roots groups is a vital issue because of their importance to progressive Church efforts and their role in encouraging opposition to military rule. No other innovation within the Brazilian Church has been so central to the efforts to create a new Church.

RELIGION, POLITICS, AND GRASS-ROOTS GROUPS: THEORETICAL NOTES

In the late nineteenth and early twentieth centuries, many leading social scientists proclaimed, and generally applauded, the demise of religion as a major force in social life.[1] At this point in history, it is not novel to point out that these predictions have not been entirely borne out. Nevertheless, until recently, the assumption that modernization would ultimately erode the basis for religious faith was common in sociological literature.[2] Religion was often portrayed as an atavism. Analyses of religion and politics frequently saw religious motives as a stepping stone to political action, without taking seriously the nature of those motives.

The past two decades, however, have once again underscored that religion remains a dynamic and important force in social and political life. Religion has spawned violent political strife in countries as otherwise distinct as Iran, Lebanon, Northern Ireland, El Salvador, South Africa, and Nicaragua. The religious conflicts in question generally are connected to other cleavages—class, region, ethnicity—but this in no sense makes the religious issues reducible to other, supposedly more fundamental cleavages. Religion has played a salient political role in many other countries around the world. Poland, where the Catholic Church has been the outstanding voice representing civil society against the claims of an oppressive socialist state; the United States, where religious conservatives and liberals alike have been prominent in public life; and Brazil, where progressive religious groups played an outstanding role in the opposition to military rule between 1968 and 1985, stand out as noteworthy cases. Even mundane examples illustrate the ongoing importance of religion in political life. In many Western democracies, religion and not class is the best sociological indicator of voting and political behavior.[3]

In response to this ongoing centrality of religion in political life, an impressive body of literature has emerged in recent years. Spanning a wide range of disciplines, methodologies, ideological perspectives, and geographic specializations, this literature nevertheless has some important common points. First, there is a consensus that religion is not necessarily a conservative force, even though it continues to be so in most instances. Second, religious values are important in their own right, and should not be treated as mere expressions of other, more fundamental (usually material) issues. Finally, religion has an extraordinary ongoing appeal, even when so many aspects of social life have become highly rationalized. Religion is important in some highly and some less modernized societies, and among highly educated individuals as well as illiterate people.

Religion's vitality reflects the fact that, contrary to Freud's hopes and expectations, science leaves unanswered many key questions of human existence. Religion addresses questions about the meaning of life and death. It also provides individuals with a set of values and norms that help structure their lives. Alternative values and norms do exist—religion is not functionally indispensable to modern society in that sense—but have not displaced those created by religion. Religion remains a powerful force in motivating human action and structuring world views.[4]

The current salience of religion in world politics also calls attention to the vitality and dynamism of many religious institutions. Churches have adapted to the challenges Marx, Freud, and Feuerbach felt would lead to their demise. They have been capable of responding to secularization, modernization, and democratization, among other social changes. They have done so in a large variety of ways, sometimes by seeking integration within a new social order, sometimes by successfully affording masses of individuals protection against some of the evils of that new order, sometimes by rejecting and defeating attempts to create a more secularized society. Among the major institutions that form contemporary society, only the family and the state could claim to have been as capable of adjusting to the challenges of the times—and such a claim on behalf of either institution would be disputable. In brief, churches, like other institutions, change to meet the demands of their times and their constituencies. They are part of society and as such respond (consciously or not) to changing social contexts, even in the case of fundamentalist groups who reject many elements of social changes. Of course, not all churches change in equally "successful" (in the limited sense of maintaining and expanding a constituency) ways. Some churches decline and even disappear; others emerge and expand. Very few, however, can survive without changing in significant ways. They may even claim that change is intended to bring the church back to the "original" ideals—but whatever such ideals may have represented in times long past cannot be duplicated today, given the radically different context.

While general and abstract, these comments are relevant to understanding the grass-roots religious communities that have played an important role in Brazil's Church and political life. It is impossible to understand such groups without reference to the powerful motivating force that religion provides. While the middle and upper strata in urban areas in Brazil often have a secularized world view, religion is an important part of the world view of many poor people, especially those who live in rural areas. Of course, this is nothing new, nor does it mean that religious people regularly participate in *organized* religious expressions. Nevertheless, the fact that a strong popular religiosity permeates major sectors of the society helps explain why CEBs have had reasonably wide appeal.

Insisting on the importance of religious motivations is crucial because the average CEB in Brazil is more conventionally religious, and less political, than many analysts have suggested. People participate in CEBs because of their faith and because they enjoy the social experience. Many people acquire a rudimentary political consciousness (often accompanied by radical rhetoric learned through primers) in CEBs, and in the most politicized parts of the country many also participate in social movements. But the vast majority of CEBs remain a haven for religious activity, above all for praying, reading the Bible and religious materials prepared by the diocese, discussing the social and political implications of Christian faith, and discussing issues of central importance in their members' daily lives.

Analyses of grass-roots religious groups often distinguish between religious and political motives for action. Among the vast majority of grass-roots participants this distinction makes little sense. Whether a grass-roots participant is praying or organizing a petition to obtain improved transportation facilities, there is a unity of logic and action that makes our neat analytical distinctions break down. In both cases, what is at stake is acting in the name of certain principles of faith.[5] To most grass-roots members who participate in collective action, such participation is every bit as religious as prayer. Conversely, the content of prayer and the way it is organized are deeply political. Many liberation theologians seem to have understood this point in recent years, as they have increasingly turned their attention to spirituality.[6]

At the same time, the Brazilian case cannot be comprehended without reverence to the unusual vitality of the Catholic Church. Arguably no Catholic Church in the world has changed in such deep ways since 1964. Clearly, religious issues would not have become as salient in political life without these changes.

One of the interesting debates about CEBs has involved the extent to which they reflect popular proclivities rather than an initiative from above. Analysts from both North and Latin America have taken both sides of the debate.[7] Here we adopt an intermediate perspective, under-scoring the interaction between pastoral agents and the grass roots,[8] al-beit with greater emphasis on the Church's control over grass-roots groups. In some senses, such groups represent a profound challenge to the institu-tional Church. In others, however, they are part of the Church, are sus-ceptible to control by institutional leaders,[9] and derive their own sense of legitimacy and affirmation from their linkages with the institution. I will expand on these remarks by first addressing the nature of the linkages between the institutional and the popular, and then considering the senses in which the popular has challenged institutional leaders.

Throughout Latin America, CEBs were created by "pastoral agents"—priests, nuns, bishops, and lay people commissioned by the Church. The linkages between CEBs and the institutional Church are enduring. In most dioceses, pastoral agents visit CEBs on a regular, although usually infre-quent, basis, and most dioceses also sponsor occasional gatherings of the CEBs found in a given parish or set of parishes. The materials used by the CEBs are produced by the diocese or by any of a multitude of Church institutes and organs. Most dioceses also hold training sessions for CEB leaders.

The central importance of the hierarchy is even more apparent in other initiatives of the Brazilian Church such as the Pastoral Land Com-mission (CPT), the Workers' Pastoral Commission (CPO), and the Indians' Missionary Council (CIMI). None of these can unequivocally be called grass-roots organizations since they are part of the National Conference of Brazilian Bishops (CNBB). However, all three organizations attempt to serve poor, marginalized people; all three function partially on the basis of small local groups not terribly distinct from CEBs. There is a conti-nuity from the CEBs to these three organizations (and others I do not analyze here) in terms of how local groups function and of their political perceptions. It is misleading in the case of both the CEBs and these other groups to say "These are (or are not) grass-roots groups." What is impor-tant to address is not *whether* we are dealing with grass-roots groups, but rather *how* the grass roots are related to the institutional Church.

The nature of clerical and episcopal leadership has been a major factor in determining the orientation and success or failure of the groups. It is impossible to comprehend their successes and limits without empha-sizing the linkages to the hierarchy. On the one hand, it was precisely the close linkages between the grass roots and the hierarchy which made the Brazilian Church so dynamic in the 1970s. Without support from the hierarchy, grass-roots pastoral agents would have been ineffectual in im-plementing innovations, and the Church as a whole would have been ineffective in defending human rights. In this sense the situation of grass-roots Church groups in Brazil differs significantly from that in Central America, especially Nicaragua, where there has been sharp conflict between progressive grass-roots groups and the hierarchy. (See the chapters by Cáceres, Crahan, and Williams.) On the other hand, the dependence on the hierarchy implies limits to these movements. The movements involve the grass roots, but they are part of what remains a very hierarchical institution. At a period when the international Church is moving in a conservative direction, this fact has significant implications for the future of these Catholic groups.

Nevertheless, it would be erroneous to infer that the official Church imposes its programs upon groups of poor people, or that the poor would prefer a more autonomous relationship vis-à-vis the Church. CEBs welcome and need their contact with the Church. Individuals and groups gain legitimacy, a sense of pride, and contacts in a society that has denied the popular classes all three. It is often though not always the case that CEBs fold if the pastoral agent who has most directly supported them departs.

While CEBs and other groups are a product of the Church, they are not infinitely malleable or susceptible to complete control. In their initial phases, CEBs tend to be more dependent on pastoral agents than they are at a later time. The CEBs attempt to develop more autonomous leadership, so they acquire a greater capacity to sustain themselves without weekly contact with a pastoral agent. This increasing autonomy also implies the possibility of conflict with the parent institution. The potential for serious conflict has occurred where conservative priests and prelates have attempted to control CEBs that have already reached an independent assessment of their needs. Such conflict has been common in Nicaragua, but in Brazil it has been the exception. Generally, relations between the base and the hierarchy have been harmonious in Brazil.

If grass-roots groups are created by and influenced by the institutional Church, and if they are less political than many people have suggested, why all the attention? In the first place, such groups are a novelty in terms of the Latin American Church, not only because of their efforts on behalf of social justice, but also because they have created a new role for poor lay people. In the past, the Church often voiced a concern about its pastoral work with the popular classes, and it made attempts to reach the masses, ranging from service work (hospitals or schools that were accessible to the poor) to lay movements. However, the poor never had such a vital role in the Church as they have acquired in the CEBs.

Although these groups in Brazil were almost universally sponsored by pastoral agents, they themselves became such an important Church constituency that they had some influence on the institution as a whole.

Once the grass-roots groups had become one of the most important, dynamic aspects of the Brazilian Church, only at a high cost (assuming it had wanted to) could the Church have failed to respond to the demands generated by the grass roots and by the pastoral agents who worked with the people. In this sense, the argument by theologian Leonardo Boff, that the CEBs were "reinventing" the Church,[10] is not entirely far-fetched. This does not, of course, mean that individual CEBs set about attempting to change the entire Church.

In the second place, although the political potential of grass-roots Catholic groups has often been overstated,[11] in the late 1970s a wide range of observers, from CEB ideologues to leaders of Brazil's military regime, were impressed with their potential for transforming society. For years, the military regime had controlled popular groups. When CEBs and other groups surfaced in the second half of the 1970s with surprising vitality, the government was caught off guard.

The nature of political involvements of base communities throughout Latin America has depended a great deal upon the broader political context. In revolutionary contexts, such as those found in Nicaragua and El Salvador, CEB participants have generally supported revolutionary struggles. Conversely, the profoundly conservative character of Brazil's transition to democracy contributed to defusing CEBs' political involvement. In a different scenario, grass-roots groups might well have played a more central political role.

Finally, these groups stimulate the development of popular leadership, encourage a transformation of political consciousness, and attempt to promote popular participation. While the short-term impact of these groups has been blunted by the character of Brazil's transition, there is some possibility that CEBs can promote long-range change by encouraging a transformation of the cultural underpinnings of political life. I return to this point later.

Too often analysts present a static picture of the activities and perspectives of grass-roots groups. In fact, these groups continuously evolve as they face new questions within the Church and within society at large. Subsequent sections of this chapter detail some of the changes Brazilian grass-roots groups have undergone since 1964, focusing specifically on their linkages to the political world. It should be noted that their internal dynamics, sense of spirituality, relationship to popular religion, and linkages to the institutional Church have also changed over time.

Two primary factors condition the political involvements and perspectives of grass-roots groups. First is the linkage between these groups and the institutional Church. In conservative dioceses where the bishop insists upon strong hierarchical control of grass-roots groups, the latter are generally less autonomous and more conservative. This point follows from our earlier discussion of the importance of pastoral agents in shaping the nature of the CEBs. Second is the changing character of politics in the society. The opportunities, dilemmas, and problems faced by grass-roots groups are shaped by what takes place in the society at large. Changes in political regime, in the party system, and in popular movements and organizations have a profound impact on grass-roots Catholic groups.

THE ORIGINS AND EARLY DEVELOPMENT OF CEBS, 1964–1974

Considering how significant CEBs have become in many Latin American countries, they had an inauspicious origin. For decades, the Brazilian Church had been concerned about a shortage of priests, seen as the Church's most important problem. Pope John XXIII shared this view and, in the aftermath of the Cuban revolution, encouraged North American and European priests to become missionaries in Latin America. There was a widespread perception that the shortage of priests prevented the Church from effectively reaching the masses. By the early 1960s, this concern was magnified by fears that if the Church did not reach the masses more effectively, Communists or competing religious groups would.

By the late 1950s even some relatively conservative clerics had encouraged greater lay initiative within the Church in response to this shortage. Given the shortage of priests and the enormous territory they had to cover in rural areas, there was no possibility of saying Mass everywhere once a week. One response to this situation was to give nuns more responsibility. Another was to encourage lay people to assume more active leadership so as to help compensate for the shortage of Church personnel. This strategy was not only practical; it coincided with the thrust of theological change at the time. The issue of lay responsibility and autonomy was salient in Brazilian and international Church discussions of the period.

During the 1950s and 1960s, an increasing number of Church leaders became interested in themes like community and social justice. In the face of a society undergoing rapid changes, Church leaders of all stripes were concerned with what they perceived as a breakdown of community. The interest in social justice issues reflected broader Church currents of the papacy of John XXIII, as well as the political effervescence in Brazil.[12]

The first base communities were created around 1963 in response to this conjunction of concerns.[13] Progressive priests working in rural areas realized that they could not come close to covering their entire geographical region on a given Sunday, so they began to encourage the peasants to hold a religious ceremony without them. Initially, these gatherings of peasants were known simply as Sunday religious services without the priest.[14] Clerics took the initiative in creating these early CEBs, and they did so more out of a desire for more effective evangelization than out of political concerns. While this initiative in lay autonomy marked a rupture from past ecclesiastical practices, the early CEBs were not very involved in politics (nor were they known as CEBs at the time).

Present almost from the outset and decisive in the dissemination of CEBs was a religious populism. Long accustomed to working primarily with elites, an increasing number of clergy "discovered" the people in the second half of the 1960s and throughout the 1970s. Some of the first wave of pastoral agents—especially the middle-class activists who had participated in Catholic Action movements—were scornful of traditional popular religiosity, seen as inimical to the formation of a critical political consciousness. Over time, however, this initial stance gave way to a veneration of popular practices that idealized *o povo* in romantic terms. The people were often seen as the bearers of humankind's potential: pure, generous, spiritual. As one cleric put it: "The true Evangelical values which the people live will lead us to a rethinking of our own beliefs. . . . In the silence of their hope and suffering, the people question us and give us lessons of faith. In the encounter with the people, we want to learn to be like the people, to have their generosity, their hospitality, their courage, their openness."[15] The search to work with "the people" led thousands of clerics and nuns to move to poor urban neighborhoods and even more destitute rural areas where, almost always with the blessing of their bishops, they encouraged the creation of CEBs.

If these diverse concerns motivated the Church's move to the people, what explains popular receptivity to this new pastoral work? Far too often the question is assumed away as if popular proclivities were endlessly malleable, when in fact the Church's many failures in reaching out to the masses attest to the opposite. Above all, popular receptivity to the Church's new pastoral line reflected the ongoing strength of popular religiosity in combination with the pastoral efforts to attain a new sensitivity to popular culture. In addition, the popular sectors valued the experiences of friendship, human warmth, community, and personal enpowerment that came in many CEBs.

While the broad set of concerns raised by Vatican II internationally and by a host of religious innovations in Brazil explains the creation of CEBs, this does not mean that the Church had a consciously formulated plan. On the contrary, CEBs surfaced without that name, independently, around the country in dozens of places, most of which were remote. Paradoxically, the term "base communities" was initially used by Church lead-

ers who had little if anything to do with the first CEBs. Responding to
Vatican II themes and to the need for more effective Church structures,
in the General Pastoral Plan of 1965 the CNBB began to use this term
to denote small groups within the parish. By no means did the bishops
envisage anything like what eventually emerged. To the limited extent that
they had an idea of what base communities were, it was as "the lowest
level expression of the Church." The bishops did not conceive the CEBs
as groups of poor people; on the contrary, they imagined that they would
be equally significant among all social classes. The early discussions of
base communities insisted on strong clerical control, and they did not
see CEBs as groups that would have a political impact.[16] The CEBs never
would have become as significant as they did if they had evolved as en-
visioned by the Brazilian bishops who called for their creation in 1965.

During the years following the military coup of 1964, a few progressive dioceses began to promote CEBs, especially in rural areas. In João
Pessoa, Vitória, São Mateus, Goiás Velho, and other dioceses, CEBs began
to appear. Nevertheless, it was not until after the Medellín gathering of
the Latin American Bishops Conference (CELAM) in 1968 that the CEBs
started to become more widespread. At Medellín, CELAM proclaimed
the base communities one of the most promising innovations in the Latin
American Church. This official endorsement helped encourage their dissemination to other dioceses during the following years.

Originally largely limited to rural areas, by the early 1970s CEBs began to emerge in a few dozen cities. The intersection of religious and political events was essential in this dissemination. On the religious side,
CELAM and the Vatican encouraged progressive innovation. The conservative retrenching in CELAM began later (in 1972), and the Vatican,
while squelching innovation in the Dutch Church, continued to support Church progressives in Brazil until the end of the 1970s. Meanwhile,
the Brazilian military government became notably more repressive after 1968. The combination of widespread repression that directly affected
Church people and a highly inegalitarian development model had a decisive impact on the Church. More and more bishops opposed the government, spoke out on behalf of social justice, and supported grass-roots
innovations.

This intersection between religious change and the rise of national
security states has been treated simplistically by many analysts of the Latin
American Church. It was not simply the case that repression generated
progressive Church change throughout Latin America. In some cases,
notably Argentina and Uruguay, repressive military regimes wiped out
progressive pockets of the Church without provoking any significant response from the hierarchy; indeed, in Argentina, the hierarchy helped

legitimize the military government.[17] In Brazil, however, the fact that there had already been a critical mass of progressives before 1964 prevented the government from effectively isolating Church radicals. Instead – and in contrast to what happened later in Argentina and Uruguay – repression against the Church catalyzed further ecclesiastical change.

Between 1964 and 1970, grass-roots innovations clearly outpaced those at the level of the hierarchy. The CNBB initially retreated from its reformist positions of the 1958–1963 period. Deeply divided, the bishops as a collective body did not begin to criticize the government until the end of the 1960s. Meanwhile, however, in many dioceses, especially in the Northeast and the Amazon region, Church change was rapid and deep. After 1970, this gap between developments at the grass roots and the CNBB narrowed as the CNBB began to criticize the military government in no uncertain terms. For example, in May 1970 the CNBB issued a denunciation of the government's repressive practices.

> We cannot accept the lamentable manifestations of violence in the form of physical beatings, kidnappings, deaths, or other forms of terror. . . . The postulates of justice are frequently violated by trials of a delayed and dubious nature, by imprisonments realized on the basis of suspicion or precipitous accusations, by interrogations that last for months, during which the person is held incommunicado in poor conditions, frequently without any right to defense. . . . We would be remiss if we did not emphasize our firm position against any and all kinds of torture.[18]

The most important impact of the repression upon CEBs was indirect; repression pushed an increasing number of bishops and pastoral agents toward a progressive understanding of the Church's mission. In turn, these pastoral agents went out and created CEBs. In addition, the repression and inegalitarian development models directly affected the lives of CEB participants. Poor people had to work longer hours to make as much money. Colleagues in unions were imprisoned and tortured. Unions and neighborhood associations were dismembered. Among the masses at large, such developments did not have a politicizing effect, but among poor people who had already organized and who were discussing issues of social justice, they did.

As the CNBB's criticisms of the military government deepened, its support for CEBs did likewise. By the mid-1970s, CEBs occupied the center stage of the Brazilian Church. Three related developments reflected the transformation of CEBs from groups in a dozen or so isolated dioceses into the leading edge of Church innovation in Brazil. First, the best Brazilian theologians turned their attention to CEBs and other issues related to the popular sectors. Second, the CNBB became actively involved in supporting CEBs. Finally, the Church sponsored national meetings of CEBs, thereby enhancing their visibility.

The years between 1968 and 1975 marked a decisive change in the direction of progressive theologies in Brazil. Some early radical Brazilian theologians, most notably Hugo Assmann, were deeply interested in the linkages between Christian faith and revolution. Belgian Joseph Comblin, who was a missionary in Brazil and had a deep influence on Brazilian theology, also flirted with this trend.[19] This particular variant of liberation theology was generally less seasoned and more vulnerable to attack than other lines that by the mid-1970s had clear hegemony in Brazil. Although this earlier line of liberation theology assumed that the poor would be the major beneficiaries of socialism, it did not extensively address popular themes.

During the late 1960s, a different line of progressive theology that focused on popular themes, including base communities, also emerged. The theologians who developed these themes had a diverse set of interests, but they usually worked with CEBs, and their reflections were influenced by this work. Popular religiosity was a salient theme. The Brazilian (and more generally Latin American) Church had historically perceived popular religiosity in an ambivalent way, attempting to encourage the deep faith found among some people, while also frequently scorning popular religious beliefs and practices. With the reforms encouraged by the Second Vatican Council, this ambivalence frequently gave way to direct attacks, especially among Church progressives, who assessed popular religiosity as a form of alienation. Pastoral agents working with CEBs, however, discovered that such an attitude posed serious obstacles to communication with the people. With Comblin and fellow Belgian Eduardo Hoornaert leading the way, some prominent intellectuals of the Brazilian Church began a reevaluation of popular religion that had a major impact on work with CEBs.[20]

The veneration of "the people" came to include admiration of their religious values. Moreover, priests who sharply criticized popular religious beliefs usually found themselves without much of a following. "The people" virtually demanded the continuation of many traditional practices— however "alienated" they may have been. As a priest from Crateús, Ceará wrote, "The people always want masses, baptisms, marriages. They forget that the major priority of the priest is to announce Christ's message through his words and his life. The people only want us to be religious functionaries."[21]

Most progressive dioceses and pastoral agents came to feel, in Eduardo Hoornaert's words, that "our action was too secularist to be understood and accepted by the people, who live in a universe whose reference points are predominantly religious."[22] The attacks on popular religion gave rise to efforts to support aspects of it, even while attempting to impart a more progressive understanding of faith. The reevaluation was strongly influenced by approaches to popular education that insisted upon the importance of respecting popular values.[23]

This reevaluation of popular religiosity is still marked by some deep tensions. Which aspects of popular religiosity should be supported and which should be criticized has not been resolved. Intellectuals of the progressive Church state that popular religion contains the seeds of liberation, but in my view, this is a mystification. The old orthodoxy that underscored the conservative, "alienated" aspects of traditional popular Catholicism is more convincing. While the tension has not been (and probably cannot be) resolved, the effort to respect popular religiosity was fundamental.

The ascendant line of liberation theology also dealt extensively with Bible themes and their relevance to CEBs. Two pioneer works stand out in this regard. In 1971, Leonardo Boff published his classic work, *Jesus Christ, Liberator*, an interpretation of Christ's life that emphasized his predilection for the poor. Although clearly aimed at an elite audience, Boff's book (as well as his prolific subsequent production) deeply influenced theological currents in Brazil. Carlos Mesters's book, *Palavra de Deus na História do Homem* [God's Word in Man's History], also published in 1971, is an interpretation of the Old Testament that emphasizes the struggle of the Israeli people for land and justice. It never achieved the international fame of Boff's book but, along with many other works Mesters produced, helped shape the kinds of materials used by pastoral agents in working with CEBs.[24]

Brazilian theologians and social scientists who worked with the Church also began to write extensively about the importance of CEBs in the Brazilian Church and society. The earliest theological discussion about CEBs emerged before Medellín, at a time when there was limited clarity about what the CEBs were. Spurred on by Medellín, theologians began to write on CEBs with a more progressive focus after 1968. Comblin was again prescient on this issue, publishing a book on ministries in the Latin American Church in 1969 and an article on CEBs in 1970.[25] The first Interecclesial Meeting of CEBs, held in 1975, spawned a number of works by the leading intellectuals of the popular Church, including Leonardo Boff, Carlos Mesters, J. B. Libânio, and Eduardo Hoornaert. In the late 1970s, several important theological books appeared on the CEBs.[26] Leonardo Boff's book *Eclesiogênese: As Comunidades Eclesias de Base Reinventam a Igreja* [Ecclesiogenesis: The Ecclesial Base Communities Reinvent the Church] (1977) captured much of the tone of the discussion, with its emphasis on the importance of CEBs. Virtually all of the leading intellectuals of the popular Church in Brazil have now written on the CEBs. This inordinate attention given to CEBs reflected changes that were already under way, but it also helped to legitimate those changes and to provide directions for further innovations.

A second reflection of the growing importance of CEBs in the life of the Brazilian Church was the CNBB's direct interest in and support for base communities. Numerous CNBB documents and three studies specifically on CEBs expressed a strong commitment. In 1982, a CNBB study on CEBs stated that "the Ecclesial Base Communities . . . express one of the most dynamic elements of the life of the Church. . . . Inspired by the teachings of Vatican II, our CEBs have become instruments of the construction of the Kingdom and of the realization of the hopes of our people. . . . We are increasingly convinced of the immense wealth the CEBs bring to our churches and to the revitalization of evangelizing activities."[27]

A third visible reflection of the importance CEBs acquired were the national encounters of base communities. In response to the proliferation of CEBs throughout many dioceses in a country of continental dimensions, a group of bishops and popular Church intellectuals decided to bring together CEB participants and advisors from all over the country. The first such meeting was held in 1975, in Vitória, Espírito Santo, a diocese that had been among the pioneers in experimenting with CEBs. The purpose was to share ideas and experiences, discover what was happening in other dioceses, and talk about progress and difficulties in the CEBs. Up until that point, there had been little systematic collective reflection about CEBs beyond a diocesan level, even though groups of bishops and popular Church intellectuals were interested in the subject. Subsequent meetings involving pastoral agents and CEB participants from all over the country were held in 1976, 1978, 1981, 1983, and 1986. These meetings generated intense interest in and reflection about CEBs. The 1986 meeting included seventy bishops and hundreds of pastoral agents among the more than 1500 participants.

If on the one hand, the CNBB's growing interest in and commitment to the CEBs implied greater support for these grass-roots groups, on the other, it also gave the bishops' conference greater control over the base communities. CEBs still function in markedly different ways from one diocese to the next—and even from one parish to the next. But the level of lay autonomy in the CEBs has clear limits. Conversely, never since the CNBB was founded in 1952 has it exercised greater influence over the Brazilian Church as a whole.

Often overlooked in the countless discussions about the new ideas of the progressive Church—liberation theology in particular—is its equally new institutionality. The progressive Church has created a variety of new structures—not only CEBs—that link the institution to the popular sectors. In the early 1970s, the Church created the Pastoral Land Commission (CPT); the Workers' Pastoral Commission (CPO); and the Indian Missionary Council (CIMI). Later, in the mid to late 1970s, human rights organizations linked to popular needs and pastoral groups for favela (slum) dwellers were also formed in some progressive dioceses. These organizations were created because of both the successes and some shortcomings of the CEBs. The pedagogy, theology, and political and religious ideals of the later organizations closely paralleled those of the CEBs, but their creation also reflected the CEBs' inability to deal with the authoritarian regime during its most repressive period. Some churchpeople felt the need for ecclesiastical organizations that could go beyond the very limited political involvement of CEBs. Moreover, they felt the necessity for organizations of a regional or even national character, both to have greater impact within the Church and to increase visibility and thereby enhance protection against repression. The CEBs grew in number, but they remained less political than the CPO, CPT, and CIMI, and they had no national or regional organizations.

The CPT and CIMI were created by pastoral agents in the Amazon region, though both organizations acquired a national identity within a short period of time. The precursor to the CPT was created in 1972 at an Amazon regional encounter. Officially created in 1975 in its present form, the CPT quickly became active in many dioceses in the Northeast, and during the rest of the 1970s began to work in other parts of the country as well. The CPT has played a leading role in defending legal rights of the peasants, documenting violations of human rights, developing religious publications for use with peasants, and encouraging peasants to organize. CIMI was created in April 1972 as a means of helping missionaries to do effective pastoral work with the Indians. Its work has ranged from defending the Indians' legal rights to holding workshops for the missionaries. Because of their work with some of the poorest people in what has been the most violent region in Brazil, both the CPT and CIMI leaders experienced significant government repression during the Médici and Geisel years. They were able to survive only due to the protection of Latin America's most progressive hierarchy.

CIMI and the CPT helped serve as a model for the creation of the Workers' Pastoral Commission and other organizations like archdiocesan commissions for favela dwellers and for the marginalized population. These organizations had a specifically Catholic character, but they were more involved in political work than the base communities. Even though the base communities have received more attention, these other Catholic organizations have also been important in Brazilian politics and in the Brazilian Church. These organizations involved pastoral agents and lay people who were interested in a Church group that would be more political than the CEBs. Among the laity, the participants were generally CEB members with the greatest interest in politics. Even though I focus primarily on the CEBs here, the existence of a vast network of different organizations and groups linking the institutional Church to the grass roots is noteworthy.[28]

GRASS-ROOTS GROUPS AND POLITICS, 1974–1979

Before 1974 Catholic groups engaged in political actions of a very limited scope. In urban areas, they occasionally petitioned the state to provide rudimentary services. In rural areas, they occasionally protested land expulsions; or in the case of the CPT and CIMI, they denounced some particularly egregious incidents of violence against peasants and Indians. Nevertheless, Catholic groups were virtually the only opposition popular organizations; other popular organizations were dormant as a consequence of the repression.

During the second half of the 1970s Church groups continued to focus primarily on religious activities and on community. However, the context in which they operated changed considerably and, as a result, their linkages to social movements, political parties, and the state changed. Two changes in the political context stand out as particularly important. First, in 1974, newly installed President Ernesto Geisel (1974–1979) began the lengthy and cautious process of political liberalization that, after many vicissitudes, finally culminated in the restoration of democracy in March 1985. Over a period of time, repression against popular organizations generally decreased, even though in vast parts of the countryside elite violence and state complicity are still rampant under the new democratic government. Second, by the end of the Geisel presidency, popular movements were burgeoning all over the country. Neighborhood movements were the first to revive, springing up in the major cities in the mid-1970s. In 1978, the labor movement in greater São Paulo exploded with the first major strike in a decade, beginning a wave of strikes that surprised the government and opposition alike. Extant peasant unions began to reorganize and new ones were created.

Grass-roots Catholic participants played a major role in the strengthening of many—though not all—popular movements. Many individuals with no prior history of political involvement became active in popular movements as a result of their work in the Church. Catholic activists emerged as leaders of a large number of movements. Although only a minority of CEB members actively participated in popular movements, most others lent passive support.

Yet the relationship between popular movements and Catholic groups was far from consistently smooth. Conservative clerics generally opposed the popular movements, and even in progressive dioceses many tensions arose. The following pages suggest the nature of some of these tensions.

Because they had arisen after the coup in a period of significant repression, the Catholic groups had never faced the problem of defining their identity in relation to popular movements. They had promoted a discourse committed to popular liberation and popular struggles, but had never needed to translate that discourse into political practice. The CEBs and other groups faced the problem of defining their own role in the new situation. What is the proper function of CEBs and other Catholic groups? To what extent should they become involved in politics? On paper, the answer was clear. All of these groups stated their support for popular movements, but they clearly enunciated a principle of not becoming the vehicle for channeling popular demands. As the CPO of São Paulo stated,

> The Workers' Pastoral Commission is not an organization to defend and struggle for workers' rights and interests. It is a Church organization for the working class. Its goal is to develop activists for the Church and not for the labor movement. . . . It often activates movements which include other groups, but it is not able to organize these groups.[29]

In practice, however, the problem was more complex: Church documents often simultaneously overstated both the political involvement of grass-roots Catholic groups and the autonomy of popular movements vis-à-vis the Church. On the former account, the greater part of the CEBs remained relatively aloof from politics. Eduardo Hoornaert described his experience with CEBs in a report for the First Interecclesial Meeting of CEBs in 1975: "The leaders are well trained, [but] without a critical consciousness in the political sphere . . . with a strong spirituality open to domestic and neighborhood problems, but not political ones properly speaking."[30]

Likewise, the autonomy of popular movements vis-à-vis the Church was often not so clear as the discourse indicated.[31] In some regions of the country, including most rural areas, the level of repression remained high. In the most conflictual regions, like vast parts of the Amazon, the peasants were incapable of organizing effective unions which could withstand the repression. There the Church, with the CPT leading the way, continued to be the only institution which could defend the popular classes. Even in developed urban areas there continued to be sporadic repression against popular movements, which were still fragile. In progressive dioceses, the Church legitimated the movements, and a significant number of leaders were Catholic activists. In many cases the same people were leaders of the local base community, the CPO or CPT, and the labor movement or neighborhood association.

The close linkages between the Church and the popular movements were apparent even in the case of the best organized and most autonomous movement, the metal workers' union in greater São Paulo. In successive years between 1978 and 1980 the union went on strike, only to incur the wrath of the state, which declared the strikes illegal, imprisoned some leaders, and attempted to intimidate the rank-and-file into returning to work. Each year the Church intervened on behalf of the union when the going got especially difficult. When union offices were closed, the Church opened its doors as a meeting place for workers. The Church's highly visible support for the workers and sharp criticisms of the government made possible a continuation of the strike. CEBs all over the country collected funds for the ABC workers, and Bishop Cláudio Hummes was one of the negotiators for the union.[32] Even in São Paulo, where popular movements were generally strongest, Catholic groups frequently served as a substitute for autonomous popular organizations. The largest unions and the largest neighborhood federation (Society of Friends of the Neighborhood) had a history of close linkages to the state which made them unreliable in the eyes of most grass-roots Church activists. Consequently, the CEBs often directly attempted to obtain urban services,[33] and the CPO was involved in efforts to transform the unions.

Church discourse encouraged Catholics to participate in autonomous popular movements. In practice, however, this issue was again more complex than the discourse suggests. A small minority of radical pastoral agents encouraged the Catholic groups to become political vehicles, neglecting the specifically religious work. In this case, Church groups would be the basis for the popular movements; thus encouragement to participate was real, but the autonomy was not. At the other end of the spectrum, many clerics who were hostile to more autonomous popular organization argued that outside groups would exploit or manipulate the people. Consequently, they discouraged people from participating in popular movements that were not controlled by the Church. In this case, there was neither real encouragement to participate in popular movements nor autonomy between these movements and Church groups.

A recurring problem in popular movements was tension between the Church and the Marxist left. During the late 1960s and early 1970s the Marxist left, decimated by the repression, began to form tacit alliances with the progressive Church. Rethinking a Leninist past, much of the left became more concerned than ever with human rights, liberal democracy, and popular organizing.[34] Because of the concomitant changes in the Left and the Church, by the end of the Médici period there was a confluence of some objectives in many progressive dioceses. Both opposed the dictatorship; both were interested in popular organization. The Church frequently provided to young leftists the space and protection they needed to do any popular organizing. By the end of the Geisel period, however, the initial harmony between the left and the Church had evanesced in many cases. With the strengthening of popular organizations, there emerged competing conceptions of how to lead the popular movements, often causing sharp conflict among forces which had earlier been allies in the struggle against the dictatorship. Some pastoral agents were concerned that participation in autonomous popular movements would subject the popular sectors to manipulation. They feared that the popular movements would coopt and undermine Church groups. Even many progressive pastoral agents criticized the politically motivated popular organizers ("external agents" in the Brazilian lexicon) for failing to respect popular values. Non-Catholics engaged in grass-roots organizing countered that these clerics simply wanted to dominate the movement themselves. They viewed the Catholic groups as somewhat naive, limited, and unrealistic in their assessment of how to change Brazilian society. In their perception, what was needed were mass organizations which could effectively mobilize large numbers of people, not small discussion groups like the CEBs.[35]

Despite these tensions, Catholic groups deeply influenced popular movements. Many leaders of Catholic groups became leaders of popular movements, and the majority of CEB participants, while not active politically, nevertheless lent passive support to the movements. Equally important, the style and values of the new popular movements frequently drew upon those of the Catholic groups. Partially in response to the failures of previous efforts at popular organization, but also partially in response to the success of the Church's work, issues like grass-roots participation, internal democracy, and greater autonomy vis-à-vis the state became more salient concerns.

The nature of the relationship between progressive Church groups and popular movements differed significantly according to diocese, parish, region of the country, and kind of movement. For example, in São Paulo, because the network of neighborhood associations was closely linked to the state, the base communities played a significant direct role in seeking urban services. In Nova Iguaçu, base communities supported the neighborhood movement, but the movement was more autonomous. In urban areas, neighborhood associations were generally more closely linked to the Church than were the labor unions. In part, this was because labor had a stronger history of previous mobilization, and many of the pre-1968 leaders contributed to the movement's reorganization in the second half of the 1970s. In addition, like the Church, neighborhood associations were organized on a territorial basis, so people who had been active in the Church groups were already well known in the neighborhood. Especially in the most repressive rural areas, Church groups remained actively involved in defending peasants' rights.

The relationship of Catholic groups to political parties and the state, which became the outstanding political dilemma after 1979, did not yet loom as a central concern during the Geisel years. Catholic groups maintained a profound skepticism regarding political parties. During the course of the authoritarian regime, the MDB, the official opposition party, had not distinguished itself by its active defense of the popular sectors. Catholic movements neither expected nor sought support from it. Prior to the 1974 elections, the issue of political parties was not even a subject of discussion in the CEBs and other Catholic groups. Basic group survival and development was the main concern. Due to the combination of the MDB's surprising victory in 1974 and the regime's decision to promote political liberalization, which enabled the opposition party to become more assertive in the ensuing years, by the 1978 elections the party question had become more important. In many dioceses, Catholic groups discussed the elections and the parties and what they both represented. While still maintaining a basic skepticism, most Catholic groups voted for the MDB. In São Paulo some went even further. Several Catholic activists, convinced of the importance of the elections, decided to run for political office, and a couple (Irma Passoni and Aurélio Peres) were elected with most of their support coming from CEBs.

During the Geisel years, these Catholic groups generally rejected the state as an arena of political action. They saw the state as corrupt and unresponsive to popular demands. They often dismissed the *abertura* (liberalization process) as a government ploy to gain legitimacy without resolving popular problems, and to a significant extent this perception was grounded in reality. While the regime made meaningful concessions in liberalizing the political arena, repression against the popular sectors did not diminish overnight.

Although their discourse generally expressed a radical rejection of the state, sometimes in practice Catholic groups had to work with it. Even the limited community actions during the early Geisel years frequently led Catholic groups to petition the state for social services. What was, however, a relative novelty was the rejection of clientelistic practices. Even in cases where Catholic groups engaged in community actions that involved making demands upon the state, they maintained greater autonomy vis-à-vis politicians than had been the practice in the past. The insistence upon avoiding clientelistic linkages to politicians and upon maintaining autonomy became one of the characteristic trademarks of the grassroots Catholic groups. In this sense, they helped introduce new practices that would affect other social movements.

GRASS-ROOTS GROUPS AND POLITICS, 1979–1985

The changing political climate created by political liberalization constantly created new challenges and dilemmas for grass-roots Catholic groups during the Figueiredo presidency (1974–1985). This is not the place for a detailed account of political changes between 1979 and 1985, but we should note briefly the most relevant evolutions. First, the use of repression declined even though it did not come to an end. Second, labor unions, peasant unions, and urban social movements were considerably more visible than they had been since at least 1968. Third, the opposition political parties became stronger—strong enough to help displace parts of the military regime by 1985. In 1979, a change in party legislation precipitated a move from a two-party system to a multiparty system, with some key schisms in the opposition resulting. Finally, electoral channels became more meaningful as state governorships were disputed in 1982 for the first time since 1965. These changes meant that Catholic groups faced a new political landscape.

As the *abertura* allowed popular organizations to become stronger and as the party debate intensified, some intellectuals of the popular Church emphasized the specifically religious identity of Catholic groups. In an article which was disseminated throughout progressive dioceses, Frei Betto argued,

> The Church cannot attempt to substitute for political parties, unions, neighborhood associations, which are the mechanisms specific to the political struggle. . . . Asking the base communities to also become the union movement, a grass-roots party organization, or a social center is a mistake. . . . The specificity of the base communities lies in their religious character. The people who participate are not motivated by professional, educational, or political interests. They are there because of their faith.[36]

In a similar vein, in 1982 an important CNBB document on CEBs stated,

> We need to maintain clearly the distinction between CEBs and popular movements. Popular movements are social movements of the poor classes and they work toward the liberation and sociopolitical promotion of the people. They are not Church movements, and they do not depend on the

Church. The CEBs must become aware of this to avoid occupying a space which is not theirs. In the same vein, the CEBs would lose their identity if they changed their mode of being and their explicit religious values to accommodate popular movements.[37]

This attempt to establish limits to the political involvement of Catholic groups and to define their specificity also reflected the changing mood in the international Church. Radical Catholic politics, liberation theology, and base communities all came under attack from the Vatican, the Latin American Bishops Conference, and conservative Brazilian prelates. The neo-conservative movement was weaker and emerged later in Brazil than most countries in Latin America, but by 1982 it became a force to be reckoned with. Conflict between the Vatican and the Brazilian Church became serious, although rarely did the Vatican directly confront the Brazilian Church until the sanctions imposed against theologian Leonardo Boff in 1985. The latter move had sharp repercussions among pastoral agents working with CEBs, as Boff was extremely well known and venerated. In a less publicized case, sanctions were also imposed against Clodovis Boff in 1984. Then in June 1985, in response to Vatican pressures, the CNBB issued a statement critical of some versions of liberation theology, addressed to pastoral agents and CEBs. Other measures, although not specifically aimed at the Brazilian Church, nevertheless were perceived (and surely intended) as warnings to progressive Church people throughout the continent. Particularly important in this regard were the September 1984 document on liberation theology, published by the Vatican Congregation for the Doctrine of the Faith, and the litany of conflicts in Nicaragua with the Vatican and the hierarchy on one side, and the grass-roots Church and the government on the other.[38]

Grass-roots groups have been one of the main objects of attack from the neo-conservative Church leaders. These leaders state that they favor the idea of such groups, but are concerned about their excessive political involvement and about an absence of spirituality and religious preparation. In this view the grass-roots groups threaten hierarchical authority lines within the Church. These lines of authority were established by Christ, and they are immutable over time. Therefore, while the neo-conservatives accept the idea of small ecclesial groups, they argue that such groups must be closely supervised by the hierarchy. As Archbishop Salles states the case, "The CEBs are Church and therefore are born from Christ; their mission is not determined by the people."[39] By 1985, the issue of how to face these pressures and sanctions had become a concern among leaders of the grass-roots Church network.

More prominent on the progressive Church agenda was the evolving relationship between grass-roots groups and politics. Some of the same issues which had existed during the Geisel period – especially the autonomy of Catholic groups vis-à-vis popular movements – continued to be present. But during the Figueiredo period, the relationship between these groups and political parties became the burning issue.

On paper, there was a consensus among Church intellectuals that the party question was important, but that the Church would not promote any particular party. But in practice many issues were difficult to resolve. Some leaders of the popular Church initially maintained that the parties were too distant from the popular classes to merit support. They argued that the parties were elitist, and that primary efforts should be directed toward popular organization. Leaders with this orientation did little or nothing to encourage the grass roots to discuss or participate in the party restructuring. They so strongly insisted upon autonomy of the grass-roots organizations that they essentially rejected the parties. This exclusive emphasis on grass-roots groups is apparent in a report about CEBs in Minas Gerais: "The poor people have to organize themselves, believing in each other, without being dependent on politicians or the wealthy."[40] In doing so, they doomed themselves to political marginalization, for the parties were becoming an increasingly important arena. Most grass-roots participants themselves were relatively uninterested in the party debate. As J. B. Libânio summarized, "Some groups refer to an aversion the people have to discussing politics. . . . The CEBs are not inclined towards party politics, but towards local and union struggles. . . . Firmly engaged in concrete popular struggles, the communities view politicians and parties with a certain discredit. They don't put much hope in them."[41]

At the opposite end of the spectrum were those who were absorbed by the parties. Many leaders of grass-roots organizations felt the party question was so important that they devoted themselves principally to partisan politics. Some of the most politically astute Catholic participants often found themselves with little time for their Church involvement. While they remained deeply marked by their Church experiences and committed to radical Catholic principles, it was impossible to actively participate in a political party, a popular movement, the CPO, and a base community all at once. By the mid-1980s, the withdrawal of former CEB leaders from Church groups was common.

This process of CEB leaders leaving the Church has provoked interesting reactions. For years, liberation theologians have insisted on the image of the Church being a service to the world. And in fact, in forming political leaders, the popular Church was providing a service. Yet not surprisingly, it has been difficult for the Church to accept these departures. It wants to claim for itself the leaders created under its own wings. A nonresolvable dilemma arises: the Church wants people to participate in politics; those who are most active in politics find they have no time or patience for the Church; Church personnel are frustrated when ex-activists no longer create time for the Church.

Compounding the divisions between those who were uninterested in parties and those who were absorbed in them was a second problem: which party to support. Most grass-roots leaders who opted for a party chose the PT or the PMDB. But a large number did not opt for any party, and others (especially in Rio de Janeiro and Rio Grande do Sul) joined the PDT, a left-of-center populist party. In the Northeast some grass-roots activists even supported the government party, the PDS.[42]

There was a particular affinity between the PT and grass-roots Church groups. Indeed, it is difficult to even imagine the existence of the PT had grass-roots Church groups not existed. The PT was inspired by progressive Catholic ideas emphasizing popular participation, grass-roots democracy, popular organization, and basic needs.[43] Like the popular Church, the PT placed greater emphasis on popular needs than on liberal concerns such as electoral arrangements. In many parts of the country, grass-roots Catholic leaders played the predominant role in the PT. In 1983, according to one study, 71 percent of CEB participants who made a party option supported the PT.[44] Nevertheless, progressive Catholic groups never uniformly supported the PT. Progressive Catholic influence was pronounced in the PT partially because the party failed to win broad support elsewhere.

Until the early 1980s, the view that parties were unimportant was still widespread among grass-roots groups, especially the CEBs. Many CEB activists perceived the parties as elitist and unworthy of support. They believed that popular mobilization, and not political parties, was the best means of effecting profound political change. As the 1982 elections approached, however, most politically aware Catholic activists, realizing that elections mattered more than in the past, became interested in, and sometimes even involved in, partisan politics. A large number of dioceses issued electoral pamphlets to be discussed among grass-roots groups. The most influential pamphlet, developed by the Archdiocese of São Paulo, noted the importance of elections:

> The distance which separates the popular sectors from the state cannot be overcome just through the dynamics of the popular movements. The living and working conditions of the great majority of the exploited and marginalized population can only be transformed if the popular classes are capable of influencing the centers of decisions and power.[45]

By the November 1982 elections, most of the CPO leaders had made party options, and a number of CPT and CEB leaders had done likewise. Even where grass-roots participants did not make a clear decision for one party or another, they were at least exposed to discussion about the significance of the parties.

Over time, the political involvement of CEB leaders deepened considerably. By the 1986 national encounter of CEBs, a Church intellectual who had earlier noted the political weakness of the base communities observed "an enormous progress in political conscience."[46] Accompanying this deepening involvement in politics was an ever clearer option in favor of the PT. But still, two critical questions linger. The first is whether the deepening political involvement is accompanied by a parallel depth in political sophistication. The second is whether the political involvement of the average CEB member has also deepened in commensurable fashion. My impression is that despite the radical political rhetoric, most CEB members have unsophisticated political views and relatively shallow political involvements. The results of an extensive study in Vitória, one of the most established progressive dioceses in Brazil, are revealing. "The Church of Vitória is seen as a politicized Church, but the questionnaires are not revealing this. Few lay people are committed to social and political service."[47]

The debate about parties at the grass-roots level had as a counterpart debates among leading Church intellectuals about the proper linkage between religion and politics. Most Church intellectuals felt that the CEBs should focus primarily on religious issues. Frei Betto was the leader of this trend, arguing that CEBs should concentrate on prayer above politics. Betto argued that Catholics should not organize as Catholics to engage in politics. Doing so, he reasoned, would reproduce the clericalism of earlier, generally conservative experiences. Moreover, he maintained that what was at stake in the political world was not a Christian project, but a political project. A minority position was represented by Clodovis Boff, who argued that the CEBs should get more involved in party politics as a means of enhancing their efficacy.[48]

By 1983 one of the problems among grass-roots Catholics was an increasing disenchantment with conventional politics. The political parties and the opposition state governments did not become as responsive to the demands of the social movements as many had hoped. The PMDB in particular moved in a conservative direction following its merger with the center-right PP in December 1981. Over time, some of the political elites who had been wedded to the authoritarian regime flocked to the PMDB or the PFL, with which the PMDB established an alliance in 1984. The PMDB thus had a constant infusion of "new" conservative blood. The PT was the only party which managed to overcome this problem, but it was plagued by an amalgam of difficulties. It maintained an image as a leftist party, committed to strong linkages with social movements, but because the party itself fared badly in the elections, it was incapable of altering the conservative character of the transition to democracy.

Many expected the victory of opposition governments to enhance the role of social movements in states such as São Paulo and Rio de Janeiro, where well-established movements existed. These expectations were largely frustrated. When the opposition came to power it was faced with the classic dilemmas of governing, which differ from those of opposing. In opposition, the PMDB and the PDT supported strong, autonomous social movements, which helped further the parties' objective of eroding the military regime. In government, they attempted to contain these movements through traditional mechanisms of clientelism and cooptation.

This disappointment was reproduced after 1985 at the federal level. The vast mobilizations for direct elections in early 1984 created the sensation that Brazilian society was becoming more politicized than it ever had been in the past. In conjunction with these broad mobilizations, the end of the military government created a widespread sense of optimism. But by 1987, when the economy took a nosedive, a profound pessimism set in. The Sarney government veered increasingly to the right; the minimum real wage reached a historic low in 1987; and popular movements faced mounting difficulties.

From the viewpoint of religious activists, the political parties (except the PT) were to blame for the breakdown in communication between grass-roots groups and the parties. Not surprisingly, party leaders took a different view. Federal Senator Fernando Henrique Cardoso of the PMDB, explaining the misunderstandings between the Church and the PMDB government of the state of São Paulo, stated in 1984, "At times, the Church demands moral solutions for a structural crisis, leading to a certain lack of communication."[49]

THE RADICAL CATHOLIC VIEW OF POLITICS

Cardoso's comments call to mind some difficulties religious activists have found in the political sphere.[50] In broadest form, these difficulties result from the absolutism of many religious activists in a sphere (politics) where absolutes are virtually impossible to obtain. There is a tension between the absolutes of religious life and the constant compromise of political life. Bringing an ethical dimension to politics can have important benefits, but it also presents tensions.

Some leading intellectuals of the popular Church have sophisticated understandings of the contemporary world but, at the grass-roots level, many pastoral agents and lay activists have sectarian political views. Motivated by strong and clear conceptions of what is right and wrong, they tend to treat political problems as moral issues. Purity is an important motivating principle for community and political action. Within this moral framework, the complexity of the political world is vastly understated. Thus anything which is not good is evil, unacceptable. The grey or intermediate spaces, in which strategy, negotiation, compromise, and political skill are essential, are rejected as "bourgeois," as compromised by the dominant order.

There is often a strong sense of righteousness within the community and among pastoral agents, not unlike the righteousness found among conservative religious groups, that leads to the attitude that the group's political views are the ones Jesus inspired, while other political positions fall short of Jesus's teachings or are sinful. Within this world view compromise can become unacceptable on moral grounds. The wisdom of the old adage "Politics is the art of the possible" is lost. Ironically, the rejection of compromise and second-best solutions has sometimes contributed to a situation in which the political center has made alliances with the right rather than the left. Especially in a country like Brazil, which has notably elitist and conciliatory political traditions, compromise and negotiation are an indispensable feature of party politics and of governing. This is not to suggest that all grass-roots Catholic activists failed to come to terms with the importance of compromise in political life, or that all opposition politicians outside the PT reneged on their commitments to popular concerns. But the conflict between the logic of moderate opposition politicians and that of religious activists was ubiquitous after 1982, contributing to ongoing tensions between democratic state governments and the Church.

For years, the notion of "liberation," with its utopian overtones, has been prominent in popular Church discourse in Brazil. In the 1970s, this notion was a vague reference, but by the mid-1980s, it became identified with socialism. Yet in practice, liberation and socialism were far from attainable. Even as the economy suffered wild vicissitudes in a generally bad decade, the capitalist system in Brazil was hardly on the verge of a collapse. Progressive Catholic intellectuals generally dismissed the significance of incremental improvements within the capitalist order, while longing for a socialist system that was a chimera in the Brazilian context. Establishing such an impossible objective almost surely contributed to political frustration at the grass-roots.

Popular Church intellectuals sketched out and encouraged a view of politics that made popular participation the primary vehicle of political change. They did not, however, address issues such as what institutional mechanisms would encourage this change, how participation would be encouraged, or how popular movements would deal with state institutions. An extreme instance of this difficulty in understanding or dealing with institutional aspects of the political world is found in a pastoral letter by the bishops of Paraíba, providing guidelines for the November 1986 elections. "People should vote for whomever has always demonstrated concern for the collectivity, for the common good, *regardless of whether he/she is a candidate.*"[51] Exactly how one votes for someone who is not a candidate, or what good it would do, is not explained. This is a clear example of the combination of uncompromising moral logic and ineffective political praxis.

Parties, politicians, and the state are frequently scorned. Politicians are generally portrayed as self-interested and self-serving, with no sincere interest in popular causes.[52] These perceptions are not entirely misguided, and indeed conform to Schumpeter's characterizations of how politicians function even in advanced democracies.[53] However, this view of the political world overlooks the fact that beginning with the 1978 elections, a number of elected officials were genuinely committed to popular causes. Moreover, it is a view that easily generates lack of interest in democratic institutions on the grounds that all politicians are the same. While this sentiment is comprehensible in light of the incomplete and elitist character of the Brazilian transition, it can easily lead to apathy in attempting to work within democratic institutions. Such apathy is worrisome in view of the fragile character of democratic institutions in Brazil.

There is one salient exception to the generalized rejection of parties and politicians, namely, the PT and its politicians. Often, the PT is treated as sacrosanct, as though God supported the party.[54] Support for the PT often acquires moralistic overtones: good people and politicians are in the PT; those who support other options are bourgeois. A deeper analysis of the problems of the PT has been lacking within Church circles.

Catholic activists tend to view politics in ethical terms. Injustice exists because the wealthy and politicians are evil or egotistic, as though the poor were never egotistic, or as though all politicians and wealthy people were. Evil and egotism, in turn, are results of capitalism. One CEB report captured this attitude in affirming that the root of the current situation (poverty, marginalization) "is egotism and the power of money. In the first instance, this is capitalism, . . . a form of exploitation where some people keep the profits and others do the work."[55]

Even among some leading intellectuals of the popular Church, analysis of capitalism has become facile. Clodovis and Leonardo Boff, for example, write that poverty is "endogenous to the capitalist system," ignoring that several capitalist countries (particularly in Scandinavia) have, by almost any measure, the lowest incidence of poverty in the world. They go on to aver that "The most that can be done in capitalism is the attenuation, not the elimination, of injustice."[56] This claim is incontrovertible, but it is universally true, not a problem limited to capitalist societies.

The perceptions about Brazilian politicians and capitalism contain important kernels of truth. Power in Brazil is patrimonial; relatively few politicians defend popular causes. The role of political parties and the Congress in the new democratic period has been lamentable. The dominant party, the PMDB, has almost completely reneged on its historic commitments. The second and third largest parties in Congress represent the center-right and the right. Politicians and the political process are widely demoralized, and for understandable reasons. Corruption, perverse and pervasive clientelism, and egregious trading of political favors have abounded. Surveys underscore how widespread disaffection with the political class is. And despite the dynamism of Brazilian capitalism between 1945 and 1980, widespread poverty prevails, and today Brazil has among the most pronounced inequalities in the world. Yet the simplicity of Catholic analysis is still striking. For example, it attributes to capitalism in general social problems that have derived specifically from Brazilian capitalism. Few other capitalist systems have generated such extraordinary inequalities. Implicit in this extrapolation from Brazilian capitalism to all capitalist systems is a view that reform is inadequate—indeed, bordering on worthless. Once again, this viewpoint easily leads to rejecting alliances with reformist forces—and often to political isolation.

In addition, there is difficulty in attributing the frustrations of the transition or the egregious socioeconomic inequalities in part to popular origins. The popular vote was responsible for electing the current congress,[57] and fragmentation among popular movements has contributed to weakening the popular presence in politics. Yet these issues have not received the deeper analysis they deserve. To the contrary: in 1986, when the labor movement and urban popular movements were generally having more troubles than five years earlier in mobilizing people, the National Encounter of Base Communities reported that popular movements "are growing all over Brazil, moving from struggles of resistance to struggles of conquest."[58] This particular statement suggests that the interpretation of empirical reality is sometimes as flawed as the broader analysis that underlies it.

Alongside the repudiation of capitalism is a generally uncritical view of socialism. At the grass roots, socialism is treated in markedly romantic ways—generally, with very little knowledge about what it means. There is considerable difficulty in grasping the fact that politics inherently involves domination, and that some individuals will strive for power in ruthless ways, regardless of how "good" or "bad" the social system is.

In a similar vein, there is difficulty grasping that some social problems are problems of humanity rather than of capitalism. Authoritarianism, inequality, war, bureaucratization, pollution, and poverty are found in capitalist and socialist societies alike, albeit in different degrees. Although it would be absurd to expect poor Catholics to have a sophisticated view of socialism, one finds a romantic conception even among many leading intellectuals of the popular Church. The fertile debates about the authoritarian character of "real socialism" have found little echo among popular Church intellectuals.[59]

In recent years, some prominent Brazilian theologians have issued highly apologetic statements about Cuba, Nicaragua, and the Soviet Union.[60] To deny the important achievements of these revolutionary regimes in the areas of health and education, among others, would be blind. But criticism of markedly militaristic and authoritarian regimes such as Cuba and the Soviet Union does not make one a bourgeois reactionary. Some of the most important thought of the European left in the past fifteen to twenty years has been extremely critical of the Soviet Union: Lefort, Castoriadis, Foucault, etc. Most of the intellectuals of the Brazilian Church seem utterly unaware of the existence of this important corpus of social theory. Moreover, they seem unaware of the criticisms of "real socialism" leveled from within the Socialist bloc itself, in which Polish thinkers (Kuran, Schaff, Kolakowski, Michnick) have played a particularly prominent role. And the problem is not only one of lack of awareness of important debates in Western and Eastern Europe. Some leading Brazilian intellectuals have also called attention to the need to invent more democratic traditions within the left. From different perspectives, Carlos Nelson Coutinho, Leandro Konder, Francisco Weffort, and Fernando Henrique Cardoso, among others, have addressed this issue, yet many prominent Church intellectuals seem unaware of these debates.

After a trip to Cuba, Clodovis Boff wrote that, "It is necessary to avoid bourgeois illusions. One of these is the belief that freedom exists only where there is party pluralism."[61] Yet what Clodovis Boff presents as a bourgeois illusion is, in my view, far more than that: party competition is an essential requisite for a democratic political regime, although it far from ensures the existence of a just society. Amazingly, Boff goes on to note, even while downplaying their significance, several reasons why the Cuban Catholic Church has been less than fully enamored with the government. It is difficult to get permission for foreign priests to work in Cuba; the Church has almost no access to the media (which is fully state owned); practicing Catholics have limited access to leadership positions in the party, in mass organizations, and in the university. Similar governmental pressures against the Church formed part of the basis for Boff's opposition to military rule in Brazil.

Similarly, there is little awareness that conflict of interests inheres in society. Politics is seen (as it also is by the Catholic Right) as an expression of the search for the common good rather than, as from a liberal perspective, an expression of necessarily competing interests. The nineteenth-century ultramontanist rejection of liberalism – not in the Brazilian sense, of a conservative anti-statism, but in the North American sense of an open (although not equal) competition of political forces – has not been entirely superceded. Among significant sectors of the Catholic Left, there is still a perception that, while class struggle is a positive force in social change, ultimately, political conflict is pernicious. This rejection of conflict is not peculiar to the Catholic Left: it affects other sectors of the left, as well as vast parts of the right in Brazil. The view that there is a "common good" can lead to the suppression of viewpoints that oppose this good. Thus, for example, the kind of criticism voiced here is often dismissed as "bourgeois." Also, among the more sectarian pastoral agents and grass-roots activists there is often an indifference toward liberal democratic institutions. One expression of this indifference is the view that the new government is no different from the military government. (It must be noted that there are indeed many continuities; the new government is not unequivocally democratic. Moreover, the capacity of even a clearly democratic government to address the abject poverty that faces millions of Brazilians, without profound structural changes, is questionable.)

Catholic activists often tend to reject outsiders, whether politicians, intellectuals, or leftist militants interested in community organizing. The "people" are pure, and they need to organize themselves for their own liberation. Outsiders, in contrast, are self-interested, unprincipled in comparison to the Catholic activists. "People from the universities always show up to do research, wanting to enter into the popular organizations. We saw that these people aren't peasants and that they want to take advantage of the people."[62] A viewpoint that followers of the faith are somehow better than other people, more worthy of trust, is still common. Of course, such a position is not unique to progressive Catholics; it exists among a variety of faiths and among many secular ideologies as well. This perception that Catholic activists are motivated by altruism, whereas others are self-interested, helps explain the existence of practices and perceptions that have led non-Catholic activists to accuse the Church of being authoritarian.

One finds among grass-roots activists a simplistic conception of society: society is divided into the rich and the poor or the oppressed and the oppressors; the rich exploit the poor; the government is allied with the rich and foreign interests[63] against the poor; the poor need to rely on themselves to change society. These characterizations contain important kernels of truth, but it is also the case that Brazilian society has become quite heterogeneous, that the class structure is more complex than a simple division into exploited and exploiters suggests, that the poor frequently have conflicting interests, and that there are meaningful divisions within the elite. Remarkably, the simplistic division into the rich and the poor, the good and the evil, has impeded the articulation of an analysis based on social classes. In this sense, the analytical tools which are sometimes used to explain social reality are not Marxist, but rather pre-Marxist, and indeed premodern.

There emerges an inchoate view of a popular utopia, of a harmonious world to be brought about by popular organization. "Someday we shall have a party of the people, formed exclusively by elements of the people, based on love of our country. The candidates of such a party will not be academics, nor wealthy people, but simple workers and peasants."[64] This kind of view is not limited to Catholic activists but it is particularly strong among them.

This quest for a popular utopia in a world without domination has probably limited the political efficacy of Catholic activists since their political activities are based on dubious assumptions. Moreover, it has surely contributed to the enormous frustration with the Sarney government. In a society in which parties and politicians rarely have served the needs of the poor, widespread skepticism among Catholic activists about traditional politics is neither surprising nor indefensible. But this skepticism made it more difficult for Catholic activists to act in the political sphere at a time when conventional politics were not challenged in broad ways.

The problem is not only one of political efficacy. There is also a real danger that because of the facile analyses of social reality, the potentially innovative character of these groups will be lost. The innovative side of the grass-roots groups resided precisely in their internally democratic character. Today, they run the risk of adopting sectarian—and ultimately authoritarian—views of the political world, even if they continue to promote grass-roots democracy.

The intellectuals of the popular Church have a responsibility to attempt to overcome this problem. For contrary to the populist claims of some Church intellectuals, these conceptions of society do not spring spontaneously from the base, but rather result, in good measure, from conceptions transmitted by pastoral agents, who in turn are strongly influenced by the "organic intellectuals" of the Church. In this sense, there is a striking deficiency within the Church. Social and political analysis has rested in the hands of distinguished theologians and bishops who unfortunately have facile conceptions of society and politics. Not that there is anything wrong with theologians or bishops engaging in social and political analysis. The problem is rather that their analyses are not well informed. The relative paucity of good social scientists working within the Church is noteworthy, as is the need for more sophisticated political analysis in an institution that has assumed vital importance as a moral critic of the political order. Being a moral critic can justly be defended as the Church's prominent contribution to the political order—but even this function requires greater sophistication in political analysis than several prominent liberation theologians have demonstrated.

While calling attention to some deficiencies in political analysis and to the inefficacy of political action, I do not mean to suggest that the Church's sole purpose should be political efficacy. Political utopias and moral criticisms have their place. More important, grass-roots Catholic groups, as indeed the Church more generally, have religious and social objectives in addition to political ones. One of the great achievements of the network of Catholic groups has been the creation of a sense of community, identity, friendship. Curiously, however, alongside the inadequate political analysis and ineffective political action, one often finds among pastoral agents an excessive concern with politics to the detriment of the more festive, religious, or communitarian aspects of group life. Calling attention to the importance of more sophisticated political analysis in no sense implies that political objectives of grass-roots groups should be more important than these other aspects.

CONCLUSION: THE POLITICAL IMPACT OF GRASS-ROOTS CATHOLIC GROUPS

Previous sections suggested some of the ways in which Catholic groups participated in the struggle for democracy: Catholic activists participated in popular movements and political parties; Catholic practices affected other social movements. Having outlined aspects of the political evolution of these grass-roots Catholic groups, now I will address some questions regarding their contributions and limits in promoting democratization.

It is difficult to argue that grass-roots movements (Catholic or otherwise) played any significant role in the military government's initial decision to promote political liberalization. Liberalization began in 1974 when popular movements were very weak and when the military regime enjoyed considerable support. In fact, elsewhere I have argued that the weakness of popular movements, although not a necessary condition, certainly increased the military's confidence that it could promote liberalization with minimal risks.[65]

The liberalization process in Brazil was remarkable for how long it took and for how well the military was able to control key aspects thereof.

Nevertheless, once liberalization began, different actors gradually pene-trated the political arena and were able to influence it. Liberalization, which began as an initiative by the government, came to involve oscillating ini-tiatives between regime and opposition, as well as negotiations between the two sides. Among the actors in this process were grass-roots movements, whether or not of Catholic origin.

Just as the opposition in general encouraged the government to make some changes so, too, did grass-roots movements. During the early 1970s, the government was concerned about and hostile toward these grass-roots organizations. However, as electoral politics became more meaningful, the regime realized that it needed broad popular support. The Figueiredo ad-ministration was less inclined to repress social movements, and more will-ing to accept them as legitimate political actors, especially in urban areas. Its strategy changed from marginalization and repression, where movements could not be marginalized, to cooptation and isolation. While generally hostile to grass-roots Catholic groups, the government attempted to main-tain popular support by responding to the material demands they raised.

It would be a mistake to attribute the government's changing poli-cies toward the popular sectors exclusively to grass-roots movements, but it seems apparent that the presence of these movements contributed to these changes. Even though these movements never involved more than a small minority of the population, they seemed to pose a threat because they were difficult to coopt. Furthermore, the government sensed that the movements could influence popular demands and expectations as a whole. Therefore, around the end of the Geisel period and beginning of the Figueiredo administration, finding a means of dealing with them became a priority. The party reform of 1979, the reorientation of economic policy, and changes in attitudes toward the popular sectors all reflected the gov-ernment's efforts to blunt the thrust of the grass-roots movements by re-sponding to just enough popular demands to maintain its legitimacy.[66]

The party reform of 1979 reflected a complex governmental strategy of going ahead with political liberalization while attempting to ensure that the regime would continue to remain in control. Party reform had long been a demand of the opposition, which argued that the two-party sys-tem imposed by the government in 1965-1966 was artificial, and the gov-ernment was able to satisfy this demand while dividing the opposition and enhancing its own electoral prospects. The party reform succeeded beyond the government's hopes in isolating grass-roots movements and the Left. But it succeeded only because the regime was willing to make concessions to some demands of the opposition, especially continuing the move toward democracy.

Economically, too, the administration pursued a strategy of making some concessions to the popular sectors while attempting to enervate the most combative popular movements. In an effort to obtain popular support, the Figueiredo administration initially promoted income redistribution toward sectors at the bottom of the income scale. In urban areas, the government built housing projects and improved services in popular districts. At the same time, its efforts to isolate the most combative popular movements were apparent in the willingness to resort to repression to deal with the ABC labor movement and in the repressive practices pervasive in the Amazon. Generally speaking however, the policy of neglecting and repressing popular demands, characteristic of the Médici years, gave rise to efforts to coopt the popular sectors through traditional clientelistic practices.

In addition to indirectly encouraging the government to change its strategy toward the popular sectors, Catholic groups encouraged opposition parties to espouse popular issues. This was most apparent with the PT and the PDT, but during one period (1979–1982), there appeared to be real potential that the PMDB would become more receptive to popular participation and popular political issues.

Finally, Catholic groups may contribute to changing elitist patterns in Brazilian society. They have helped develop leadership qualities among people who were previously afraid to speak out; have promoted participation and group equality; and have encouraged people to feel that, as citizens, they have basic rights that the state should respect. In a society that is still marked by the remnants of slave culture, this represents a significant change, at least for the people involved in these groups. The general significance of these changes for democracy is debatable. At a minimum, however, it seems clear that cultural patterns in Brazilian society have reinforced elite political domination, and that CEBs represent a challenge to those cultural patterns.[67]

By the March 1985 inauguration of a democratic government, Catholic groups had lost part of their political impact, both as a result of their own political ingenuousness and of the consolidation of a traditional Brazilian pattern of elitist style politics. Yet while Catholic movements became marginalized during the political struggle of the first half of the 1980s, this certainly does not mean that they have lost their relevance. The political issues they raise remain as important as ever in Brazil. Questions of popular participation, grass-roots democracy, and socioeconomic justice have been relegated to a secondary role in the last years of Brazilian politics, yet it is evident that these issues have hardly been resolved. If anything, twenty-one years of military rule reinforced the inegalitarian and elitist nature of Brazilian society.

The difficulties confronting these Catholic groups in encouraging the transformation of Brazilian politics in a progressive direction are great. They represent a small minority of the population in a society with powerful conservative elites. The groups themselves have continued to be uncertain about what to do politically. The relative weakness of popular movements, the electoral failures of the PT, the conservative character of the Sarney government, and the absence of political allies were salient concerns for many leaders, but they did not know how to respond. And finally, the naive character of the dominant analysis of society, while not a great obstacle in fighting the dictatorship, became one when different conceptions of democracy were at stake.

On top of all this were the criticisms against the popular Church in Brazil coming from the Vatican, CELAM, and conservative Brazilian prelates. The neo-conservative ecclesiastical movement could have a profound impact upon the grass-roots groups. Consequently these groups have begun a new period in Brazilian democracy, caught between an increasing marginalization in politics and in the Church. But this marginalization should not detract from the significant impact these groups had in working toward the reestablishment of democracy, nor from the importance of the questions they continue to raise about the quality of that democracy.[68]

NOTES

1. Tocqueville, however, went against the grain. In the 1830s, he wrote that "Eighteenth-century philosophers had a very simple explanation for the gradual weakening of beliefs. Religious zeal, they said, was bound to die down as enlightenment and freedom spread. It is tiresome that the facts do not fit this theory at all." *Democracy in America*, ed. J. P. Mayer (Garden City, N.Y.: Anchor, 1969), p. 295.

2. David Martin's *A General Theory of Secularization* (New York: Harper & Row, 1978) is among the best works in this genre. Leading theologians shared the viewpoint that secularization is inexorable. See, for example, Dietrich Bonhoeffer, *Letters and Papers from Prison* (New York: Macmillan, 1971); Harvey Cox, *The Secular City: Secularization and Urbanization in Theological Perspective* (New York: Macmillan, 1965). In Brazil, Michel Schooyans, *O Desafio da Secularização* (São Paulo: Herder, 1968), was representative of this line of theological inquiry. My own view, which is close to Weber's, is that secularization has occurred in many societies, but it does not, as many assumed, imply the demise of religion. In part, this is because secularization is uneven and incomplete and allows for nonsecular spaces of public interaction. In part, it is because secularization creates new problems or recasts old ones in different terms that reinvigorate religion and other nonsecular forms of interaction.

3. See, among others, Juan J. Linz, "Religion and Politics in Spain: From Conflict to Consensus above Cleavage," *Social Compass* 27 (1980): 255–277; Charles Glock and Rodney Stark, *Religion and Society in Tension* (Chicago: Rand McNally, 1965), pp. 185–229; Vincent McHale, "Religion and Electoral Politics in France: Some Recent

Observations," *Canadian Journal of Political Science* 2 (1969): 292–311; Richard Rose and Derek Urwin, "Social Cohesion, Political Parties, and Strains in Regimes," *Comparative Political Studies* 2 (April 1969): 7–67.

4. Durkheim's words on this point are of enduring value. "[The believers] feel that the real function of religion . . . is to aid us to live. The believer who has communicated with his god is not merely a man who sees new truths of which the unbeliever is ignorant, he is a man who is *stronger*. He feels within him more force, either to endure the trials of existence, or to conquer them. It is as though he were raised above the miseries of the world, because he is raised above his condition as a mere man." Emile Durkheim, *The Elementary Forms of the Religious Life* (New York: The Free Press, 1965), p. 464. Durkheim, however, also agreed with the view that religion in its traditional form was declining: "The old gods are growing old or already dead, and others are not yet born" (p. 475).

5. This point is developed by Karen Fields, writing on a quite different religious experience, in her recent *Revival and Rebellion in Colonial Central Africa* (Princeton, N.J.: Princeton University Press, 1985), especially pp. 3–23.

6. See, for example, Gustavo Gutiérrez, *We Drink from Our Own Wells* (Maryknoll, N.Y.: Orbis, 1984); Jon Sobrino, *La oración de Jesus y del Cristiano* (México: Centro de Reflexión Teológica, 1981); Segundo Galilea, *The Future of Our Past* (Notre Dame, Ind.: Ave Maria Press, 1985).

7. For analyses that see CEBs as an institutional initiative, see Thomas Bruneau, "Basic Christian Communities in Latin America: Their Nature and Significance (Especially in Brazil)," in Daniel H. Levine, ed., *Churches and Politics in Latin America* (Beverly Hills, Calif.: Sage, 1979), pp. 111–134; Thomas Bruneau, "The Catholic Church and the Basic Christian Communities: A Case Study from the Brazilian Amazon," in Levine, ed., *Popular Religion, the Churches, and Political Conflict in Latin America* (Chapel Hill, N.C.: University of North Carolina Press, 1986), pp. 106–123; Cândido Procópio Ferreira de Camargo, et al., "Comunidades Eclesiais de Base," in Paul Singer and Vinicius Caldeira Brant, eds., *São Paulo: O Povo em Movimento* (Petrópolis: Vozes/ CEBRAP, 1980), pp. 59–81; Francisco Cartaxo Rolim, *Religião e Classes Populares* (Petrópolis: Vozes, 1980); José Ivo Follmann, *Igreja, Ideologia e Classes Sociais* (Petrópolis: Vozes, 1985); William Hewitt, "The Structure and Orientation of Comunidades Eclesiais de Base (CEBs) in the Archdiocese of São Paulo," Ph.D. dissertation, McMaster University, 1985. For analyses that emphasize popular proclivities in the CEBs, see Frei Betto, *O que E Comunidade Eclesial de Base* (São Paulo: Brasiliense, 1981); Gottfried Deelen, "The Church on its Way to the People: Basic Christian Communities in Brazil," *Cross Currents* 30 (Winter 1980–81): 385–408.

8. The argument that follows owes much to discussions with Daniel Levine. See our "Religion and Popular Protest in Latin America," Kellogg Institute Working Paper #83 (October 1986), to be published in Susan Eckstein, ed., *Protest and Resistance: Latin American Experiences* (Berkeley: University of California Press, forthcoming). Several of Levine's recent contributions on this subject are fundamental. See, for example, "Conflict and Renewal," in Levine, ed., *Religion and Political Conflict in Latin America* (Chapel Hill, N.C.: University of North Carolina Press, 1986), pp. 236–255.

9. On this point see especially Vanilda Paiva, "Anotações para um Estudo sobre

Populismo Católico e Educação Popular," in Paiva, ed., *Perspectivas e Dilemas da Edu-cacão Popular* (Rio de Janeiro: Graal, 1984), pp. 227–266; and Roberto Romano, *Brasil: Igreja contra Estado* (São Paulo: Kairos, 1979).

10. See his *Eclesiogênese: As Comunidades Eclesiais de Base Reinventam a Igreja* (Petrópolis: Vozes, 1977).

11. Among many examples, see Frances O'Gorman, "Base Communities in Bra-zil: Dynamics of a Journey" (Rio de Janeiro: FASE-NUCLAR, 1983); João Carlos Pet-trini, *CEBs: Um Novo Sujeito Popular* (Rio de Janeiro: Paz e Terra, 1984); Clodovis Boff, "A Influência Política das CEBs," *Religião e Sociedade* 4 (1979): 95–119.

12. I discuss the Church's evolution at length in *The Catholic Church and Poli-tics in Brazil, 1916–1985* (Stanford, Calif.: Stanford University Press, 1986). See also Thomas Bruneau, *The Political Transformation of the Brazilian Catholic Church* (New York: Cambridge University Press, 1974); Thomas Bruneau, *The Church in Brazil: The Politics of Religion* (Austin, Texas: University of Texas Press, 1982); Ralph Della Cava, "The Church and the 'Abertura,' 1974–1985," in Alfred Stepan, ed., *Democratizing Bra-zil* (New York: Oxford University Press, forthcoming).

13. In my view, the best work on the origins of CEBs in Brazil is Marcello Azevedo, *Basic Ecclesial Communities in Brazil* (Washington, D.C.: Georgetown Univer-sity Press, 1987). Azevedo's book is essential reading on CEBs. An extensive and care-ful analysis of the origins of CEBs, but one whose central argument I question, is Faus-tino Luiz Couto Teixeira, "Comunidade Eclesial de Base: Elementos Explicativos de Sua Gênese," M.A. thesis, Pontifícia Universidade Católica, Rio de Janeiro, 1982. See also Luiz Gonzaga Fernandes, "Gênese, Dinâmica e Perspectivas das CEBs no Brasil," *Revista Eclesiástica Brasileira* 42 (1982): 456–464. Many people date the first CEBs back to the late 1950s, but this oft repeated viewpoint seems wrong to me.

14. The earliest discussion of these Sunday services without a priest are Ber-nardo Leers, "A Estrutura do Culto Dominical na Zona Rural," *Revista da Conferência dos Religiosos do Brasil* 99 (September 1963): 521–534; and Antônio Rolim, "O Culto Dominical e os Religiosos," *Revista da Conferência dos Religiosos do Brasil* 100 (October 1963): 631–636.

15. Report from the diocese of Goiás, *Uma Igreja que Nasce do Povo* (Petrópolis: Vozes, 1975), pp. 76–77.

16. Examples are Raimundo Caramuru de Barros, *Comunidade Eclesial de Base: Uma Opção Pastoral Decisiva* (Petrópolis: Vozes, 1968); and José Marins, *A Comunidade Eclesial de Base* (São Paulo, n.d.).

17. See Emilio Mignone, *Iglesia y dictadura* (Buenos Aires: Ediciones del Pensa-miento Militar, 1986).

18. Statement of the CNBB's Eleventh General Assembly, *SEDOC* 3 (1970–71): 85–86.

19. Assmann's most important work was published in Spanish. See his *Opresión-liberación: Desafio a los Cristianos* (Montevideo: Tierra Nueva, 1971). By Comblin, see *Théologie de la Pratique Révolutionnaire* (Paris: Editions Universitaires, 1974).

20. Joseph Comblin, *Os Sinais do Tempo e a Evangelização* (São Paulo: Duas Cidades, 1968); Joseph Comblin, "Prolegômenos da Catequese no Brasil," *Revista Ecle-siástica Brasileira* 27 (1967): 845–874; Eduardo Hoornaert, "A Distinção entre 'Lei' e 'Religião' no Nordeste," *Revista Eclesiástica Brasileira* 29 (1969): 580–606; Eduardo

Hoornaert, "Problemas de Pastoral Popular no Brasil," *Revista Eclesiástica Brasileira* 28 (1968): 280–307.

21. *Uma Igreja que Nasce do Povo*, p. 83.

22. "Comunidades de Base: Dez Anos de Experiência," *SEDOC* 11 (January–February 1979): 727.

23. Leonardo Boff, "Teologia à Escuta do Povo," *Revista Eclesiástica Brasileira* 41 (1981): 55–119; Clodovis Boff, "Agente de Pastoral e Povo," *Revista Eclesiástica Brasileira* 40 (1980): 216–242; Frei Betto, "A Educação nas Classes Populares," *Encontros com a Civilização Brasileira* 2 (1978): 95–112.

24. Boff's book, now available in English, was published in Portuguese as *Jesus Cristo, Libertador* (Petrópolis: Vozes, 1971). Mesters's book was also published by Vozes. A recent book brings together many of Mesters's most important subsequent contributions. See *Flor sem Defesa: Uma Explicação da Bíblia a Partir do Povo* (Petrópolis: Vozes, 1983).

25. *O Futuro dos Ministérios na Igreja Latinoamericana* (Petrópolis: Vozes, 1969); "Comunidades Eclesiais de Base e Pastoral Urbana," *Revista Eclesiástica Brasileira* 30 (1970): 783–828.

26. Clodovis Boff, *Comunidade Eclesial, Comunidade Política* (Petrópolis: Vozes, 1978); Almir Guimarães, *Comunidades de Base no Brasil* (Petrópolis: Vozes, 1978); Alvaro Barreiro, *Communidades Eclesiais de Base e Evangelização dos Pobres* (São Paulo: Loyola, 1977).

27. *As Comunidades Eclesiais de Base na Igreja do Brasil* (São Paulo: Paulinas, 1982), pp. 5, 11, 32. The other CNBB studies are *Comunidades: Igreja na Base* (São Paulo: Paulinas, 1977); and *Comunidades Eclesiais de Base no Brasil* (São Paulo: Paulinas, 1979).

28. There are few secondary sources on the creation and development of the CPT and CPO—an interesting lacuna, especially when compared to the mass of literature which has been produced about the CEBs. On the CPT, see Ivo Poletto, "As Contradições Sociais e a Pastoral da Terra," in Vanilda Paiva, ed., *Igreja e Questão Agrária* (São Paulo: Loyola, 1985), pp. 129–148; and Cândido Grzybowski, "A Comissão Pastoral da Terra e os Colonos do Sul do Brasil," also in Paiva, ed., *Igreja e Questão Agrária*, pp. 248–273. On CIMI, see Fany Ricardo, "O Conselho Indigenista Missionário, 1965–1979," *Cadernos do ISER* (1980); and Paulo Suess, "A Caminhada do Conselho Indigenista Missionário, 1972–1984," *Revista Eclesiástica Brasileira* 44 (Sept. 1984): 501–533. More broadly on pastoral efforts with indigenous populations, see also Erwin Krautler, "Povos Indígenas e Pastoral Indigenista Hoje," *Vozes* 79 (May 1985): 281–286; and Paulo Suess, "Alteridade-Integração-Resistência," *Revista Eclesiástica Brasileira* 45 (September 1985): 485–505.

29. Mimeo, May 1975.

30. In *Uma Igreja que Nasce do Povo* (Petrópolis: Vozes, 1975), p. 62.

31. See Luiz Gonzaga de Souza Lima, "Notas sobre as Comunidades Eclesiais de Base e a Organização Política," in José Álvaro Moisés, et al., *Alternativas Populares da Democracia* (Petrópolis: Vozes/CEDEC, 1982), pp. 41–72.

32. On the Church's role in the strikes of 1978–1980, see *Religião e Sociedade* 6 (1980): 7–68; Centro Ecumênico de Documentação e Informação, "1980: ABC da Greve," *Aconteceu* (May 1980); Centro Pastoral Vergueiro, "As Greves do ABC," *Ca-*

dernos de Documentação 3 (December 1980); Francisco Cartaxo Rolim, "A Greve do ABC e a Igreja," *Revista Eclesiástica Brasileira* 44 (1984): 131–151.

33. On the relationship between Church groups and the neighborhood movement in São Paulo, see Anna Luiza Souto, "Movimentos Populares Urbanos e suas Formas de Organização Ligadas à Igreja," in ANPOCS, *Ciências Sociais Hoje* 2 (Brasilia, 1983): 63–95; and Paul Singer, "Movimentos de Bairros," in Singer and Brant, eds., *São Paulo: O Povo em Movimento*, pp. 83–108. Paulo Krischke and Scott Mainwaring, eds., *A Igreja na Base em Tempo de Transição* (Posto Alegre: L&PM/CEDEC, 1986) offers a collection of articles on the relationship between the Church and neighborhood movements in different parts of the country.

34. No single source details these changes in the Brazilian Left, and given the significant heterogeneity of the Left, it would be misleading to generalize too much. A good overview is provided by Robert Packenham, "The Changing Political Discourse in Brazil, 1964–1985," in Wayne Selcher, ed., *Political Liberalization in Brazil: Dynamics, Dilemmas, and Future Prospects* (Boulder, Colo.: Westview, 1986), pp. 135–173; and Bolivar Lamounier, "Representação Política: A Importância de Certos Formalismos," in Lamounier, Francisco Weffort, and Maria Victória Benevides, eds., *Direito, Cidadania e Participação* (São Paulo: Tao, 1981), pp. 230–257. Statements by leading Marxist intellectuals which imply a significant change in thinking about democracy are Leandro Konder, *A Democracia e os Comunistas no Brasil* (Rio de Janeiro: Graal, 1980), and Carlos Nelson Coutinho, *A Democracia como Valor Universal* (São Paulo: Ciências Humanas, 1980). Many ex-guerrillas have written memoirs highly critical of the vanguardist approach to politics; see, for example, Alfredo Sirkis, *Os Carbonários: Memórias da Guerrilha Perdida* (Rio de Janeiro: Global, 1980).

35. See, for example, Ricardo Abramovay, "Marxistas e Cristãos: Pontos para um Diálogo," *Proposta* 16 (March 1981): 11–20.

36. "Da Prática da Pastoral Popular," *Encontros com a Civilização Brasileira* 2 (1978): 104, 95. On the Church's attempts to define its role in the new political conjuncture, see also Paulo César Loureiro Botas, "Aí! Que Saudades do Tempo em que o Terço Resolvia Tudo," *Tempo e Presença* 26 (March 1980): 3–10; Frei Betto, "Prática Pastoral e Prática Política," *Tempo e Presença* 26 (March 1980): 11–29; Frei Betto, "Oração: Uma Exigência (Também) Política," *Revista Eclesiástica Brasileira* 42 (September 1982): 444–455; Antônio Alves de Melo, "Fé em Jesus Cristo e Compromisso Político-Partidário," *Revista Eclesiástica Brasileira* 42 (September 1982): 562–587.

37. CNBB, *Comunidades Eclesiais de Base na Igreja do Brasil*, p. 29.

38. I discuss the post-1982 demise of the popular Church at length in chapter 11 of *The Catholic Church and Politics in Brazil*. See also the important article by Della Cava, "The Church and the 'Abertura'."

39. "Comunidades Eclesiais de Base," *Boletim da Revista do Clero* 19 (September 1982): 21.

40. *SEDOC* 14 (September 1981): 200.

41. "O IV Encontro das CEBs," *SEDOC* 14 (September 1981): 153, 154, 155.

42. On the relationship between CEBs and political parties, see Ricardo Galleta, *Pastoral Popular e Política Partidária no Brasil* (São Paulo: Paulinas, 1986); Bruneau, "The Catholic Church and the Basic Christian Communities"; Luiz Alberto Gómez de Souza, *Classes Populares e Igreja nos Caminhos da História* (Petrópolis: Vozes, 1981), pp. 247–

268; Ivo Lesbaupin, "As Cartilhas Diocesanas de 1981-1982," in Lesbaupin, ed., *Igreja, Movimentos Populares, Política no Brasil* (São Paulo: Loyola, 1983), pp. 57-74.

43. On the PT, see Margaret Keck "From Movement to Politics: The Formation of the Workers' Party in Brazil," Ph.D. dissertation, Columbia University, 1986; Emir Sader, ed., *E Agora, PT?* (São Paulo: Brasiliense, 1986).

44. Galleta, *Pastoral Popular e Política Partidária no Brasil*, p. 25.

45. Comissão Arquidiocesana de Pastoral dos Direitos Humanos e Marginalizados de São Paulo, *Fé e Política* (Petrópolis: Vozes, 1981), p. 29. Over the years, SEDOC has published a large number of electoral pamphlets from various dioceses.

46. J. B. Libânio, "CEBs: Igreja em Busca da Terra Prometida," *REB* 46 (September 1986): 504.

47. "Pastoral à Luz da 'Grande Avaliação'," *SEDOC* 19 (May 1987): 1100.

48. See the interesting debate in Clodovis Boff et al., *Cristaos: Como Fazer Política* (Petrópolis: Vozes/IBASE, 1987).

49. "Igreja e Montoro se reaproximam mas ainda existem divergências," *O Globo*, July 29, 1984.

50. I make some related points in chapters 9 and 10 of *The Catholic Church and Politics in Brazil*. See also Pásara's chapter in this book.

51. "Carta pastoral dos Bispos da Paraíba," *SEDOC* 19 (April 1987): 961.

52. "In some CEBs, there is an infiltration of politicians. In others, the politicians are not infiltrating but the communities are reflecting on why politicians are taking advantage of what the people have." Fourth Intereclesial Meeting of CEBs, *SEDOC* 14 (September 1981): 181.

53. Joseph Schumpeter, *Capitalism, Socialism and Democracy* (New York: Harper & Row, 1950), pp. 240-302. Schumpeter's emphasis on the limited responsiveness of politicians to popular demands has, of course, often been challenged.

54. See the provocative essay by Paulo César Loureiro Bottas, "Sou do PT porque Ele Está no Plano de Deus," *Comunicações do ISER* 8 (March 1984).

55. Third Intereclesial Meeting of CEBs, *SEDOC* 11 (October 1978): 432.

56. Clodovis Boff and Leonardo Boff, "A Igreja Perante a Economia nos EUA," *REB* 47 (June 1987): 363, 367.

57. In this regard, it is interesting to note the "radical critique of the Constitutional Congress" by leaders of base communities. The constitutional Congress "reduces the elaboration of a new Constitution to representatives elected through political parties. A participatory conscience demands the direct participation of members of the oppressed classes." See Manfredo Araujo de Oliveira, "CEBs e Constituinte: Um Desafio à Modernidade," *Revista Eclesiástica Brasileira* 46 (September 1986): 609. The constitutional process can be criticized on many grounds, but it is important to note that the representatives chosen through political parties were elected by popular vote!

58. "CEBs: Povo de Deus em Busca da Terra Prometida," *REB* 46 (September 1986): 485.

59. The outstanding exception is Luiz Alberto Gomez de Souza, one of Brazil's most creative social scientists. Rubem César Fernandes, while not a Church intellectual, is linked to ISER, a research center on religion, and has also been a prominent figure in addressing the authoritarian character of "real socialism."

60. Frei Betto, *Fidel e a Religião* (São Paulo: Brasiliense, 1986); Leonardo Boff,

"Teólogos brasileiros viajam à União Soviética," *Revista Eclesiástica Brasileira* 47 (September 1987): 678–686; Clodovis Boff, "Carta Teológica sobre Cuba," *Revista Eclesiástica Brasileira* 46 (June 1986): 348–371.

61. C. Boff, "Carta Teológica sobre Cuba," p. 356.

62. Fourth Interecclesial Meeting of CEBs, *SEDOC* 14 (September 1981): 181.

63. "The government, oriented by the Trilateral Commission, carries out the party reorganization. Japan, the United States, and Europe decide what policies will be applied for the Brazilian people." Fourth Interecclesial Meeting of CEBs, *SEDOC* 14 (September 1981): 220.

64. *Boletim da Pastoral da Terra* 19 (November-December 1978): 2, quoted in Azevedo, *Comunidades Eclesiais de Base e Inculturação da Fé*, p. 124.

65. Scott Mainwaring and Donald Share, "Transitions Through Transaction: Democratization in Brazil and Spain," in Wayne Selcher, ed., *Political Liberalization in Brazil* (Boulder, Colo.: Westview, 1986), pp. 175–215.

66. For discussions of the impact and limits of grass-roots popular movements, see Renato Raul Boschi, "Movimentos Sociais Urbanos e a Institucionalização de uma Ordem" (Rio de Janeiro: IUPERJ, 1983); Ruth Cardoso, "Movimentos Sociais Urbanos: Balanço Crítico," in Bernardo Sorj and Maria Hermínia Taves de Almeida, eds., *Sociedade e Política no Brasil Pós-64* (São Paulo: Brasiliense, 1983), pp. 215–239; Scott Mainwaring, "Grassroots Popular Movements, Identity, and Democratization in Brazil," *Comparative Political Studies* 20 (July 1987): 131–159.

67. For a fine recent work on religion and politics that argues for the fundamental importance of cultural patterns, see Jean Comaroff, *Body of Power, Spirit of Resistance* (Chicago: University of Chicago Press, 1985).

68. I would like to thank Caroline Domingo, Frances Hagopian, Margaret Keck, Daniel Levine, Alfred Stepan, and Alexander Wilde for helpful suggestions.

Social Movements and the Catholic Church in Vitória, Brazil

Ana Maria Doimo

This chapter analyzes the relationship between the Catholic Church and two social movements that developed in Greater Vitória[1] in the late 1970s: the Vila Velha public transportation movement and the construction workers' movement. The data, information, and documents used were assembled during the course of my direct involvement with both movements and through interviews conducted with their main leaders.

The need for researching this topic arose from the attempt to analyze the relationships established between the neighborhood and the labor movements and from the assumption that repression and government control of unions makes neighborhoods the main locale for workers' organization. It has been the belief that organizing around demands related to "urban problems" influences the organization of demand-oriented struggles in the area of production. My studies, however, revealed that these movements each developed an individual dynamic consisting of their own spokespersons and their own specific demands. What they had in common were their organizational principles, values, and political-cultural proposals. These dynamics were transmitted through particular organizational agents — among them the Church — thus solidifying their relationships and growth processes.

This chapter was written for the purpose of analyzing these two social movements in terms of their relationship with the Church's pastoral action. The progressive sectors of the Church developed new strategies in the late 1970s for the redirection of the Church's relationship with social movements. These Church strategies influenced the development of specific movements and, while seeking to maintain the united nature of the Church institution, they did not ignore the need for the encouragement of more innovative forms of organization. This complex process gave rise to contradictions and ambiguities. This study also reveals that, as an expressive component of the Brazilian culture, religion has been a powerful force in the bringing together and the motivating of sociopolitical participation and organization.

GREATER VITÓRIA, ITS SOCIAL MOVEMENTS, AND THE ARCHDIOCESE

Rio de Janeiro and São Paulo, the most dynamic regions in the country, began to accelerate their process of industrialization and urbanization in the 1930s. However, the state of Espírito Santo, bordering the state of Rio, did not begin this process until 1970. In 1960 industry accounted for only 7.9 percent of the state's income with an economy still based on coffee. Real industrialization began in the late 1960s as a result of two converging processes. The first of these, begun in 1962 and accelerated in 1966, was the Coffee Plantation Eradication program,[2] which in addition to agricultural consequences, forced more than 50,000 rural workers from their subsistence activities, creating a migration of approximately 150,000 people from the countryside into the urban areas, with most of them moving to Greater Vitória. The other process was the establishment of state-sponsored, large-scale industrial projects in the early 1970s (steel, parachemical, and port complexes).[3] These were intended to bring development to the state. These projects attracted many more immigrants from the countryside and from the neighboring states of Minas Gerais and Bahia. The immediate consequence of both processes was a rapid increase in population in Vitória and its adjacent municipalities, known as Greater Vitória. The region's population increased from 194,200 in 1960 to 368,338 in 1970 and has continued to grow, reaching more than 900,000 in the 1980s.

The unrestrained, disorderly process of urbanization was a result of the governmental priority on investing in the infrastructure demanded for the reproduction of big capital and was detrimental to the type of investments in collective infrastructure (transportation, education, sanitation, housing, etc.) needed for the reproduction of the labor force. As the industrial projects took shape, injecting new life into the building industry—which absorbed a large number of unskilled migrants from the countryside—Greater Vitória begin facing countless "urban problems." "Boomtowns" mushroomed and transportation became a crucial problem, due both to the shortage of vehicles and to the 30 percent average increase in travel. The inability of the poor to acquire adequate housing led to the growth of shantytowns on the hillsides and river shores. From

1970 to 1977, the number of permanent houses increased 24 percent while the number of shacks grew 46 percent.[4] As far as basic sanitation needs were concerned, a 1977 survey carried out by the State Planning Department revealed that 25 percent of the region's households were without running water, 13.2 percent without toilets, 34 percent without sewers, and 16 percent without electricity. In terms of education, the illiteracy rate was estimated at 14 percent. While the majority of the population faced serious problems in "urban space," it was even less fortunate in the productive sector. This same survey showed only 63 percent of the workers as having regular jobs with signed contracts, indicating a high rate of part-time unemployment.

The style of industrialization promoted in Greater Vitória was consistent with the economic model adopted by the federal government: an excessive concentration of income and centralization of capital. These policies, along with the increasing penetration of monopolist/oligopolist foreign capital, succeeded in generating and accentuating the blatant social disparities evident within the contours of the urban space (made visible by the "black holes" of the poverty-stricken areas).

The long period of military dictatorship imposed by the 1964 coup d'etat impoverished the working class under the aegis of wage-cutting policies and the institutional and police control over the trade-union and associative organizations. It was not until the late 1970s, during the beginning of the redemocratization process, that the working class and the poor made their presence felt on the political scene. Then they came on strong in the defense of their interests. In both the productive sector and the residential areas countless movements were organized to protest and to demand improvements in the existing living and working conditions. In 1978, nearly 70,000 workers went on strike in São Paulo's ABC region:[5] 10,000 walked out at the Volkswagen plant and Ford workers struck for a whole week. In the city of São Paulo, the rank-and-file metalworkers movement ran a strong opposition platform in the election for the leadership of the largest union in Latin America, which had been controlled by a single president—considered friendly to the bosses—for the previous ten years. Bank employees nationwide held a Congress and denounced the falsification of the figures by which their wage adjustments had been kept below the inflation rate in 1973–74. Metalworkers in Contagem (Minas Gerais) also mobilized in order to return to earlier, higher wage levels.

The wave of strikes and protests spread with varying degrees of intensity to several of Brazil's states. In Espírito Santo, these movements resulted in strikes by bus drivers, cashiers, high-school and university professors, doctors, and construction workers.

Resistance movements against wage cut-backs and the awful conditions of urban living flourished in residential areas. Neighborhood associations, street commissions, assemblies, cooperative efforts, and land take-overs were common forms of organization which, through banners, posters, marches, petitions, and conferences with authorities, poor people expressed myriad demands: price freezes on basic consumer goods, public transportation, legalization of land titles, water, sewers, clinics, childcare, etc. These urban movements were particularly effective in Greater Vitória. There were at least twenty land take-overs, which while invariably accompanied by police violence, also carried the support of the opposition sectors, most notably the Justice and Peace Commission of the Archdiocese of Vitória, whose legal department won the right to grant land deeds in some cases. At this time other urban movements were taking place in Vitória. The water movement organized residents of twenty-one neighborhoods and won the fight for running water. It then reorganized into the Vitória pro-sanitation movement, demanding other improvements such as sewers, garbage collection, and the construction of hillside stairways. The public transportation movement began in Vila Velha and eventually reached a total of twenty-six neighborhoods. In the neighboring city of Serra, small grass-roots neighborhood organizations developed into the establishment of legally registered neighborhood associations that were totally autonomous and independent in their relation to the public authorities.

One of the most significant aspects of these social movements was the organizational link sustained with grass-roots groups of the Catholic Church. These groups were known as Ecclesial Base Communities (CEBs). The establishing of CEBs started in the interior of the state in 1960 and reached Greater Vitória in 1973. By early 1980 there were approximately 1,000 CEBs in existence throughout the state, about 250 of them located on the outskirts of Greater Vitória. The process of the creation of these base communities in Espírito Santo was extremely intense, so much so, that the first two national conferences of CEBs took place in Vitória during 1975 and 1976.

The renewed Church in Espírito Santo is a complex structure. In the Archdiocese of Vitória, the upper level of the structure is occupied by the Pastoral Council of the Archdiocese of Vitória (COPAVI) and is made up of representatives of the six local councils from the areas covered by the Archdiocese: Greater Vitória, Colatina, Linha ITA, BR 101, Benevente, and Serrana. Each of these councils, in turn, contains representatives from a number of other organizationally and hierarchically related councils. The Greater Vitória Pastoral Council, for example, has representatives from three other councils: the CEBs Council (also known as the Periphery Council), the Council of Parish Seats, and the Environmental and Services Pastoral Council, each of which is made up of representatives from a number of the other sub-councils, commissions, and groups spread throughout their respective areas of action. Between the Periphery Council and the CEBs alone, there exist sectoral councils within the cities of Greater Vitória that cover groups of five or six contiguous neighborhoods representing the CEBs in each area. The CEBs, for their part, consist of several work teams (finances, liturgy, cleaning, women, youth, children, marriage, eucharist, baptism, songs, neighborhood problems, etc.), each of which is led by an "animator" and with representatives on the neighborhood council. This intricate structure, which covers the entire state, is organizationally decentralized at the grass-roots level thus creating new decision-making bodies made up of lay people, while maintaining the hierarchical and bureaucratic structure where the clergy (priests and bishops) carry more weight.

In the Archdiocese of Vitória, Archbishop Dom João Batista Motta de Albuquerque and Auxiliary Bishop Dom Luiz Gonzaga Fernandes have incorporated the precepts of liberation theology, principally the "preferential option for the poor," and have encouraged critical reflection on the local socioeconomic situation through the ecclesiastical prism view of the Church. With this basis of support, the growing number of small groups soon began to see the results of their efforts to organize to fight for their rights. These results were embodied in the social movements that burgeoned in the late 1970s.

THE PUBLIC TRANSPORTATION MOVEMENT AND THE CEBS

The public transportation movement of Vila Velha was launched in April 1978.[6] Bringing together the residents of twenty-six neighborhoods, the movement lasted until November 1979. Its decline, not by chance, coincided with the reorganization of political parties that occurred at the end of the same year.

During nearly two years a considerable number of people attended countless weekly meetings to debate how best to struggle for better public transportation and how to act against the Alvorada Company's monopoly over the transportation services in their city. During this period (considered a long time for an urban movement to last), the public transportation movement went through the stages of beginning, ascent, apex, and decline. This was an apparently "normal" cycle, which conformed to the "nature" of such movements. Yet the movement did not arise merely out of the existence of a public transportation problem, nor did it end following the exhaustion of some "normal" cycle. Its development clearly revealed the existence of a cohesive group united around main organizational principles. The group's identification with the Church's Periphery Pastoral gradually became more evident despite successive declarations that the movement had not come out of the Church and that the two could not be linked. Yet there was no way to deny that the movement did grow out of Church groups. Neighborhood residents commented that the movement "smelled churchy," and the city authorities seethed at the insistence of those "people from the communities" in holding public demonstrations and marches that upset the "normal" functioning of their offices.

The Church's base communities did play a fundamental and decisive role in the creation, organization, mobilization, and maintenance of the public transportation movement. They not only provided the organizational model and the settings for discussion, but they also guaranteed the unification of the movement throughout the twenty-six neighborhoods involved by the means of a network of relations which enabled the main leaders to clearly recognize the internal dynamics. This recognition, however, only extended to those who had ties to the pastoral work.

Although it was some time before the movement's link to the Church was publicly recognized, the religious connection of the movement's supporters, based on interpersonal community relations, could be traced before the existence of the movement itself. The discussion in all the local CEBs of the CNBB document "Christian Requirements for a Political Order"—published jointly in a popular version by the Archdiocese of Vitória and the Diocese of São Mateus (another progressive diocese in the state of Espírito Santo)—was what turned the scales in favor of the organization of an issue-oriented movement.[7] In Vila Velha, the problem of public transportation had been viewed as an issue capable of unifying the interests of all the neighborhoods. In an interview, one pastoral agent gave this explanation for the emergence of the movement:

> The public transportation movement came out of a document called "Christian Demands for a Political Order," which was discussed by all the communities during the second semester of 1977, and covered the rights and duties of Christians within a capitalist social structure. Much emphasis was placed on the question of the participation of the people and the need for the people to be involved in the decisions that directly affected them.[8]

Another pastoral agent said that

> this document led people to commit themselves to reality and to try to change it. Even when the training process was still beginning we already knew that concrete demands would come out of it. It was hard to believe! Everyone started to show desire to fight for their rights. It was then that

we observed that transportation was the key issue. Early in 1978 transportation was part of the annual report of the CEBs from Vila Velha.[9]

In April 1978 the movement was ready to be launched. About 700 people decided to discuss the problem and to create a General Commission, representative of all the neighborhoods, in order to organize the work and present the solutions proposed at a grass-roots level. They created neighborhood commissions to carry out a citywide survey, conducted by the residents, on the transportation problem. Tasks were proposed, assigned, and taken on collectively over a four-month period. When the survey was finished, its five pages of conclusions were filled with details and analyses of specific problems. Once it was approved by an assembly attended by 200 residents, the document was condensed into a petition, then circulated throughout various neighborhoods. Forty thousand signatures were obtained. In October of that same year another assembly of 700 residents, between the singing of one "spirited hymn" and another, selected the public authorities who were to be sought out and pressured to meet the demands. Five commissions were created, of six to eight members each, to discuss the petition directly with each of the targeted authorities (City Hall, state government, Transit Department, Highways Department, and the Secretary of the Interior and Transportation). The Alvorada Company and the politicians, including the City Council and the State Legislative Assembly, were vehemently rejected as targets for discussions. Then formal interviews were scheduled and the contacts were made following a lot of coming and going, an expression used so much that it inspired the name of the movement's newsletter (*Vai e Vem*) that was created in a later assembly with the objective of informing and holding the movement together.

The results of the talks with public authorities were disheartening. Nothing was achieved except for a promise from the Transit Department to carry out a technical study of the movement's voluminous document. But the participants were not discouraged. Their objective was to break Alvorada's monopoly on the bus lines between Vila Velha and Vitória (the capital). This would have to wait for the results of the Transit Department study and, since the movement could not afford to demobilize in the meantime, they decided to organize around the destruction of the monopoly on bus lines within the city of Vila Velha as well, targeting City Hall. Following demonstrations, marches, manipulations, bribes from the companies, and more, the mayor finally gave in and announced that he would accept bids for companies from other states. The first victory came in early 1979; the intra-city monopoly was broken with the entrance of the Verdun Company. The success was commemorated with festivities, but the main objective was still on the agenda. But it remained so only until the majority of the pastoral agents, in one of their regular meetings held separately from the General Commission, decided to reduce as much as possible the agents' participation in the commission in order to give it "greater representativity of the neighborhoods themselves." At this point the movement's relationship with the CEBs was publicly recognized, since the time had arrived to end it. In the language commonly used at the time, the public transportation movement needed to enjoy greater autonomy and develop its own means of self-reliance since the Church was cramping and limiting its development.

On November 4, 1979, at the height of the debate over reform of the political parties, an assembly of neighborhood commissions was organized to decide what in fact had already been resolved: the end of the movement. Interestingly, all the neighborhood transportation commissions —which were virtually indistinguishable from the CEBs—were already involved with other specific problems in their respective neighborhoods. It became a matter of each neighborhood looking out for itself or, in other words, of decentralizing the popular struggle, of protecting the CEBs' territory, and of clearing out intruders who had shown up along the way. It became evident later that these behavioral changes were part of a larger strategic reorientation started by progressive sectors of the Church at the close of the 1970s in order to reorient its relationships with the social movements.

THE CONSTRUCTION WORKERS' MOVEMENT AND THE PASTORAL WORKERS COMMISSION

The construction workers' movement arose shortly after the beginning of the public transportation movement and also had the issue of transportation as its detonator. On April 26, 1978 the Christiani Nielsen company—a construction company contracted by the Vale do Rio Doce Company (CVRD)—suspended free truck transportation for its employees between the outlying areas of the cities of Vila Velha and Cariacica and the job sites at the Tubarão port. Launched around this specific transportation issue, the construction workers' movement broadened its concerns six months later during the yearly contract negotiations, which that year focused on demands for wage readjustment and a raise in entry-level pay. Originating out of an extremely impoverished category of workers, the movement expanded considerably, culminating in a tradewide strike in September 1979. The movement also successfully ran a slate in the union elections of August 1980.[10]

The constructions workers' movement was extremely significant in the context of the social struggles in Greater Vitória in the late 1970s. Representing the region's largest category of workers, whose last strike had been in 1934, it was the first organized strike movement to occur in the state of Espírito Santo since the 1964 coup d'etat. Its massive and attention-catching events mobilized local press coverage and attracted the avid interest of several political organizations and groups. The movement polarized positions and was a conduit for evaluating and confronting political policies. It articulated ties of solidarity among sectors of the trade union movement, and between the union and popular movements in general. During the September 1979 strike, for example, nearly all the organized neighborhood movements throughout Greater Vitória—particularly those tied to the Church—joined the strike-fund campaign and raised substantial contributions for the workers. The public transportation movement, specifically, organized meetings in neighborhoods all around Vila Velha to discuss and support the strikers' demands. These meetings produced letters of solidarity which were enthusiastically read at the workers' assemblies and occasionally published in the major local newspaper. Support was forthcoming from all sides—the Church and various sectors of the MDB (the opposition party), clandestine leftist organizations, other more combative sectors of the union movement, various professional associations, and the neighborhood movements. This process created a political catharsis as the dictatorship began its process of political liberalization, creating an atmosphere which visibly strengthened the movement.

The strike of September 1979 surprised many people, especially the press, with its spontaneity, vigor, and size. The most common explanations for the outbreak were the precarious working and living conditions, the wage cut-backs suffered over fifteen years of authoritarianism, and the economic crisis. Such explanations gave economic and circumstantial factors responsibility for the strike. Actually, other reasons had occurred during the time between the initial demand for transportation and the strike for higher wages.

The movement's leaders were part of a cohesive group which shared common goals and styles of action. They consisted of fifteen to twenty workers, three or four of whom stood out on the basis of their ease and self-assurance when speaking in public and defending their positions. Who were they, what were their positions, and where did they get their sense of identity?

Some preliminary information comes through in interviews with the three main leaders:

"We were members of the Pastoral Workers Commission, and it was there that we organized the union struggle.[11]

> The movement started around the issue of transportation at Christiani Nielsen . . . and at the time we were discussing things in the Pastoral Workers Commission. . . . I joined the Pastoral Commission in 1974. . . .[12]

> Before we were union leaders—you know because you were around while we were putting out the *Posição* newspaper—when we were workers but not union leaders, we were capable of holding meetings with 500, 600, even 1,000 people. . . . I don't mean just members of the Pastoral Workers Commission. In fact there was a group of workers, of comrades, that put out a lot of effort and worked seriously.[13]

It would certainly be impossible to evaluate the construction workers' movement without taking into consideration its leaders' involvement with the Church through the Pastoral Workers Commission. In publications of the Workers Commission, worship programs are combined with agendas for workers' meetings; strike leaflets with Church newsletters, and convocations for plenary sessions of the Pastoral Council of the Archdiocese of Vitória with calls for union assemblies. The documents provide rich evidence of the symbiotic relationship of religious faith and political action. For example, the report on training courses held in October–November 1977 lists the following subjects of discussion: "We and Our Family; We and Our Neighborhood; We and the Ecclesial Base Community; We and the World of Work; Our Role in Response to this Reality." These discussions were led with group dynamic techniques in order to stimulate the participation of all, and they raised issues and reflections on the creation of new values and attitudes in the relationships between the Church and the social movements.

The following are the conclusions of the groups' discussions on "We and the Base Community":

> THE CHURCH BEFORE: the people did not participate; the priest turned his back on the people; the priest wore a cassock and spoke Latin; the priest was on top and the people were below; the people thought the priest was God.

> THE CHURCH TODAY: the people participate in the celebrating of mass, etc.; the priest is a friend of the people, he lives with them; there is not much division.

> WE ARE THE CHURCH: each are at the service of the other (helping, collaborating); giving all the chance to speak, to say what they feel.

> TO THIS END: we must not be imprisoned in our little world of prayer; we must be present in the struggle of our brothers; we must not throw water on the bonfire but rather discover the reason for the fire.[14]

Made obvious here is the expressed need for transformation within the Church itself, as well as the preparation of its members for activity in the outside world. The conclusions of the discussions on "We and the Neighborhood" and "We and the World of Work" reveal a concern with the understanding of the historical and social reasons behind the existence of rich and poor, of wage-earners and bosses. In these meetings and in many others held inside the Church, the workers' group gradually incorporated the idea that they had to educate and organize their fellow workers.

> We'd work until six and head straight to the meetings. On the job site we'd have meetings at lunch time. We also had meetings on Saturday in rooms that were offered at Cáritas (an agency that deals with problems of the poor) or at the Pastoral Commission office, in order to decide what we would do on Monday with the other workers. We even had discussions at soccer games: we'd come in and tell them that soccer games were used to divert their attention. It was hard getting that idea into their heads.[15]

The local Church ratified the ideas and actions of its working-class faithful thus providing an official reference. The minutes of the plenary sessions of the Pastoral Council of the Archdiocese of Vitória (COPAV) provide detailed analyses of the development of capitalism in the state of Espírito Santo—both in the cities and in the rural areas. It characterizes workers in the following fashion:

> 1. Their production is social in nature; 2. they produce surplus labor; 3. [their work is] oriented towards others; 4. their needs are defined by capital; 5. they are characterized by their antagonism; 6. they are subject to the internal conflicts of capitalism; 7. their consciousness is determined by the alienated nature of labor; 8. they can become a class in itself and for itself; 9. solution: overcome exploitation. Achieve the future.

Those minutes were distributed to the Church's grass-roots groups with the following introductory paragraph:

> In the various COPAV sessions, the council members have been reflecting on personal and community commitment to building the Kingdom of God on the ground we walk on. Therefore the situation of poverty, which impedes the building of this Kingdom, has been a concern of the leaderships committed to the Church's work in Vitória.[16]

This language clearly illustrates the utopian and prophetic nature of the Church's organizational work which is based on liberation theology, taking into consideration concrete and historically determined circumstances. Liberation theology uses faith as a uniting factor, thus the worker is able to find inspiration for his participation in the organizational processes. While it is faith that moves one to participate, it is the political significance of the symbols of faith that leads one to reflect upon social contradictions, and thus to become aware of the historical nature of the problems that affect survival. The organizational structure of many small groups helps to encourage the "right to choose, to speak, and to be respected like human beings." In this sense, the following outlook was proposed, in 1977, for "community work":

> Each member of the group has personal objectives, and each one proposes their personal objective as an OBJECTIVE FOR THE GROUP. The agent also has objectives FOR THE GROUP. On the basis of these objectives FOR THE GROUP, the members arrive at the objectives OF THE GROUP, integrating all the objectives. It is important, in group work, that people take on tasks that are related to everyone's objectives.[17]

Within the dynamic of the working groups, the worker feels respected and recognized as a person, which does not occur for the individual in the everyday experience on the job. Feeling that they can participate in decision making, workers are able to leave the shell of their private and individual sphere and gain the insight that they are able to act in a public and collective sphere. This provides a new source for their motivations that will then guarantee the continuation of their participation.

The workers involved in the Pastoral Commission gradually became more anxious to actively participate and organize. No longer satisfied with the small meetings held at Church, they now wanted to actually apply their organizational experience and awareness. The means for this did not take long to appear. The metalworkers' Union Opposition* was at this time expanding rapidly in São Paulo and its ideas found fertile ground among the construction workers. Having been led for over a decade by the same president, the construction union had few members and did little more than administer the workers' benefit programs. With help from the Pastoral Workers' Commission, from FASE (a popular education organization), which had also been a steady contributor to the movement, and from the auxiliary bishop of the Archdiocese of Vitória Dom Luiz Gonzaga Fernandes, the small group of workers were put in contact with Union Opposition leaders in São Paulo,[18] from whom they received written material to study. A movement leader stated in an interview:

---

*The Union Opposition (*Oposição Sindical*) refers to a part of the labor movement that focuses largely on factory level concerns. It has generally criticized the official unions for playing the bosses' game. In turn, it has been accused of undermining the unions and focusing exclusively on factory organization.—Ed.

We started studying those documents in group meetings out in Porto de Sant'Ana. G. also took copies out to Rio Marinho. And everyone studied. There was another group in Campo Grande. That was when we got the idea that we should take over the union and throw out the one that was there.[19]

The movement leaders thus began a period of criticism of the official union structure, which was dependent on the Ministry of Labor. The struggle aimed at increasing the awareness of the need to change the union structure, to create an autonomous and independent union movement, organized rank and file from the bottom up. Their language was so emphatic and so radical that it impeded the struggle for more specific demands and resulted in isolating the movement from the other political forces emerging both in the parties and in the labor movement.

While the language assimilated by the Union Opposition stimulated segregationist practices, the behavior of the external agents (the Pastoral Commission and FASE) significantly reinforced the same type of attitudes, with blatant manifestations of protectionism, political purism, and the preservation of these organizations' influence over the group. These circumstances, along with the changing of the political situation at the turn of the decade, began to reveal certain contradictions and ambiguities in the "Church's work" with social movements.

A NEW POLITICAL SITUATION AND NEW STRATEGIES FOR PROGRESSIVE CHURCH SECTORS IN RELATION TO SOCIAL MOVEMENTS

During the 1970s, the Church was the only channel of popular expression capable of confronting police and institutional repression. It not only stimulated a variety of issue-oriented social movements, but it also gave all its support to the struggle for political amnesty and for human rights. It was during this period that the Church played the part of a political party identified with popular interests and with other organizations more fit to represent the specific interests of individual social sectors.

The political situation at the turn of the decade, with its promises of greater political freedom and the reorganization of the parties, led the Church to redefine its strategies for action in its relation to the social movements, and to encourage their formal organization outside the Church structures. A text written by Frei Betto in November 1979 entitled "Political Practice and Pastoral Practice" is representative of this change in strategy and appears to have been used as a guide and point of reference by the Church's grass-roots agents. Frei Betto says:

In these new circumstances, within this new political process, pastoral work with the popular classes must redefine its role in civil society and reformulate its relationship with political action. With the political "opening," which reflects the regime's need to reset its course in response to a new international situation and the qualitative advance of the popular and workers' movement, Brazilian civil society has been reordered. The popular movement and the workers' movement have been emancipated from the need for ties with Pastoral Commissions.[20]

Frei Betto thought that pastoral work ought to remain in a specifically ecclesiastical dimension. Popular movements should be channeled through their own means. Pastoral work should avoid the "tendency of Christian specificity"; rather, it should articulate itself dialectically with society's other organizational forms: neighborhood associations, unions, parties, etc.

Despite the political coherence of this proposal, it reflected the desires of a person with a broad view of the political process more than it did the desires of the majority of activists in social movements dependent on the Church. Sharing a generalized antipathy toward politicians, trade-union leaders, and institutional politics, these sectors found it very hard to make the leap toward the emancipation from their ties to the pastoral commissions. It was not easy for the "animators" of urban movements already organized around specific demands to suddenly redirect their actions into gaining control of extant neighborhood associations. Nor was it simple for the many Union Opposition groups to accept the idea that they should work within the unions. The difficulties were located not only in the formal aspects but, above all, in the formal break with symbolic and cultural characteristics of the social movements identified with the Church's organizational agenda.

Another urgent issue at this time for pastoral agents and movement activists was the need to work with political parties. Frei Betto made it clear that this was of the utmost necessity in enabling the popular forces, CEBs, and activists in community and labor movements to unite into a new political channel. He argued that:

> This political channel should not be simply the sum of the grass-roots movements, but also the politically structured consequences of the action of the people's movements. . . . The idea is to assure the autonomy of the grass-roots community and workers' organizations (from mother's clubs to factory commissions) and, at the same time, to create the conditions for them to have an impact, through a political channel, on the system of legislative, judicial and executive powers.[21]

The reorganization of the party system in 1979 shook up the political forces and confused the movement activists who had not been identified with either the government party (ARENA) or the opposition party (MDB) and who had not been especially interested in political parties as a short-term priority. Yet the political situation was now raising the urgent demand for decisions in this area in order to simultaneously preserve both the Church and the integrity of the local bases of social movements that were tied to it. Never before had there been so much talk of *autonomy* and *independence* for the social movements in their relationship with the political parties and the state.

The idea of "emancipating the social movements from the pastoral commissions," along with that of the creating of a party that would act as an instrument for the expression of the movement's interests in the political arena, revealed the two sides of the intricate issue of the Church's relationship with the social movements. The progressive grass-roots party was already being created through efforts to bring together the three types of political and social forces existing mainly in the ABC region of São Paulo: progressive sectors of the Church; remnants of the 1960s' leftists who were critical of certain forms of struggle and organization; and the sector of the Brazilian labor movement, self-identified as combative and independent, together with the union opposition movements.

This party was the PT, the Workers' Party. Its structure was based more on a nucleus factor than on an effort to circumvent the antidemocratic nature of the new Law for Party Organization. This center-based structure enabled the political party of the Church's own CEB-based structure to then spread throughout neighborhoods, trades, professions, and rural areas. Not that the PT was an entirely Church-sponsored project. Rather, it represented the desire of sectors identified with the struggles of the people and presented them with a certain kind of organizational work. The PT would provide the political framework for all these sectors, preserving the unity and the institutional limits of the Church, and at the same time giving political support to the goals, values, and organizational style of a broad array of social movements.[22]

There was more to the political architecture aimed at safeguarding the respective interests of the Church and the social movements. What was needed was a broad space for the articulation of the social movements themselves. And in early 1980, months after the political party reform law—and for the first time since the authoritarian regime had come to power—representatives of social movements met with the objective of organizing a national network. This *sui generis* gathering would bring together a diversity of movements and, organizationally, would provide the decisive and fundamental embryo of what, three years later, would become the Unified Workers' Confederation, the CUT (Central Única dos Trabalhadores).

In February 1980, important representatives of the Brazilian labor movement, professional associations, and several Church pastoral commissions met in João Monlevade (state of Minas Gerais) to establish some basic orientations for trade union actions, as well as to encourage "cooperation between the labor movement's struggles and those of the people's movement (neighborhoods, land, etc.) in the cities and in the countryside."[23] In June 1981 this network, significantly broadened, adopted the name ANAMPOS (National Network of Labor and People's Movements). When the second encounter was held in June 1980, the grouping still had no officially sanctioned name as its fundamental interest was in defining its own territory, not wanting to be even remotely confused or associated with the various organizations or parties related to the union and its social movements. The participants wanted to create the atmosphere that would enable the movements to meet each other, to exchange experiences, and to coordinate specific struggles, without compromising each individual group's autonomy.

Our aim here is not to point out or to analyze in their entirety the consequences of this network. Our interest lies more in the network's relationships with the Church and with the conceptions it developed regarding the organization of the people's workers movement. Present at the meeting of the Second Encounter, held in Taboão da Serra, São Paulo, were twenty-six representatives of urban and rural unions of varying political and ideological inclinations, alongside of twenty-three representatives of other kinds of social movements that were tied—directly or indirectly—to the Church, from various regions of the country. Twelve of the latter were representing worker or land pastoral commissions and CEBs; two were representing union oppositions; two were members of FASE; and five were metal workers connected to union opposition activities. All in all, there were fifty. I was the fiftieth, the only person who was neither a union member nor tied to the Church. I was simply a participant in the popular movement of Vila Velha.[24]

ANAMPOS's conceptions regarding the organization of popular movements were put into practice within the dynamic of the meetings themselves. Here, decision making arose from small-group discussions where all were able to speak and participate as equals, explicitly encouraging not only the movement's own internal democracy, but also distribution of power within the group. This organizational style sought to reproduce and reinforce the day-to-day characteristics already present in most of the social movements represented. Among these characteristics were certain principles already evident in activities underway at the time, and already being shared by a broad range of social movements, especially by those stimulated by the Church.

These characteristics and principles can be summarized by the following points: (1) maintenance of the autonomy and the independence of the social movements in their relation to the parties and the state, while always respecting their participants' freedom of choice regarding party affiliation; (2) mobilization from the bottom up, and maintenance of respect for rank-and-file decisions; (3) horizontal structuring of the organizations, with the leadership acting as the instruments and spokespersons of the interests expressed by the rank-and file; (4) stimulation of the exercising of direct and participatory democracy (in the unions, through horizontal union organization, for example, in factory commissions; and in popular movements, through direct relations between the movement and the state); (5) inter-linking, solidarity, and cooperation between the union movement and the other popular movements.

This set of observations acquires greater significance from the point of view of the Church's relations with the social movements beginning in 1980. While it took great care to maintain its unity and cohesion during the period of political flux and confusion, the Church carefully created solid spaces and channels which enabled it to maintain certain practices, principles, and values espoused within the social movements. The Church thus reinvigorated its specific functions, but did not renounce its influence over the orientation of these movements.

The effects of the new orientation for pastoral work in relation to the social movements were not immediately obvious in a direct or linear sense because each movement had its specificities that created different responses to external influences. Nonetheless, due to the strength of the organizational initiator—the Church—the movements gradually followed this orientation.

We saw how the public transportation movement was abruptly and deliberately disarticulated despite having survived for nearly two years, and despite the fact that its goals were still unrealized. From the view of the new orientations for pastoral work, however, we can find a plausible explanation. For the transportation movement to regroup specifically around Church work, at that moment, would have meant an intensification of care for the grass-roots level groups. This would have removed them from the broader movements which, over a period of time, had already been influenced by other leftist political forces. As a result of this participation in the broader movements, internal disputes within the leadership group had erupted, leading to a split between those whose activities were oriented by the CEBs and those who were active in the popular movements, whether or not these movements had any ties to the Church. This latter group, which included people who had been involved with the Pastoral Commission's work, began accusing the Church of "not helping the struggle to advance" and joined an underground organization called MEP (Movement for the Education of the Proletariat). The timing of the split was not by chance, but was one of the effects of the new orientation, which aimed at, among other things, "winnowing out" the movement. However, the consequences for the public transportation movement were discouraging. First of all the leadership's lack of resolve discouraged grass-roots work and had weakened the movement's capacity for strong mobilization and pressure. Secondly, the "need to opt for genuinely Church-oriented work" led to the pastoral agents' withdrawal from the transportation movement's General Commission with the justification that it would now have to stand on its own legs, independent of the CEBs. The veiled objective was to decentralize the struggle by involving the grass-roots groups with other, more localized, demands, thus preserving the Church's own maneuvering room.

This set of factors led to the total decline of the movement, which became totally inviable with the increasing involvement of its constituency with other urban problems: sewers, drainage ditches, garbage collection, pavement, construction, legalization of land deeds, etc. The need to win over formal community movements within the various neighborhoods was also to become one of the main priorities from that time on.

As has already been stated, specific movements will respond to the Church's general orientations in their own way. However, one can conclude that the new orientations of the progressive pastoral sectors from 1979 on were largely responsible for the general decline during the years of 1980, 1981, and 1982 of what were previously broad and massive urban movements. Other factors (such as the party reform and the 1982 elections) also were responsible for this decline but their influence can be viewed as minor when compared to that of the Church.

As for the construction workers' movement, the impact of the new orientations and of the above-mentioned strategies was reinforced by the tendency of the Union Opposition to favor parallel unionism, i.e., to focus on neighborhood level organizing outside the union structures. This tendency was promoted by activists from FASE and from the Workers' Pastoral Commission. Here discrepancies arose because other activists defended the idea of fighting for a new union structure by working within the union itself. In other words, instead of organizing outside the sphere of production (in the neighborhoods, where workers' associations actually were created), organizing ought to take place on the job site and in union assemblies and the aim would be winning control of the union. These discrepancies ended up confusing many working-class leaders and took the wind out of struggles for specific demands. Once again, demands were used to promote "politicization" and consciousness building through language that reaffirmed the need to participate and organize.[25] This time the aim was changing the official union structures.

In contrast to the public transportation movement (whose social base was not specifically limited to the quest for better transportation), the mobilized rank-and-file construction workers were strongly motivated more by the tangible prospect of wage gains than by the effect of consciousness-building language. They pressured their wavering leaders who, whether they wanted to or not, were then obliged to draw up clearly worded proposals which incorporated concrete interests. The workers' interest in this was so vital that it led to a general strike of the building trades, a strike led out of necessity by the union opposition after the refusal of the local union leadership to do so. Within months, the union opposition group put together a platform on which to run in the local elections. At this same time its main leader was actively participating in ANAMPOS and was planning to adopt their principles of action. The tendency to favor work outside the union structures was gradually dispelled and disappeared completely after the opposition won the union elections.

Although other factors contributed to the demise of the mistaken notions of parallel union movements (i.e., outside the official unions) within the Brazilian labor movement, the orientation, given by the Church's progressive sectors to its pastoral commissions in the years 1979 and 1980, made an extremely important contribution to this change in posture.

As for the relationship between the public transportation movement and the construction workers' movement, the factors that had brought them together were not of the nature of economic demands but consisted more of sets of political principles, propositions, and values which flowed together through specific channels: initially through the Church and, later, through the PT and the ANAMPOS.

AMBIGUITIES AND CONTRADICTIONS
IN THE CHURCH'S RELATIONS WITH SOCIAL MOVEMENTS

Several questions have arisen from observng the Church's presence within social movements. The most common questions include the following: Does the Church help or hurt? Does it stimulate the movements or hold them back? Is it really interested in the independent creation of popular organizations or does it organize people only to reinforce itself as an institution?

These same questions are studied in treatises by Church theoreticians and theologians. Roberto Romano is extremely skeptical in his evaluation of the Church's actual commitment to transforming the structure of class society. According to him, the restructuring of the Church merely reflects a formal change, expressed in bureaucratic modernization under "the sign of a revolutionary position."[26] He states that its real aim is to "renew the instruments of domination" through its criticisms of the state. The Church does not intend to question the state's intrinsically repressive character, but rather to strengthen itself and reaffirm itself in relation to the state. Romano goes on:

> The division of society between oppressors and oppressed, between owners of production goods and people robbed of the fruits of their labor, between antagonistic social classes, conveys confrontations, struggles and violence. How, then, can one live out evangelical charity and also opt in favor of one social class? Unity, in fact, is one of the Church's keynotes and class struggle divides people. Are the unity of the Church and class struggle compatible?[27]

The questions and concerns raised by Roberto Romano are valid and are easily perceived within the two experiences described. We need only to return to the strategies implemented by the Church in response to the new circumstances that arose at the turn of the decade, when its primary goal was maintaining its organizational and institutional unity. These concerns and questions, however, can be made relative by observing that the same strategies that were preserving the Church were also influential in the advancing of the national articulation of social movements. We have seen, for example, how these concerns contributed to the creating of a national network of people's movements (ANAMPOS) as well as helping in the weakening of the practice of parallel trade unionism. Yet despite these advances it becomes clear that the Church's retreat, and the internalization of its action at the time, were a setback for the social movements, especially for the urban movements most dependent on the Church.

These situations reveal a profound ambiguity within the Church's relationship to the social movements. This ambiguity, however, is mitigated first by the recognition and admission that religiosity (as a cultural element) is the principal link to be maintained and preserved and that it guarantees the basic conditions for survival of the movements. And secondly, that the preservation of religiosity implies a defense of the institution which guarantees its existence. These observations make more sense when we look at the decision-making process happening within the Church-related social movements. At the higher levels of the pastoral commissions, goals and orientations for action are established "for and with" the base. The people at the base, on the other hand, must forward their decisions to the many intermediate and higher levels in order to establish "common points" and achieve the united action of all the sectors involved. This flow of information illustrates an important peculiarity of the decision-making process, that is, the *sacred* dimension of the institution actually invests the decisions with a higher force, which is capable of imposing and nurturing the group identity necessary for political and social participation. Moreover, the openness of the Church to critical reflections on social problems and to the popular interests that arise within its ranks are seen by many as a means for transforming the institution itself. Bruno Pucci's study deals with these aspects in an attempt to understand the Church's new line of action.[28]

The institutional transformations began in the 1960s when certain sectors of the Church began dedicating their lives to the oppressed, exploited, and impoverished, especially to the peasants of the North and Northeast, always with a view toward their organization. At the same time, there was a growing concern within the Church about the increasing influence of the Pentecostal and Umbanda sects, while its own ritual forms were remaining traditional and authoritarian. Its fears at the prospects of a dwindling clientele gradually intensified and led to an awareness of the weakness of its missionary and proselytical work, as well of its inability, in ideological terms, to provide a reasonable explanation for the ever increasing impoverishment of the people.

These factors led many of the religious clergy to engage in organizing work. While some were motivated more by the desire to drive away the phantom of communism, there were others whose actual interest was the transformation of society. Their critical actions and reflections culminated in the creation of the MEB (Grass-Roots Education Movement) and its appeals for social reform and, later in the Catholic Action movement, which espoused more radical positions. The workers' and peasants' movements of the 1960s increased the awareness of the intermediate sectors of the Church, who then aroused the members of the hierarchy, thus progressively bringing into being the incorporation of different and antagonistic world views. In 1964, while the majority of the episcopate were defending the coup d'etat, political persecution was affecting the priests and others involved in religious orders. Members of the JUC (Catholic University Youth) were imprisoned and the majority of bishops did nothing in their defense. However the links with the workers' and student movements did not disappear, and the hierarchy usually found itself obliged to take up the defense of these sectors. While conservative sectors were attempting to construct a dialogue between Church and state, the new progressive sectors were demonstrating against the regime. The intensification of repression thus pressured the CNBB to speak out in the defense of human rights, what Pucci calls an "educational process in which the grass roots educate their leaders. . . ." "The conscious participation of Christians in popular movements, the appearance of the popular Church as a result of that participation and the subsequent theoretical efforts—although only in their first step throughout Latin America—were to be fundamental elements in the Second Conference of the Latin American Episcopate (2nd CELAM) in Medellín and would have an overwhelming influence on the Church's actions in the 1970s."[29]

Yet the observation that the Church, over the past twenty years, has been permeable to popular interests and sensitive to their organizational needs does not negate the affirmation that its relationship with the social movements is contradictory. The ambiguity inherent within the Church's stance of preserving its own unity while having to defend the specific interests of one class (the dominated class) ends up creating tense and conflictive relationships in several areas: within its own ranks (the sanctions against theologian Leonardo Boff, for example), in its relationship with the state and with its pastoral agents, and finally, in its relation to the social movements themselves, our main concern here.

The contradiction in the Church's relationship with the social movements is made evident, for example, when Church activists—imbued with their commitment to social and political action—interacted with parties and organizations who offered more attractive prospects for participation in social reality and promised to free them from the control exerted by the Church. This explains how several underground political organizations arose and/or increased their membership with former Church activists. These groups, although "bothersome," are no threat to the Church since the language they use seldom finds great popular receptivity when contrasted to the Church's discourse. This is why it is so common to hear vehement criticisms of "Church work" coming from those who have left the Church and even from those who are still reluctant to break their ties with it. The following interview bears significant witness to this situation:

> I was a member of the Pastoral and I still am. But I have a lot of criticisms. The problem is that our observations are not taken into account. Before, with Father Fugerre, Dom João, and Dom Luiz as bishops, we were really strong, with moral and political support. This gave a lot of strength to the construction workers' movement at the time. Today the Church in Vitória has totally changed. The Church helped and still helps us to advance. But it has a limit: it's capitalistic. It accepts capitalism, even though the more progressive sector doesn't think that way. They can think what they want, but the Church accepts capitalism, you know? . . . The Church is a public business; anyone can join. And for the Church, you're a potential client,

you're a Christian. It has a vision of saving you, as a Christian, as a child of God or whatever. . . . The Church either has to take the responsibility when it says the opposite of what society says or else it has to get out. You grow when you start realizing that you're exploited by a boss. If you stay put in the Church, you won't grow beyond this point.[30]

This statement, made by one of the main union leaders of the civil construction workers in early 1985, reveals the tension that inevitably results from the contradiction inherent in the Church's need to maintain its own unity while being committed to the actions of social transformation. In practice, this means that while it encourages participation in public affairs and politics by promoting critical consciousness-building, the Church at the same time places priority on its demands for the practice of faith and religious services, thus securing the presence of these members within the flock.

RELIGIOSITY AND SOCIAL MOVEMENTS

One of the main concerns frequently observed in the meetings of social movements and in their encounters is "How can we keep the movement going?" In other words, how to guarantee and maintain continuity of mobilization, and how to encourage participation in the face of the many situations and values that lead people in the opposite direction?

Here the weight of the lengthy heritage of populist and paternalist practices becomes visible. It is difficult in this context to awaken a sense of collective action of daily reinforcements of the ideology of individualism and social ascent. Trying to encourage forms of community identity under the weight of the impersonal and depersonalized relationships engendered in such urban settings has become an endless challenge. How can you take people, tired after a day's work, away from their television sets when this is their most important leisure activity? How can you take them away from their scant free time to ask them to participate in the organizing of initiatives around community needs? Very strong motives are needed. The silent and for the most part painless adaptation of broad sectors of the population is an impressive phenomenon, as is the passivity that pervades the daily lives of the outlying impoverished neighborhoods when confronted with problems that affect their very survival.

During the two years that I was on the board of the neighborhood association of the most polluted (from coal and iron-ore dust) neighborhood in Greater Vitória, where the pollution was posing an immediate and a serious threat to the health of residents, we had to do veritable song-and-dance routines to promote public demonstrations that would pressure the polluters, one of whom was a major state-owned company, the Vale do Rio Doce Company. Following the occasional mass mobilizations, we were always left with the same few people who, for one reason or another, always assumed responsibility for keeping alive the association.

Other specific factors fragment the population, making community organizing difficult. Rather than considering themselves residents, thus perceiving the characteristics of exploitation contained in this sociological category,[31] the inhabitants of neighborhoods—even the ones most directly involved in community problems—define and identify themselves with smaller groups. These small groups consist of immediate neighbors, religious sects, different age groups (especially the elderly and the youth), groups evolved around leisure time activities (soccer teams, tournaments), and local political party organizations. These groups overlap, interrelate, and at times are mutually hostile, illustrating part of the diffuse movement which obscures and even annuls the category of *resident* as being a valid category meaningful for collective political action. A neighborhood association, for example, though defining itself as representative of the residents of a given neighborhood, is usually nothing more than a tight circle of relationships which only give unity and cohesion to a specific group. The great difficulty of neighborhood associations, from the sociological point of view, lies in the maintaining of a mobilization based on common urban problems and their underlying contradictions in the face of other diverse interests and expectations. This difficulty is exacerbated by the neighborhood's sociological heterogeneity (ranging from retired, unemployed, students, housewives, and workers in any number of professions, to small businesspeople and merchants).

Permanent motivations must arise from within this culturally multifaceted and socially heterogeneous population if the residents are to be organized. These motivations must cut across differentiated interests and expectations, and they must involve diverse groups. They need to be strong enough to impose themselves and take shape above the small cleavages and the disintegrating and individualistic ideological forces. Moreover, they must provide symbolic identity of actions. The action of several of the left-wing currents armed with "the truths" and slogans, have a revolutionary rationality, but their discourse does not appeal to the popular sectors. The historical configuration of Brazil's development, which is marked by varying modalities of domination and repression, has produced ideological and cultural traits adverse to political parties equipped with that kind of revolutionary rationality.

However, religiosity has provided a force for unifying people and maintaining group identities. Religion enables the residents to overcome differences, problems, and cleavages. It also equalizes different interests by offering unity in action and by keeping the local populations relatively mobilized and predisposed to participate in demand-oriented and protest social movements. While not true of all forms of religiosity, this is true of the religiosity already deep-rooted in the Brazilian people's consciousness and culture, and practiced through new ritual forms created and encouraged by sectors of the Catholic Church. These new decentralizing and participatory ritual forms confer to religious symbols a critical dimension identified with the interests of the people.

Among the workers, where disintegrating and conformist ideologies had prevailed for years, religion also acts as a unifying force and provides a space for reflection upon their real condition of oppression and exploitation. Countless CEBs, acting jointly with the Workers' Pastoral Commission, produced groups of workers who, while initially moved by faith, came to perceive the importance of organizing, of struggling to change the conditions imposed on them by exploitation and poverty. The real base of support for the cost-of-living movement, active in working-class neighborhoods of São Paulo between 1973 and 1978 despite the support of other social and political sectors, came out of mothers' clubs of the Church and the CEBs. It is significant, too, that the major strikes in São Paulo's ABC region also had the total support and backing of these particular groups along with that of the Workers' Pastoral Commission. In Espírito Santo, the construction workers' movement grew out of a group tied to the CEBs and to the Workers' Pastoral Commission; just as the public transportation movement in Vila Velha was basically structured around and sustained by the CEBs.

The importance of the Church's involvement with the social movements that arose in Brazil from the 1970s on and in the motivational role of religiosity in the establishing of commitments to participation and organization is undeniable. A wealth of documentation produced by the Church itself attests to this reality. In particular, the Document "Christian Demands for a Political Order," produced in 1977 by the CNBB, and discussed by all the CEBs in the country, issued strong appeals in this very sense. It encouraged participation and organization as components of faith and as the duty of Christians.

When, for example, a housewife and mother of eight like Dona Maria Clara, who became a symbol of the Vila Velha CEBs through her active participation in social movements, gets up on a platform and speaks to a gathering of demonstrators of her daily suffering; denounces capitalist exploitation; and calls for the social justice and equality achieved through the participation and organization of the people; she speaks in the name of her faith. Her cry was for a better existence in the name of the struggle for liberation and in the name of Christ. The political and utopian ideology of her discourse is colored by the religious and Christian faith that comes from the depths of her being. All those who hear and identify with her, through the concrete privations of their own lives and faith, are able to share and assimilate the political sense of her utopia.

This points out a process of sacralization of the profane: politics. The practice of politics by the people will enter the domain of faith. The need for a "critical reflection on reality," for participation and for organization is now an attribute of faith. The struggle for a just, egalitarian society, one without exploitation—in religious language—gains a prophetic and utopian dimension, not just in the sense of the unattainable but also in the sense of what is lacking. Thus the quest for a different kind of existence acquires a real bodily significance for those who are transformed through their contact with symbols that have been re-created and have taken on new meaning.

None can deny that the new organizational methods that the Church is putting into practice are creating major transformations for those who are assimilating them; nor can it be denied that such stances are altering the daily reality of practical actions, and of political and cultural conceptions. Denying this means denying the existence of most of the social movements that have arisen in Brazil and that have high value on interpersonal ties, solidarity, mutual aid, participation among "equals," collective decision making, etc. These characteristics conflict with some of the fundamental values of capitalism (competition, individualism, dispersion, etc.) and with the Brazilian political tradition (centralization of power, populism, paternalism, etc.). These movements, whether urban, rural, or working-class, are organized around the communitarian model, and have promoted significant changes in terms of political culture, with visible effects on the political process itself.

CONCLUSION

The observation of the Church's vital and outstanding presence in the social movements that have occurred in Brazil since the 1970s leads us, from the epistemological standpoint, to the suggestion that the analysis of social movements need not be restricted to the movement of capital (the existence of social contradictions) and/or political circumstances.[32] The social and political actors (the organizational subjects) generating the impulse for these social movements must also be taken into consideration. With their principles of action, behavioral values, and organizational norms for the process of change and transformation, they have an overwhelming influence on the shaping of social movements, and on the eventual social, political, and cultural impact of these movements. This impact, of course, also depends fundamentally on the behavior of the movements' antagonists.

According to this epistemological approach, it is impossible to account for innumerable social movements without first considering the Church as the decisive organizational subject. Nor can social movements be understood without transcending certain sociological considerations (since structural contradictions alone are not a sufficient condition for the occurrence of social movements) to grasp a number of concepts developed by anthropology: cultural dynamics, political culture, and identity. Among similar studies[33] I will point out the excellent contribution of Eunice Durham, who had the sensitivity to apprehend and categorize the types of organizational models that cut across the social movements present in Brazil over recent years.

Durham perceived the existence of two basic organizational models, one formal and the other "communitarian," which are usually mutually exclusive but at times overlap. The formal model requires clear representational mechanisms and certain bureaucratic conditions for its recognition by the state, and also requires the election of a group of leaders responsible for the promoting of mobilizations and of representing the population's demands. This model is often supported by the state due to the fact that official agencies expect the presence of "official representatives." While it may not have arisen out of the social sectors it represents, it is part of the population's cultural heritage. Typical examples of this model are neighborhood associations and trade unions.

The novelty, however, pertains to the emergence of the "communitarian" model. It avoids the institutionalizing of its representation and demands the ongoing participation of all, both in the making and in the execution of decisions. Emphasis is placed on equality—a symbolic recourse for building group identity—as a means for achieving the goal of collectivity. Thus, according to Durham, "This experience of community, that is, the collectivity of equals created by the joint action of all, takes place in a dimension of its own which implies an even more important novelty: recognition of the person in public rather than private terms."[34]

She points to the CEBs as an example of this latter model. I would conclude that, far beyond the CEBs themselves, the Church itself—with its new proposals for organization and for political action—has been the foremost organizational subject responsible for adoption for the communitarian model by such a large number of social movements. Yet while they are flourishing and moving toward this model, these movements are also subject to countless ambiguities and contradictions that deserve a further study, one avoiding *a priori* and hasty assessments.

I conclude by raising the following hypothesis about the contradiction between the need to preserve the unity of the Church and the need to stimulate the kind of social movements we have described. While these movements are dependent on the Church, thus subject to fluctuations within its power structure, they also open room for organization, creating political channels for participation and generating changes in popular political culture.[35] These latter developments may well take on their own life and strength and make it possible for decisive pressure to be brought to bear on class structures and on the interests of conservative sectors within the Church itself.

NOTES

1. Greater Vitória is made up of five contiguous municipalities: Vitória (capital of the state of Espírito Santo), Vila Velha, Cariacica, Serra, and Viana.

2. The Coffee Plantation Eradication Program was an initiative of the state government, with the object of eradicating inefficient coffee plantations and modernizing production. By 1968, approximately 300,000 hectares or 52 percent of the total area where coffee was grown had been eradicated. While the program had also called for crop diversification, fiscal incentives, and support for cooperatives, 70 percent of the eradicated area was turned into pastures for livestock raising, an activity which requires little labor.

3. Investments in these "large-scale industrial projects" were projected at around four billion dollars and were expected to create direct employment for 10,421 skilled workers. All the projects were export-oriented, were based on joint ventures between the government and foreign capital, and used advanced technologies.

4. In 1983, according to the Archdiocese of Vitória, 47 percent of the population lived in shantytowns; 41 percent of these were located on private land, 22 percent on federal government land, 20 percent on city-owned land, 7 percent on state-owned land, and 10 percent on land with disputed ownership. The occupation, or "take-overs," of urban land grew substantially from 1975 to 1983. It is estimated that 100,000 people became squatters during that period, not without confronting police violence, evictions, and resistance.

5. The ABC region of São Paulo refers to the highly industrialized municipalities neighboring the city of São Paulo to the south (Santo André, São Bernardo do Campo, São Caetano, and Diadema). The area concentrates the largest single contingent of the Brazilian working class.

6. For a more detailed description of the organizational dynamic of the Vila Velha public transportation movement, see Ana Maria Doimo, *Movimento Social Urbano, Igreja e Participação Popular* (Petrópolis: Vozes, 1984). Several ideas on religiosity and social movements are developed further in my book.

7. The CNBB document "Exigências Cristãs de uma Ordem Política" ("Chris-

tian Requirements for the Political Order") issued in 1977, in addition to being highly critical of the authoritarian regime, emphatically advocated the emergence of the need for participation and for popular organization. "Every person is a social being," and as such is always involved in organizing. Youth, for example, organize their outings, parties, and dances just as the workers, in their unions, "unite to struggle for their rights." Farther on, it affirms that "a request presented by a commission, along with a petition signed by all the residents, is worth much more than the request of just one member of a community." Moreover, "people and social groups have duties to society, such as the duty to participate in politics. . . . Society, which is full of injustice, needs to be totally transformed. . . . The role of all Christians is to participate in building this new society." Note the constant appeal to participation and organization as values and duties, and a sacred duty at that, if we consider the nature of the institution which speaks and the receptive spirit of the faithful who hear. The document was published in Luiz Gonzaga de Souza Lima, *Evolução Política dos Católicos e da Igreja no Brasil* (Petrópolis: Vozes, 1979), pp. 255–266.

8. Interview, spring 1980.

9. Interview, spring 1980.

10. In this chapter, I will not go into the historical meanderings of the organization of the construction workers' movement, nor into the conflicts with the local union leadership who were seen as sold-out, devious, and paternalistic. I will restrict myself to the movement's relationship with the Church, through the Pastoral Commission.

11. Interview, March 7, 1985.

12. Interview, March 4, 1985.

13. Interview, March 3, 1985.

14. Equipe Coordenadora de Cursos da Arquidiocese de Vitória, "Relatório da Semana de Formação (17 a 21–10–77)," mimeo, 1977.

15. Interview, March 7, 1985.

16. Minutes of the 23rd plenary session of the COPAV, mimeo, Vitória, June 21–22, 1980.

17. "Questões e Reflexões sobre a Reunião da Diretoria do Conselho Pastoral da Arquidiocese de Vitória," mimeo based on November 1, 1977 meeting.

18. There is still no systematic study of the Union Opposition movements in Brazil, nor will we attempt to do one here. The Union Opposition is a segment of the Brazilian labor movement that arose out of the need to break out of the official trade-union structures, which are dependent in a top-down fashion on the Ministry of Labor. The first timid appearance of the movement came in 1968 during the strikes at Osasco and Contagem, but its most significant growth has been since 1977.

19. Interview, March 4, 1985.

20. Frei Betto, "Práctica Pastoral e Práctica Política," in *Cadernos do CEDI*, Supplement No. 26 (Rio de Janeiro: Tempo e Presença, March 1980), pp. 12, 15. I consider this text as a reference document since, according to pastoral agents in Vitória, it was widely disseminated and discussed by leaders of the pastoral commissions, thus playing the role of transmitting and generating new political behavior and actions with regards to the social movements.

21. Betto, "Práctica Pastoral e Práctica Política," p. 21.

22. Certain sectors interacting with the workers' movement in the ABC region

of São Paulo had drawn up plans for a new socialist party. In late 1979 this project was merged into the proposal under discussion by the ABC Workers Pastoral with which the metalworkers—especially their leaders—were most identified.

23. "Documento de Monlevade," João Monlevade (mimeograph, 1980).

24. The fact that I was merely a member of a specific movement (I was on the board of my local neighborhood association) which was not part of the web of Church movements was probably why I was not invited when the network's Third Encounter was held in Vitória in 1981. One reason for my surprise at not being invited was that I had received the report distributed by the Second Encounter (the *Documento São Bernardo*, Taboão da Serra, São Paulo: mimeograph, 1981) to all the local social movements. But my initial surprise gave way to an understanding that I and "my" movement were insignificant from the point of view of the interests of the Church sectors involved in the national network. Their objective was to either win back people and "Church movements" that had been "grabbed" by and/or deviated to other values and political tendencies.

25. The two specific movements discussed in this article exemplify a style of action prevalent in the social movements of the 1970s, in which the satisfaction of demands seemed to be less important than the goal of participation and organization. The cost-of-living movement was another eloquent example of this; see Ruth Cardoso, "Movimentos Sociais Urbanos: Balanço Crítico," in Bernardo Sorj and Maria Hermínia Tavares de Almeida, eds. *Sociedade e Política no Brasil Pós-64* (São Paulo: Brasiliense, 1983), p. 234. In more recent movements promoted by the Church we find a greater balance between the value given to the process of participation and organization and that given to satisfaction of the demands themselves. A close analysis of the movement against unemployment—especially in Curitiba—is an example. In these experiences, the state is no longer a mere target of denunciations, "against which we must struggle." It represents an arena where real political and economic victories can be won and an arena for negotiation, where popular interests must be well formulated and presented in order to prevail in the face of other interests also present in the same space.

26. Roberto Romano, *Brasil: Igreja contra Estado* (São Paulo: Kairós, 1979), p. 204.

27. Ibid., p. 219.

28. "A Nova Práxis Educacional da Igreja," Ph.D. Dissertation, University of São Paulo, 1981.

29. Ibid., pp. 71–74.

30. Interview, March 4, 1985.

31. See Manuel Castells, *La Cuestión Urbana* (México: Siglo XXI, 1974).

32. I refer here to theoretical developments inspired by the analyses of Castells, *La Cuestión Urbana*, and Jean Lojkine, *O Estado Capitalista e a Quesão Urbana* (São Paulo: Martins Fontes, 1981).

33. See Tilman Evers, "Reproduçao da Força de Trabalho e Movimentos Populares: O Caso dos Loteamentos Clandestinos em São Paulo" in Paulo J. Krischke, ed., *Terra de Habitação X Terra de Exploração* (São Paulo: Cortez, 1984); Eunice Durham, "Movimentos Socialis: A Construção da Cidadania," in *Novos Estudos*, No. 10 (October 1984); Eliane J. Vasconcellos Godoy and Paulo J. Krischke, "Igreja, Motivações

e Organização dos Moradores em Loteamentos Clandestinos," in Krischke, ed., *Terra de Habitação* X *Terra de Exploração*; Ana Maria Doimo, *Movimento Social Urbano*: Cardoso, "Movimentos Sociais Urbanos." Renato Boschi and Licia do P. Valladares, "Problemas Teóricos na Análise de Movimentos Sociais: Comunidade, Ação Coletiva e o Papel do Estado" (Nova Friburgo, ANPOCS, 1981) also provides important theoretical contributions for the analysis of issues such as community, collective action, and the role of the state.

34. Durham, "Movimentos Sociais," p. 28.

35. I see "culture" not as a product but rather as a set of symbols and values through which human beings orient and give meaning to their actions over the course of historically determined social, economic, and political processes. In this sense, culture is a dynamic universe of symbols, signs, and meanings subject to re-elaboration and re-creation in response to new conditions (material or otherwise) of existence.

Catholic Base Communities, Spiritist Groups and the Deepening of Democracy in Brazil

Rowan Ireland

This chapter explores the possibility that religious groups at the grass roots of Brazilian society might contribute to the deepening of democracy in Brazil. The Brazilian Catholic Church has expressed the hope that its primarily religious grass-roots ecclesial communities (CEBs) might contribute to the building of a Brazilian society that is more just, more participatory, more consonant with human freedom. While focusing on the CEBs, I also refer to the other popular religious groups found in the northeastern coastal town of Campo Alegre which I selected for a case study in the relationships between religion and politics in Brazil. In a broader study I investigate how the religions of the town, while being shaped by the political economies of Brazil, also contribute to the construction of social structures and what Clifford Geertz has called "cultural paradigms" with political and economic implications.[1] Here I pursue a question that is included in this broader investigation: Structurally and culturally, how does the group life of the CEBs and Afro-Brazilian cult groups of Campo Alegre affect the chances of its citizens contributing to a deepening of democracy?

Let me provide some conceptual and theoretical maps for the journey. The notion of "deepening of democracy" emerges by implication from critiques of democracy as it has been and is in Brazil. Formal democracy in Brazil, enhanced in the recent transition from military to civilian rule, has been seen by some Brazilian social scientists to be shallow—shallow in the sense that Brazil's modern periods of populist democracy, alternating with authoritarian regimes, have never included the lower classes except on terms manipulated from above. Shallow democracy, never allowing real participation in the political process below the urban middle classes, has in this view contributed to the steady advance of elite-controlled state power over civil society.[2]

Granted that critique, a deepening of Brazilian democracy would imply not only an opening of political structures from the top down but a building of structures from the grass roots up. Unrepresentative democratic politics and bureaucratic authoritarian politics escape challenge and succeed one another as long as lower-class and marginalized interests and values are not effectively articulated. The granting of more formal democracy, when, for example a military regime responds to elections and allows a civilian government to take office, does not of itself achieve a deepening of democracy.[3]

Effective articulation of interests and values for a deepening of democracy requires the construction and emergence into the political arena of grass-roots collectivities where private troubles may be seen to be public issues; where lower-class identity, values, and visions can be lived and rehearsed. I call such collectivities "intermediate groups"—*intermediate* in the sense that they stand between and allow for two-way communication between the structures of the state and citizens at the grass roots.

Intermediate groups, then, are not just any grass-roots groups. As an ideal type, they must have the following overlapping characteristics. First, they must be autonomous vis-à-vis local and national elites, in the sense that their development proceeds primarily from the expressed needs and decisions of members themselves and is not, primarily, a function of the needs of elites and elite-managed institutions. The concept of autonomy becomes clearer by negative example. Intermediate groups are autonomous from control by elites *unlike* the official unions granted the working classes by Getúlio Vargas that incorporate while extending state control; *unlike* a local religious brotherhood, incorporating the poor in the patronage of local landed or commercial or clerical elites in return for a respectable burial. Second, the autonomy of intermediate groups must not be merely national: their members must be engaged in articulation of grass-roots identifications, values, and interests, rather than in the transmission of hegemonic ideas from the state and the institutions of the dominant culture. Third, intermediate groups must operate as inclusive communities rather than as exclusive clubs. As such, their principle of internal organization cannot be ascriptive hierarchy or the expert-client relationship, reflecting and reproducing the dominant society. The intermediate group's internal organization, including its leadership, must maximize participation of individual members.

Placed in the historical realities of Brazil, this ideal-type of an intermediate group might seem to have little chance for real existence. The sheer momentum of paternalistic institutions, the securities offered the poor by corporate structures, the economic achievements of authoritarian regimes, the "culture of despair"[4] at the grass roots—all these factors might make it unlikely that intermediate groups should develop at the grass roots of Brazilian society. Indeed, contemplating Brazil from the top down and with a macrohistorical perspective, it is tempting to indulge the pessimism of overdetermination—to conclude that a deepening of democracy in Brazil has been preempted.

I believe that I can argue, albeit a little tentatively, against this pessimism. There are signs in the CEB movement that real and important changes have taken place at the grass roots over the last two decades. A diversity of groups, including some religious groups, demonstrate intermediate group characteristics. In focusing on religious groups I am not arguing that they are alone nor that all is well for a deepening of democracy through them. In fact I want to draw out ambiguities and pinpoint the fragility of intermediate groups as intermediate. But it is impossible to point to the religiously informed creativity that generates intermediate groups at the grass roots.

Years ago Emilio Willems suggested possibilities along these lines for Pentecostal groups.[5] In the face of conventional wisdom about Pentecostal conservatism I believe that there is some evidence to keep Willems's position alive, but I want to concentrate on the CEBs of the Catholic Church and suggest some comparisons with Afro-Brazilian groups. It may be *because* these groups are primarily religious and not political that they have a long-term potential to contribute to a transformation of Brazilian politics. But that line of speculation is not pursued here: it would involve an examination of linkages and overlap between grass-roots groups about which very little is known.[6]

THE POTENTIAL OF THE CEBS

For those familiar with the ways in which the Catholic Church in Latin America has traditionally served the status quo, it might come as a surprise that grass-roots intermediate groups might emerge from the Brazilian Church. But there is no doubt that the Church has changed profoundly over the last two decades, and the outstanding product of that change, the CEBs, do promise to function as intermediate groups and to help generate other intermediate groups, despite the hostile environment and internal problems of the Church.

The Brazilian National Conference of Bishops (CNBB) has adopted a "preferential option for the poor," implying that the Church should assume a new identity as promoter of the liberation of the poor. In analyzing why the Church should have adopted this option, some have seen its quest for institutional maintenance and influence as the prime motivation.[7] By the late 1950s, and thereafter at an accelerating pace, the attempt to maintain influence by institutional alliances with the state and through concentrating resources and personnel on the urban middle classes was failing. A marginalized Church, in this view, turned to the people at the margins of society for its new constituency—the uprooted peasants, the new urban masses. And a shortage of clergy (about one priest for every 9,000 people) called forth new methods, such as the creation of the CEBs run by lay leaders, to exert influence. One implication of this explanation of change in the Church is that the CEBs themselves might, after all, be a new mode of grass-roots aggregation initiated by elites for the ends of what remains an upper-class institution. Some of the ambiguous rhetoric in Church documents and some accounts of CEBs as "co-opting" agencies support this position.[8]

On the other hand, ideas and not the quest for influence have persuaded many clergy and laity that the building of CEBs is what the Church should be doing—even at the cost of influence as usually conceived. And these ideas anticipate that the CEBs, although essentially religious and certainly not political party groups, should develop as intermediate groups. Those members of the Church who have actually practiced the "preferential option for the poor" seem, from what they say about what they do, to be motivated by religious ideas which they and a majority of bishops consider faithful to recent papal teaching, the Vatican Council, and the declarations of the Latin American bishops assembled at Medellín, Colombia, in 1968 and Puebla, Mexico, in 1979. Those ideas include the definition of the Church's mission as being to the whole person, not just to some separated spiritual part—hence the concern with issues of justice and equity. The Church aims to encourage human fullness not only through the promotion of a consonant individual morality but by the struggle for a consonant social order. Salvation is conceived not as much in individual terms as in social terms: it is believed to involve the individual in participating in the transformation of society so that human potential revealed and called for in the Bible might be better achieved. Further, there is the belief that social transformation of the poor cannot be achieved by elites but only through the building, by the poor themselves, of communities in which new understanding of the Bible informs action to change society and transformative action informs religious understandings. The CEBs would not themselves be cells, as it were, within a movement for change, but they would move and motivate members to join or form other intermediate groups for change—new union formations, neighborhood associations and cooperatives, mothers' clubs, and the like. New ministries performed by laity from the lower classes are considered not simply to be filling in for the lack of priests, as would be consistent with the institutional-influence approach, but expressing a new understanding of the Church as "the people of God."[9]

If plans and vision could be translated into reality without any problems, the estimated 80,000 CEBs, composed mainly of rural and urban poor, would certainly qualify themselves as intermediate groups. What is intended of the CEBs by episcopal authorities and by Church clergy and laity in the field is outlined in a great number of documents and reports from 1965. I will cite here from one of them, an official report commissioned by the Brazilian National Conference of Bishops (CNBB) and presented to the Conference by Bishop José Freire Falcão in 1979.[10]

The new communities are expected to be autonomous within the Church in the sense that they communicate their own insights and programs for action to the Church as a whole. They are not just acted upon. They are expected not just to be recipients of religious messages but articulators and transmitters to the Church as a whole of an understanding of the Gospel that only the poor, it is believed, can have:

> The more oppressed class, of the factory worker, the small farmer, the Indian, becomes the privileged location of the message [of God] — because it is a class more sensitive to the need for union and more open to give welcome to the Gospel's message of liberation. It is notable that in the middle class the process [of welcome] is more difficult; there the message is often received and applied only in the solution of isolated, individual or family problems and never arrives at the community level to achieve a dedication to the transformation of the whole environment in which one lives.[11]

Further, they will not duplicate and reproduce the hierarchical relationships of the dominant society. Involvement in CEBs converts individual members to think and act communally and to reject subservience either to experts or patrons. In the communities individuals are converted away from the habits of dependence:

> The change, or the conversion, transforms relationships. No longer is it the relationship of the expert who teaches that the student might learn; of the rich who pay that the poor might receive; of the patron who commands the passive obedience of the employee. Instead it is a relationship between brothers, sharing among themselves their own material and spiritual goods and recognizing only one Master, before whom all are students. . . . Lacking power, expertise and riches, the communities are a challenge to the world and to the social system that dominates in our continent.[12]

The life of the communities is expected to be directed outward:

> Discovering the grandeur of life, the communities set out to restore dignity to it, uniting members, therefore, to struggle against everything that degrades and oppresses man. From the community's living of the Gospel values, members draw energy, courage, and inspiration, and in the environment in which they live, they join with others with whom they might transform the world, in accordance with the will of God.[13]

These hopes for the CEBs from on high are shared by at least some of their ordinary members. Cláudio Perani quotes a member of a CEB in Pernambuco defining as its purpose "that the people might see with their own eyes, think with their own heads, speak with their own mouths, and walk with their own feet."[14] That asserts clearly enough the intent of autonomy and critical articulation of experience.

Reports compiled by CEB members suggest, further, that at least some CEBs actually function as intermediate groups.[15] Some groups are founded and encouraged along in earlier stages by laity from established CEBs. Many groups conduct their own liturgies and Bible discussion groups. Nearly all report the effort to articulate local values and experiences in the light of what is learned from the Bible discussions. Many report a variety of CEB organized activities in their neighborhoods: housing projects for the destitute, the setting up of mothers' clubs and health stations, the compiling of information on a local problem.[16] Often, these activities involve members in clashes with the authorities—e.g., representatives from the forty-four rural CEBs in the diocese of Barreirinhas who appeared "en masse to select the board of directors of the rural union, despite the organization of a terrorizing police apparatus."[17]

These reports deserve more careful analysis than I can give them here. Not only their explicit content but their authorship (cleric or lay member?), theological assumptions, omissions, and other features must be assessed before they can be used as data in determining the extent to which CEBs actually function as intermediate groups. It should be noted that there are published reports for only a very small proportion of the 80,000 said to exist. Data from Thomas Bruneau's survey of eight dioceses in different regions of Brazil suggest considerable disagreement among dioceses about what might be said to constitute a CEB—in some dioceses it would seem likely that very traditional clerically controlled devotional groups might be counted as CEBs.[18]

Analysis of the small number of reports in Barreiro's book suggests the fragility of many CEBs as intermediate groups. Quotations from the report on CEBs in the extremely poor area of Tacaimbo, Pernambuco, leaves little doubt that, for the moment, these are genuine intermediate groups. But their continued existence, let alone any impact in their immediate environment, is threatened by the effects of worsening absolute poverty:

> The poor do not believe that they can emerge from this situation in which they are living. They cannot believe in improvement. They can only believe in worse conditions until the end. . . . People are now observing the poor uniting, but it remains to be seen whether the unity is merely a pretense. The poor person does not have a chance in the local society.[19]

The report from the Barreirinhas CEBs underlines the same vulnerability.[20]

Other reports point to another source of vulnerability that will probably have occurred to the reader of the quotations from the report to the CNBB cited earlier. That is the vulnerability of local lay groups to clerical good intentions. Some of the language of the plans and the reports written by clergy suggest that some clergy know exactly what values and perceptions the CEBs should be heading toward; and as they impose their knowledge they undermine the potential of *their* CEBs to become intermediate groups.

My study of Catholicism in the town of Campo Alegre may help us grasp the interaction and depth of these problems which stand in the way of easy realization of ideals for CEBs as intermediate groups. On the other hand, the appreciation of those difficulties in our case does not amount to a dismissal of CEBs as intermediate groups. Indeed, the full story—of persistence, of transformations in individual lives, and of the slow development of grass-roots lay leadership in and through Campo Alegre's fragile CEBs—might encourage interest in the potential of CEBs even in situations where all of the odds would seem to be stacked against their functioning as intended.

Some of those odds may be discussed in terms of Campo Alegre's economic situation and social structure.[21] It is a town of 12,000, triple its population twenty-five years ago. In 1950, it still had an economic role in a backwater of the northeastern sugar industry which had not been absorbed, as other production areas had long since been, in the *usina* system of sugar production. Campo Alegre served as a port and trading town for sugar estates in sad decline but still needing it for communications and trade with the capital city. That capital was close by, but because the area had been bypassed by railways and good road systems, it was difficult to reach except by the old *barcacas* that carried trade along the northeastern coast.

An intricate social system of local patronage still, in 1950, focused around the Brotherhood of the local patron saint. The town of Campo Alegre had grown up on a corridor of land deeded in the early nineteenth century to the Church (or to the saint, as many old locals preferred to see it). The Brotherhood, constituted in 1870, administered the patrimony, and its board maintained in the town what were regarded as the amenities of civilization. Initially sugar mill–owners had dominated the board but through the twentieth century they had come to share power with the local commercial elite. Whatever its composition, the board was the institutional focus of town life and the center of the town's patronage structure.

By the 1970s, the town had in a manner of speaking, fallen apart. It had lost its focal economic role as the sugar mills had gone out of existence and road transport had improved. Many erstwhile Brotherhood patrons had left town for jobs in the city and the Brotherhood was unable to incorporate a larger and much more diverse town population in its web of patronage. In any case, the Brotherhood had been displaced from most of its functions by various state agencies and by the town's first resident priest.

The town's population had swollen with refugees from the rationalization of the sugar industry in surrounding areas, so that only a quarter of Campo Alegrenses had always been residents of the town. With good roads and a regular bus service, daily commuting to the capital city and to nearby factories was possible. So as well as being mixed in terms of residential history, Campo Alegre's population was extremely varied in occupational profile by 1970. A declining minority of Campo Alegrenses by residence and recent occupation could and did still identify with the world of the *coroneis* and the sugar trade and recalled with nostalgia the times when the Brotherhood had been a valued link to that world. Others were struggling to maintain their small plots, threatened by new, rationalizing landlords. Others again were part of the capital city's drifting unskilled labor force for whom Campo Alegre was a place of cheap residence. No one institution had emerged to articulate the diversity of interests and modes of attachment to the place. The priest and his helpers found the social melange hard to manage. It was difficult to encourage neighborhood leadership where there were few social bases for neighborhood unity.

The problems arising from social structure were exacerbated by cultural heterogeneity. As Campo Alegre was incorporated at least partially into modern urban-industrial Brazil, its population became more religiously diverse. Though only about 12 percent of families had one or more practicing members, the Assembly of God was on many indicators the largest organized religious group in town. There were also fourteen different Afro-Brazilian cult groups of varying size. Probably even more difficult for a priest attempting to develop CEBs was another layer of cultural diversity. Moving in different sectors in Brazilian society, open to a variety of ideological influences, Campo Alegrenses had come to be very diverse in the range of their "cultural paradigms" for negotiating everyday life, and for assessing the claims and projects of politicians—and of priests. Some Campo Alegrenses still seemed to make sense of their world and assess it through the symbols and myths of the world of *coronelismo* (traditional landowners and political bosses). Others negotiated with the symbols and myths of populism; others again with the symbols and myths of the military regime. The priest's CEBs carried with them their own cultural paradigm; and conversion to it was no easy matter.

Even within the majority Catholic population of Campo Alegre, Father Eduardo—it is time to give him a name—encountered problems of conversion in this sense. One set of problems arises from elements in the folk Catholicism of the area—a Catholicism that has itself been shaped by clericalism of the past, by the struggles of the poor to make a succession of political economies work for them, and by the attempts of generations to find meaning and hope in the hard life.[22] Folk Catholicism in Campo Alegre is not all of a piece, any more than it is in the whole of Brazil.[23] One stream of folk Catholicism, still manifest in *festas* and pilgrimages and protested from the heart by many of my interviewees, predisposes those who profess it to patronal attachments. Another stream, more "privatized," orients toward a highly individualistic definition of problems and solutions. Both streams, however, through different logics of myth and symbol, tend to preclude interest in CEBs.

A second set of problems arises from the Church itself: its buildings, which at the town's center still proclaim the Church's centrality in an institutional matrix pervaded by patronage;[24] its patrimonial holdings, which made the priest appear a landowner, whether he liked it or not; its recruitment and training of clergy, which gave the town a young priest who, despite his intentions, spoke and acted as a man from a cultural world very different from that of the poor of Campo Alegre. These aspects of the Church in Campo Alegre made it difficult for the priest to be understood when he urged the need for CEBs.[25]

The convergence of these two sets of problems undermined several of the priest's attempts to establish the sorts of CEBs that might qualify as intermediate groups, at least in the short run. Father Eduardo hoped that if he could get a group of farmers together as a CEB, it might develop to the point where the farmers themselves would organize their own challenge to a local landowner who was expelling small farmers from land they rented on his property without the compensation required by law. If only the farmers could define their problem clearly enough for themselves, and draw sufficient motivation to unite and act from their shared faith, then the political and economic forces ranged against them might be defeated.

An extract from my wife's description of one of this group's few meetings suggests some of the reasons for the failure of this vision. The meeting was held in a shed used for processing manioc and which was owned and managed by one of the tenants, Manoel Davi, who had received a dismissal notice:

> Some thirty or forty people sat expectantly awaiting the arrival of the priest. . . . Eventually, the priest drove up in his car. . . . He addressed the meeting, sitting formally on the chair, earnestly developing the text for the day—the importance of sharing this world's goods with one another, especially the needy; the great promise that the poor would inherit the earth, so clearly prefigured in Christ's washing of his disciples' feet. This feast would be celebrated during the coming week, the priest reminded his listeners, and he personally planned to wash the feet of six farmers and six fishermen at the local ceremony. Now and then the priest elaborated his lesson, coaxing his audience to suggest examples from their own lives which paralleled the gospel story. For most of the time the audience was silent, now and then shuffling their feet. Occasionally, one of the men would mutter a comment or suggest an example, his eyes hardly leaving the ground in front of his feet. Often the priest's questions remained rhetorical. The restrained conduct of the audience and their halting speech contrasted oddly with the animated debates about prices, wages, and bosses, the jokes about manioc roots and marriage, and the incessant bustle that normally took place in this space.[26]

The portents of the group's short-term failure as a CEB may be easily discerned in this description. The group is waiting for a leader and is reduced to inarticulateness on his arrival. Father Eduardo feels forced, awkwardly because he had hoped it would be otherwise, to draw the lessons from the Gospel story. Deference to him has defeated the autonomy and communality which he believes the Gospel should elicit.

In another attempted CEB, subversion of intent occurred in a different way. This CEB was led not by Father Eduardo but by a man named Carlos. It did not fold early but had been meeting for five years when I first attended. While I was in Campo Alegre, on most Sunday afternoons a group of from ten to thirty would gather in a private house or in the local non-Church primary school where Carlos was a sort of voluntary caretaker. At these meetings, which Father Eduardo did not attend and at which up to half of those present did not go to Mass, Carlos dominated. He would always summarize, usually quite accurately, Father Eduardo's sermon of that morning and attempt to lead a discussion on it. He spoke all the time and without Father Eduardo's characteristic hesitance. In these discussions and in the meeting as a whole, it appeared to me that only some aspects of Father Eduardo's message had taken hold in Carlos' consciousness. At first I had a general, puzzled feeling that this was so, but after participation in a number of congregation meetings, some basic thematic differences became clearer.

First, Father Eduardo's moral values became, with Carlos and in the congregation, a moralism. Moral judgments about social and public issues which were intended to evoke social action for change became moral judgments applied against individuals (e.g., the landowner) who were singled out for condemnation. The concern in the congregation was with clarifying right from wrong, with distinguishing wrongdoers from victims of wrongdoing. And two reactions were evoked. The congregation must right wrongs by assisting its members who were among the victims. Individual members must also in their own lives strive to be innocent of whatever was being condemned. Second, the congregation was still operating with the notion of the Church as law rather than Father Eduardo's notions of the Church as liberator. Carlos and the congregation were much more concerned than Father Eduardo about the Pill, the errors of Protestantism (false law), and so on. Third—and as I interpret things, underlying the previous two differences—the congregation operated with a basically different image of Jesus than the one held by Father Eduardo. His image was of Jesus the liberator, the model liberator, the model of liberation who calls us forth to battle oppression. The congregation's image was of Jesus the lawgiver, the judge who orients us in our quest for salvation.

One interesting aspect of these meetings, then, was the mistranslation of Father Eduardo's message, which I have analyzed elsewhere.[27] Here my interest is on the nature of the group. It seems to me that as Father Eduardo had withdrawn, Carlos had reentered as a very clerical figure. Speaking for the priest, the sheer volume of Carlos's contributions in the form of leading questions and then very long replies to his own questions tended to drown out other contributions. And at that point his message becomes of interest again. As a new sort of Church authority (Father Eduardo placed great hopes in his leadership and encouraged it), he preached old moralisms and activated old symbols which prejudiced any new Gospel-inspired articulation of values and perceptions which other members of the group might have brought forward.[28]

This is not all there is to tell about the CEBs of Campo Alegre.[29] When I returned in 1982, I interviewed three people who had been in both of the groups sketched here. All three had remained at the center of resistance to the expulsions from the land. All three insisted on the importance of the groups in providing the initial motivation, energy, and information that led to their resistance. Two of the three continued in yet a third CEB composed of ex-farmers. All three insist on unity—which on probing turns out to be engagement of a greater number of ex-farmers in a CEB, if advance is to be made on the land question. None thinks it is the job of the priest to enlarge the CEB or get another going—although all praised the help now given by a nun and a seminary student.

In the long haul, some of the problems of the Campo Alegre CEBs seem to have been overcome. But not even the clergy involved consider that all is rosy. Four years after my first encounter with them, Father Eduardo and the nun who works with the fisherwomen's CEB worried about what they saw as little progress. The nun, in particular, was worried about continued dependence on her as leader. The Campo Alegre cases illustrate some of the problems that stand in the way of CEBs functioning as intermediate groups even when the priest initiating them attempts to be nonmanipulative.

Under less difficult circumstances than those prevailing in the Northeast in such places as Tacaimbo and Campo Alegre, the prospects would seem to be better. The famous Catholic commentator Alceu de Amoroso Lima, in a column in the *Jornal do Brasil*, argued that at the national level one indicator of the success of the CEBs is the fear and opposition they elicit from agencies of national security and conservative groups in society. He began his article by asking "Why is there so much fear, such distrust and such concern with the famous CEBs?" And his answer, basically, is that it is because they actually work as non-party but politically effective alternatives to structures of privilege in Brazil.[30]

CEBs have received national and international attention—and not only as a religious phenomenon. General Golbery e Couto, the architect of Brazil's security network, adviser to military presidents and ideologue of the national security doctrine, affirmed, from his different perspective, the long-term political importance of the CEBs as part of a wider popular movement. In a 1980 lecture at the Superior War College, General Golbery observed of the new groups that comprise the popular movement that:

> The real active forces [os *verdadeiros agentes*] in the political field have become these conglomerates, much more than the one party of the opposition. And in these conglomerates, because of their traditional prestige and the protection they can offer, the religious and para-religious organizations have assumed an outstanding, almost hegemonic, position.[31]

It seems less obvious that the Afro-Brazilian spiritist cults should be assessed in the same framework. They have not attracted the same sort of attention as the CEBs for their transformative role. And their leaders do not claim a long-term transformative role for their groups in Brazilian society as do the protagonists for the CEBs. Nevertheless a brief review of some recent literature and my own research may help, on the one hand, to refine the notion of intermediate group and, on the other, suggest the rich diversity among religious groups at the grass roots of Brazilian society.

AFRO-BRAZILIAN CULTS: THE DEBATE

Do the Afro-Brazilian cults, which in one way or another may involve as many as thirty million Brazilians, function politically as the CEBs are supposed to function? There would seem to be some basis for an affirmative response. Although there are various federations of Umbanda and other Afro-Brazilian groups, the small local group does seem to be the basic unit. Insofar as the cults represent a continuity with the African past, they keep alive a history and a set of identifications which provide a basis for resistance to pressures for ideological conformity organized for political purposes by the ruling elites of both the representative and authoritarian systems. As voluntary organizations with grass-roots leadership, they might constitute groups intermediate between the isolated individual and the state. In other words, there would seem to be a *prima facie* case for an affirmative response to the question.

But the response of many recent studies of Afro-Brazilian cults among the poor has been a resounding negative. Renato Ortiz, justly one of the most influential scholars of the cults, argues that the family of Umbanda cults possesses an ideology formulated largely by whites that functions to extend the hegemony of white elites. Umbanda is the largest, regionally most extensive, and fastest growing of the cults. Ortiz argues that in ritual, organization, and mythology, Umbanda achieves "the white death of the black shaman."[32] In terms of the categories I have been using, Umbanda groups are not autonomous but manipulable, and dependent— ultimately—on the resources and direction of dominant elites. Umbanda ideology does not encourage the articulation of critical awareness and values among the lower classes, but expresses—through its scientism and its placing of African spirits and practices at the bottom of an evolutionary scale—white, upper-class hegemony. As it expresses, so does it socialize: its members enter modern society, not as members of a grass-roots community but as individuals competing for often illusory upward mobility.

At the end of his book, Ortiz speculates that the state, no longer finding Catholicism congenial as a legitimating power, might turn to Umbanda.[33] Other studies suggest ways in which Afro-Brazilian cults, and especially Umbanda, short of becoming an official legitimating religion, may yet serve either or both the patronal-representative and bureaucratic-authoritarian political economies rather than prove a grass-roots base for an alternative politics.[34]

Yet other studies, and my own research in Campo Alegre, do not allow me to agree that these cases reveal the whole of the political story of the Afro-Brazilian cults. In fact, the diversity to be found among them allows for no simple political equations concerning their contributions to Brazilian politics. There is a tendency in the studies cited to assume that as the cults become less African, they will take on new myths, symbols, and rituals from the dominant culture and on terms that guarantee the hegemony of political economic elites. But it seems not to be the case that the decline of explicit African-ness is the same as the loss of cultural and structural bases for the articulation of evolving critical awareness and evaluation is viable communities. While they might prompt us to abandon a certain foreigner's romanticism in the great Roger Bastide's interpretations of the Afro-Brazilian cults, these facts still demand respect for his observation about the creativity, religious and political, to be found in them:

> It is always easy enough to see through hindsight how economic or social systems are reflected in religion, but one forgets that there was a factor of creative freedom, that substructural aspects are determinative but not compelling and that the people confronted with them can either reject the old values that no longer seem to fit the new social situations or invent new meanings for the old symbols they do not wish to reject completely and thus be forced to find an original solution.[35]

The diversity cannot be avoided; the difficulty is to typologize it validly and with thematic relevance. With Bastide's observation and the concerns of this paper in mind, the typology presented below might be helpful. It brings out the association between various class situations and distinctive types of Afro-Brazilian spiritism. It also suggests how each of the types of spiritism involves the formation of groups which vary markedly on the dimensions of autonomy, articulation, and communalism[36] (i.e., on the extent to which they might be said to constitute intermediate groups).

Several observations need to be made of the diagram and drawn from it. First, on the nature of the typology. Each column and, indeed, each box represents an exercise in ideal typification. That is, the entries represent deliberate dramatic exaggerations of trends noted in the literature. The case studies constituting the literature also show that reality is more complex than the typifications suggest. Many groups, although predominantly classifiable in one column, display some characteristics listed in other columns.[37] These ambiguities should be well appreciated by the time I have referred my own cases from Campo Alegre, themselves grossly simplified here, to the categories of the diagram.

The distinction between types 1 and 2 emerges with great clarity

Typology of Afro-Brazilian Religions

	CONSTRUCTION FOR/BY WHICH GROUP:		
	Type 1	Type 2	Type 3
Characteristics of Group	Old sub-proletariat	New sub-proletariat	New urban upward mobiles
Form & content of syncretism:	White patronal content in Afro forms	Constant variations on Afro-Brazilian forms & themes	White hegemony in Afro-caboclo mestre symbols and myths
Ritual features:	Afro & Portuguese language. Blood sacrifices	Portuguese only. Blood sacrifices rare	Portuguese only. Sacrifices for individual
Autonomy structural:	Continuity with patronage hierarchy in dominant society. Internal hierarchy in dominant society	Discontinuity with dominant patronage structures. Internal egalitarianism	Continuities with patronage and bureaucratic structures. Expert-client relationship
Autonomy ideological:	Acceptance of racial/class harmony myths. Frozen syncretism for acceptability	Rejection of harmony myths. Development of Afro & other folk myths	Acceptance of Brazilian national-security myths
Articulation of developing perspectives & values:	Articulation to conserve a space reserved: no interest in critical perceptions & values	Articulation of critical perceptions & values	Articulation of received ideologies vs. articulation of critical perceptions & values
Communalism vs. individualism &/or bureaucratic relationships:	Concern to construct & maintain sub-group within accepted structure	Concern to construct & maintain alternative community	Concern for advancement of individual clients & maintenance of medium's prestige

in Colin Henfrey's comparisons of spiritist groups in Salvador, Bahia.[38] In certain areas of Salvador, the descendants of slaves are still engaged in traditional occupations such as domestic service in the households of the bourgeoisie. It is these people who join the traditional Candomble groups, beloved of tourists and tourist agencies. These groups, like their members, serve the upper classes in a variety of ways and have upper-class patrons as paying participants. They compete for rewards provided by patrons and the Department of Tourism, and rewards are proportional to success in exemplifying the tradition as it is hallowed by the patronizing classes. The result, expressed in my terms, is summarized as type 1. The groups are low on structural and ideological autonomy. For their members they are environments which structure experience in ways that duplicate the structuring of life in the society at large.[39] They are environments which rehearse a set of myths and values which freeze the past for the reward of an assured niche in the dominant society. In a sense, despite their exotic Afro appearances, they are kept groups, almost the opposite of intermediate groups on all criteria.

In great contrast are the cult groups which Henfrey studied in the bairro of Liberdade. The characteristics of these and similar groups are sketched as type 2. Liberdade is, in terms of its location, history, and the "informal-sector" occupations of its inhabitants, much less integrated into bourgeois society. The cults, as well as samba groups, reflect and maintain the distance. On all dimensions, as environments structuring experience and as groups preoccupied with the creative conservation of a counter-culture, they seem to function as intermediate groups. Like some of the CEBs with similar features, their concern with autonomous community-building seems easily to lead members into political activities against the status quo.

Type 3 seeks to encompass features of the Umbanda groups studied by Renato Ortiz, Diana Brown, and others. These groups, as the previous discussion of the literature made clear, can in no way be considered intermediate groups. On the contrary, they contribute to the reproduction of both patronage and bureaucratic authoritarian Brazil. They do this through structure and ideology. Structurally, they are groups which integrate lower-class urbanites into the patronage formations of middle-class Brazil. Ideologically, they teach and rehearse a vision of Brazilian history and a mythology of its heroes and villains which legitimates upper-class patronage and national security values and encourages competitive individualistic responses by the poor to the problems of everyday life. But the point of presenting the typology was to make something of a case for the claim that these sorts of Afro-Brazilian cult groups are only one among other types.

That claim may be elaborated through a brief resume of cases from my study of the fourteen Afro-Brazilian cult groups of Campo Alegre. The questions I had in mind as I studied the biographies of members and group rituals were these:

(1) To what extent do the cults of Campo Alegre adopt and re-
    hearse ideologies akin to the national security ideology promoted
    by the bureaucratic authoritarian sectors of the Brazilian State?[40]
    Are the cult groups of Campo Alegre exactly as the hegemonic
    interpretation of Afro-Brazilian spiritism claims them to be?

(2) To what extent do the cult groups constitute intermediate groups,
    resisting hegemony and rehearsing, in viable community, per-
    ceptions and evaluations that may be constructing alternative
    Brazils?

A contrast between several very different groups may serve to illustrate the range and complexity of answers to these questions.

Case 1. The leader of the most self-consciously African cult group in Campo Alegre is popularly known as Pai Fuló. Fuló's is one of the Xangô family of cults. The spirits of his house are exclusively the African spirits—he will have nothing to do with the Indian spirits of Jurema or the various other spirit lines of Umbanda.

When I was first getting to know Fuló and the group, he was at pains to point out his respectability, his good relations with the police, his sons who had done well, his allegiance to the Holy Roman Catholic and Apostolic Church, the parallel identities of the African spirits and Catholic saints (e.g., Xangô as St. John the Baptist). I might initially have classified the group under type 1. And, indeed, many details about the group would justify that placement.

But the fit is not neat. Having protested respectability, Fuló would come to point out that he was not of the *cultura alta,* the high white culture of modern Brazil but of *Brasil selvagem,* literally, savage Brazil. He and members of the group would maintain and self-consciously construct that identity for themselves with pride: they did not accept it as a low or inferior status. In that and in aspects of their social relations, Fuló and the members of his religious "family" are profoundly countercultural in a society where, even at the local level, authority claims legitimation through formal qualifications and expertise. Fuló exercises traditional authority— authority based on wisdom passed on through the generations in deep personal relationships. Fuló does not intend, nor is he expected, to hoard this wisdom as an expert for specific functions; rather his standing relies on his transposing his wisdom from his life to as many other lives as he can. His proudest boast to me was that he has left communities of *filhos* and *filhas de santo* all over Brazil—he has fulfilled his roles as "ambassador of the spirits" and *zelador* (watchman) of the wisdom of Africa and *Brasil selvagem.*

I do not want to suggest that Fuló's group is an antithesis of modern Brazilian society, or that its encodings of reality exactly negate the national security code. Fuló and members of his family in even greater degree are ambivalent toward a *cultura alta* that is itself multivalent. Fuló, I would say, is teacher/father in a counterculture—but counter to what? If entirely counter to rational-bureaucratic authority, then for some members it is only an alternative locus wherein to realize the continuing motif of patrimonialism in the *cultura alta.* Counter to the *exclusive* pretensions of those who accept white, scientific, rationalist Brazil lock, stock, and barrel, Fuló's Xangô does not yet arm for resistance, unless it is with a potent sense of independence and confident apartness grounded in ritually nurtured alternative history. But it is precisely that sense, evident in interviews with Fuló and a core of cult members, which would lead me to rate the group high on the dimensions of autonomy and articulation. In that sense, the group, while the nearest in Campo Alegre to the type 1 Candomble groups studied by Henfrey, manifests some features of type 2 spiritism and in those features has some potential as an intermediate group.

Case 2. Dona Rosária's group is profoundly different from Fuló's and much closer to type 3 outlined in the diagram. Dona Rosária is a different sort of leader. She comes as a regular visitor to her spiritist center from the state capital, 30 kilometers away. She bring a message to the poor from her upper-class suburb of the *cultura alta.* In the center, she dispenses enlightenment, therapy, and goods to the needy. Where Fuló's rituals are conducted in his house, Dona Rosária operates from a large barn that was made available to her and the Umbanda Federation by the state prison authorities. Dona Rosária and visiting dignitaries speak from the table to an audience seated in rows—in my view the arrangement of furniture and partitions made in the converted barn induce passive reception of messages from experts.

Dona Rosária's spirit world is tidily arranged. It is elaborately structured from higher spirits, with Jesus Christ at the top, through the great departed thinkers of Western civilization, down through lower spirits—old slaves, cowboy spirits, the spirits of the street, and the inarticulate *caboclo* and African spirits—and finally down to the evil spirits of darkness, including the African *Exus.* She professes the beliefs of the Umbanda cult, although among Umbandistas hers is of the kind most heavily influenced by the nineteenth-century European spiritualist Alain Kardec and the least continuous with more African cults such as Fuló's Xangô or Bahian Candomblé. Her exemplar is the great white medium Chico Xavier, whose portrait hangs on a screen behind the table. Xavier has published books of prayers and revelations communicated by superior spirits. And the superior spirits are not the African spirits of Xangô or the *caboclo* Indian spirits, the cowboys, ex-slaves, and street spirits of the Umbanda groups—but spirits of departed white, professional representatives of *cultura alta.*

Much of Dona Rosária's discourse departs from a framework of oppositions: spirit vs. flesh; whiteness, light, lucidity, science, and Christ vs. blackness, darkness, ignorance, superstition, and Satan. Like most *Umbandistas,* she has borrowed the notion of Karma: success in this life is to prepare the spirit, in whatever walk of life, for a higher, purer existence in the extraterrestrial plane and in the next incarnation.

Regular attenders in Dona Rosária's group are trained to accept the superiority of the experts, in whose hands lies the possibility of a better material future, and to work toward purification of their spirits. In many ways the provisions of the national security ideology are translated in the group into a meaningful world view. Dona Rosária, gentle soul, has become a medium for what Harvey Cox calls "the seduction of the spirit" in more ways than one.[41] Where Fuló's group hovers between types 1 and 2, Dona Rosária's displays features associated with type 3 and it is difficult to imagine in it any potential as an intermediate group. It involves a network of relationships in which an outside expert controls patronage. In it there is preached and enacted a world-view which can only encourage effective acceptance of Brazilian national security myths. It in no way encourages the articulation of critical perceptions and values.

Case 3. Dona Paula's is one of the two most "up-market" of the spiritist establishments in Campo Alegre in terms of the number of wealthier clients she attracts (some from out of town) and the size and appointments of her *salão.* Many of her clients, however, are fishermen and workers in the informal sector. Unlike some of the other mediums in town, Dona Paula does not try to build a core group of disciples. She does not regard herself as a teacher, though she believes she serves her clients well as a medium working with the spirits of Umbanda. Eschewing the teaching role and working with lower spirits like the gypsy Pombagira, she stands in contrast to Dona Rosária; but her group is perhaps even closer to an exemplification of type 3.

Dona Paula's family connections allow her to be classified as "new urban upward mobile" in the social context of Campo Alegre. She is married to a recently retired middle-level bureaucrat in the state government who worked in the capital city. He is now deputy mayor (*sub-prefeito*) and, in 1982, a member of the government party bloc in the municipal government. In a variety of ways, his politics intertwine with her practice as a medium. One of her sons is an engineering student and he brings friends from the capital and a nearby holiday resort to the Umbanda *toques* in his mother's *salão.* Dona Paula herself is very conscious of the need to maintain a certain respectability and she employs various means to ensure it. The commercial and political elites of the municipality are invited to the major Umbanda ceremonies; drunkards and *marginais* are carefully excluded; the *salão* itself, larger and more solid than most of the residences of Campo Alegre, is kept freshly painted, well lit, and ventilated with electric fans. She makes the connection herself between these factors and her respectability; and she points out that Fuló and other mediums are less respectable because they don't cultivate her sort of connections, they allow *marginais* to participate, and their *salões* or *terreiros* are a shambles.

Dona Paula makes one further point as she distinguishes herself as a respectable medium from others. Though she works with spirits who are not completely "developed," her Umbanda spirits can be manipulated, their strengths exploited and the weakness controlled, by a properly trained medium like herself. She claims a sort of specialist expertise. If someone should be brought to her suffering under the malign influence of a completely undeveloped African *orixá*, she would send them off to Fuló; she does not know or want to know how to deal with such entities.

Dona Paula is quite frank in confirming what this observer concluded from attendance at several *toques* and celebrations in her *salão*. The various ceremonies are meant, above all, to establish her credentials as a qualified, successful, and respectable medium. Manifesting as Pombagira or Comadre Florzinha, she distributes cake and champagne to the guests of the house, with strict regard to a pecking order of prestige: military, politicians of the governing party, and guests from the holiday resort first; the local commercial elite second; at the end, regular clients from among the poor of Campo Alegre. That recognition of hierarchy ensures respectability and confirms reliability in a chain of patron-client exchanges. As she manifests a variety of spirits, Dona Paula always steals the show, retiring from the floor when *manifestada* to reemerge magnificently arrayed to display her spirit. That helps establish credentials as a powerful medium.

Regular clients whom I have interviewed are proud of the spectacle provided. Poorer clients value the ambience of another class that Dona Paula invites them into, the exchanges between classes as well as the exchanges between powerful spirits and the living which she mediates. Above all, though, Dona Paula is valued for her powers in divining which spirits are causing harm and why. Most of her clients come with a story of specific suffering: a husband straying, illness, a string of inexplicable accidents. They come in the belief that much human suffering is caused by spirits whom the sufferer has offended or who have been turned against the sufferer by some other person. Dona Paula, as a manifestly powerful and successful medium, is able not only to diagnose but to remedy. If the sufferer has provided the provocation directly but unknowingly, she can prescribe the remedy which will appease the spirit. If a provocateur has been involved, working perhaps through another medium, Dona Paula, it is expected, will be able to summon more powerful spirits or negotiate with the spirits causing the trouble so that the harmful activity is neutralized or stopped.

Biu, an occasional client and a neighbor in Campo Alegre, helps illustrate the medium-spirit-client relationship and the world-view that sustains it. Biu habitually attributes events, particularly mishaps in her life, to the actions of the spirits upon her. As an eighteen year old, living with a young man who could gain only intermittent employment as an unskilled laborer, she became pregnant and felt very ill. Iemenjá acted upon her, she says, drawing her into the water, where she would have drowned if not restrained. Then, when the child was born, it was frequently ill, and she was anxious about her lack of resources to care for her child and herself. At this time, she says, a spirit kept impelling her to kill the baby. Later, when the baby was healthy, her husband had to leave her behind while he went to work in another town. She was convinced that he would not return but go off with another woman who would employ the power of the spirits to ensnare him.

In all these events, Biu sees herself the passive victim of spirits' actions. In each case she goes to one or all three of her preferred mediums for help, for which she must pay a fee. She favors Dona Paula above the others, in part because she does not urge her to participate in a spiritist group but provides prompt diagnoses of the roots of the problem, appropriate remedies, and generally correct prognostications. Dona Paula has usually confirmed Biu's diagnoses, though not in the case of the supposedly errant husband. In that case Dona Paula divined, there was no spirit at work to draw her husband away and he'd be back. He was. Dona Paula's authority and apparent success seem to reinforce Biu's own diagnoses and mode of dealing with crises in her life.

My interpretation of the medium-spirit-client relationships involved in the case of Biu helps justify the claim that Dona Paula and clients exemplify some features of the type 3 Afro-Brazilian religion in Campo Alegre. The expert medium encourages the client in her predisposition to interpret her problems in individualistic terms; the private trouble and competitive relationships are emphasized rather than any public issue that might be discerned and any communal solution that might be appropriate. The predisposition to pathos, to interpret suffering as being acted upon and about which the sufferer can do nothing, at least not without expert help, is also encouraged and enacted in the relationships described. Interpreting her problems episodically, individualistically, and with pathos, Biu links herself with existing patronage structures and a mode of interpreting everyday life that rather precludes the articulation of critical perceptions and values.

Of course it is easy to over-interpret along these lines. There *are* such things as private troubles and appropriately individual modes of addressing them. The political sociologist must beware of judging Biu of misperception of her problems and concluding that her life will be determined by her misperceptions. In fact, over the years, it has become apparent to this observer that Biu has not been set in or determined by her interpretations and actions of 1977. The example is not meant to establish tight causation nor assert correct political vision but only to demonstrate how a particular spiritist world-view and the social relations involved in a type of spiritist group might steer those involved away from the perceptions and responses that are encouraged in groups approaching the ideal type of an intermediate group. That something of the kind is a possibility within the spiritist family just as it is within the developing Catholic traditions is suggested by the final case to be briefly outlined.

Case 4. Maria Pretinha's small group is much more unequivocally an exemplification of a type 2 group than Pai Fuló's. Maria is another of the cult leaders whom Biu consults, but she sternly rejects the pathos with which Biu negotiates her world. Anyone may be acted upon by the spirits, usually for the better, but, as Maria Pretinha argues, and proclaims in her well-organized, if poverty-stricken life, people are ultimately responsible for their own actions, for their control over the spirits, for the purification of their own spirits. Maria Pretinha negotiates her world with irony, interpreting even her own sufferings as, in part at least, due to the still unconscious weaknesses or deficiencies in herself that she must discover and control. She goes out from her cult to assess and conduct life in a way that is strikingly similar to that of many members of the Assembly of God: insisting sternly on the necessity of traditional morality and self-discipline, allowing efficiency and order as the only legitimations of accepted hierarchy and political authority. Unlike most members of the Assembly, however, Maria Pretinha seems predisposed by her religion to distrust the claims of experts and professionals to a monopoly of wisdom. She is medium for a spirit who in his "terrestrial" life was a sort of city slicker, a wily Afro-Brazilian operator from the urban lower classes who, despite his sins, picked up much wisdom and who has developed as a spiritual and practical guide for the living through his relationships with other spirits since his death. Maria criticizes her spirit for his remaining rough edges, but also proclaims his merits as a sort of lower-class hero who has battled upward from vice and ignorance to a higher plane of development. She insists that he knows and understands what many a learned doctor will never learn, and points out that he dispenses counsel without pretensions and at a cheaper rate than the officials from the higher classes. He is also wiser than they are: he calls his clients not just to bandage immediate problems but to turn to a new way of life, and most of his remedies, passed on through Maria Pretinha, involve clients in some sort of activity for their own spiritual development.

Maria herself insists that consultations with clients to deal with immediate problems is the lesser part of her work. The more important part is the building of a small community of those who will study with her to banish "mystification" from their lives and develop spiritually even as they help the spirits themselves to develop through exchanges with them. Like Fuló, her chosen role is *zelador* of the spirits for a group which will work hard over the years to overcome ignorance about identity and purpose in life. But like Fuló, she also finds it difficult to attract members who will persist with the effort she requires.

CONCLUSIONS

There are many dimensions on which these cases of the Afro-Brazilian religions in Campo Alegre might be compared. It might be noted, for example, that Dona Paula's and perhaps Dona Rosária's groups encourage a certain pathos and an episodic approach to life's problems among members, whereas Fuló and especially Maria Pretinha encourage individual responsibility and the location of episodes in a life and even a communal history. But the point is to determine how the groups stand in relation to the ideal type of an intermediate group and, finally, to compare the potential of the Afro-Brazilian groups as intermediate groups with the CEBs — primarily in Campo Alegre, of course, but by reference to a growing literature, in Brazil as a whole. Here, it is possible only to *suggest* reasonable conclusions, even for Campo Alegre, given the slight detail that can be presented in a short article.

Within Campo Alegre, spiritist groups vary enormously in their potential and performance as intermediate groups. Fuló's and Maria Pretinha's groups, in terms of the mode of conceiving life's problems and the sense of personal and communal identity which their leaders encourage, provide a countercultural base for intermediate group formation. The group life they encourage and the networks of association they foster are at least consonant with the intermediate group structure. In these same cultural and structural terms, Donas Rosária and Paula encourage and rehearse their rituals, identifications, perceptions of problems, and forms of association which are antithetical to intermediate group life.

This variation in Campo Alegre corresponds with variations between spiritist groups noted in the literature. The Campo Alegre cases cannot be fitted neatly and exactly into our tentative typology. But as we refer the Campo Alegre cases to that typology, it does seem possible to claim that they illustrate and amplify a varying potential for intermediate group formation among spiritist groups found in Brazil.

The Campo Alegre case studies suggest that there is an enormously rich and varied group life at the grass roots in Brazil. The CEBs are part of this life and their potential for contributing to the deepening of democracy in Brazil, as conceived in this paper, may be critically assessed by comparing them with the Afro-Brazilian groups. How do the fledgling CEBs of Campo Alegre compare with the groups of Fuló and Maria Pretinha in their potential as intermediate groups?

By contrast to the base communities in Campo Alegre these two groups, because of their lack of association with an erstwhile establishment institution like the Catholic Church, are well able to resist certain pressures toward cooptation into hegemonic culture and politics. Comparison with Dona Rosária's and Dona Paula's groups, however, suggest strengths even of the rather underdeveloped CEBs of Campo Alegre. Dona Rosária's group is firmly nested in an institutionalized Umbanda that socializes members and relates them to structures of power in much the way that Ortiz has foreseen. Dona Paula's group tends to atomize its membership and encourages competitive patron-client solutions to private troubles rather than communal solidarity. In contrast, the CEB is linked to an institution and to elites committed to nonmanipulative, antiauthoritarian relationships and to the building of relatively autonomous local communities. Moreover, where Fuló's and Maria Pretinha's groups seem unlikely to survive their leaders, one can be fairly sure that Campo Alegre has only seen the beginning of Catholic Church attempts at the formation of intermediate groups in the area.

Though I do not believe that the data I have reviewed allow the euphoria of some Church apologists for the CEBs, some important claims can be made for them. They may be considered part of a little-studied mosaic of religious-based intermediate groups at the grass roots of Brazilian society. That they are *not* alone, I would argue, increases their chances of viability and feeds hope for a richly pluralistic alternative to authoritarian or traditional representative politics. At the same time, their unique combination of institutional attachment and antiauthoritarian ideology and structure suggests that, more than other groups, the CEBs have a chance of contributing to changing relationships between civil society and the state in the longer term and on a national scale.

NOTES

The author would like to express his gratitude for the hospitality and stimulation provided by the Woodrow Wilson International Center for Scholars, Washington D.C., in the preparation of an early version of this paper and the larger work of which it is a part.

1. Clifford Geertz, *The Social History of an Indonesian Town* (Cambridge, Mass.: The M.I.T. Press, 1965).

2. For contributions to this critique, see Aspásia Alcântara de Camargo, "Autoritarismo e Populismo: Bipolaridade no Sistema Político Brasileiro," *Dados* 12 (1976): 22–45; Simon Schwartzman, *Bases do Autoritarismo no Brasil* (Rio de Janeiro: Editora Campus, 1982).

3. I do not want to discount the importance nor deny the difficulties of an opening from the top down. Such an opening includes granting of access to the lower

classes to institutions with real power in the distribution of economic resources. For
an account of how such access tested the limits of formal democracy in 1963, see Ken-
neth Paul Erickson, "Populism and Political Control of the Working Class in Brazil,"
in June Nash, Juan Corradi, and Herbert Spalding, eds., *Ideology and Social Change
in Latin America* (New York: Gordon and Breach, 1977), pp. 200–236.

4. See Shepard Forman, *The Brazilian Peasantry* (New York: Columbia University Press, 1975) for a development of this notion.

5. Emilio Willems, "Religious Mass Movements and Social Change in Brazil,"
in E. N. Baklanoff, ed., *New Perspectives of Brazil* (Nashville, Tenn.: Vanderbilt University, 1966), pp. 205–232.

6. Knowledge and ideas about religious groups and grass-roots social forma-
tions have been greatly extended by Carlos Rodrigues Brandão, *Os Deuses do Povo*
(São Paulo: Brasiliense, 1980) and Francisco Cartaxo Rolim, *Religião e Classes Populares*
(Petrópolis: Vozes, 1980).

7. The most important contribution to the influence approach but one which
is subtle and sympathetic to reformers in the Church is Thomas Bruneau, *The Church
in Brazil: The Politics of Religion* (Austin, Texas: University of Texas Press, 1982).

8. Jether Ramalho, "Algumas Notas sobre Duas Perspectivas de Pastoral Popular," *Cadernos do ISER* 6 (March 1977). The theme of cooptation of grass-roots religious
groups by upper-class religious functionaries and not just Catholic clergy is well analyzed in Brandão, *Os Deuses do Povo*.

9. Almir R. Guimaraes, "Comunidades de Base–Busca de Equilibrio entre
Ministérios e Comunidade Cristã," *Revista Eclesiástica Brasileira* (REB) 88, 149 (March
1978).

10. *Comunidades Eclesiais de Base no Brasil: Experiências e Perspectivas*, 23 (São
Paulo: Paulinas, Estudos da CNBB, 1979).

11. Ibid., p. 20.

12. Ibid., p. 14.

13. Ibid., p. 15.

14. Cláudio Perani, "Comunidades Eclesiais de Base e Movimento Popular,"
Cadernos do CEAS, no. 75, pp. 25–33.

15. Reports are collected and presented at the "Interchurch meeting [*encontro*]
of Base Communities." These reports may be found in the journal *SEDOC*. The first
of these *encontros* was in 1975 and the fourth, the last for which I have read reports,
in 1981. Reporters of the meetings have noted their progressive declericalization. By
the third meeting, and even more in the fourth, the theologians and bishops were
listening. The speaking, analyzing, and organizing of the *encontro* was in the hands
of CEB members from all over Brazil. See L. Boff, "Comunidades Eclesiais de Base–
Povo Oprimido que se Organiza para a Libertação," *REB* 41, 162 (June 1981): 312–320.
In the following paragraphs, I will quote from a study now available in English which
draws from the reports in *SEDOC*: Alvaro Barreiro, *Basic Ecclesial Communities: The
Evangelization of the Poor* (Maryknoll, N.Y.: Orbis Books, 1982).

16. For some detailed accounts, see Barreiro, *Basic Ecclesial Communities*, chaps.
2 and 5.

17. Ibid., p. 42. The chronology section of *REB* under Leonardo Boff's editor-
ship is a valuable record of reported clashes between CEBs and police or hired gunmen.

18. Bruneau, *Church in Brazil*, chap. 8. Scott Mainwaring, *The Catholic Church and Politics in Brazil, 1916–1985* (Stanford, Calif.: Stanford University Press, 1986) is now an indispensable source on the history of the CEBs and the conflicts concerning them.

19. Barreiro, *Basic Ecclesial Communities*, p. 56.

20. Ibid., p. 44.

21. My main sources for the nineteenth- and twentieth-century history of Campo Alegre are the *Atas*, or minutes of the Brotherhood, interviews with older residents, and the thesis of Mary Aitken Ireland, "Leaseholds on Life: A Study of Land and Lives, Campo Alegre, Northeast Brazil – 1814–1977" (unpublished Ph.D. diss., La Trobe University, 1982).

22. I have drawn out some of these interactions in R. Ireland, "The Prophecy That Failed," *Listening: Journal of Religion and Culture*, 16, 3 (Autumn 1981): 253–264. For profound considerations of the formation of popular religiosities in Brazil, see Francisco C. Rolim, "Religião do Pobre e seu Anúncio," *REB* 41, 164 (December 1981): 745–776.

23. The special issue of the *Revista Eclesiastica Brasileira* 36 (March 1976) remains a landmark in the consideration of variety of Brazilian folk Catholicism. See also Eduardo Hoornaert, *Formação do Catolicismo Brasileiro* (Petrópolis: Vozes, 1974).

24. One very traditional but poor Catholic thought that the Church was fine but lamented the fact that the priest was encouraging meetings out and away from it. He yearned for the days when the Church and the *quartel* (the barracks) stood close to one another and the priest and the other authorities could get together to maintain law and order.

25. I have analyzed the problems of communication closely in "The Prophecy That Failed."

26. Mary Aitken Ireland, "Leaseholds on Life," pp. 373–374.

27. "The Prophecy That Failed," 259–264.

28. The obvious question is: "Would other members of the group have come up with anything but the prejudices of folk Catholicism?" The obvious reply is that we don't know but that in CEBs in the same diocese very interesting new liturgies and analyses of urban slum life were emerging.

29. I have not even listed them all. Another comprises fisherwomen. Yet another is composed of high school students.

30. Tristão de Athayde (nom de plume), "O Mundo das Comunidades," *Jornal do Brasil*, June 25, 1981.

31. Quoted in Perani, "Comunidades Eclesiais de Base e Movimento Popular," p. 30.

32. This is the title of two of Ortiz' analyses of Umbanda: *A Morte Branca do Feiticeiro Negro-Umbanda: Integração de uma Religião numa Sociedade de Classes* (Petrópolis: Vozes, 1978); and the article of the same title in *Religião e Sociedade* 1 (May 1977): 43–50.

33. Oritz, *A Morte Branca do Feiticeiro Negro-Umbanda*, p. 197. Compare Maria Helena Villas Boas Concone, "Ideologia Umbandista e Integralismo," *Ciências Sociais Hoje* 1 (Brasília: CNPq, 1981), pp. 379–395. Concone draws out the very considerable overlap between Umbanda and integralist ideologies in the 1930s. Many elements of

those ideologies are alive and well in the national security ideology of the modern military and in modern Umbanda.

34. Diana Brown has shown how Umbanda may restore patronage systems in urban areas. Patrícia Birman traces parallels and relationships between submission to certain spirits and submission to centralized, bureaucratic power. Leni Silverstein examines how Bahian Candomblé groups enable lower-class survival through incorporation into an upper-class, white, patronage system. See Diana Brown, "O Papel Histórico da Classe Média na Formação de Umbanda," *Religião e Sociedade* 1 (May 1977): 31–42; Patrícia Birman, "A Celebração do Poder: Um Ritual Umbandista," *Ciências Sociais Hoje* 1:403–408; Leni Silverstein, "Mãe de Todo Mundo: Modas de Sobrevivência nas Comunidades de Candomblé de Bahia," *Religião e Sociedade* 4 (October 1979): 143–169.

35. Roger Bastide, *The African Religions of Brazil* (Baltimore, Md.: Johns Hopkins University Press, 1978), p. 397.

36. As I typologize in this way, I am taking up a question raised by Anani Dzidzienyo about conservative vs. dynamic adaptations of Africanity in Latin America. See his "African (Yoruba) Culture and the Political Kingdom in Latin America," in I. A. Akinjogbin and G. O. Ekemode, eds., *The Proceedings of the Conference on Yoruba Civilization Held at the University of Ife, Nigeria, July 26–31, 1976*, (University of Ife, 1976), vol. II, chap. 17. In a fuller exploration of the question, the sociology of the cults must be done with the aid of Thomas Skidmore, *Black into White: Race and Nationality in Brazilian Thought* (New York: Oxford University Press, 1974).

37. Maggie Velho's study of conflict in a Rio cult group brings out combinations of types 2 and 3 in the one group. Yvonne Maggie Velho, *Guerra de Orixa* (Rio de Janeiro: Zahar, 1977).

38. Colin Henfrey, "The Hungry Imagination: Social Formation, Popular Culture and Ideology in Bahia," in Simon Mitchell, ed., *The Logic of Poverty: The Case of the Brazilian Northeast* (London: Routledge and Kegan Paul, 1981), p. 108.

39. An excellent study of the internal organization of these groups is Vivaldo da Costa Lima, "A Família-de-santo nos Candomblés Jeje-Nagos da Bahia: Um Estudo de Relações Intragrupais," (Master's diss., Federal University of Bahia, 1971–1972).

40. José Comblin, *The Church and the National Security State* (Maryknoll, N.Y.: Orbis Books, 1979), chap. 4, provides an outline of the origins and content of the national security ideology (NSI) promoted in modern Latin American military regimes. I consider that the ideology actually transmitted to the grass roots in Brazil is not the complete NSI that Brazilian generals such as Golbery e Couto have helped to formulate, but a mixture of elements from that ideology together with evaluations and perspectives that elite modernizers have been formulating and teaching since at least the 1930s.

41. Harvey Cox, *The Seduction of the Spirit: The Use and Misuse of People's Religion* (New York: Simon and Schuster, 1973).

PART III

Peru

The Peruvian Church: Change and Continuity

Catalina Romero

In recent years, the Catholic Church in Peru has become one of society's main protagonists, a dynamizing factor in social change and element in the nation's cultural identity. Once considered one of Latin America's most conservative Churches and a central force in the structures of domination ever since colonial times, the Peruvian Catholic Church has undergone remarkable changes, often thought to have been produced by exogenous factors, such as the country's social reality or the Church's own reorientation at a worldwide level. Many political analysts have thus attributed changes in the Church to a necessary adaptation to the changes arising from reforms implemented by civilians and the military in the 1960s and 1970s, as well as to the emergence of an organized people's movement which, by changing the demands of the Church's own clientele, might also have forced the institution to change its policies in order to survive or to go on exercising some degree of influence in society. Another perspective, often present within the Church itself, frequently cites the Vatican II Council and the Medellín gathering of Latin American bishops as the most direct sources of change in the Peruvian Church. While these factors must be taken into account in any analysis of the change in relations between the Church and society, they are insufficient to explain the radical nature of the change and its consequences, especially considering that not all Latin American Churches changed.

What we present in these pages is an analytical framework utilizing a macrosocial perspective. More than simply describe the process, we present an overview of change and a tentative approach to understanding the process. The chapter, accordingly, is divided into three sections: (1) a brief survey of the thirty-year period of change, subdivided into three distinct moments;[1] (2) the nature and the meaning of the changes that oc-

curred during this period; and (3) the social and religious factors contributing to the process of change.

    This ambitious objective has left certain imprecisions and gaps, com-
pensated for here simply by references to other articles and complemen-
tary sources on Peru and the Church which offer a more detailed and
descriptive view of the process, as well as an indication of the areas which
require further study.[2]

    My hypothesis here is that the Catholic Church in Peru changed
its social involvement and its Christian vision of social reality, and incorporated these changes institutionally into its pastoral work and its
theology. The result of this process has placed the Church in a new relationship with society, characterized by the autonomy acquired through
its critique of prevalent social relations. I view this autonomy in sociological terms and in relation to the dynamics of Peruvian society in particular. The Church's autonomy finds its roots in its universality or international dimension, in its historical continuity, in its hierarchical organization,
and in the transcendental nature of its message, whose beginning and
end is the Word of God. This final element—transcendency—is usually
ignored in sociopolitical analyses, but is nonetheless essential for gaining
an overall comprehension of the process and its central aspects. It is the
starting point both for the Church's understanding of itself and for its
judgment of the historical reality in which it acts.

THIRTY YEARS OF PERUVIAN SOCIETY
AND OF THE CHURCH

    Analysts of Peruvian history all agree that the 1950s brought the
beginning of a process of qualitative change in society, manifest in a range
of social indicators such as migration, modifications in the productive and
occupational structure of the population, the involvement in politics of
new middle sectors, etc. Very few, however, have looked at the religious
factor and Church organization as relevant variables in an analysis of that
period, perhaps because of their scant immediate impact on our society.
It is possible, nonetheless, to speak of the Catholic Church as one of the
institutions participating in the process of change underway since that time.

    Both the political arena, as an expression of society's social and po-
litical processes, and its accompanying ideological manifestations reveal
a clearly defined period of change in Peru. In general terms, the 1950s
and early 1960s were a period of crisis for the system of oligarchical domination, progressively broken down by the modernization of society. The
advance of industrialization and urbanization represented a challenge to

the underpinnings of oligarchical power, based on agriculture and oriented toward commence and exports. The internationalization of Peru's economy and culture also made its contribution. New power blocs began to arise and, though without destroying their forerunners, call for changes in class alliances. New social groups also arose, struggling for their own economic and social expansion, with repercussions in politics as well. The birth of new political parties like the Christian Democratic Party (PDC) and Popular Action (AP), in 1955 and 1956 respectively, are both significant in that regard. Both presented themselves as modernizing and reformist alternatives to the Odriísta National Union (UNO), with its traditional *caudillo* base and supported by the oligarchy, and to the Peruvian Aprista Party (APRA), which with its myriad alliances moved between reformism and conciliation. The APRA-UNO coalition during the Manuel Prado government (1956–1962) was criticized as weak-kneed even within the APRA. Also important during that period were popular protest movements in the countryside and in several Peruvian cities. Though lacking in nationwide impact and organization, they expressed the fiercely repressed demands of many sectors of the masses.

The 1960s were marked by the emergence of middle sectors and of a class fraction with interests in industry, both demanding strong policies for modernization of the country. They called for agrarian reform and for a greater participation in the nation's life both of the peasantry and of middle sectors and workers, who until then had been excluded. Though far from calls for structural reform, they displayed a clear perception of the need for profound transformations in Peruvian society in order to make the leap toward economic development. The international context contributed to this perception, both in the form of the Alliance for Progress and in the appearance of insurrectional movements inspired by the Cuban revolution, raising urgent demands for change throughout the continent.

Nevertheless, expectations for change in Peru, with its deep-rooted inequalities and problems, were soon frustrated by the predominance of the interests defended by agribusiness, business groups, and international capital. The primacy of these groups was also visible in the political disputes and splitting of the ruling parties, AP and PDC, divided between socialist or communitarian groups on the one side, and pro-capitalist groups on the other. The split in the AP gave rise to Socialist Popular Action (APS), today close to the political front known as the United Left (IU), while PDC dissidents organized the Popular Christian Party (PPC), currently situated at the right end of the political spectrum.

The 1968 military coup led by General Juan Velasco Alvarado once again opened a period of reform in Peru, this time more radical and with the objective of reaching the masses in general. Early in the regime, important reforms were carried out in agrarian structures, industry, banks, commerce, education, and the press. But by 1974 the brakes were being put on reform. A political reaction by the sectors affected began gaining both ideological and political expression during the second phase of the military regime.

One important achievement during the 1968–1974 period was the organizational and ideological advance of the masses, which became new social protagonists at the head of an amalgam of major social sectors unified by their class interests, in the broad sense of the expression. During the first phase of the military regime there was progress in organizing the country's urban poor. Through the National System of Support for Social Mobilization (SINAMOS), the military government sought organizational support for the regime and its social reforms. Yet much of this effort was later converted into a people's resistance movement, seeking autonomy from the government for its organizations. The economic crisis, the contraction of real income for the working class, and the presence of the new left—with its organizational and ideological work among the masses —all contributed to structuring an identity for the masses around interests other than those of the government or of the ruling classes. During the second phase of the military regime, the people's manifestations brought this burgeoning popular identity into the open.

Rolando Ames has analyzed the presence of this social movement and its importance in a critical and far-reaching evaluation of the country's left:

> The recent people's movement has not faded; though affected by dispersion and the lack of political centralization, it seems to us to have kept alive the potential for becoming a major national force, if we are able to harness the demands and the levels and forms of organization that are now its main instruments for achieving that objective. . . . Evaluations of the present must take into account all the characteristics of this vast process of development of the people's movement. Ideologically, it has acquired a new self-image, a beginning of confidence in its own capacity which has won over more sectors of the masses; there is growing direct participation by the people in organizations, and experience has taught the need for such organization if demands are to be won. The horizon reveals a society freed from the control of big capital and based on people's power as an impelling utopia, raising the hopes of many simple people who are now politically lost as the result of false promises and the repressive threats of the ruling system.[3]

This development of a mass movement must be taken into account in order to understand the major changes transforming the country during that period. The poor ceased to be submissive and passive objects of pity to become active participants alongside other social groups.

That period ended, politically and socially, when a new constitution came into effect and, in 1980, the Popular Action party returned to power, no longer under the banner of change but heralding the recovery of a lost ideal condition, ideologically identified with the concepts of democracy and legality. Its lack of an analysis of the nation's new situation, its alienation from the process of change which took place in the 1970s and its IMF-inspired economic adjustment policies left the government isolated, as seen in its defeat in the 1983 municipal elections.

Within the tensions between change and restoration, the impulse for change in the 1980s continues to flow basically from the popular masses, now more organized and conscious of the need for urgent transformations, within a democratic perspective. On the other hand, the appearance of a terrorist organization which is present and very active in some areas of the country, now under military control, reflects a desperate attitude of a few sectors that no longer have confidence in legal forms of achieving changes.

For some analysts,[4] these thirty years brought the crisis of oligarchical domination, with that ruling bloc—in Gramscian terms—giving way to the emergence of a reformist historical bloc unified around a developmentalist economic program aimed at integrating society, broadening the political participation of previously excluded sectors but maintaining control in the hands of an industrial and exporting class fraction closely tied to international capital, while incorporating or allowing the manifestation of national cultural values previously restricted to very limited expressions. Perhaps the most novel and particular aspect is the incipient constitution of a people's historical bloc, identified with interests opposed to those of the ruling class, which has begun to reveal its own national and popular identity and its own program for society.

These political changes and the diversification of class interests in society have been accompanied by religious and ecclesiastical changes. In other articles I have described in detail these changes in the Church's relation with society, divided into specific stages over the past thirty years. The first period covers the years 1958–1968, beginning with a pastoral letter from the Peruvian bishops, "On the Social Question," which was the first clear sign of a concern with the country's social problems. This pastoral letter pointed out existing social differences and the way in which the Church's social doctrine could contribute to understanding the country's problems. That period ended with the bishops' meeting at Medellín, co-chaired by Cardinal Landázuri from Peru and marked by the active presence of Peruvian bishops and of theologians such as Father Gustavo

Gutiérrez. Gutiérrez's liberation theology was also presented for the first time in 1968.

The second period, from 1968 to 1974, began with the above-mentioned events and culminated with the Bishops' Assembly on Evangelization, Peru's contribution to the Synod in Rome. The admission of new advisers to the Bishops' conference and the new rules established for the regional assemblies—with greater authority for the bishops—were indications of a turning point in the Peruvian Church, which thereafter sought to attenuate the dynamism arising from the parishes and communities and felt throughout the Church structures.

The third period is constituted by the time leading up to the Third Assembly of Latin American Bishops in Puebla in 1979. The conservative document presented by the leadership of the Latin American Bishops' Conference (CELAM) for discussion before the Puebla meeting called for a change in the analysis of Latin American reality, and was severely questioned by a number of specific Churches. Contributions to the document from several of Peru's dioceses and from the hierarchy reflected the tensions experienced by Christians involved in a society in transformation who examine their faith on the basis of that experience. The confirmation of the Latin American Church's option for the poor allows us to identify the end of that period as 1984, when Gustavo Gutiérrez's liberation theology was questioned, along with much of the Peruvian Church's pastoral work, as evidenced by the convocation of the entire bishops' assembly to Rome in October of the same year.

This latter period has been marked by internal tensions within the Church. Specific tensions began in 1983 when the Sacred Congregation for the Doctrine of Faith requested that the Peruvian bishops issue a declaration on liberation theology. The procedure adopted by the Sacred Congregation was unusual, since comments are not usually made on a theology in general but rather on the theological expressions of individual authors, which are analyzed directly by the Congregation. In this case the request was addressed to the Peruvian Church through its hierarchy, and not to a specific theologian.

The Peruvian bishops met in three extraordinary assemblies to discuss the matter, but a year later had come to no agreement on a unanimous declaration. This lack of consensus reflected the existence of different interpretations of the significance and the viewpoints of liberation theology. For one major sector of the Church, this theological reflection is closely tied to the Peruvian Church's pastoral orientations in recent years. Disapproval of liberation theology was felt by this sector to be a criticism of their own pastoral work. On the other hand, some of the media launched a campaign of personal attacks against liberation theologians and even against bishops identified with the same perspective; this contributed to breaking down any atmosphere for dialogue and promoted a confrontation of positions.

The April 1984 bishops' assembly finally produced two drafts, reflecting different stances of two sectors of the episcopacy. Both documents were sent to Rome, and the Peruvian bishops were invited to assemble at the Vatican to seek consensus on the matter. Since it was a year of *Ad-Limina* visits—made by every country's bishops every five years—some observers interpreted the trips as normal. Yet the inclusion of bishops who had already made their regular visits, as well as the presence of auxiliary bishops who are not normally invited, made it clear that this was a very special occasion.

The document on liberation theology finally approved by unanimity of the bishops in Rome referred throughout its four sections to the many valid aspects of that theology and recognized that "this message of liberation has in recent years inspired Peruvian Church life and many of the Episcopacy's documents." The second section delves into "the hard reality of Peru." It mentions the growth of poverty, violence, and indiscriminate repression and points to the personal and structural causes of this situation, which it calls "a cry for justice," constituting a challenge for faith and for the Church. In the third section, the bishops deal with the "need for discernment" regarding three issues: history and society, praxis and truth, and the Kingdom of God and human action. The document concludes with pastoral orientations.

The crisis provoked by the Congregation of Faith's request to the Peruvian Church was thus overcome in the tradition of its best documents. Considering the heights which the conflict had reached, this document was a real achievement for Peruvian Church's promoters of unity. Nonetheless, room was left for promoters of internal division to renew the conflict in the realm of practice, in which recourse to hierarchical jurisdictional power is easier.

This context of internecine tension in Peru can be better understood with a few references to other events affecting Latin America as a whole. For several years the Latin American Bishops' Conference and the Vatican had been raising alerts regarding certain facts in the Latin American Church. The International Theological Commission met for a detailed analysis of liberation theology, and its observations were couched in moderate tones. At Puebla, the discussions stressed the integral nature of liberation and warned against possible reductionisms. Interestingly, the Puebla document used the concept of liberation in the terms defined by Gustavo Gutiérrez in his 1971 book.[5]

At Puebla and later in Haiti, following the Pope's visit to Central

America, the question of a "people's Church" was dealt with, and warnings issued regarding the risks of a parallel Church which might adopt a class alignment. Yet it was recognized that the term could also be understood in a positive sense. In neither case did the Peruvian hierarchy feel itself to be the target of such warnings. Following the CELAM meeting in Haiti, Cardinal Landázuri declared to the press that in Peru there was no "people's Church" in the terms defined by the Pope as inadmissible. Christian communities in Peru had developed with close ties to parishes and to the hierarchy, due in part to the major pastoral efforts mentioned elsewhere in this chapter. The theoretical development of liberation theology is also very clear in affirming its ties to the Church and to tradition.

What was being questioned, therefore, was neither the ecclesiality of the communities nor the Catholicism of theology in Peru, but rather the Catholic religious movement growing at the time. The questioning came from outside the Peruvian Church, first from CELAM and more recently from the Congregation of Faith. It found echo in Peru among bishops from various positions, but all of them tied in one way or another to a new conservative religious movement, also Catholic, which first appeared around the Puebla meeting.

In a certain fashion, it was the Peruvian Church's own recent history that was being questioned by Rome when the bishops were convoked to the Holy See and asked to make a declaration on theological developments present in their jurisdiction. The public repercussions of these internal Church problems also reflect the social influence of the Catholic religious movement characterized by liberation theology. Egged on by members of *Opus Dei* and by a new organization which also has international ties—*Sodalitium Christiane Vitae*, with integralist and totalitarian traits and a liberal pro-capitalist ideology—the media has heated up the debate around liberation theology, singling out bishops and accusing priests of various errors, with the objective of achieving a clear condemnation of liberation theology.

The public declarations of Archbishops like Msgr. Ricardo Durand and Msgr. Vargas Ruíz de Somocurcio, as well as the former military vicar Alcídes Mendoza (now Archbishop of Cuzco), condemning liberation theology, represent a break with the Peruvian bishops' traditional discretion regarding internal affairs and, thereby, with their external unity. *Sodalitium* members no longer speak of liberation theology without interjecting the epithet of Marxism, in addition to linking the Peruvian experience to that of Central America. They are thereby seeking to transpose conflicts peculiar to the Central American Churches—which arise from quite different social and political contexts—to the reality of Peru, which is now living through a very special moment of political definition.

THE MEANING OF THE CHANGES

Several studies on the changes in Latin American Churches have interpreted their meaning and importance as ideological contributions, legitimizing or delegitimizing particular political regimes, and acting politically as a pressure group to defend human and democratic rights undercut by the *de facto* regimes implanted in several countries around the continent. Others attribute the changes to a rationale of adapting and adjusting to structural changes with the aim of survival.[6]

While these aspects are certainly part of the overall meaning of the changes, I believe that the process is actually much more radical from the Church's point of view, involving a fundamental change in its way of understanding its own Christian identity and of relating to society. Although this may not have been totally clear over the entire thirty-year period we have referred to, the current reaction occurring inside the Church has fully revealed this to be the case.

The change has been progressive; initially the fruit of isolated efforts with converging objectives, it gained strength and identity out of the Church's moments of collective reflection, such as the Latin American Episcopal Conferences and, in the case of Peru, the national bishops' conference. It is a broad-ranging process, encompassing theology, doctrine, organization, and pastoral action, and has rallied a growing number of Christians around a new ecclesiastical experience which places very concrete demands on their individual lives. The overlapping of these aspects meant that the process was not rooted only in the communities nor in the advanced groups of Christians conscious of the faith and the reality it has been their lot to live, nor in the creative theologians or prophetic hierarchies alone; rather it is a process which involves all these forces in the common search for evangelical answers to their historical moment.

The core of the change is the Church's option for the poor, and its novelty is to conceive of the poor as subjects in our continent's history. To understand the history of humanity and of salvation from the standpoint of the poor as subjects changes one's categories, filling them with new meanings which, though present in Catholic tradition, have often been obscured by commitments made at different points in time.

The inequities of Peruvian society cut across all human and social relations, tinging them with the oppression and domination that are integral parts of the nation's collective consciousness. Even more than in other Latin American countries—since Peru was the center of the Conquest and Spanish colonization—this situation is expressed in many ways in the identity of Peruvian men and women. The clearest differences are those regarding Indians, and relate not only to race but to their social and economic situation as well. Stripped of their land, traditions, and customs, the Indians are foreigners in their own country.[7] This state of affairs also holds for the "natives" (indigenous populations living in the jungles). Living outside of the national society, their process of colonization is now bringing problems with the expropriation of their lands, the extermination of their natural habitats, and the loss of their culture.

Urban inequities are of similar proportions, though less apparent. Mountain people are not the same as those from the coast, those of rural backgrounds are quite unlike the capital-city dwellers, the blacks and mixed-bloods are different from the whites, and men are on a different plane than women. People treat each other in a way that makes these inequities manifest, especially during moments of social conflict. The differences are internalized and expressed in the social role played by each. The Peruvian often speaks openly among his or her peers, but is silent in the presence of anyone seen to be different, as a defense and protection of his or her own identity. The poor in Peru are the indigenous, those from the rural and mountain regions, the mixed-bloods, the women of the popular classes, the workers, the sick, those who have no influential friends, those who have no work, and those with little income.

The Church, in its daily practice of attention to the people's spiritual life, administration of the sacraments, liturgical celebrations, and social work aimed at human promotion and development, has perceived this situation of inequity. Its option for the poor has not meant the exclusion of the non-poor, but rather a vocation for real fidelity to the Gospel, which invites all to a life of fraternity. This dimension, not taken into account in the analyses of social scientists, is at the heart of the meaning of that option.

The Peruvian Church has been able to accompany this process of turning the poor into historical subjects capable of speaking for themselves by respecting their autonomy, taking them in, and interceding on behalf of their rights when such intervention was requested. During the most repressive period of the military dictatorship, from 1976 to 1979, twenty-two of Peru's forty-one dioceses issued denunciations and protests against abuses committed by the authorities and against the social costs provoked by the government's economic policies.[8] The denunciations from the South Andean and the Jungle regions stand out, frequently presenting their analysis of the situation and the Christian reflections underlying their concrete acts of solidarity with people's movements in their regions.[9] The ONIS (National Office for Social Information) priests' movement issued eight declarations during the same period, denouncing government measures and defending the people's right to organize and to protest against an unjust situation. Christian Communities from around the country also put out the same kind of declarations. An overview of all the public expressions in favor of the poor during that period reveals a vast movement encompassing half of the Church's dioceses.

The defense of the poor on such a large scale can only be explained by a very clear pastoral motivation, since the bishops and pastoral agents participating in these expressions of solidarity cannot all be identified with a single ideological, political, or even ecclesiastical current. It is a reasonable hypothesis that this solidarity was only possible due to the nonpartisan nature of the people's mobilizations—we have already seen the low degree of political and organizational centralization. The Church, therefore, did not confront an ideological movement that might be called communist nor a political movement that could make it back away from involvement. In this broad social movement the protagonists were the country's poor. Their new ties to the Church encouraged them to resort to this institution in order to strengthen their positions, and in fact they met with a receptive reaction to their requests.

The option for the poor was thus understood as a practice of solidarity with them and of protest against poverty.[10] This meaning of the option for the poor, developed in liberation theology and in the writings of the bishops, became the basis for a new and blossoming spirituality in the Latin American poor. Gustavo Gutiérrez outlined the notion as follows in his most recent book:

> The irruption of the poor (referred to at the beginning of the chapter) is expressed in the conscious identity and in the organization of the oppressed and the excluded of Latin America. From now on Latin American society is judged and will be transformed from the outlook of the poor. An entire people has begun its march to build a world where people are more important than things, and where all may live in dignity. A society respectful of human liberty at the service of an authentic common good, with no constraints at all. This is what we call the historical process of liberation, which with its ebb and flow is stalking the entire subcontinent. The spirituality being born in Latin America is that of the Church of the poor, that of the ecclesiastical community seeking to make real its solidarity with the world's poorest. Collective ecclesiastical spirituality; marked by the religiosity of an exploited people of believers.[11]

The people emerge as a new collective subject, with an active role in the society whose historical process of liberation they have become part of, contributing their myriad qualities, their Christian spirituality and their faith. This occurrence is new in the history of modern-day people's movements. In Europe, the proletariat became a class in the context of a secularized society, rife with the atheism characteristic of a rational and scientific mentality and of the practice of the capitalist ruling classes, against whom the Catholic Church reacted defensively. In Peru and in Latin America, the evangelical work of the Church and its choices in doctrine and practice have turned the Christian community and faith into an element of identity which contributes spiritual strength to the people's process of liberation and an opening to transcendency.

FACTORS OF CHANGE IN THE CHURCH

As the Church moves closer to the poor, it makes room for them by opening a new level of participation. To speak of the factors of change, we must distinguish between those arising from within the Peruvian Church and those which come out of the Church in its international dimension. We shall only touch briefly on the latter, since they recur throughout Latin America. Though they do not explain differences between one country and another, they certainly influence the course of events when combined with the processes underway within each country's Church. The Vatican II Council is the most important of these factors, but papal encyclicals like *Populorum Progressio* and CELAM's Latin American meetings in Rio de Janeiro (1955), Medellín, and Puebla shaped the meaning of the change. Also influential were the situations in other countries' Churches and outstanding actions by bishops, although to a lesser degree. Examples of this would be the situations of the Cuban and Nicaraguan Churches, as well as that of El Salvador. Personalities such as Msgr. Romero and other bishops like Helder Câmara, Leonidas Proaño, and Méndez Arceo bear witness well beyond their national experiences. These factors originating in the international Church have influenced the processes underway in the Peruvian Church, three of which we will discuss here: the Christian communities, liberation theology, and the opening of the institutional framework to take in the new developments.

The Christian Communities

No research has been done yet on our country's Christian base communities, but it is possible to attempt a description and evaluation on the basis of some experiences of work with them. First of all, we must account for their differences, or the heterogeneity of the groups commonly called Christian communities.[12] On the one hand, we have the groups organized as movements of the lay apostolate. They appeared in Peru during the 1940s and have displayed exceptional staying power compared to other similar movements in Latin America, since they are still active in the Church today. With lay communities active among workers, secondary and university students, and independent and professional sectors, these movements are characterized by their methodology, based on an analysis of reality, reflections in the light of the Bible and Church teachings, and a resolution to act. Many priests and religious have put this model to work without being tied to specific movements, since it offers a clear work method coming out of experience with community Revisions of Life Events.

Alongside these experiences, which have taken on their own character, adapting their work methods to specific environments, other communities have arisen out of everyday parish work and efforts to incorporate a greater number of lay people into Church life. This category encompasses the majority of our country's communities, which – in urban areas – can also be subdivided into at least three types, depending on their origin.

The first are those organized around the ministry of sacraments, with an emphasis on preparation to receive the sacraments, following the directions issued by the Vatican Council and implemented by the Peruvian bishops in their 1969 General Assembly. When they participate in a group preparing for the sacraments, studying together, and discussing their responsibility as Christians, parents (in the case of Baptism and First Communion) and youth (in the case of Confirmation) often constitute Christian communities that want to continue their existence. For most this is not the case, yet there is a significant number of communities that have arisen out of this experience in parish life.

Another source of Christian communities is also linked to the experience of preparation for the sacraments, but led by lay people who have taken the responsibility for this work. The average number of inhabitants per parish in Peru is 15,000 and there are half that number of people per priest.[13] The need to rely on lay people for presacramental education has led to the creation of groups of cathechists and liturgical teams which, alongside the parish councils recommended by Vatican II, have given rise to ongoing groups of parishioners who assist the priests and religious in all their activities. The ongoing nature of this work facilitates the formation of a human community whose sharing in evangelical tasks often gives rise to Christian communities. The pastoral agents (lay and religious) nonetheless differentiate clearly between those who are actually a community and those who are simply members of work groups. Christian reflection and commitment are two aspects used in this distinction, and also allow members to identify themselves as such.

Yet another source of Christian communities is found in the Church's growing involvement in different forms of social work. As Christians have become engaged in neighborhood problems like health (street cleaning, demands for effective health care from public agencies, etc.), they have created the role of health agents, who meet to discuss their work as Christians at the service of the population. As social conflicts have intensified, solidarity groups have been organized to support striking teachers, arrested workers, injured squatters, etc. Mercy missions like feeding the hungry or visiting prisoners have led to participation in community kitchens and involvement in the defense of human rights, visiting prisoners in jail, taking them food, washing their clothes, writing them letters, and communicating with their relatives. Any of these tasks are well within the reach of neighborhood women, young people, the unemployed with free time, and those who are designated by supportive unions and associations. More recently, the need to organize people's restaurants and community kitchens in response to the spread of hunger in shanty towns has brought the active participation of Christians. Since these groups are organized to meet neighborhood problems, a Christian participates like any other person. Christian communities arise out of these experiences, organized by those who see in this work a sense of fidelity to the Gospel and a sign of the presence of God. Lay identity is greater in these and in other similar groups less involved in the traditional tasks of the clergy.

One dimension to be emphasized in the study of Christian communities is their dynamism. A group organized around catechism may soon move into center stage in neighborhood solidarity work, and another involved in social work may come to concern itself with making the Church's liturgy more meaningful to the people attending Sunday Mass. Lay people participating in Christian communities acquire the ability to analyze reality, as well as an awareness of neighborhood problems. They quickly begin to stand out through their embodiment of virtues respected by the people, such as honest, hard work and commitment, and they are soon asked to take responsibilities in their neighborhood association or at their workplace. This is a real challenge for the communities, which must adapt to the new demands of their members, even at the risk of dissolving as a community. This kind of situation is not at all exceptional in our reality, due to the vitality of the people's organizations. The Christian community is a privileged forum for collective experiences, training, and free-flowing encounters, but it is not the only one, and the outside environment places high demands on its effectiveness and witness. Perhaps this is what has led the communities to affirm their ecclesiastical identity amid the people's other organizations, rather than seeking to replace them, as has been the case in other countries where the political situation has placed Church groups in exceptional situations.

To complete this overview of the Christian communities, it is important to note that in rural regions—both the Andean area and the jungle—the experience has been somewhat different. In relatively small social communities, the formation of small groups, no matter how diverse, may promote internal differentiation or division. Therefore, although there are catechists, Delegates of the Word, or liturgical readers, more emphasis is placed on a relationship with the entire population, with a system for electing those who will be Delegates of the Word or liturgical readers and attempts to achieve broader forms of participation among the population as a reflection of faith. Since the heterogeneity of these regions is much greater, I will simply point to the complexities involved.

It has been principally through these experiences with Christian communities that the Church's official representatives have come to recognize that the people have a more mature faith than was expected, given the people's social and cultural background. Affirmations like "The people are bearers of the Gospel," repeated at the Puebla meeting in 1979,[14] arise from this experience of working with the poor and from the discovery of the gold mine of faith that exists in them as part of the Church. The announcing of the Kingdom of God as a kingdom of plenty and of life, and the faith in the resurrection from a situation of crisis and misery retrieve the deepest meaning of the announcement of Christ from the cross. It is more than the hope for political victory or for achievement of material success. The Gospel is made present with the discovery that, despite the defeats, humiliation, and death, faith speaks with strength and the commitment is unwaning.

The social and political consequence of this process of organization of Christians in the poor sectors of the cities and the countryside is that the poor find in the Church a space for personal freedom, human development, and identification as a people with their own identity and history, which implies responsibilities. In other words, they become aware of their active role in history and of their possibilities for collectively becoming an agent for social change. The specific means by which they will be able to play their parts remain open to their own decision, in the context of political pluralism needed to guarantee the universality of the Christian message. The goal of the search, in any case, is oriented by the overall option for the poor.

Theological Reflection

There have also been important theological changes within the Peruvian Church. While the best-known aspect is the development of liberation theology, beginning with the book by Gutiérrez which gave it its name, theological activity has been further developed in other writings by the same author, as well as in the discussions of the Christian com-

munities and in the documents of the Church hierarchy. Biblical themes
such as charity, poverty, the Kingdom, and classical themes in theology
such as Christology and Ecclesiology have all been areas for contributions. The recourse to philosophy and to the social sciences to achieve
a better knowledge of the historical situation and to enrich theological
reflections are present in this production. The creativity of its development comes out of Church tradition and the Church's written teachings,
in the spirit of freedom opened by Vatican II. This new theological production has become a conscious factor orienting the practice of the Church
and of Christians as the basis for the search for a Christian way of living
in a situation of social transformation.

Liberation theology offers not only a subject for theological reflection, but a key for understanding the history of salvation and of humanity as a part of that salvation, or, in other words, for recognizing the liberating dimension of Christ's message as a whole. What is the relation
between salvation and the process of man's liberation throughout history?
Or, more precisely, in the light of the Word, what is the meaning of the
struggle against an unjust society, the creation of a new man? These questions are raised by Gutiérrez in his book. The answer goes beyond the
traditional dualism between sacred and profane history, without reducing
one to the other.

> The history of salvation is the very heart of human history.[15]

> The eschatological promises have been fulfilled throughout history,
> but this does not mean that they can be simply or clearly identified with
> specific social realities. Their liberating work goes beyond what was fore-
> seen and leads to new and unexpected possibilities. The full encounter with
> the Lord will put an end to history, but it is already taking place partially
> within history.[16]

In his reflection on poverty, he recognizes both its spiritual and its
material dimensions:

> Material poverty is a scandalous state. Spiritual poverty is an attitude of
> opening up to God, of spiritual infancy. The precise notion of these two
> conceptions of the term poverty clears our way and allows us to advance
> in the understanding of the Christian witness of poverty, thanks to a third
> sense of the word: poverty as a commitment to solidarity and to protest.[17]

The strength of theology in this conflict-ridden country and continent has made it a very significant part of intellectual development. For
those accustomed to repeating theories learned abroad, liberation theology opens an original perspective which is faithful to a genuine Christian

tradition, adding to it new content born of Peruvian and Latin American reality, characterized by the suffering and happiness of a people that does not flee from the reality of conflict and that in the midst of that conflict seeks to be loyal to its faith.

The Peruvian hierarchy also reflects this theological thinking in its documents. The four most important of these documents, from the perspective of the option for the poor and liberation, are the Conclusions of the 26th Episcopal Assembly, the contributions to the Synod on "Justice in the World," the document on the "Ministerial Priesthood," and that on "Evangelization." A few quotes from these writings will reveal the nature of the positions taken by the episcopacy, which are also present in lesser documents and in relation to other issues.

The first document, from January 1969, says in relation to lay people:

> Considering the indisputable situation of poverty, injustice and oppression in our country, a situation harmful to the dignity of the human person, this Episcopal Assembly expresses the desire to confront, frankly and decisively, the concrete problems of the Peruvian man. To make our society more humane is to contribute to the Church's redeeming mission.[18]

The document on "Justice in the World," in 1971, went further:

> Building a just society in Latin America and in Peru means liberation from the present situation of dependency, of oppression and of plunder in which the great majority of our peoples live. Liberation, on the other hand, will be a break with all that makes it impossible for man to fulfill himself either personally or in community; on the other hand, it means building a new society, more humane and fraternal. Christ's salvation is more than political liberation, which finds its place and its true significance in the total liberation announced unendingly by the Holy Scriptures, leading man to his dignity as a child of God (Medellín, Justice, 3). . . . For the Peruvian ecclesiastical community, this implies opting for the oppressed and the excluded, as a personal and community commitment. This choice excludes no one from our charity; rather, to opt for those who today are experiencing the most violent forms of oppression is for us an effective way of also loving those who, perhaps unconsciously, are oppressed by their situation of oppressors.[19]

So as not to extend these quotations, I will take the last one from the document on Evangelization, which won the praise of the Congregation of Bishops of Rome for its "development of the concept of liberation" in the context of theological reflection "in conformity with the repeated teachings of the Holy Father."[20] This document states that

The evangelical mission of the Church demands that we announce here and now the Good News of the liberation of everyone, so that all men may commit themselves to participating in the action of God in the world, recognizing Christ as Lord of the Universe. The history where the People of God are located is the history of humanity in which Christ saves men; it is the history of salvation. This is not a peaceful process but, as analysis of reality tragically shows us, advances in the midst of enormous difficulties. When the People of God today accept the same mission as Christ, they are consciously accepting a liberating mission.[21]

And, in another section:

Precisely because the Church's mission is to save man, it must also commit itself to establishing a social, economic and political order capable of sustaining and encouraging the promotion of man. . . . The task of redemption cannot, therefore, be indifferent to the prevailing social order.[22]

These quotations in themselves reveal how the Peruvian Church understands its mission. It revolves around man in Peru and his concrete problems of oppression and poverty, and it announces here and now a salvation which also encompasses the political dimension. The mission of liberation seeks to integrate the transcendental dimension with the history of human liberation. The option for the poor, which excludes no one, is a demand of that mission. A long road has been walked since the Archbishop of Lima declared in 1937 that "poverty is the most certain road to human happiness. Only the state which is successful in making the poor appreciate the spiritual treasures of poverty will be able to resolve their social problems."[23]

The Institutional Framework

To round out these factors of change in the Church, it is important to include the institution's organizational dimension. The nationwide body representing the Peruvian bishops is the Peruvian Bishops' Conference, which acquired its present structure following the First General Conference of the Latin American Bishops, held in Rio de Janeiro in 1955, which led to the creation of CELAM, based on the national bishops' conferences.[24]

Its present definitive form, approved by Vatican II, goes back to December 1967, when the statutes approved by the Assembly of Bishops were ratified by the Holy See. The purpose of the conference is "to study ecclesiastical problems of common interest and to promote the progress and coordination of Catholic activities in the country."[25]

The documents quoted above were issued by the Plenary Assembly, the highest organ of the Conference. The assemblies are generally attended by theologians who, as expert advisors, work as consultants to the bishops. These advisors have included people like Gutiérrez, Ricardo Antocich, S.J., José Luis Idígoras, S.J., and many others. This ongoing dialogue with theologians in a pluralist setting has enriched the bishops' meditations, as is reflected in their documents. All the more so in the case of theologians involved in pastoral action and not isolated in the academic milieu, because the reality of the people of God was even more embodied in their contributions.

The most important organizational changes took place during the 1970s and led to broader participation in the assembly by priests, religious, and the laity as guests. The January 1972 Assembly on Joint Pastoral Work in Peru was attended by fifty-six guests, double the number of bishops. That same year, the country was experimentally divided "into nine zones, in order to hold zonal or regional assemblies of bishops and pastoral agents, to achieve a greater and more concrete knowledge of Peru's disparate realities."[26] The assembly held the following January was attended by forty-eight prelates, three delegates from the Conference of the Religious of Peru, and thirty-six representatives of the regional assemblies: priests, religious, and lay people, plus six experts for each commission. Although the bishops met alone once during the event, this broad participation at the assembly was a clear sign of organizational opening within the Church. In many dioceses and regions, the lay representatives at the assembly were elected by the communities, resulting in the participation of a significant group of Christians committed to their social milieu.

Following 1973, eight ecclesiastical regions were organized, along with regional assemblies. These bodies opened discussion regarding common decisions of the Church to diocesan and religious clergy, nuns, and the lay representatives of the Christian communities. It was also agreed that half of the members of the clergy sitting on the Presbyterian Councils would be elected, thus making it possible for priests with highly regarded pastoral work to participate in diocesan responsibilities.

The 1974 Assembly brought up the need to regulate the regional assemblies, although still recognizing their utility, "in order to safeguard the exclusive responsibility of the region's bishops for the conclusions to be sent to the General Assembly."[27] New regulations for those assemblies were approved in May of the same year, recognizing the indicative value of the participation of laity, priests, and the religious. These new regulations also established a preparatory commission to set the meetings' agendas, the number of grass-roots delegates to be elected (but approved by the bishop), and a number of other norms for the meeting itself which assured control, when necessary, over the members' participation in the assemblies.

Subsequent National Assemblies received preparatory working papers presented by the regional assemblies for the discussion and approval of the bishops. The degree of opening to participation of pastoral agents now depended on the bishops of each region. In general, this decentralization allowed for the increasing consideration of the country's regional situations in decisions taken by the General Assembly of Bishops, and represented the creation of very important communication channels between pastoral agents and the hierarchy.

These channels are still open, although no longer used so regularly. In 1978 the regional assemblies participated actively in the preparation of documents for Puebla, and later for the Synod on the Family. In 1983 the text of the Encyclical *Laborem Excercens* was discussed, but the regional assemblies did not meet, and each diocese channeled its contributions through the Episcopal Commission for Social Action.

Since Peru is a centralized country, concentrating in the capital not only the main seats of political and administrative power but also the country's economic resources, the Church's efforts at decentralization implied a greater attention to the regions and the incorporation of their particular problems in its vision of the nation. This is especially significant with regard to two regions: the Jungle, which is united geographically but the size and cultural diversity of which encompass a very heterogeneous reality largely unknown by the rest of the country; and the South Andean region, centered in Cuzco, which through the Andean Pastoral Institute has managed to develop overall pastoral work for the area's peasants. The fact that its regional identity had preceded its designation as an ecclesiastical region, as well as the pastoral care demanded by the situation of its peasants and indigenous peoples, had led bishops, prelates, and pastoral agents into very close collaboration, with joint training courses and the publication of very important declarations about local realities and on the urgency of solutions for its most serious problems.

Alongside the Peruvian Church's formal structures, which we have just described, the decade also brought the development of many informal groups for the sharing of experiences and Christian reflection. Some arose from the experience of meetings of the regional assemblies and others came out of common lines of pastoral action. Among these informal groups known to the hierarchy is the priests' organization called ONIS (National Office for Social Information), which was a channel for exchanging information and education regarding national and ecclesiastical events for many Peruvian and foreign priests. It was well known for its public expressions in response to the country's problems at times of social tension. For the laity and for pastoral agents, the encounters of Faith and Action in Solidarity would allow for communication among Christian communities from around the country.

More formal types of organization included the national encounters of the various movements of the lay apostolate, as well as the meetings of those responsible for pastoral work with peasants, human rights, and health called by the Episcopal Commission for Social Action (CEAS). As was the case of the regional assemblies, these meetings allowed for closer relations between pastoral agents and bishops in discussions of the country's concrete problems and the tasks of evangelization.

Initiatives for the training of the laity and pastoral agents also took place during the same period. The days of Theological Reflection organized by the Department of Theology at the Catholic University are one example of this work, begun in 1970 and still underway. This experience has included around 3,000 people from the entire country and neighboring countries in the study of theology. The School of Theology of the Archdiocese of Lima and other religious studies institutes have also organized educational activities, thus strengthening the intellectual aspect of lay commitment.

All these activities contributed to the dynamism of the Catholic Church in Peru during a period of intense social change, accompanied by an equally intense rhythm of change within the Church. To conclude, we can say that Peru's Catholic Church displayed its own dynamic of change, encouraged by Vatican II and by the theological currents present there; by the pastoral practice of the Catholic Church in Latin America as expressed in Medellín and later in Puebla; by the social reality of Peru, marked by profound social inequities inherited from centuries of injustice and the social reform processes undertaken during the 1960s and 1970s; by the search for pastoral responses and Church renewal on the part of Peru's bishops and pastoral agents; by the participation of a people of believers in the Church's common quest; by the theological production best represented by the works of Gustavo Gutiérrez; and, finally, by the opening up of the hierarchy to the world, in the best post-conciliar spirit, an attitude which contributed to the renewal of the Church in Peru during a crucial period in its history.

The conjunction of these multiple factors conducive to renewal and change was a propitious moment for the Church's contribution in Peru. During the new period which has now begun, the Church appears torn between the strength gained from opening up to the world and the impulse to draw back into itself, strengthening its hierarchical structures and its dogmatic principles. The unfolding of this tension in the future will continue to be important for building the Peruvian nation, in which the

Church has played a role promoting both the domination and the liberation of its people.

NOTES

1. Catalina Romero de Iguíñiz, "Cambios en la relación iglesia y sociedad en el Perú, 1958–1978," in *Debates en Sociología*, Department of Social Sciences, Catholic University, No. 7, 1982.

2. The author is a member of a research team studying the Church at the Instituto Bartolomé de las Casas-Rímac.

3. *El Diario de Marka*, March 28, 1982.

4. Henry Pease, *El ocaso del poder oligárquico* (Lima: Desco, 1977).

5. For the conclusions of the Puebla meeting, see *Evangelization at Present and in the Future of Latin America: Conclusions* (Washington, D.C.: National Council of Bishops, 1979). See also Gustavo Gutiérrez, *Teología de la liberación: Perspectivas* (Lima: CEP, 1971). The English version is *Theology of Liberation: History, Politics, and Salvation*, trans. and ed. Caridad Inda and John Eagleson (Maryknoll, N.Y.: Orbis, 1973).

6. Authors such as Carlos Astiz, "The Catholic Church in Latin American Politics: A Case Study of Peru," in David Pollock, ed., *Latin American Prospects for the 1970s: What Kinds of Revolutions?* (New York: Praeger, 1973); Julio Colter in his brief reference to the Church in *Clases, estado y nación en el Perú* (Lima: EP, 1978); and others have made contributions in this area.

7. Gutiérrez refers to this experience in his book *Beber en su propio pozo* (Lima: CEP, 1983). The English translation is *We Drink from Our Own Wells* (Maryknoll, N.Y.: Orbis, 1984).

8. This data comes from various issues of the magazine *Páginas* during that period.

9. See, for example, "Recogiendo el clamor," Pastoral letter from the bishops of the Southern Andes region, July 1977.

10. Gutiérrez, *Teología de la liberación*, p. 368.

11. Gutiérrez, *Beber en su propio pozo*.

12. In Peru, the name "Christian communities" is used as it was at Medellín; the term "base ecclesial communities" is less frequent, although it refers to the same reality.

13. *Directorio Eclesiástico del Perú* (Lima: 1984).

14. *Conclusions de Puebla*, document, no. 1147.

15. Gutiérrez, *Teología de la liberación*, p. 189.

16. Ibid., p. 215.

17. Ibid., p. 368.

18. Document by the Episcopacy, Lima, 1977, p. 17.

19. Ibid., pp. 146–147.

20. Ibid., p. 17.

21. Ibid., p. 189.

22. Ibid., p. 192.

23. Quoted by Julio Colter in *Clases, estado y nación en el Perú*, p. 308; and by Fredrick Pike in *Modern History of Peru* (London: Weidenfeld and Nicholson, 1967).

24. *Iglesia en el Perú*, No. 52, June 1977.

25. *Directorio Eclesiástico del Peru* (Lima: 1984).

26. *Iglesia en el Perú*, No. 3, February 1972.

27. *Iglesia en el Perú*, No. 15, February 1974.

Peru: The Leftist Angels

Luis Pásara

The Catholic Church landed in Latin America with the Spanish and for centuries was part of the order that both they and their successors imposed. Yet the Church is one of the institutions that has undergone significant changes over the last two or three decades. One of these changes is the appearance within it of radicalized groups which, in several Latin American countries, have played important roles both within the Church and in the political arena as a whole.

This chapter will look at the changes taking place in the case of Peru, often mentioned as an important example. Peru produced one of the best-known names in liberation theology—Gustavo Gutiérrez—and it would be hard to explain the recent development of the Peruvian Church, or even certain aspects of the country's political evolution in the past twenty years, without referring to the impact of the presence of radical Catholic sectors.

We shall attempt here to describe the context in which the radical Catholic tendency appeared as well as the conditions which allowed it to develop, to characterize what has been called the radical Catholic style and its projection into the sphere of political action and, finally, to explain the apparent involution in recent years whereby the radicals—who had managed to occupy strategic advisory positions in the hierarchy and to exercise decisive influence over its public stances—find it difficult today to be even tolerated and seem to have lost the initiative to the conservative wing of the Church.

The crux of our analysis is that the Peruvian Church did not go through any dramatic institutional change transferring the political benefits of its action from right to left, but experienced rather an internal process of diversification of political and religious positions. This process has brought alongside traditional defenders of the reigning order those who, in the name of the Gospel, question that order and the Church's complicity in its maintenance. Major changes in Peruvian society that were

276

accelerated by a military government which put an end to the old oligarchical order helped expand Catholic radicalism both among the clergy
and the laity. In the wake of these changes the traditional sector realized
that this radicalization was being translated into political benefits for the
left, and therefore—from its dominant position within the Church as a
whole—retook the initiative which for a time it had lost. The confrontation between the two forces seems to arise from their common inability
to live together in the same institution, thus making it impossible for the
institution to adopt democratic and pluralistic forms.

Regarding sources for this article, it is prudent to mention the author's own personal experience during one stage of the process under examination, as an activist in the Catholic university movement. In terms
of information, we have analyzed the main publications of Peru's radical
Catholic sectors—including the entire collection of the magazine *Páginas*
—and carried out a series of interviews with Gustavo Gutiérrez and twelve
others selected as informants on the political evolution and actions of
radical Catholics; half of them were selected from among non-Christian
political leaders who, during their left-wing party experience, witnessed
the outbreak of Catholic activism.

BREAKING WITH TRADITION

It is hard to say exactly when the first signs appeared of a sector
of Peruvian Catholics in the process of radicalization but the early moments were decisively influenced by the advent of the Cuban revolution,
which put social transformation on the order of the day as not only a
desirable but an achievable goal. "After Cuba, Christian Democracy was
just too tight a fit," as one noted Christian intellectual, a former DC sympathizer, observed. "Revolution" and "Reform," promoted respectively by
Fidel Castro and by the Alliance for Progress, appeared to be Latin America's two available options for social transformation in the early 1960s.
This was the backdrop for the early process of radicalization of a group
of activists, most of them members of the Catholic university movement,
the National Union of Catholic Students (UNEC), and of two related
organizations, the Young Catholic Students (JEC) for high-school students
and the Young Catholic Workers (JOC).

The possibility for an opening of Catholic movements to social issues and at least an implicit questioning of the Church's traditional behavior in Latin America was enhanced by the fact that important changes
were also underway in Rome. Three years after his 1958 election, Pope
John XXIII published the encyclical *Mater et Magistra*, whose contents

encouraged Catholic activists to give priority to social problems and the urgent search for solutions.

The process of change among Latin American Catholics was facilitated, but not generated, by the "aggiornamento" sought by John XXIII for the Church. The UNEC's first "national seminars," aimed at deepening study of the nation's problems, with the participation of many non-Catholic specialists, actually coincided with the first signs of renewal coming out of Rome. Within the Peruvian process, the most crucial role would be played by a man soon to be recognized as one of the world's leading liberation theologians: Gustavo Gutiérrez Merino.

Following his education in Santiago, Chile, in Lyon, and in Louvain, Gutiérrez returned to Lima in the late 1950s and became head of the UNEC advisory board. The weight of his influence in developing the line to be followed by that movement over the next two decades could hardly be exaggerated. That process, which deserves a detailed study of its own, merits a reference to some of its main characteristics.

First of all, under the intellectual leadership of Gustavo Gutiérrez the UNEC carried out activities in the 1960s (frequently with the participation of non-UNEC members of the university elite) in which the main subjects for discussion were national problems, university reform, and the confrontation between Marxism and Christianity. We would underline the significance of the presence of non-Christians among those invited to these activities – both as speakers and as listeners – thus permitting dialogue between them and the university Catholic activists. More specifically, these were the first encounters not only with Marxism – one of the priority themes for discussion – but also with the Marxists themselves: university professors and students.

A second characteristic is that the UNEC's theological underpinnings at that stage were based on "the distinction between planes," a European contrivance aimed at questioning severely, from an ecclesiastical perspective, the social-Christian banners unfurled by Christian Democratic Parties around the world. Gutiérrez, perhaps due to his experience in Belgium – "Where there were two self-sufficient worlds: one Christian, including the Church, and the other worker and socialist" – says that he never adhered to this manner of understanding the relationship between faith and politics. The theological alternative available at the time made a distinction between the secular and the strictly religious planes, and Gutiérrez used this conception to set out the basic ideas which would define that stage of the UNEC, thereby creating internal tensions in the UNEC between Christian Democrats and those who did not share this second affiliation. In contrast to the Chilean experience at the time – where the equivalent Catholic action movement (the AUC) was a PDC seedbed — Peru's Christian Democrats were vexed by the theological conceptions professed by this movement advisor as the institutional theological position.

The third aspect to be underlined is that, as the decade went by, university issues as such lost steam as a priority concern. The practical impossibility of achieving in the university real changes capable of dealing satisfactorily with its myriad shortcomings and limitations led to the conclusion that the roots of the problems could only be understood through an analysis of society as a whole. As a result — in a movement paralleled by left-wing university organizations — the UNEC progressively withdrew its field of action from the university. The movement began timidly with summer camps in the countryside so that the urban, middle-class activists could make contact with social reality. In 1970, a national seminar held in Ica finally decided to make "work with the people" the movement's priority, explicitly downgrading work within the university.

By the early 1970s the situation in Latin America had moved well beyond the relatively symbolic influence of the Cuban revolution, which had highlighted the beginning of the previous decade. Che Guevara had died in Bolivia in 1967 in an unsuccessful attempt to create one of the "Vietnams" then seen as part of revolutionary strategy. And even earlier had come the death of Gustavo Gutiérrez' personal friend Camilo Torres who, since his return to Colombia from the University of Louvain, had experienced a rapid process of radicalization, left the priesthood in 1965 in order to do political work and, in 1966, was killed in a confrontation with counterinsurgency forces, only a few months after he had joined the guerrillas.

The 1970s opened a process for both lay people and the clergy which, in the case of Central America, has been well described by Berryman.[1] Begun by "going to the people" — which often meant giving up personal comforts in order to move physically into poor urban or rural areas — this course was marked by a relationship with sectors of the people who were first of all to be "conscientized" and then organized. For a better understanding of this reality, which these Catholics were now encountering first-hand, the most appropriate conceptual instruments they found were those which, still in terms of confrontation, they had learned from Marxism. For university students, this factor was reinforced by the upswing of the social sciences in the preceding years, heavily influenced by Marxism in Latin America. Concepts such as "class," "domination," and "dependency" acquired real meaning in the experience of these Catholic activists with the people. Finally, the modest attempts to improve the living conditions of the poor ran head on into the almost invincible resistance of the established order, thus confirming that the basic problem actually was the social system itself and—for these Catholics on the road to radicalization—tipping the scales toward adopting the "revolutionary" path and rejecting the "illusions of bourgeois reformism."

The politicizing effects of this process are obvious. In a report presented by representatives of the ONIS priests' movement at the Latin American Encounter of Christians for Socialism in April 1972, the radical Catholics themselves criticized as ingenuous any "apolitical" attempts to renew the Church and denounced them as linked to the kind of modernizing developmentalism that does not question the social system.[2] Some years later, two intellectual activists in Peru's radical Catholic movement developed the same point better when they sustained that a central element of the process by which "movements of the secular apostolate . . . [undergo] a process of radicalization" is the fact that "commitment to the poor leads to political awakening because it demands a social analysis of reality and gives a political dimension to faith."[3]

During most of the 1960s, Catholic radicalization in Peru revolved around the movement of the lay apostolate. A new phase began in 1968 with the appearance of a movement of radical priests that soon became the visible locus of Catholic radicalization and projected, to a certain extent, the image of a "new Church."

In a gathering in early 1968, the initial group of about thirty priests "interested in taking on their pastoral mission in response to the problems of the nation," issued a declaration energetically denouncing the country's chronic injustices, backwardness, and immorality. They pointed to the unjust distribution of property, the take-over of national resources by foreign capital, and the oppressive role of the media as some of the undesirable expressions of capitalism. Their declaration concluded with a call to "fight the battle against exploitation and oppression."[4] According to Maloney,[5] the main organizer of this first gathering was the Jesuit Romeo Luna Victoria, a man who for years had been waging a solitary ideological struggle against the old social structures. The group of priests led by Gustavo Gutiérrez did not attend the meeting but did sign the final declaration and joined the coordinating body created there, to be known as ONIS, the National Social Information Office. This version is to some degree corroborated by Gutiérrez, for whom that movement "was always unclear theoretically, but was accepted pragmatically." In the next and much better-attended ONIS meeting, in July 1968, it was Gustavo Gutiérrez who presented the first outline of what would soon come to be known as liberation theology. Over the following decade, the ONIS—with the tacit approval of Cardinal Juan Landázuri—was to play a key role not only for radical Catholics but for the public image of the Peruvian Church itself.

According to Macaulay's detailed study of the ONIS movement,[6] its membership displayed some clearly distinctive traits. They were much younger than the rest of the clergy. Only 45 percent of them worked in poor parishes—most of them urban—and 80 percent of the membership was concentrated in Lima, Arequipa, Trujillo, Chiclayo, and Chimbote. The majority was made up of foreigners, as is the clergy as a whole in Peru, but an overwhelming number of these were from the U.S., Canada, and France.

The participation of U.S. citizens was very noteworthy in the ONIS; when the group consolidated at a little over a hundred members, 40 of the 150 U.S. priests working in Peru at the time had joined. During the 1960s, at the request of Rome, U.S. dioceses had taken on the commitment to supply a massive number of priests to countries like Peru, where they were in scarce supply. Those who came were deeply moved by their new ecclesiastical experience, so dramatically different from their own and also sharply differentiated from that of the Spanish and Italian priests who until then had predominated among Peru's foreign clergy. As a result, many U.S. priests returned home after relatively brief stays. "For those who had still not left, the personal crises provoked by this pointless invasion of Peru led to the decision to find a new Peruvian identity,"[7] and joining a group like ONIS could significantly help them in this process. It offered them, on the one hand, a group identity and, on the other, a radical definition toward which those who had decided to stay were probably already inclined as a result of their encounter with Peruvian society and its exasperating inequalities.

The ONIS as a movement distinguished itself from its contemporaries in Latin America in terms of relations with the Church hierarchy—a point we will come back to—but Dodson has identified several other traits that all these movements had in common.[8] They all questioned the widely accepted premise according to which it was possible to expect the poor countries to develop within the framework of international capitalism; having recognized that premise as false, a Marxist frame of analysis could provide a more appropriate conceptualization for understanding the development of the Latin American crisis. This option was not clear in the first ONIS documents published following 1968, and for a number of years they contained no allusion at all to socialism, for example. Macaulay, however, registered the fact that from 1970 on the movement's declarations were addressed to the "popular sectors," emphasized the theme of revolution, and contained fewer references to the teachings of the Church.[9] While the first four ONIS declarations dealt with specific problems of the moment, the next four proposed overall alternatives and criticisms, consistent with those of the left, of the reforms being introduced by the military government.

The report presented by ONIS representatives at the April 1972 meeting of radical Latin American clerical groups held in Santiago, Chile, had this to say about the priests' movement: "Its influence is on the rise. Conscious of class struggle in Peruvian society, they feel that faith demands them to opt for the oppressed classes and for the building of socialism. . . . Since [1968] there has been an increasing tendency towards relations with left-wing groups and towards personal commitments to them as well."[10]

The ONIS had definitively abandoned the language of "development" to take on the language of "liberation." Gustavo Gutiérrez argues that, by assuming this position publicly, the movement was responding to "the need for one group in the Church to remind the Church as a whole of its social commitment." The ONIS, nonetheless, spoke more to an outside than to a Church audience, playing a role of denunciation and prophecy in the political arena, where—rather than harmony and consensus—it emphasized social conflict and exploitation, a characteristic trait of the movements of radical clergy.[11]

From this perspective, one of the most sensitive issues to be dealt with was obviously violence. ONIS declarations frequently quoted the 1968 Medellín resolutions by the Latin American Episcopal Conference, which condemned the social system of "institutionalized violence" against the poor. Yet, as Macaulay has observed,[12] the ONIS did not condemn the use of violence as a response, which was also sanctioned by the Medellín document. To avoid a direct confrontation with the hierarchy on the subject, they restricted themselves to frequently repeating that violence, as a response to injustice, was inevitable, but without coming down for or against it. Yet ONIS members did have an opinion on the recourse to "revolutionary violence." In a 1974 survey, more than two-thirds of the ONIS priests who answered the question said they were in favor of violence as a response to "institutionalized violence," while only 19 percent of the clergy as a whole responded favorably.[13]

Ten years after its first appearance, the ONIS started cutting back on its public statements until it virtually fell into permanent silence. The explanation offered by Gutiérrez is that "the reason for making declarations was that the poor had no voice; the idea was always that once they gained their own voice, the ONIS could remain silent." It may be useful to look more closely at this reasoning. First of all, those who have taken up the "voice of the voiceless" are now the left-wing parties which—either directly or through the social movements they control—have become the advocates of the people's needs, demands, and expectations in much the same fashion as the ONIS during its period of public activity. Objectively, the ONIS performed what in terms of the Church's teaching mission could be called a "supplementary role," considered to be necessary as long as the country's left did not yet have the projection and representativity finally achieved in 1978, when it received a quarter of the ballots cast in the Constituent Assembly elections. From then on the left would be able to fulfill the part played by radical priests.

Yet another factor should also be taken into account to explain the silencing of the ONIS: the growing internal conflict within the Church. Here, public statements could exacerbate tensions with bishops who had not been moved previously to react directly to this other voice of the Church, parallel to their own.

This radicalization process would probably have been impossible without its doctrinal pillar of support: liberation theology. This theological development came out of a criticism of the theology of distinction between planes, which had been convenient for the Church's objective of "being as present as possible in the situation, but with minimal institutional commitment to it."[14] The demand arose for an approach more appropriate to the needs of this new style of commitment taken on by Catholics in the process of radicalization and to the Latin American context itself, where, as Sanks and Smith point out,[15] democratic processes are often interrupted, the gap between rich and poor widens, and society is increasingly polarized between right and left. It was time to formulate a theology not for "reformism"—as promised by an already clearly limited Christian Democracy—but for revolution.

The Church had historically asserted a clear distinction between Church and world, and consequently of action appropriate to clergy and lay people. Liberation theology broke down this distinction in the affirmation that "the history of the struggle of the oppressed, the weak, the poor is the history of salvation, of the redeeming action of the Lord."[16] It is from this perspective of social conflict as the history of salvation that liberation theologians warn that "it would be ingenuous to believe that armed struggle is a thing of the past."[17] Having adopted a Marxist interpretation of society, they conclude by proposing "a society in which private property over the means of production is eliminated."[18]

This political commitment—which includes both involvement in the social struggles of the oppressed and adherence to the proposal of socialism as a solution—binds religion and politics. For liberation theologians, this fusion is not only possible but indispensable because "The Church in this process—the people and their struggles—is responsible for announcing how God . . . impregnates this process from within and unifies the political dimension with the dimension of faith."[19]

A FAVORABLE ATMOSPHERE

The appearance and development of a radicalized sector among Peruvian Catholics were possible due to the occurrence of relatively important changes both in the Church and in the country. Both factors contributed heavily to the influence gained by the radical Catholics and to their ecclesiastical and political prominence.

As for the Church, Romero points out that in the late 1960s the Peruvian hierarchy had entered a period of what she refers to as "social distance": a withdrawal from the positions close to the worldly powers which the institution had maintained for more than four centuries.[20] To an equal or even greater extent than the rest of the continent, the Church that landed in Peru with the conquistadores became an active ally of the social order they imposed. Except for a brief crisis at the time independence was declared, Catholic institutions were always allied with the ruling elite. The alliance demanded that the hierarchy and the clergy remain silent regarding the less acceptable aspects of the established order. As in the rest of Latin America, whenever circumstances caused that order to be or to appear threatened in any manner, the Church came out openly in its defense.

This orientation of institutional Catholicism in Peru led one author who studied the role of religious elites in Peruvian politics up to the 1960s to conclude with a projection that conditioned social change in the country to "Catholic faith stopping its ideological justification of the status quo" and to add, with extraordinary foresight, that "this step will only be possible with new interpretations of a large amount of dogma."[21] This was precisely what would come to pass.

By the early 1960s, the Peruvian episcopate had moved the Church into a position favorable to the social changes needed to correct existing inequalities. In practice—at least rhetorically—this meant staking out their distance from the groups dominant in Peruvian society at the time who were completely opposed to change. A born member of the national oligarchy, Manuel Prado, had been president until 1962. And although the president elected in 1963, Fernando Belaúnde, had promised social and economic reforms, his administration soon showed that no real change would come during his mandate. Only in 1968 would the military government of General Velasco Alvarado actually impose social reforms, that is, ten years after the bishops had begun to face up to social issues, allowing part of the Catholic elite to line up with sectors demanding a transformation of the country's old traditional order.

Several changes in emphasis also accompanied this process. One of them was that the anticommunist theme lost its prominence in the bishops' official statements and was soon virtually dropped. Another was that the solutions proposed for the problems denounced had gained in complexity. At first, the solution prescribed was simply that the powerful urgently and voluntarily renounce part of their privileges and wealth; this ingenuous discourse would later be replaced by calls for changes to be implemented by the government: redistribution through tax reform, expropriation of land, etc.

Catholic support for the reforms started coming in on October 9, 1968, only six days after the civilian government was forcibly removed, when the military government expropriated the U.S. company that exploited the country's petroleum. "The cardinal congratulated the new government for that measure [although] the same communiqué requested a return to constitutional normality through democratic elections."[22]

From then on, each important reform dictated by the regime was officially supported by Church spokespersons. Three weeks after the agrarian reform was promulgated in July 1969, the episcopate issued a clear declaration of support which called on Catholics to "collaborate actively for its full implementation." A similar attitude was taken in 1972, when the education law met with resistance from heads of family at Catholic schools. In 1974, when the military government expropriated the newspapers, the episcopate came out in favor of the right of the majority of access to the mass media, the same principle used by the government to justify its action.

The identification between the Church elite and the program of the military was established and reinforced by a number of mechanisms. First of all, at least some of "the officers who headed the Peruvian Revolution were clearly influenced by the Catholic Church, more specifically by progressive priests and lay people." In addition, "numerous bishops, priests and lay people imbued with Catholic social teachings collaborated as government advisors."[23]

Although the Church as an institution did not decisively influence the orientation of the process of changes forcibly set in motion, it did look favorably on the process and offered its endorsement. Nonetheless,

> This did not mean that all Church people enthusiastically supported the reforms. . . . During that period, with their frequent use of the oppression-liberation terminology, the declarations of the national bishops' conference displayed the heavy influence of the ONIS and Cardinal Landázuri. Out of deference to Landázuri, some bishops signed declarations they did not

completely agree with. They did not dissent publicly, nor did they vigorously implement the declarations.[24]

Whether these bishops' attitude was taken out of deference to the
cardinal or, more realistically, in response to the *de facto* nature of the changes
imposed by the dominant political forces, the relevant fact is that there
was already dissonance among the episcopate. While the discrepancies
were still not expressed openly—creating, by omission, the appearance of
a Church uniformly mobilized in favor of radical social changes—once
the country's situation changed they would surface and reveal a divided
Church.

As time would tell, the evolution of the Church's official positions
coming out of the 1960s, which allowed it to be fairly consistent in its
endorsement of the military's reforms, did not really reflect a change either
in the hierarchy as a whole or, much less, by Peruvian Catholics. It was
precisely the institutional weakness of the Peruvian Church—unable to
exercise influence through its mass of believers, who see themselves as
Catholics but are not actively organized in the Church, thus making it
hard for their nominal pastors to sway their opinions—that had always
led it to relate to the state through what Maloney has called an "exchange
of resources." Due to its inability to act through the millions of Catholics
who formally make up its flock—a situation growing out of problems ranging from the scarcity of priests to difficulties in recognizing the heterodoxy
of "popular" religiosity—the Catholic Church has always worked the in-
ner circles, pressuring the elites toward the creation of a "Catholic atmosphere" to facilitate its tasks. Thus, for example, it has been much easier
to have the state decree religious education classes in schools than to train
its own Catholic teachers.

This Christendom pastoral approach was simply rejuvenated during
the period of military rule, when the points of agreement between the
military reform program and the new outlook adopted by the bishops once
again made it possible—in a very different atmosphere from old times—
for Church authorities to return to their traditional lobbying of the state.
In exchange for respect, budget allotments, and legitimization of their
religious practices from government authorities—who of course reaffirmed
their allegiance as "Catholics" and let their presence lend an official seal
to religious ceremonies—the Church could thus provide its own approval
of the new social order in the process of creation.

It was in this context of a changing discourse from the Catholic hierarchy and a political atmosphere of drastic social reforms being imposed
at double-step by the military government that the radical Catholic sector came out in the open with the ONIS priests' movement. McCurry's

evaluation of these circumstances, which he termed a "fortuitous conjuncture," highlighted the beneficial consequences for the work of the radicals: "In the 'ambience' created by this new ideological conversion of political and ecclesiastical structures, the ONIS has found a receptive audience."[25]

During that period, however, although the ONIS movement took to the field within the general political guidelines established by the bishops (with the active contribution of ONIS leaders themselves), the movement also carried its own colors. Arguing that they "were in a position to speak more freely than the hierarchy," since "their words were not the official voice of the Church," and conscious that, nonetheless, the ONIS "is sufficiently representative of the Church to be influential and important," the movement's declarations "often went beyond [the bishops] in demanding respect for an active role of the people in the reforms."[26] Strictly speaking, this subtlety corresponded to a political strategy different from that of the hierarchy, since, although the ONIS coincided with the hierarchy in abandoning the traditional ruling sectors, it did not totally underwrite the military's program and made criticisms of it similar to those raised by left-wing groups. In other words, the radical priests tried to gain a foothold out of the internal differences within the Armed Forces and chose to give selective support to those measures aimed at eliminating the old order. At the same time they reserved the right to criticize others they considered too timid or conciliatory toward interests opposed, as they saw them, to those of the people.[27] This perhaps may actually have been a "resource exchange" strategy with a different political actor: a revolutionary left which only some years later—and with the contribution of the radical Catholics—would become a major political force.

The radical sector's activity did allow for the occurrence of a few cases of conflicts between priests and military government authorities. The most important took place in 1971, between Msgr. Luis Bambarén—at the time bishop of Lima's poorest neighborhoods, the *barriadas*—and the military government's Minister of the Interior, General Armando Artola. During a Mass that followed a massive land takeover in Lima, Bishop Bambarén said that "the squatters could be considered *conquistadores* demanding the right to housing. After the Mass the bishop was arrested and detained for several hours."[28]

Maloney concludes from this and other examples that differences between the Church and the Velasco government arose from the military's authoritarianism, incompatible with recent developments in the Church's thinking. This interpretation magnifies such incidents and, to explain them, concedes excessive weight to the rhetoric of Church declarations. As for the Church supposedly being concerned with authoritarianism, we should note that Maloney, in a 1974 survey of priests in Lima, found that two priests out of three believed that Peru was not a country where a political regime with political parties and regular elections would work.[29] The significance of these run-ins was not so much that the Church called for "people's participation" while the military government tried to contain it, but that some of the radical Catholics' actions had undermined government control. These actions were part of the ministerial work among the people, based on liberation theology, which was already underway.

These few incidents did not bring a break-off between the Church and the Velasco Alvarado government. With the leaf turned on problems like Bishop Bambarén's, once the government had backed down, the normal institutional position was of support for the military reform program as a whole, tempered by occasional minor criticisms from the bishops and somewhat larger discrepancies raised by radical priests, the latter coming from the left. And the Church's support was profitable for the ruling military: as long as a few criticisms here and there could not be turned to the advantage of the conservatives—who for so long had enjoyed the Church's unconditional support and now found themselves ideologically orphaned in the face of the military's radicalism—the official and unofficial Church voices raised in favor of the changes contributed, even unwittingly, to "legitimizing the government's actions. The ONIS has been efficient in this role with regards to the [present] military *junta*."[30]

The support for radicalism was mutual. "The breakdown of the country's traditional powers doubtless created favorable conditions for the process of change within the Church."[31] The bishops not attuned to the Church's new outlook, having fallen into disgrace with the social sectors with which they felt most identified, had been neutralized. Temporarily free of their conservative ballast, the Peruvian hierarchy quickly moved into advanced positions within the Latin American Church. In 1969, a year after the military government had taken power, the Episcopal Assembly endorsed the new rulers' judgment of the country's situation, and pointed to the causes:

> This unjust situation . . . is the result of a world-wide process characterized by the concentration of economic and political power in the hands of very few and by the international imperialism of money, which operates in complicity with the Peruvian oligarchy.[32]

Two years later, in August 1971, the document presented by the Peruvian Church at the Synod of Justice in the World espoused "the search for our own path to a socialist society, with a humanist and Christian content,"[33] in terms that echoed those used only three weeks earlier by

General Velasco Alvarado to define the doctrinary grounds of the "Peruvian Revolution." With that step, the official position of the Peruvian bishops moved into the vanguard of ecclesiastical renewal in Latin America. According to a survey conducted by Mooney, the majority of the clergy did not believe that this implied any illegitimate mixing of religion and politics.[34]

The evolution in the episcopal declarations did not reflect a drastic radicalization of the members of the institution as a whole. In fact the position of the clergy did not really coincide with the one adopted formally by the bishops. Maloney's 1974 survey of priests in Lima reached the conclusion that only 15 percent of those surveyed held positions favorable to the military government, and only one in three declared any attraction for liberation theology,[35] which was the inspiration behind the bishops' declarations. This latter figure is consistent with the number of priests' signatures collected on public declarations promoted by the radical sector. Although two-thirds of those answering the survey displayed an anti-Marxist or anticommunist position, the majority could not really be considered conservative: 58 percent did support the official position of the bishops regarding the need to break with the old economic system, but without identifying that change with the rejection of capitalism.

Analyzing the 1968–1975 period, Klaiber holds that "The Peruvian Church followed a double strategy with the goal of promoting reforms within a Christian context. It sought, on the one hand, to influence the military government towards incorporation of Christian ideals in its reform plans. On the other hand, it worked to identify with the marginalized classes."[36]

We could add that, with the coexistence of dissonant positions within the same institution, the distribution of tasks between one line of work and the other must have been facilitated. While the "centrist" tendencies identified with the changes promoted by the military government and collaborated actively with it, the ministries taking their inspiration from liberation theology were implementing consciousness-raising and organizing projects among the poor that were unprecedented in the Peruvian Church's history.

The change of government in 1975 led to a subsequent intensification of the work with the people. Velasco Alvarado's reformist government was replaced by another military regime headed by General Morales Bermúdez, who by 1980 had turned back the tide of the preceding period. His stabilization policies had a high social cost and the resulting popular protests were severely repressed. The Church kept its distance from the new government, preferring to take the occasion to strengthen its positions in the people's ministries.

Between 1976 and 1979, twenty-two of Peru's forty-one dioceses issued declarations or statements denouncing the social situation and/or
abuses committed by the ruling authorities. "The ONIS priests' movement issued eight proclamations during those years . . . in defense of the
people's right to organize and to protest against that situation of injustice."[37] While there was "no lack of priests" who denied their support
for labor or neighborhood struggles, even authorizing the police to expel groups of demonstrators from their churches,[38] the gestures of solidarity with the people's mobilizations coming from the Church were clearly
manifold.

Romero de Iguíñiz has underlined the fact that the bishops' declarations were signed by prelates from a range of positions along the spectrum of the Church's internal dispute.[39] This is understandable, since the
dispute had not yet come out in the open and because the protests they
were enduring at the time were social in nature. Only in 1978 would these
protests begin being channeled by the left, and the open identification
of the radical Catholics with the United Left would only come a couple
of years later, at the turn of the decade.

In Idígoras' view,[40] "When it resolved to denounce the rulers' abuses,
the Church inexorably broke its links with the power it might receive from
them," a totally new turn in the history of the Peruvian Church. This
had important consequences for the ways the Church rooted itself socially, since "the Church managed to acquire a remarkable degree of moral
legitimacy and acceptance among the popular classes, to an extent rarely
achieved in Peruvian history."[41] This "change in strategy," according to
Idígoras, "does not mean an outright total renunciation of power, for in
our society the power of the masses is actually more influential every day,
as they become more aware of this situation; the Church is turning to
the oppressed and to their power."[42]

This change in strategy arose from the recognition of the decline
of the sector that had controlled power in Peruvian society until the
early 1960s, an objective factor to which both the military government
and the radical Catholics had added their proposals for a new social order. The hierarchy thereafter fell into line, tacitly admitting the possibility of new alliances that might even include the left, as the radicalized
clergy and laity were now openly beginning to propose. As we shall see,
however, the 1980s brought quite a different political atmosphere, marked
by a revival of conservative sectors and the consolidation of a bloc of
left-wing parties. In this new period the turnabout in the Church's discourse twenty years earlier and the theological and pastoral advances
achieved by the radical sector would be called into question from within
the Church.

THE RADICAL CATHOLIC STYLE

The style of activity of a well-established group of people gathered around a given motivation is significantly related to the beliefs that inspire its members. Yet there are nonrational factors which characterize and distinguish the behavior of any group and which depend on social origins, education, and the type of socialization that its members bring to the group or—even more importantly, in the case of the latter two factors—that they receive from it. Throughout this section we will attempt to isolate the most significant traits of Peru's radical Catholics in terms of the relevance of their influence on the group's political activities. Some of these traits are peculiarities of any Catholic activist—and are shared by other Church groups—while others are specific to a given institution like the UNEC, which gave rise to the initial (and hegemonic) nucleus of radical Catholics.

One trait associated with beliefs, but which strongly affects attitudes and behavior, is utopianism. All religions, of course, possess utopian elements and Catholicism could not get along without them. For the radical Catholics, however, utopia has its own particularities, well synthesized in this quotation from a 1975 ONIS declaration, which refers to a peasant conflict:

> The Gospel's promise of full liberation, the Good News of a Kingdom of love among men, confirms both our hope and our commitment to make it an historical reality today.[43]

This singular utopianism imagines that the immediate realization of a "Kingdom of love among men" is not only possible but inevitable, and commits the active pastoral work of clergy and laity to its achievement; since this work is eminently politicizing for them, their utopianism will color the resulting political activity with radicalism.

Of particular importance in this utopianism is the consideration it gives the poor as subject. As the favorite theme of Latin American Church rhetoric over the past two decades, the poor are collectivized as subjects by radical Catholics—influenced both by the Bible and by Marxism—and presented as the leading actors of history. By privileging the collectivity of the poor, radical Catholic utopianism fits into Weber's characterization of politically oppressed peoples, among whom—according to Weber—it is precisely their suffering and hopes for redemption that are collectivized.[44]

To enhance this thesis, the radical Catholic discourse holds that the people do not seem to be suffering from the same crisis of values prevalent in the rest of society. "One finds among them the sense of brotherhood preached by the Gospel,"[45] no matter how miserable the living situation of peasants and the urban poor. No matter how desperate the situation of the poor, their behavior is exemplary: "Despite the defeats, humiliations and deaths, the expression of faith is strong and the commitment unwavering."[46] The people's *fiestas*, for example, are no longer hotbeds for sinful excesses, as the rural priest traditionally had preached, but rather, according to Irarrázabal,

> In the *fiesta*, particularly in the peasant world, there is a social reciprocity and a happiness of the poor which are harbingers of a new form of life. . . . [They bring] a strengthening of egalitarian ties amongst the poor, of shared responsibility and of gratuitous happiness. The forms of festive reciprocity are contradictory to relations of exploitation and the drive for individual advancement.

Therefore, for those who postulate the presence of a revolutionary force among the poor,

> This happiness is also subversive. . . . That is why the *fiesta* points the way to a new and egalitarian world, a different life of happiness and reciprocity with a paschal significance.[47]

This also explains the frequent reaffirmation by the radical Catholics of the idea that "the workers' and people's movement is not only the revolutionary subject of the present, but it is also the paramount agent of evangelization."[48] This view of the people, heavily laden with radical Catholic utopianism and seemingly forgetful of the Christian notion that selfishness and sin will inevitably accompany human nature, was explicitly mentioned by two of the informants interviewed for this study. One of them, a leftist militant who has worked intensely with the people's movement, defined it as "a romantic search for what is popular, which leads to paternalistic relationships," and the other, a leftist member of parliament with a long history of party work, underscored how this trait impedes comprehension of the people's real life experiences and behavior.

We will go into the political effects of this utopianism below after first looking at the potential contained in the interaction of the radical Catholics' religious utopia arising out of liberation theology with the political ideals of the left. In this encounter, the religious utopia of a final immaculate society where men can once again be naturally good seems to project itself historically into revolutionary society. This montage not only reinforces a revolutionary utopia with a religious basis, it also arouses in those who have received an early religious education the profound sentimental aspiration for a society where human relationships are not contaminated by the issue of good and evil. This religious feeling extrapolates the Marxist utopia of communism, moving it even further from reality, and thus contributing to the unfettered radicalism of the Marxist-Christian militant, exercised in the name of the imminent and secure advent of the society of revolutionary Kingdom Come.

Utopianism, of course, is not peculiar just to Peruvian radical Catholics. The same trait has also been identified in similar Latin American movements. In Brazil, for example the JUC's utopianism arose out of the conjunction between Christian principles and the social analysis of reality, characterizing that movement's "historical ideal." Later, when this social program was adopted by Popular Action—the political action group created by the Catholic University Youth laity—the utopianism crystallized into the notion that it was "possible to reach a final 'purification' of the world, eliminating from it all that is 'diabolical,' the hunger for power, domination, individualism and alienation. After the revolution . . . the contradictions known by society would disappear."[49]

As De Kadt has observed regarding Brazil,[50] the utopian approach led to a well-defined political option, as opposed to the range of options offered at the time by the Church social doctrine's "intermediate principles"—a series of social, economic, and political postulates presented as derived from the Gospel which, through papal encyclicals, restricted but did not impose partisan options. Utopia, much narrower and more precise, is therefore more persuasive in its call for a deeper and active commitment. At the same time, this utopianism probably has a reductionist effect: the problem of man and of the world is the social problem, to be resolved through politics, which means class struggle. This perspective of reduction and simplification has been identified by Fontaine as one of the behavioral characteristics of Chile's leftist Catholic militants during the 1970s.[51]

Utopianism leads to a curious reading of reality, tinged by radicalism. Utopia, therefore, is not a reference point but an immediate and urgent demand which orients present-day political behavior. A logical consequence is the political inability to negotiate acceptable terms, since they would represent an intermediate point between the present situation and that which is desired. On the contrary, political action comes to be judged by all-or-nothing criteria which are not always explicit. Any partial victory is unimportant, since when the people's movements "in given political circumstances achieve certain concessions [these are no more than] partial advantages within the adversary's field."[52]

At the same time, utopianism leads to a reading of reality whereby defeats are actually victories, and signs presented as negative should be interpreted as positive. In Gutiérrez' analysis of the Latin American panorama in the late 1970s characterized by severe repression under authoritarian military regimes, he paraphrases Don Quixote: "We can say with realism, though not without sorrow: 'Repress, it is a sign that we are win-ning our freedom'."[53] According to the "realistic" interpretation of social events, perhaps the severe repression suffered by the Chilean people since 1973 contains a happy and valuable message, for it surely announces the coming of freedom. In personal, and certainly even more extreme terms, death also has a positive character for the radical Catholic committed to the struggles of the people. Therefore,

> Christians . . . must be ready to die because of their unconditional love and because of the hate that this will arouse in the blindness of the powerful. Their witness will be the sign of salvation and the builder of true history.[54]

The second trait of the radical Catholic style relevant to our analy-sis is *clericalism*. This factor no doubt derives from the origins of these radical groups, born out of priests' movements throughout Latin Amer-ica. We should recall that "Catholic Action is not a lay movement but rather a mobilization of the laity under the leadership of the Church."[55] The reach of this valuable definition was explained by Pope Pius XII, one of the popes most dedicated to the development of Catholic Action. In a February 1954 speech to an auditorium of lay movement advisers, he reminded them that the essence of their task was to

> discover these souls in order to put them at our service once they have been solidly edified by us. To this end it will be necessary to know who they are, what they can do and how they can be efficiently employed. . . . We must not, of course, neglect their "human" edification, especially since a well-finished development of one's natural talents makes apostolic action more effective. You must give particular attention to the "intellectual" train-ing of your collaborators. . . . Nonetheless, their spiritual edification must be pursued above all. . . . Then, you should put them to work. Be demand-ing in showing them their tasks and in pressuring them to carry through. . . . Leave them enough room to develop a spirit of fervent and inspired activity; this way, they will also be happier, more active and more eager to collaborate with you.[56]

It would be hard to find a more explicit and complete presentation of the Church's orientation for decades of work with Catholic Action movements. For anyone who was active in these apostolic movements for a time, the reading of papal directives issued several years earlier is a key to interpreting that experience. The contents of the adviser-leader and adviser-activist relationships thus cannot be attributed to the personal characteristics of specific people, as some of us used to believe, but rather are part of explicit Church policy.

This style of ministry — as revealed by Poggi's excellent study on Italy's

Catholic Action—meant that the lay activist in apostolic movements submitted to the clerical adviser and accepted his orientation, enthusiastically or not but always passively. There are different levels for priests and
laity in the Magisterium of the Church, and the lay person must express
his or her Christian self-denial in the form of a Catholic militant's readiness to serve the hierarchy. This generous readiness, which is the fundamental quality for the lay person, in due time will be rewarded by the
hierarchy through promotions up the institutional ladder. At least two
characteristic traits of the lay activist arise from this socialization process:
insecurity and inferiority in relation to the adviser. "A sense of rigid and
totally acritical devotion to the spirit and letter of The Truth held by the
Church," as transmitted by the advisor, is the guarantee that control will
remain in hierarchical hands and that the activist will gain a certain security, though at significant personal cost.[57]

In such an institutional setting, with the adviser usually working
full time at his tasks, it is not surprising that he himself will magnify the
definition of his work, since he can rely "on an official charisma in the
eyes of the organization's members and lay leaders to place himself to a
certain extent beyond control and criticism."[58] He thus takes on supervision not only of spiritual but of secular activities as well, including even
the most personal activities of the apostolic movement's membership. This
circuit of relationships between advisers and lay activists was depicted ex-
traordinarily well in a novel that is a classic insight into the operation
of elite Catholic groups, *The Clown*, by the German Catholic Heinrich
Böll, whose writings were awarded a Nobel Prize in literature. The adviser
of a group of Catholic activists, who keeps a discrete but rigorous watch
on the intimate lives of each of his Catholic charges, one day declares
to the husband of one of the group members, "You will grant me the right
to impose certain orders in which I believe and which I represent."[59]

The Catholic Action "adviser," despite the term used to designate
his function, is actually the organization's main leader. In the Catholic
organizations where the emphasis is more temporal—as in Peru's UNEC—
the adviser also leads the activists in areas of activity that are not directly
religious, even though he must resort to "using the abilities of any politi-
cian," as *L'Assistente Ecclesiastico* had warned the Catholic Action clergy
in Italy.[60]

In Peru, Gustavo Gutiérrez' role in radicalizing UNEC members included both intellectual and political leadership. One of the persons interviewed recalled that early in the 1970s Gutiérrez organized a study and
reflection group made up of outstanding Peruvian intellectuals who were
or had been Catholic activists, in which the agenda and orientation were
clearly designed to encourage left-wing party militancy. Vallier, one of the

first to study the changes in the Latin American Church, from the very beginning perceived this "clerical radicalism," which issued from the "abolishing of frontiers between religion and the world," and which would be accepted by Latin American laity since tradition "had accustomed [them] to letting the clergy define their political responsibilities." To Vallier, "this action is very old and traditional in nature. . . . Clerical radicalism is the appropriation of old means to serve new ends."[61]

Clericalism is also partly responsible for the third characteristic trait of the radical style, its *elitism*. The majority of Church movements which went through the radicalization process in the 1960s recruited out of the well-to-do sectors of Latin America's rigidly stratified societies. This probably had less to do with social discrimination, a Church at the service of society's dominant groups, than with a frank choice to work with the cultural elites, which obviously meant the upper and upper-middle classes.

As for Peru, Astiz had already noted before the open appearance of radical Catholicism that "the upper class has not shed its wealth to remedy the economic evils, as Catholic dogma and the clergy counseled them to do."[62] Yet, while that study was being published, a process was already underway in Peru which also occurred in other Latin American countries: the indolent behavior of the upper sectors of society in the face of the prevailing poverty and social injustice was being rejected by a large part of the generation entering the university or finishing high school at the time Fidel Castro marched triumphantly into Havana. This dissatisfaction was not a phenomenon restricted to a handful of individuals. In Peru, hundreds of offspring of the upper and upper-middle classes—educated in Catholic high schools and many of them enrolled at the Catholic University of Lima—began to radicalize, some of them as Catholic Action activists, toward alignment with leftist political positions. This process grew out of a number of factors, among them the preaching in both high schools and the university of a Catholicism more alert to social problems precisely at the time these problems were breaking out into the open in the very capital of this oligarchically structured country, progressively besieged by the migration of the rural poor to urban shanty-towns.

Many of those who crossed over from the elegant neighborhoods of Lima into the impoverished other side to do their first social work projects, followed by experiences in popular consciousness-raising and finally political proselytism, ended up in the 1980s as leading leftist personalities. A good many of them are still members of Catholic organizations. They were generally marked by guilt feelings caused by their social background —"We carry all the ambiguity of a 'middle-class' or petit-bourgeois position."[63] This recognition may have been a condition self-imposed to purge what was seen as a weakness, thereby confessed and redeemed, to be able to assume the role of vanguard of the oppressed, in whose ranks they had not historically participated.

In analyzing the style of Catholic activists working as vanguard, it is illustrative to look at the part played by the ONIS priests' movement during its period of political activity. The first significant element is the vehicle most often employed by the group: declarations or press releases. Neither the writing of these documents nor their publication in the newspapers were within the reach of the masses in whose interests the movement had issued them. Replete with quotes from Church teachings and pontifical documents laden with dense sociological categories, this form of public expression could be characterized as the means used by one elite group to address another. The audience was therefore not the people but the Church hierarchy, the intellectuals, and governing circles.

The ONIS took advantage of the relatively privileged background of its members in a profoundly discriminatory society to speak as equals with ecclesiastical, cultural, civilian, and military powers, as part of what Klaiber has called an "elitist" strategy.[64] As they took positions on each of the Velasco Alvarado government's most important measures—even anticipating the reform, in the case of the new agrarian law in 1969—the radical priests used the same approach of pressuring at the top of the power structure which had always characterized the Latin American Church.[65] Their support for social change employed the same means used by the Church since the founding of the republic to hold back change, this time operating as a pressure group on those who could actually implement the demands for structural modifications. As we will see below, the ONIS theologians' approach within the Church followed a similar pattern, aimed at exerting direct influence at the highest level on documents issued by the hierarchy.

But why address the elite if the active subject of social transformation, according to the radicals' own theology, was not the elite but the people, who in this fashion are not even advised of the message? Macaulay suggests that their need to assert credentials as part of the elite, using markedly intellectual means, in order to exert concrete influence on real politics outweighed both the idea of working with the oppressed and their prophetic utopianism. Whereby, he concludes that "in terms of class, the ONIS really had more in common with the privileged than with the oppressed."[66]

The Peruvian radical priests' tactics kept them within the Church's tradition of sophisticated theoretical discussions among the anointed few. This elitist option has simultaneously reinforced their clericalism, since "for the majority of those who have received primary education, Catholic dogma is what the local priest says it is."[67] This combination of elitism and clericalism led peasants in certain areas around Cuzco to rebuff the base communities promoted there by radical Catholics.[68]

This elitism characterized other radical Catholic groups as well, in contexts quite different from those that gave rise to the ONIS. Even workers in Brazil's JUC, forced underground by the military government's repression, rapidly adopted a typical behavioral trait of the Catholic elites, intellectualization. Their emphasis on study, and their consequently deeper understanding of politics, put a distance between them and the average worker.[69]

Intellectualization is a characteristic trait of all Catholic elites, and is what Heinrich Böll had in mind when he had his protagonist observe that "when [Catholics] think someone is intelligent they hope for a quick conversion."[70] This led Peru's radical Catholics to give priority to intellectual activities aimed at theological and political-social education, leaving traditional and popular religious practices—so full of emotion and irrationality—disdainfully aside. Activists thus gained a religious faith that was above all the fruit of knowledge. Revelation became the central concern and, as liberation theology expanded on this, the distinctive characteristic of Catholics came to be that *he knows*, having gained access to the sources of revealed truth. It has even been suggested that evangelical efficacy be measured by intellectual criteria, arguing that "the preaching of this liberating ideology must be extremely intelligent, precise and clear,"[71] a criterion by which action should focus on rational communication. The high drop-out rate among radical Catholics is not incongruent with this faith rooted mainly in reason, aimed at inspiring the activist's personal commitment through a knowledge of the Gospel message and an understanding of the underlying causes of social problems.

This intellectualization adopted as part of the radical Catholics' elitism inspired Moltmann's broadside against the liberation theology groups in which he reproached them for taking to be "popular" whatever sociology said about the people, adding that Marxism and the social sciences "do not lead the theologian to the people but, at least at the beginning, to the Marxists and the sociologists."[72] It is a reasonable hypothesis that, despite its intentions, Catholicism's radical current—the tributary of an intellectual approach to the religious question—provokes a certain estrangement among the Catholic masses, since the content of liberation theology is not only hard to understand but also represents an entirely different perspective than the emotion-laden outlook of the people's religiosity.

The final relevant trait of the radical Catholics is their *verticality*. The apostolic movements' typical socialization process can give rise both to overwhelming arrogance—since the revealed truth has resolved all their

human doubts—and to an authoritarianism which in fact denies any form
of democratic practice.

Böll's novel gives the tone for a description of the self-sufficiency
present in elite Catholic groups. As his protagonist says of them,

> They're the most presumptuous people I know. . . . They retreat behind the
> wall of their dogma and bombard the world with dogmatic principles, but
> when you confront them seriously . . . the smile turns sarcastic, as if they
> were coming out of a visit to the Pope and he had given them a piece of
> his infallibility. . . . How rude and conceited are these 'eminent' German
> Catholics. . . . [with their] "principles" . . . they use any resort.[73]

In his careful study of Italy's Catholic Action, Poggi traced the implicit assumptions behind the attitudes and behavior of Catholic activists. One premise attributes to the Church a religious charisma which
should be placed by the world in the center of social life, since it contains
a normative standard by which to determine authoritatively how society
should be. To overcome the distance between this normativity and social
reality, it is requisite that Catholic activist groups, urgently and necessarily, "in- fluence social reality and above all the political process," acting
basically as pressure groups. The author also underscores the idea that,
since this approach is more a mentality than an ideology, "it may be the
common denominator for a range of alternate interpretations."[74] In other
words, the Catholic positions, both allied and opposed to the prevailing
social order, can flow equally out of this same approach.

In Peru, Macaulay's thesis on the ONIS reveals equivalent attitudes
and even the explicit proposition of an elite dedicated to political action
as a necessary step toward overcoming the alienation of the people. Such
a vanguard would be composed of those who remain immune to noxious
ideological influences due to their benefiting neither economically nor socially from the system, and being capable therefore of identifying with
the masses.[75] Straddling the Catholic action conception of the leavening
of humanity and the Leninist notion of the revolutionary party, this is
the strategic conceptualization needed to give the Catholic elite privileged
responsibilities and positions within the process of social change. As Idígoras has observed, in this interpretation they assign themselves a "moral
power over the masses and the confidence of feeling their support," which
runs the risk of generating "new forms of messianism."[76]

This self-sufficiency, so vigorously cultivated with the instruments
of intellect—to the point of attributing to themselves a pivotal role in the
advent of a new social order—is perfectly compatible with the activist lay
leaders' insecurity, which is generated by hierarchical subordination to the
adviser and which completely rules out any possibility of democratic rela-

tions within a Catholic organization. As we have already seen, the lay
activists' insecurity arises from the fact that their reference group for institutional behavior is that of the advisers, a status to which a lay person
cannot accede. The advisers are a qualitative step above the lay activist.
This superiority is expressed not only in acquired professional knowledge
and a full-time dedication to religious tasks but also in the advisers' exclusive access to the seat of institutional power, the bishops. They have
the authority, including the authority to name movement leaders. Thus
the lay person cannot address the movement's rank and file in his or her
own right, but as the holder of a mandate delegated from above, always
with fairly imprecise limits and authority. Achieving a degree of security
in these conditions suggests renewing one's commitment to the institution and sticking as close as possible to the available source of authority,
namely the adviser.

This kind of socialization is not an education for democracy, the
absence of which in radical Catholic groups is the final aspect to bring
out among the characteristic traits of their style. Nothing in the apostolic
movements comes from below; no one is legitimized in their function on
the basis of majority approval. Authority is firmly constituted by delegation, and the hierarchical distinctions—between the pope and the bishops, between the bishops and the clergy, between the priests and the laity
—are insurmountable. As a result, Poggi affirms that there is no political
leadership among lay activists. There are religious inspiration and organizational leaders, but no political leaders who draw up, propose, and
choose strategies.[77] This function is restrained to the other hierarchical
levels between the people and God: the bishops and the priests.

Catholic activists see themselves primarily as Catholics. This means
that their personal conduct will be guided by a "heroic degree of self-denial,"
since it implies a multitude of not only heavy but unpleasant obligations.[78]
This self-denial, which is the counterpart of their readiness to serve (the
adviser, the hierarchy, and ultimately, through these worldly mediators,
God), is the extreme opposite of recognition of a value central to individual rights, which is the theoretical basis for one's becoming an active subject in a democratic regime. Concomitantly, the kind of practice which
derives from such a mentality is no preparation at all for democracy. This
state of affairs is conspicuous both in the authoritarian dynamics of the
radical Catholics' apostolic movements and in the internal life of the
Church that harbors them, where no rights are guaranteed by the majority opinion of the faithful. We can presume that this regressive legacy is
carried by Catholic activists into their political activity, as Maloney's 1974
survey of ONIS priests has also suggested: 79 percent of the priests sur-

veyed maintain that elections and party politics are inappropriate in a country like Peru.[79]

POLITICAL ACTION

Both the Church in general and Catholic movements in particular have always had a political impact; in Peru, we need only recall that "priests and friars took active part" in the post-independence political struggles.[80] This reminder is pertinent, since detractors of the radical Catholics often resort to accusing them of having politicized Catholicism. True, here the politicization is explicit, all the way from discourse to action, yet—as opposed to other more intimate forms of religiosity—Catholicism had never renounced the exercise of political influence, although at certain times and places it found it best to do so discreetly.

As was the case with their Latin American counterparts, once Peru's radical Catholics had denounced the pact between the Church and the traditional elites, they did not set out to depoliticize the Church but rather raised the need to "shift its alliances to promote the interests of the poor and the dispossessed."[81] This new proposal contained not only an ethical aspect, counterposed to the historical relationship of complicity between the Church and the ruling powers, but also potentially fundamental political consequences. It is thus not surprising that the first signs of ecclesiastical renewal immediately caught the attention of outstanding Latin American radicals. Che Guevara predicted that the revolution would be "invincible" once the Christians firmly embraced the cause, and Fidel Castro proposed not only a tactical but "a strategic alliance between religion and socialism, between religion and revolution."[82]

Paraphrasing Karl Marx, radical Christians had decided that it was no longer enough for the Gospel truth to interpret the world; it must now seek to change it. Therefore, they oriented their pastoral actions "towards manifesting how political liberation can be a sign of eschatological liberation" and formulated a new type of social commitment posited on the premise that "God's action is manifest in man's ability to create, according to the Promise, a more just and fraternal society." In this perspective, obviously, "the political dimension of the Gospel takes on a new face."[83]

Hart has observed that the utopian element of this new outlook would have to become a dynamic and mobilizing force in history, since it could only be validated once it gave rise to action.[84] Radical Catholics announce that "we are objectively . . . part of the ideological struggle," but their role is no longer limited to rhetoric. "Practice and communication, gestures and words, all are messengers of the life we wish to share."[85]

Out of this reworking of the contents of their Christian identity came a complete transformation of pastoral tasks. "It is there [in the people's struggles] that we must be present to do effective evangelization."[86] And evangelization means revolutionary politicization, in the clear words of a member of Chile's Christians for Socialism movement who, after the 1973 coup, became a frequent contributor to the Peruvian magazine *Páginas*:

> A solidarity strike, the expression of an alternative form of education or membership in organizations of the oppressed class are some of the concrete steps of the people's struggle. One dialogues about them, discussing their immediate possibilities and how they lead to a revolutionary breakthrough in order to initiate a new society.[87]

An initial criticism, such as Sanders's, might find that relatively imprecise notions such as "liberation" or "the promise of the Kingdom of God" would shed confusion rather than light when introduced into the political arena with their normative pretensions. The actual contents of the radical Christians' new political program, however, would not derive directly from these justificatory theological invocations, but rather would be taken from a Marxist analysis of Latin American reality. The contents would thus be neither vague nor ambiguous; despite the utopianism in their inspiration, they would be quite clearly defined in terms of contemporary leftist politics.

The reasons why radical Catholics were attracted to Marxism go beyond its impact on the social sciences used by liberation theologians as an analytical instrument. Sanders, quoting from Niebuhr, points out some of these reasons:

> With its "scientific" interpretation of society, [Marxism] strengthens and intensifies their utopia, in its tendency to place people and social systems in categories of good or evil. The complex structures of social classes, interest groups and contending powers in the Latin American countries, as well as the changes that occurred in this century, are reduced to the dichotomy of oppressed and oppressors. Nations are either "capitalist" or "socialist," a terminology that precludes an understanding of their various forms of economic development and their political options. The attribution of responsibility for regional problems to foreign "domination" obscures the real characteristics of Latin American dependency . . . [and] these nations' responsibility for and sovereignty over their own decisions.[88]

Enchanted by Marxism's all-encompassing comprehensiveness, including the possibility of a "faith" concerned with worldly affairs (now made perfectly compatible with the original faith by means of liberation theology), radical Catholics were now prepared for a political experience within the Marxist left. Their only encumbrance may have been the fact that they were Christians and might be considered "second-rate revolutionaries," but they were ready to make up for that handicap with their indubitable radicalism. To "win their place in the revolution," they would have to produce a drastic and convincing turnabout in the secular behavior of a Church whose demonstrably conservative background had, for example, led the Cuban Communist Party to bar Christians from its ranks.[89] With their all new social responsibility they could add an ethical sense of commitment to the area of political work, which Drekonja put on a par with the Puritan ethic described by Weber as essential to capitalist development.[90] The radical Catholics would be the salt of the earth, a moral ingredient in the revolutionary leavening. This religious manner of living politics, where "the attitude corresponds . . . totally to the obligation of the crusade," has historically given rise to "the genuine Puritan revolutions."[91]

In Peru, as we have seen, the ONIS was the first of the radical Catholic sector's political protagonists. Its main political contribution was in the creation of a space to the left of Velasco Alvarado's nationalist military regime. Whether intentionally or not, this led to a certain legitimization of the military reforms, since the radical priests publicly recognized the need for the drastic social changes imposed from above, no matter how insufficient they considered them to be. Invested with the force the Church has in a Latin American country and running no risk of persecution, the ONIS also legitimized left-wing positions that had not previously enjoyed public recognition in Peru. In terms of an ecclesiastical strategy of alliances, this amounted to "setting side-by-side the two poles: the Church and the radical forces."[92]

If the Church were actually to take the side of the forces favorable to restructuring society, two important consequences would be assured. First, the process would be somewhat less conflictive (than in Mexico, for example) since the privileged sectors would not have the Church's help to resist it. Traditional anticommunism, to which the Church had made a significant contribution, was severely affected by this new alignment. The second consequence would be an unprecedented chance for a new kind of "resource exchange," no longer between the conservative sectors of the ruling powers and the Church, but between the latter and the new power blocs emerging to the left of the political spectrum. As in the traditional exchange, both parties—the renewed Church and the left—would benefit from a reciprocal legitimization, facilitating the former's penetration among the people and the latter's acceptance by the middle and upper classes. The ONIS, in the arrangement, would be the bridge toward these achievements.

Yet, in addition to their public role as a pressure group, the pastoral work of radical priests and lay people since the early 1970s had been channeled mainly into furthering the process of politicization among the poor, already induced by the military's social change programs. This context was enhanced by the radical Catholics' strategic evaluation of Latin America in the wake of the failure of the approach embodied by Camilo Torres, a martyr of the armed struggle which had been seen in the 1960s as the only legitimate revolutionary path. What arose in its place was another way for Christians to contribute to the revolution: "political participation in organizing the masses, through consciousness-raising of the people in order to eliminate the ideological blocks created by traditional religion in the consciousness of the continent's Christians."[93]

This pastoral approach assumed that "liberation theology (theory) and the priests dedicated to organizing social change (praxis) were linked in a single prophetic action."[94] This relationship between the Church's radical sector and the people led Klaiber to affirm that "only the Church has been successful in penetrating the politicized reserves of the popular classes."[95] This achievement came basically out of the tactic of "accompanying the people in their militant protests and working the grass roots with consciousness-raising and organization."[96]

One of the new strategy's main channels is the base communities, essentially characterized in liberation theology by their "reflection and commitment," which lead their members to take "consciousness of their role in history and of their potential to become a collective agent of social change."[97] The resulting educational experience combines religiosity and politics. In Gutiérrez' words, "When people become politically alert they live their faith better, and when they are freed as Christians they awaken politically." Collective organization is a crucial outgrowth of the radical Catholics' commitment because, among other things, it places the laity and clergy in "a direct relationship with *concrete liberation movements*";[98] or, in more explicit terms, in touch with left-wing political organizations.

Since at least 1978 the left has been an important political force in Peru. In that year's elections, the left-wing parties together won nearly 30 percent of the vote, and in three of the four subsequent elections through 1985 they garnered between a quarter and a third of the total, now representing the country's second largest political force. Since 1980 most of them are members of a front called the United Left which, despite its internal differences, elected its secretary general as the mayor of Lima in 1983: Alfonso Barrantes, a Marxist attentive to the lessons of the Sandinista revolution and, in his own words, zealously respectful of Catholic tradition in Peru. This agglomeration of parties ranges from the pro-Soviet Communist Party to a gamut of groups born in the 1970s under the inspiration of the Cuban or Chinese revolutions. The most significant factor in the rapid growth of the Peruvian left comes from their control over many of the people's organizations—labor, neighborhood, and peasant movements—which appeared during Velasco Alvarado's military regime.

A review of the magazine *Páginas*, the main vehicle of communication used by the Peruvian radical Catholics, leaves no doubt as to the importance placed on giving their activists political analysis and orientation in a setting marked by the left's weighty presence. Nor is there any doubt as to the leftist nature of the orientation, which aligned these Catholics with positions also assumed by the left-wing parties. Thus the demand was raised in 1974 for "the expropriation without payment" of a North American mining company as a "demand of justice," with a proposal that "class organizations . . . lucidly use their power . . . to turn the present balance of forces to their favor."[99] In 1978, the analysis of Peru's first national strike in history concluded, in relation to the Communist Party's labor confederation, that " the CGTP is indispensable in a call for the nationwide united action of the proletariat," and warned that organization that "in order to avoid becoming isolated it will have to call another strike."[100]

The left itself has often been dealt with by the magazine, which regrets that the organized masses encounter "weakness in political development as such, that is, in the organization of the left."[101] Referring to the results of the 1980 elections, Rolando Ames—who would be elected to the Senate by the United Left five years later—published an evaluation in *Páginas* which lamented "the left's self-inflicted weakness," and concluded that "the left has not been defeated."[102] Regarding the alternative of armed struggle proposed by Sendero Luminoso, *Páginas* also put forth a clear position in 1982: "We do not find these terrorist actions to be positive and solid."[103] Once the tendency was established, a 1984 issue brought the assertion that "We believe that the IU [United Left] is the political expression of the process by which broad and varied sectors in the country organize themselves autonomously."[104]

This definition may be congruent with Gustavo Gutiérrez' affirmation that "the great majority of the people in base communities have no political position," in that the United Left political front includes both political parties (Marxist and non-Marxist) and "independent" citizens, not affiliated to any of the parties. In the 1985 elections two outstanding

Catholic leaders were elected to parliament on United Left slates as "in-dependents"—that is to say, not as representatives of any of the member parties but at the invitation of the front's leader and presidential candi-date, Alfonso Barrantes. Manuel Piqueras was elected as a deputy from Lima and Rolando Ames was elected to the senate. Working, therefore, through the so-called "independent" sector of the IU, radical Catholic lead-ers had found a channel for their "political action" aimed at "transform-ing the world into the Promised Kingdom." Ames himself had issued this kind of a call in *Páginas* in 1981, in which he said that the task began in "the base communities of the people . . . forums for elaborating the people's critical and autonomous consciousness, forums for experiencing and encouraging real democracy from the bottom up."[105]

Before attempting to play their own card through the United Left in 1985, Peru's radical Catholics had spent about fifteen years as members of left-wing parties, and had left a mark that is worth examining in order to better understand the kind of political impact that radical Catholics can have.

To begin with, it is important to bear in mind two aspects that arise from the now-refurbished theoretical groundwork accompanying the mem-bers of this sector of the Church. One is that Catholics take up political action to respond to the need for validation both of their own reflections and of the utopia around which their religiosity revolves. In other words, the radical Church utopia is proven valid to the extent that it moves the believer into political action, rather than on the basis of its results. In addition, as Poggi has noted,[106] the Catholic activists bring into political action an "ethic of intentions" which does not care so much about results —nor the efficacy displayed in them—as about the coherence and integ-rity with which they have sought to put the principles into practice. Both aspects converge to make the radical Catholic's political action an activity where the fruits are secondary.

The kind of political activity adopted by Peru's radical priests seems to differ from that elsewhere in Latin America, since few clergy, though often collaborating with left-wing parties, have actually become mem-bers. One key element behind this has probably been the ONIS' "clear and theologically based orientation against such membership, for very important reasons of convenience." Yet by no means has this kept ONIS members from taking clearly leftist positions, as shown in Maloney's 1974 interviews, when 90 percent of them were in agreement with Allende's frustrated socialist experience in Chile.[107]

Among the laity, we must put in a separate category the experience of Catholic Action activists who renounced that affiliation and thereby opened themselves intellectually to replacing their Catholic global conception of the world with the no-less globalizing world view offered by Marxism. This substitution most likely replaced not only one absolute interpretation with another, but also a certain form of faith as well. Thus they probably carried over the certainty offered by the perception of a world that could achieve an ideal order obased on a coherent and all-embracing truth, offered both by Christian faith and by Marxism. For these activists, "class criteria" were as comforting a guide as the good and evil so unmistakably discerned by religious morals.

Others, however, maintained their Catholic activism and, with the creative application of liberation theology, amplified their Church activity to include membership in Marxist political groups. While these, strictly speaking, are the main concern of this article's analysis, the former group has also undeniably imprinted its political practice with the mark of an intense experience as radical apostles. In the interviews done for the analysis that follows, the informants sometimes clarified that the people they referred to as "Catholics" may no longer have been so confessionally, but all shared the distinctive background of membership in Catholic Action groups prior to their affiliation with left-wing parties.

Asked about the political effects of Catholic activism, and particularly the impact of the apostolic method of "recapitulating one's life" as an evangelical gauge for the activists to examine and judge their worldly activities, Gustavo Gutiérrez limited these effects to "a critical, nonsectarian attitude that relativizes certain things, in addition to a concern for the poor as real people," aspects which he believed made it possible for radical Church activists to maintain "a similar humane attitude" in the left.

Other informants gave more specific answers. One distinguished Catholic intellectual, a non-partisan left sympathizer, recalled that the UNEC's apostolic work

> always gave rise to political alternatives: the social progressives versus the Christian Democrats, the MIR against the Revolutionary Vanguard, the Communist Party against the Revolutionary Vanguard and, today, the 'independents' versus the parties in the United Left.

A long-time leftist party leader was more precise and traced out a specific trajectory of the radical Catholics through a series of left-wing parties:

> They followed a clear itinerary: from 1970 to 1972 they threw in with the MIR; when they left they regrouped around the [magazine] *Crítica Marxista Leninista*; in 1973 they joined the VR and took part in the 1976 split that gave rise to the PCR. In 1978 some of them broke off and showed up again as 'independents' within the United Left.

This double (Catholic and leftist) militancy was mentioned in several interviews as a situation conducive to concrete relations between the two sides. "In the MIR, I always had the feeling they worked together, as if they had already had this discussion somewhere else," said one. "I have the impression that party splits were discussed in the other militancy," recalled another, who closely followed the Catholic radicals' participation in the PCR. Another informant assured that, within that same party, "the Christians stood out for their loyalty to Manuel Dammert," a Catholic Student Youth movement leader and a left-wing deputy since 1980.

One of the most frequently mentioned traits of the leftist Catholic activists was that of being "people with a high intellectual level" who raise "a demand for political culture and acute rationality," "have an exceptional command of theory" and bring to bear "a greater presence of sociological data." Thus endowed, Catholic radicals in a political party are reinforced in their self-image as leftist militants "blessed with truth." This Catholic contribution to the left quite probably had significant roots in the markedly intellectual training process characteristic of Peru's radical apostolic movements. The presumption of truth, whether intellectually apprehended from the Bible or from the Marxist classics, was pivotal for these activists. This also leads to the elitization, both of lay movements and of party cadres, since this kind of outlook inevitably displaces and finally shunts aside individuals whose social backgrounds handicap them in handling the written word; anybody coming from the lower economic strata was thus the victim of an indirect—and insurmountable—discrimination.

This "high intellectual level" also goes hand in hand with a demand for rationality, the nature of which was described by a leader with twenty years of left party experience:

> These people expect a hierarchy with rules, a hierarchical order that will help give them a rational justification for their acts. . . . The Catholics establish a rational but solid loyalty. . . . This need for order helps a lot in the functioning of party organs. . . . It is a style that fits well with Lenin's rule-making.

This is not surprising since such traits can easily be traced to the kind of socialization conferred by Catholic Action movements: hierarchically constituted and organized in general and, where radicalization came mainly through intellectual channels, highly rational in their training and style.

Conversely, political militancy for leftist Catholics means principally teaching and giving witness to their truth-bearing ideology. It is interesting that the magazine *Crítica Marxista Leninista*—founded by a group of Catholic dissidents from the MIR on their way to the VR—asserted that "the first task (of a militant) is to learn Marxism,"[108] thus replicating attachment to the written word as a form of initiation. Once acquired intellectually, this truth must be shared with others. While the left's denunciation-laden style cannot be credited to the radical Catholics alone, they probably helped reinforce this persistent leftist political attitude, bent on "unmasking the class nature" of an event so that the people will supposedly be able to act accordingly.

The witness-bearing sense of Catholic commitment becomes even more important in the Peruvian left. "The Christians in the cell voted on the basis of what was good or bad, rather than the possible efficacy of the results," in the words of one informant. A logic of political action heavily weighted by utopian religiosity does not concern itself with practical results; moreover, as we have already seen, radical Catholic utopianism inverts reality and turns defeats into victories. Carried over to the realm of political affairs, this exonerates them from worrying about efficacy. And radical utopians are suspicious of partial victories: those who appraise triumphs by the specific value of a demand that has been met chain their politics to these demands and put off the total transformation of society. The real goal, on the contrary, is not what is to be gained concretely through struggle, but rather the purification of the combatant.

Providentialism is another element—a kind of Biblical overlay superimposed onto the Marxist belief in the inevitability of socialism—reassuring radical Catholics that, when all is said and done, Divine Revelation has guaranteed victory:

> Socialist revolution and the transition to communism are historically inevitable.[109]

> There may be temporary defeats and setbacks; yet the objective upward tendency will once and again allow the fighting resurgence of the only forces capable of resolving the country's critical problems, that is to say, the forces of the national popular-democratic revolution.[110]

Providentialism is a poor counselor of efficacy, since it lets the course of history rest less on the action of people than on a logic that transcends reality and, in its radical version, guides it toward the revolution. This attitude produces what one interviewee called "an illuminist or messianic sense of politics," in which the political activist is defined as a prophet:

> While they are the most implacable critics of the old world, they are the most abnegate builders of a new world: communism. [The activist] is not just another member of the masses, but one who has been morally and ideologically edified.[111]

The profile of the Catholic leftist militant also includes a personal style described at length by one informant with regards to a person known in the party cell as "the bishop":

> The Catholic militant does not seek confrontation. As opposed to the average leftist, he beats around the bush and never uses insults, but he never concedes a point to his adversary either. . . . There may be even greater obduracy in this, but it is well concealed.

Another informant posed a comparison: "The Christian and the Stalinist think in black and white"; and an experienced leader suggested that the "same form—that of dogma—is used to channel different contents, whether Marxist or Christian." Yet the most distinctive trait of radical Catholics is their "profound guilt feelings [which lead them to live] in an excessively anguished way."

Rigidity and anguish would seem to explain a radical Catholic attitude which "precludes in the militant anything that is not serious, like jokes, parties, and drinking"—an attitude which certainly must lead the leftist Catholic to keep a critical distance from "the poor as real people" despite the basically political approximation sought for their redemption. In the words of one leftist activist:

> Although the morals of good and evil might appear to fit politics well, when you start working with the people, that approach isolates you from them. . . . The Christian thus establishes a two-faced relationship with the people, because it is hard to understand them in all their complexity, so, for example, they censure the people's drinking and brawling.

Finally, the left-wing Catholic activists present a paradox: on the one hand, they construe the poor intellectually as an object of concern for whose sake they are willing to make personal sacrifices and even take hazardous commitments; yet having visualized the poor in ideal terms— albeit intellectually—in order, religiously and politically, to award them redeeming functions, they are incapable of assimilating habits of the flesh-and-blood poor which upset their preconceived notions. We have already discussed the attempts to overcome this contradiction, also in intellectual terms: the organic intellectuals of radical Catholicism systematically breed a version of "the people" which nourishes this idealization and suppresses bothersome characteristics.

Finally, it is important to reiterate that this radical Catholic behavior pattern leaves little or no room for the exercise of democracy. One informant pointed out that left-wing Catholic militants "stigmatize heterodoxy and discrepancies as heresy; political disagreements can cost friendships." This is not surprising, although authoritarianism cannot be imputed to the socialization process in Catholic groups alone; this process actually reinforces an old tendency of the Leninist left and also undoubtedly corresponds to certain deep-rooted traits of Peruvian society. Both in the left and in the Church movements, legitimacy arises and is achieved through knowledge of the truth and the use of its authentic interpretation. A majority decision cannot, therefore, prevail as an appropriate method for choosing who is best. The new leader is always selected by the knowledgeable, which is to say, those who are already in the leadership bodies. In Catholic Action and in the Leninist left, to attain formal leadership of the movement means being coopted. The militant, therefore, is not delegated by the rank and file, but rather—at a given moment—is called from above to exercise a leadership responsibility. This mechanism encourages the submission of the rank and file, the cultivation of which is the only way to ascend, at some point, in a setting where no one is formally authorized to openly compete for power and where—as opposed to what is normal in a democratic institutional setting—aspirations for power are perceived as gluttonous appetites.

The absence of democratic mechanisms rests on the assumption that someone, or some people, are true repositories of a knowledge that is the backbone of the movement's faith. In Catholic Action movements, this figure, hierarchically distinguished, is the priest, whose education makes him a professional knower of the truth, qualitatively distinct from the rest. There is no comparable ranking in left-wing parties, but here the very roots of power make it hard for the highest offices to change hands. Thus, in many of Peru's left-wing parties the office of secretary general tends to be held for life. The justification for this is that the basis for exercising the office is the accumulated knowledge of the group's truth; it would be difficult for anyone to take over the leadership from one who has achieved the requisite level of knowledge. Given the mechanism of calling leaders up from below, such a substitution would also demand the voluntary withdrawal of the person in command, since competing openly with him is impossible under prevailing ground rules.

These remarkable similarities between Church organizations and those of the organized left lead us to believe that the impact of radical Catholicism has probably strengthened the authoritarian distribution of power within the parties of the left. This brittle authoritarian structure explains the left's constant splitting, experienced by the militants as heretical break-offs. There is no room to compete openly for power, since winning the support of a significant or even majority sector of the comrades does not give one the right to take control of the organization, and since any disagreement with what the leadership has decided amounts to a punishable deviation, then any concrete attempt to achieve a position of power means planting the seeds for a split. These nondemocratic mechanisms, on the one hand, keep the truth proclaimed by the leadership from being subjected to any genuine discussion and possible amendment by the rank and file while, on the other hand, they rule out any open competition among those who aspire to the organization's leadership. The final upshot is a muffled struggle for power under the guise of discussions around "party line." The penchant of the new Peruvian left for splitting thus seems to have been enriched by an added religious ingredient.

ADVISERS TURNED DEFENDANTS

When we counterpose other radical Catholic experiences in Latin America to the growing criticisms of Peru's radical sector in recent years, the obvious question is why these criticisms did not surface earlier. The answer, among other things, has to do with the Peruvian radical Catholics' characteristic behavioral traits in their relations with the rest of the Church.

First of all, the ONIS gave priority to its relationship with the hierarchy, established through the use of two main channels. The first of these were the movement's public declarations, an important part of whose target audience were the bishops. Armed at all points with quotes selected from the Church's teachings, these texts were tacit and intelligent reminders to the prelates of commitments assumed by the institution which they, as a result, were obliged to respect.

Mindful of their audience, ONIS' documents carefully avoided taking positions apt to imply confrontations with the bishops or open to being interpreted as a subtle form of doctrinal parallelism. We have seen, for example, how the ONIS distinguished its position on revolutionary violence from that of the bishops without openly contradicting them; the differences were imperceptible. The movement's declarations also always contained explicit reiterations of obedience to the hierarchy. As Gustavo Gutiérrez put it, "The work of the Church structure was always respected and Church formalities maintained."

The other channel refers to the ONIS' and radicalized lay leaders' systematic efforts to contribute to developing the Church's new teachings, both inside Peru and throughout Latin America. In their descriptions of assemblies held in the 1970s by the Peruvian episcopate to discuss the Church's positions, two of the radical Catholics' organic intellectuals depict this participation:

Often the lay movement activists, leaders of Christian communities, and the more active priests and religious brought their voices to the assemblies. So to speak of the hierarchy's documents is not to speak of words that come from above nor of an episcopate wrapped up in itself. . . . The laity, the clergy, and the religious who are committed to the daily tasks of evangelization, who accompany the people in their growing awareness and mobilization, have a chance to be heard and to participate in the Church's collegiate discussions.[112]

Gustavo Gutiérrez participated personally in drafting the text issued in Medellín at the Latin American Episcopal Conference in 1968 (which condemns "institutionalized violence" in the social order), the declaration of the 26th Peruvian Episcopal Conference (which in 1969 deepened the orientations of Medellín) and in the contribution by the Peruvian bishops to the document "Justice in the World," prepared for the 1971 Synod. The latter marked the high point of the radical sector's influence over episcopal documents:

Construction of a just society in Latin America and Peru means liberation from the current situation of dependency, oppression, and abandonment in which the majority of our people live. Liberation will mean breaking with all that impedes mankind's full realization in both personal and communitarian terms, as well as the building of a new, more humane and fraternal society. Christ's salvation is more than political liberation, but the latter finds its place and its true meaning in the total liberation announced unendingly by the Holy Scripture, making mankind worthy of being the son of God.[113]

That document demonstrates a trait noted by Dodson in radical priests' groups: "the degree of influence that an organized and active minority can carry within the Church."[114] On the other hand, very few conflicts were registered between ONIS priests and the bishops. As Gutiérrez assured us, the movement "never adopted a trade-union role, standing by a priest in relation to his bishop, nor did it ever create an intraecclesiastical problem." This perspective on institutional work—ignored by Dodson and Montgomery,[115] who classified the ONIS as one of the Latin American priests' movements that simultaneously confronted both political and religious authorities—is a key consideration in the activity of the Peruvian radical sector.

The only incident of note took place in March 1969, a few months after the movement was founded, when a group of ONIS members in the city of Trujillo, supported by seminarians, defied the authority of Archbishop Jurgens, who had decided to expel three Spanish priests from the diocese. The three, also members of the group, not only had supported a metal-workers' strike but had publicly condemned a luxurious social club in the city, inaugurated by the archbishop. The papal nuncio also joined the fray, called the accused "rebel priests," and held the ONIS' national leadership responsible. One hundred fifty priests then addressed a public letter to the nuncio in defense of the three priests, while a "Manifesto of the Young Church" was released in Trujillo. The incident came to a close when Archbishop Jurgens cancelled the expulsion orders. Macaulay, after a lengthy analysis of documents relevant to the incident, concluded that the ONIS priests had the luck of enjoying the support of Cardinal Landázuri,[116] who—according to McCurry[117]—had to "publicly remind the nuncio that ecclesiastical discipline was the responsibility of the Peruvian hierarchy," after which the papal envoy left the country.

The role played in the radicals' strategy by the Archbishop of Lima, Msgr. Landázuri, should not be underestimated. At the same time he accepted the movement's development and turned to its members as theological advisers, he assured the unequivocal respect for his authority in a Church whose hierarchy he saw as comprehending yet firm: "above all, the spirit of initiative and the exercise of personal charisma must be reasonably exposed under the sign of authenticity, that is to say, submitted to the judgment of authority."[118]

This definition of authority was compatible with the radicals' strategy, exemplified in the behavior of Gustavo Gutiérrez, their leading personality. At the same time that an extremely radical theological and pastoral orientation was being developed, not only was confrontation with the hierarchy avoided but efforts were made to convince the bishops of ideas increasingly critical of the status quo that could be disseminated throughout the entire Church. This probably meant compromises and concessions for the radicals, who thus declined both Camilo Torres' path of rupture in Colombia and the option of the Christians for Socialism in Chile, who were soon to be sanctioned by their own hierarchy.

Thus, what at first glance might have smacked of opportunism was actually a sophisticated strategy in which Peru's radical Catholics carefully gauged the impact of their proposals on the Church as a whole, without renouncing either their principled position or their will to transform the Church accordingly. This strategy led Macaulay to argue that "the ONIS does not operate as a revolutionary force . . . but strictly . . . as a lever, as an influence, as a reformist element."[119]

Aside from their cautious relationship with the hierarchy, another key element in this strategy was to avoid participation in political parties, which became an explosive issue in Chile and Nicaragua. Avoiding this problem, and posing no direct threat to the hierarchy, the posture adopted by the ONIS offered some advantages for the Catholic as a whole due to the fact that "a Church group had come out for radical social, political, and economic reforms without compromising the Church itself." This created "the impression of a move towards the creation of a new Church ... at the same time letting the Church proceed at a more cautious pace," and avoided the radical Catholics' departure from the institution (as had occurred in Colombia), maintaining the Peruvians in their dissident positions but under hierarchical control.[120]

This give-and-take was entirely compatible with the radical priests' objectives of establishing ties between the Church and the left wing of the political spectrum, thereby helping to legitimize revolutionary goals through the use of whatever was appropriate in Catholicism to that objective. Working toward these ends from within the Church meant the possibility of enjoying not only the legitimacy they needed but also a certain protection from police repression. The radicals' project also opened an attractive possibility for the institution, that of reinstating the influence of Catholic ideas in the country, although it also ran the risk that this "'Third World' Catholicism akin to Marxism" might finally be swallowed by the latter.[121]

In early 1985, a Peruvian bishop, Msgr. Durand, published a book entirely dedicated to an analysis of doctrinal orthodoxy in the extensive writings of Gustavo Gutiérrez. In it, he presented in great detail the reasons for his recommendation to

> the faithful of Callao, with the support of the Instruction from Rome and our most recent document, both of them based on earlier Documents of the Teachings, that they not use Liberation Theology in its Marxist version, since this ideological current has not been sufficiently discerning in the use of Marxist analysis as a social force, but rather has taken from it elements that clash with the Gospel.[122]

What had happened to the harmonious coexistence of diverging positions which had lasted more than a decade in the Peruvian Church? The turnabout, obviously, was not a sudden occurrence. As early as 1972, the ONIS' report on the national situation presented at the Christians for Socialism conference in Santiago, Chile, had indicated that when the subject of people's liberation had been introduced in documents from the 1969 Episcopal Assembly and for the 1971 Synod, "there arose an unprecedented hostility on the part of rightist Catholic sectors." The surprising part of the report, however, is that those who were so careful in their delicate handling of the country's radical movement, in order to preserve by all means that fragile but crucial balance which allowed them to continue advancing toward changes in the institution, publicly affirmed in encouraging tones that that reaction "will help polarize opinions and options within the Church. It will make it clear that class struggle cuts across the Church community itself."[123]

The aggressiveness cultivated in the radical Catholics' positions sought to disqualify other forms of being Catholic. As one informant put it, in practice "the option for the poor is radicalized to exclude and oppose the non-poor." The writings of the radical sector solidly reinforce that impression. Gustavo Gutiérrez has argued that the new theological approach "imposes a rereading of the Gospel," out of which he discovers the "God of the oppressed,"[124] and coincides with the Peruvian novelist José María Arguedas "when he said that 'the God of the *Señores* is not the same God.' He is not the God of the poor."[125] In *Páginas*, the believer has been defined as "one who believes practically. One who believes the Lord is present in the History of a people's liberation and who contributes to achieving that liberation using all the means within his reach."[126] Whereby they demand of the Church that, "if it wishes to be worthy of salvation . . . it must take up the desires for liberation,"[127] a perspective which definitely imposes "the constant recreation of a true people's Church."[128] And a perspective which clearly excludes conservative Catholics.

For one Jesuit author, the passage from diversity to conflictiveness was provoked by the behavior of certain Catholic radicals:

> the involvement of many of these pastoral agents in the realm of politics brought party divisions into the hierarchy itself. . . . When those priests entered a terrain so different from that of religion, they adhered to extremist parties with religious and messianic fervor. This gave rise to contention within the Church itself, not for religious but for political motives, although it also gave rise to a new theological dissidence in the form of interpreting the Gospel.[129]

While this approach identifies the problem, it is far from a satisfactory explanation. Strictly speaking, the theological dissidence had been on the table since 1968 and did not in itself give rise to contention. Nor are there any indications of actual party membership by radical priests who, quite the contrary, were generally careful not to carry their politicizing of religious commitment to the point of joining a party. Why, then, this internal breach?

In 1970 Gutiérrez had written an article in which he reviewed changes then underway and mentioned that they had occasioned some conflicts with bishops and nuncios. He predicted that "unless there are radical changes, these conflicts will multiply and worsen in coming years," and then added another complicating factor toward which he did not take an explicit position. "Many priests also felt obliged in good conscience actively to commit themselves within the realm of politics. And in Latin America these days priests are frequently called 'subversives.'"[130]

After observing that "most of the Church is still tied in many ways (conscious or unconscious) to the established order," the analysis of the most important theologian of radical Catholicism in Peru situated the causes of a profound division of the Latin American Church:

> The polarization of options and the hardening of the situation have placed some Christians amongst the oppressed and others amongst the persecutors, some amongst the tortured and others amongst the torturers. Out of this emerges a serious and radical confrontation. In the process of liberation, the Latin American Church finds itself strongly divided. In these circumstances, life in the midst of a Christian community becomes particularly difficult and conflictive. . . . It will be impossible in the future not to face up to the problems arising from such a division amongst Christians."[131]

But Gutiérrez considered that conflict not only difficult but probably necessary—as the 1972 text presented in Santiago would also suggest —in the following cautious but significant words:

> Participation in Communion, for example, is seen by many in its present form as an act bereft of any basis in the real human community; it takes on fictitious appearances. . . . Couched in lyrical terms, a call for the union of all Christians that does not account for the deeper causes of the present situation or the real conditions for the common construction of society is no more than an evasion. We are moving towards a new conception of unity and of Communion in the Church.[132]

The radicals probably harbored a somewhat contradictory ambivalence. On the one hand, they seem to have entertained a very cautious general strategy for institutional integrity; yet at the same time they betrayed a doctrinal position which not only revealed the inevitability of internal conflict but also led them to believe that this conflict could be turned to their advantage. This is more than a mere recognition of objective differences. It is undeniable, as Mainwaring has observed,[133] that the development of these radical positions demonstrated the ongoing subjectivity of the concepts of both institutional interests and pastoral tasks; that the Church contained different and conflicting ways of understanding its mission and an analogous diversity of forms of political action within the institution; and that "change in the Church is the result of struggles between different groups with differing conceptions of faith." The problem, however, was how to set tolerable limits on plurality within the institution or, in other words, to what degree contending viewpoints could accept each other. The radicals' theoretical response was hardly pluralist.

Whether it was the radicals' exclusionist aggressiveness or not, however, this sector's positions were not winning over the majority of the institution. Mooney's study of the Peruvian Church in the mid-1970s found that a substantial number of priests disapproved their ONIS colleagues' forays into politics and their acritical acceptance of Marxism and the theory of class struggle, and that they were worried by certain consequences of that posture. They particularly feared that liberation theology would intensify conflicts among the bishops, and that the pastoral priority on base communities would reduce the experience of Christianity to small and isolated minorities, giving rise to excessively autonomous, politicized, and elitist organizations.

The radical Catholic movement catalyzed "a very strong coordination of the clergy's more conservative sector," whose development and presence quite likely contributed to a retreat by the hierarchy. A study of the content of Peruvian episcopal declarations observed that the number of "progressive" declarations dropped from 98.8 percent in 1969 to a mere 39 percent in 1975. 1975 also brought a rift between the bishops and the ONIS, when the movement was unsuccessful in exacting an episcopal statement against a mass deportation of Velasco Alvarado's opponents, and then went ahead and published the declaration on its own, virtually forcing the bishops into silence.[134]

The Peruvian Church's internecine tensions certainly went back further than the creation of the ONIS or of the "Church in Solidarity," a movement of clergy and laity known since 1971 as "Faith and Action in Solidarity." McCurry noted as early as 1972 that "the ideological struggle in the heart of the movement [of *cursillos*, which had been very successful among officers of the armed forces] upset the Church structure so much that their meetings were officially prohibited."[135] But the shock waves caused by the radicals were much greater than that. Conservative Catholics decided to air their differences openly, and for several years beginning in 1975 published the weekly *Opinión Libre*, as an ongoing denunciation of "the communist infiltration" supposedly underway in the Church. In 1978, the book *Como lobos rapaces* (*Like Ravenous Wolves*) by Alfredo Garland was published as a systematic accusation against the radical sector.

Another development was also decisive in promoting internal reaction against the institutional orientation devised by the radical clergy and laity: "the new strategy" included a partisan identification which became clear once the left achieved the standing of a political alternative, to the point of becoming the country's second largest electoral force in 1985. The Church's turn to the poor under the guidance of liberation theology had meant building ties with organized sectors of the people, whose process of politicization was given very special colors by radical Catholics in their pastoral work. In Klaiber's words, as a result of the new pastoral approach, "In the Church . . . the popular classes found a familiar and protective atmosphere, where it was easy for them to assimilate, within their own traditions, the new idea of revolution."[136]

This process was underway at the same time that the country's left-wing parties were growing and moving, through the United Left, into the center stage of Peruvian politics. The radical Catholics in this context made no bones about their option for the left (an option much more significant than that of individual Catholic members of left-wing parties, which went back farther and had produced little public impact). They assumed leadership roles in the United Left and organized a sector within it that might assume a leading part in its development. The context for radicalization had clearly changed substantially, giving a new meaning to the initial "option for the poor."

The result can be conceptualized as a politicization of religious differences, but it might also be useful to think of it as a religious reinforcement of political differences which, as Vallier warned, "produces irreconcilable fissures."[137] Once the political outgrowths of popularizing pastoral work were perceptible, and the military's reform experience had given way to a revival of *belaundismo* (symbolizing an impossible return to the past, a reference to President Belaúnde Terry, overthrown by the military in 1968), the long-coming reaction of those who had opposed drastic changes from the outset and had virtually been accused by the radicals of being false believers could be contained no more. Since 1973 – the point where Romero located the first indications of "internal differentiation" – until the 1985 publication by a bishop of a book denouncing the theological works of Gustavo Gutiérrez, the public confrontation between the two Church factions had been gaining momentum.

The radicals recognize that the conservative reaction stopped the swing to the left accompanying the active mobilization of that sector:

> The effects of social conflictiveness on the Church itself, directly attacked by the supposedly Catholic right, are beginning to be felt by the Peruvian Church and to restrict the participation in Church life of important sectors of the laity . . . of the clergy and of the bishops themselves.[138]

The concrete impact of this process on radical Catholics meant, for example, that the "Catechetical Guidebooks published by the CEP (Center for Studies and Publications, an agency tied to the radical sector] . . . were withdrawn in 1979 following a statement by the Episcopate,"[139] in one of the first (critical) responses to the ten-year-old reform movement.

It was not only the local conservative sectors that reacted to the growing process of Catholic radicalization in Latin America. Rome also expressed its concern: "Pope Paul VI warned against tendencies in small base communities, which make them 'fall victim to a political option . . . and then into a system and even into a party.'" The Latin American bishops, in a documents sent "to the Third Synod of bishops, which met in Rome in October 1974, recognized the continent's 'aspirations for liberation'" but also "warned against a 'superficial politicization of faith.'"[140] Later, both Rome and the CELAM—dominated by conservatives since 1972— would use the 1979 gathering in Puebla to reiterate their warnings and to make it clear that the attention given by the Church to popular sectors ought to be understood as a "preferential option for the poor," not excluding other social sectors.

The interpretation of the radical Catholic movement, however, was that "The questioning came from outside the Peruvian Church. First from the CELAM and more recently from the Vatican, and it was echoed in Peru by bishops with a variety of positions but tied in one way or another to a new religious movement, also Catholic, which appeared around Puebla."[141]

As a result, the Peruvian Church openly displayed its differences and harbored movements and organizations from both sectors: on one side *Opus Dei* and *Sodalitium Christiane Vitae;* and on the other ONIS, Faith and Action in Solidarity, the Center for Studies and Publications, and the Bartolomé de las Casas Institute.

Since the early 1980s, Peru's bishops have been in a difficult situation, which Levine has also identified in several other Latin American episcopates: "Trapped in the center, the bishops are trying to keep the Church and the Catholic community together, in the face of enormous divisive pressures."[142] Peru's ecclesiastical problems mounted in 1983, when the Holy Congregation for Doctrine and Faith requested that the country's bishops speak out on liberation theology; following three extraordinary assemblies, they did not reach agreement. What apparently happened was "that the subject was not dealt with in an atmosphere of dialogue but rather left the conflicting positions at loggerheads. In their April [1984] assembly the bishops arrived at two different drafts, expressing the diverse stances of the two sectors of the episcopate."[143]

This outcome revealed a serious internecine division within the Peruvian Church, including its bishops. This demonstrates that the radical sector's strategy was a success, or at least more of a success than in any of the other Latin American experiences with radicalization.

Once the two documents produced by the episcopal assemblies had been sent to Rome, the bishops were summoned to the Vatican by Pope

John Paul II, for a meeting in October 1984. There, with the pope's intervention, they managed to agree on a single document which, in its most relevant paragraph, invited "particularly those dedicated to liberation theology, to evaluate their own studies and publications in the light of that Instruction [Rome's Instruction on Liberation Theology] and of this document. And, after apprising the Episcopal Conference, to make it, if approved, public, in the spirit of communion and ecclesiastical service."[144]

Nothing happened, despite the bishops' mandate. In April 1985 one of them, Durand Flórez, published a book with his critical observations on the thought of Gustavo Gutiérrez, whom he accused of adopting approaches and topics of Marxism incompatible with the teachings of the Church. With the public airing of discrepancies, internecine splits will certainly not be healed but rather will tend to be aggravated in this new stage.

The radical Catholics have in fact become the target of attacks within a process aimed at condemning liberation theology. At the same time, a power struggle is being waged around the top posts in the hierarchy. In the past few years, the Vatican has systematically named conservative priests as bishops, and all eyes are now turned to the coming succession of Archbishop Landázuri. Although his administration as primate of the Peruvian Church has been permeable to the influence of radical Catholics, he has managed to maintain the institution's pluralism, publicly advocating respect for groups at the opposite extreme such as *Opus Dei*.

These days it is hard to agree with Romero de Iguíñiz that the experience of the Church in Peru "is a global process [summoning] a growing number of Christians to a new ecclesiastical experience." Her description fits the radical sector well, but not the institution as a whole. Nor is her contention accurate that "The Catholic Church in Peru has changed its social practice and its Christian vision of social reality, incorporating these institutional changes into its pastoral work and theology. The result of this process has been a new relationship between the Church and society, based on an autonomy acquired from its criticism of prevailing social relationships."[145]

This did actually happen at one stage of the Peruvian Church's development over the past twenty years (specifically from 1976–1980), but that period's standard cannot be simply projected as the outcome of a process still underway. The only visible result—as clear as it is provisional—is the onset of sharp internal differences which have not given way to harmonious relations among the differing sectors. On the contrary, they have produced institutional fissures, in addition to a certain paralysis which contradicts the role of the Church a decade earlier. How else could one explain the silence of these bishops—from the same episcopate which had come out in favor of socialism in 1971—when confronted with the phenomenon of mass disappearances during the antiguerilla struggle since 1983?

At some point in the future, some kind of relationship between the Peruvian Church and its society will surely be established out of the current morass of internecine confrontations and out of the interaction of this ecclesiastical struggle with the sociopolitical context of the country as a whole. The new relationship will replace the Church's traditional identification with the ruling powers—made impractical by the end of the oligarchical state and its substitution by a regime of political plurality. And it will also replace the transitional forms of experimentation with new ways of conducting the Church's relations with society, forms seen as more advantageous by one sector of Catholics than by others—a situation that has ended up undermining the Church's unity, the greatest threat of all to an institution which, above all else, values its own survival.

NOTES

Most of this study was made possible by the generous opportunity granted to its author by the Kellogg Institute at the University of Notre Dame to spend a semester working full-time on research, with the encouragement and support of the Institute's academic staff.

1. Phillip Berryman, *The Religious Roots of Rebellion: Christians in Central American Revolutions* (Maryknoll, N.Y.: Orbis, 1984), p. 31.

1. John Eagleson, ed., *Christians and Socialism* (Maryknoll, N.Y.: Orbis, 1975), pp. 125–126.

3. Catalina Romero and Cecilia Tovar, undated, unpublished manuscript, "Cambios en la Iglesia peruana," Part II, p. 12.

4. Ibid., Part 1, p. 15.

5. Thomas James Maloney, "The Catholic Church and Peruvian Revolution: Resource Exchange in an Authoritarian Setting," Ph.D. Dissertation, University of Texas at Austin, 1978, p. 149.

6. Michael Gregory Macaulay, "Ideological Change and Internal Cleavages in the Peruvian Church: Change, Status Quo, and the Priests; The Case of ONIS," Ph.D. Dissertation, University of Notre Dame, 1972.

7. Dan C. McCurry, "Las misiones en Perú financiadas por las Iglesias norteamericanas," in Daniel A. Sharp, ed., *Estados Unidos y la revolución peruana* (Buenos Aires: Sudamericana, 1972), p. 561.

8. Michael Dodson, "Prophetic Politics and Political Theory in Latin America," *Polity* 12, no. 3 (Spring 1980): 398.

9. Macaulay, "Ideological Change and Internal Cleavages."

10. Eagleson, *Christians and Socialism*, p. 126.

11. Michael Dodson, "The Christian Left in Latin American Politics," in Daniel

Levine, ed., *Churches and Politics in Latin America*, (Beverly Hills, Calif.: Sage Publications, 1979), p. 207.

12. Macaulay, "Ideological Change and Internal Cleavages," pp. 103, 105–106.

13. Maloney, "The Catholic Church and Peruvian Revolution," pp. 443–444.

14. Gianfranco Poggi, *Catholic Action in Italy: The Sociology of a Sponsored Organization* (Stanford, Calif.: Stanford University Press, 1967), p. 48.

15. T. Howland Sanks, S.J., and Brian Smith, S.J., "Liberation Theology: Praxis, Theory, Praxis," *Theological Studies* 38, no. 1 (March 1977): 7.

16. *Páginas* no. 27 (1973): 12–13.

17. Gustavo Gutiérrez, "Notes for a Theology of Liberation," *Theological Studies* 31, no. 2 (June 1970): 250.

18. Gutiérrez, "Praxis de liberación y fe cristiana" (Lima: Centro de Documentación de MIEC-JECI, 1973), p. 13.

19. Jorge Álvarez Calderón, "Descubrir la espiritualidad del pueblo," *Páginas* (1980): 3.

20. Catalina Romero, "Cambios en la relación Iglesia-sociedad en el Perú: 1958–1978," *Debates en Sociología* 7 (1982): 118.

21. Carlos Alberto Astiz, *Pressure Groups and Power Elites in Peruvian Politics* (Ithaca, N.Y.: Cornell University Press, 1969), p. 179.

22. Romero and Tovar, "Cambios en la Iglesia peruana," Part II, p. 7.

23. Maloney, "The Catholic Church and Peruvian Revolution," p. 158.

24. Ibid., p. 234.

25. McCurry, "Las misiones en Perú," p. 569.

26. Romero and Tovar, "Cambios en la Iglesia peruana," Part II, pp. 11–12.

27. Carlos Alberto Astiz, "The Catholic Church in Latin American Politics: A Case Study of Peru," in David H. Pollock and Arch. R. M. Ritter, eds., *Latin American Prospects for the 1970s: What Kinds of Revolutions?* (New York: Praeger, 1973), p. 141.

28. Romero and Tovar, "Cambios en la Iglesia peruana," Part II, p. 9.

29. Maloney, "The Catholic Church and Peruvian Revolution," pp. 424, 445.

30. McCurry, "Las misiones en Perú," p. 570.

31. Romero and Tovar, "Cambios en la Iglesia peruana," Part II, p. 3.

32. *Cronología Política*, Vol. I, p. 54.

33. *Cronología Política*, Vol. I, p. 300.

34. Mary Helen Mooney, "The Role of the Church in Peruvian Political Development," M.A. Thesis, University of Windsor, Canada, 1976, p. 128.

35. Maloney, "The Catholic Church and Peruvian Revolution," pp. 450, 408.

36. Jeffrey Klaiber, *Religión y revolución en el Perú: 1824–1976* (Lima: Universidad del Pacífico, 1976), p. 221.

37. Catalina Romero de Iguíñiz, "Iglesia peruana: cambio y continuidad," Kellogg Institute Working Paper #48, 1985, pp. 17–18.

38. Romero and Tovar, "Cambios en la Iglesia peruana," Part III, p. 13.

39. Romero de Iguíñiz, "Iglesia peruana: cambio y continuidad," pp. 17–18.

40. José L. Idígoras, S.J., "La Iglesia y el poder," *Debate* 9 (July 1981): 61.

41. Klaiber, *Religión y revolución en el Perú: 1824–1976*, p. 222.

42. Idígoras, "La Iglesia y el poder," p. 61.

43. *Páginas* no. 50 (1975): 66.

44. Max Weber, *Sociología de la religión* (Buenos Aires: Ed. La Pléyade, 1978), p. 14.

45. Romero and Tovar, "Cambios en la Iglesia peruana," Part III, p. 9.

46. Romero de Iguíñiz, "Iglesia peruana: cambio y continuidad," p. 25.

47. Diego Irarrázabal, "Las clases populares, evangelización, ¿como?," *Páginas* 5, no. 28 (March 1978): 16 (original emphasis).

48. *Páginas* 2, no. 43 (1982): 5.

49. Emmanuel de Kadt, *Catholic Radicals in Brazil* (New York: Oxford University Press, 1970), pp. 89–90.

50. Ibid., p. 78.

51. Pablo Fontaine, "Algunos aspectos de la Iglesia chilena de hoy," *Mensaje* 24, no. 239, (June 1975).

52. *Páginas* 2, no. 1 (1976): 3.

53. Gustavo Gutiérrez, "The Irruption of the Poor in Latin America and the Christian Communities of the Common People," in Sergio Torres and John Eagleson, eds., *The Challenge of Basic Christian Communities* (New York: Orbis, 1981), p. 109.

54. *Páginas* no. 42 (1974): 14.

55. W. von Loewenich, *Modern Catholicism* (New York: St. Martin's Press, 1959), pp. 115–116.

56. Poggi, *Catholic Action in Italy*, pp. 242–243.

57. Ibid., pp. 79, 240.

58. Ibid., p. 107.

59. Heinrich Böll, *Opiniones de un Payaso*, p. 124.

60. Poggi, *Catholic Action in Italy*, p. 106.

61. Ivan Vallier, "Radical Priests and the Revolution," in D. Chalmers, ed., *Changing Latin America: New Interpretations of its Politics and Society*, (Montpelier, Vt.: Capital City Press, 1972), pp. 21, 18, 17.

62. Astiz, *Pressure Groups and Power Elites in Peruvian Politics*, p. 177.

63. *Páginas* no. 27 (1973): 7.

64. Klaiber, *Religión y revolución en el Perú: 1824–1976*, pp. 221–222.

65. John William Hart, "Topia and Utopia in Colombia and Peru: The Theory and Practice of Camilo Torres and Gustavo Gutiérrez in Their Historical Contexts," Ph.D. Dissertation, Union Theological Seminary, New York, 1978.

66. Macaulay, "Ideological Change and Internal Cleavages," p. 37.

67. Astiz, "The Catholic Church in Latin American Politics," p. 137.

68. Mooney, "The Role of the Church in Peruvian Political Development," p. 102.

69. Scott P. Mainwaring, "The Catholic Youth Workers Movement (JOC) and the Emergence of the Popular Church in Brazil," Kellogg Institute Working Paper #6, 1983, p. 39.

70. Böll, *Opiniones de un Payaso*, p. 131.

71. *Páginas* 2, no. 1 (1976): 11.

72. Jürgen Moltmann, "An Open Letter to José Míguez Bonino," *Christianity and Crisis* 36, no. 15 (March 29, 1976): 60.

73. Böll, *Opiniones de un Payaso*, pp. 74, 131, 177, 242.

74. Poggi, *Catholic Action in Italy*, pp. 128, 130, 136–137.

75. Macaulay, "Ideological Change and Internal Cleavages," p. 154.

76. Idígoras, "La Iglesia y el poder," p. 63.

77. Poggi, *Catholic Action in Italy*, p. 96.

78. Ibid., pp. 41–42.

79. Maloney, "The Catholic Church and Peruvian Revolution," p. 445.

80. Luis Lituma, "La Iglesia peruana en el siglo XX," in José Pareja Paz Soldán, ed., *Visión del Perú en el siglo XX* (Lima: Ed. Librería Studium, 1963), vol. 2, p. 520.

81. Daniel H. Levine, *Religion and Politics in Latin America: The Catholic Church in Venezuela and Colombia* (Princeton, N.J.: Princeton University Press, 1981), p. 30.

82. Sergio Arce Martínez, *Cristo vivo en Cuba* (San José, P.R.: DEI, 1978), pp. 27, 170.

83. Raúl Vidales, *Cuestiones en torno al método en la teología de la liberación* (Lima: MIEC-JECI, 1974), pp. 5, 12, 7, 23.

84. Hart, "Topia and Utopia in Colombia and Peru," pp. 214–215.

85. *Páginas* 2, no. 1 (1976): 4.

86. *Páginas* no. 34–35 (1973): 26.

87. Irarrázabal, "Las clases populares, evangelización, ¿como?," p. 7.

88. Thomas Sanders, "The Theology of Liberation: Christian Utopianism," *Christianity and Crisis* 33 (1973): 170.

89. Juan Hernández Pico, "The Experience of Nicaragua's Revolutionary Christians," in Sergio Torres and John Eagleson, eds., *The Challenge of Basic Christian Communities* (New York: Orbis, 1981), pp. 69, 70.

90. Gerhard Drekonja, "Religion and Social Change in Latin America," *Latin America Research Review* 6, no. 1 (Spring 1971): 63.

91. Weber, *Sociología de la religión*, p. 81.

92. Macaulay, "Ideological Change and Internal Cleavages," pp. 134–135.

93. Samuel Silva Gotay, "La transformación de la función política en el pensamiento teológico caribeño y latinoamericano," Centro de Investigaciones del Caribe y América Latina, Universidad Interamericana de Puerto Rico, Documentos de Trabajo, no. 7, 1983, p. 10.

94. James Michael Dodson, "Religious Innovation and the Politics of Argentina: A Study of the Movement of Priests for the Third World," Ph.D. Dissertation, University of Indiana, 1979, p. 119.

95. Klaiber, *Religión y revolución en el Perú: 1824–1976*, p. 205.

96. Silva Gotay, "La transformación de la función política," p. 10.

97. Romero de Iguíñiz, "Iglesia peruana: cambio y continuidad," pp. 21–25.

98. Irarrázabal, "Las clases populares, evangelización, ¿como?," p. 13.

99. *Páginas* no. 40 (1974): 3.

100. *Páginas* 3, no. 18 (1978): 7, 9.

101. Ibid., 8.

102. *Páginas* 4, no. 30 (1980): 4–5.

103. *Páginas* 3, no. 44 (1982): 4.

104. *Páginas* 9, no. 59 (1984): 6.

105. *Páginas* 5, no. 34 (1981): 8.

106. Poggi, *Catholic Action in Italy*, p. 96.

107. Maloney, "The Catholic Church and Peruvian Revolution," pp. 443–444.

108. *Crítica Marxista Leninista*, no. 4, (June 1972): 4.

109. *Crítica Marxista Leninista*, no. 7 (January 1974), original emphasis.

110. *Crítica Marxista Leninista*, no. 11 (September 1976).

111. *Crítica Marxista Leninista*, no. 5 (November 1972).

112. Romero and Tovar, "Cambios en la Iglesia peruana," Part II, p. 17.

113. Ibid., Part II, p. 15.

114. Dodson, "Prophetic Politics and Political Theory," p. 397.

115. Michael Dodson and T. S. Montgomery, "The Churches in the Nicaraguan Revolution," in Thomas W. Walker, ed., *Nicaragua in Revolution* (New York: Praeger, 1982).

116. Macaulay, "Ideological Change and Internal Cleavages," pp. 88–97.

117. McCurry, "Las misiones en Perú," p. 568.

118. Cardinal Juan Landázuri Ricketts, *Instrucción pastoral a todos los sacerdotes de la arquidócesis*, Lima, August 10, 1968, CIC.

119. Macaulay, "Ideological Change and Internal Cleavages," p. 101.

120. Ibid., pp. 132–133.

121. Jorge Basadre, "Para la historia de las ideas en el Perú: Un esquema histórico sobre el catolicismo ultramontano, liberal, social y el democratismo cristiano," *Scientia et Praxis* 11 (November 1976): 62.

122. Ricardo Durand Flórez, S.J., *Observaciones a teología de la liberación: La fuerza histórica de los pobres* (Callao, 1985), p. 14.

123. Eagleson, *Christians and Socialism*, p. 126.

124. Gustavo Gutiérrez, "Movimientos de liberación y teología," *Páginas*, no. 46 (1974): 8.

125. Gutiérrez, "The Irruption of the Poor," p. 123.

126. *Páginas* 2, no. 3 (1976): 11.

127. *Páginas* no. 6 (1972): 11–12.

128. *Páginas* 2, no. 1 (1976): 13.

129. Idígoras, "La Iglesia y el poder," p. 62.

130. Gutiérrez, "Notes for a Theology of Liberation," p. 251.

131. Ibid., p. 86.

132. Ibid., pp. 252–253.

133. Mainwaring, "The Catholic Youth Workers Movement," pp. 11–15.

134. Mooney, "The Role of the Church in Peruvian Political Development," pp. 55, 117, 173.

135. McCurry, "Las misiones en Perú," p. 595.

136. Klaiber, *Religión y revolución en el Perú: 1824–1976*, p. 222.

137. Vallier, "Radical Priests and the Revolution," p. 17.

138. Romero, "Cambios en la relación Iglesia-sociedad en el Perú: 1958–1978," p. 138.

139. Durand Flórez, *Observaciones a teología de la liberación*, p. 16.

140. Brian Smith, *The Church and Politics in Chile: Challenges to Modern Catholicism* (Princeton, N.J.: Princeton University Press, 1982), p. 27.

141. Romero de Iguíñiz, "Iglesia peruana: cambio y continuidad," pp. 10–11.
142. Levine, *Religion and Politics in Latin America*, p. 51.
143. Romero de Iguíñiz, "Iglesia peruana: cambio y continuidad," pp. 10–11.
144. Durand Flórez, *Observaciones a teología de la liberación*, p. 9.
145. Romero de Iguíñiz, "Iglesia peruana: cambio y continuidad," pp. 15, 2.

INDEX

Index

CELAM (cont.)
  Rio de Janeiro meeting (1955), 264,
    270
Center for Agrarian Education and
  Promotion (CEPA) (Nic.), 67
Center for Multiple Services (CSM),
  71, 98–99 n.15
Center for Social Studies and Popular
  Promotion (CESPROP) (El Salv.),
  106
Center for Studies and Publications
  (CEP) (Peru), 319, 320
Central America, 156, 260. See also
  countries by name.
Central American Common Market,
  65, 110
Central Única de Trabalhadores (CUT;
  Unified Workers Confederation),
  207
Centro Antonio Valdivieso (Nic.), 47,
  49
Centro de Estudios Religiosos (Nic.),
  50, 61 n.16
Cerezo, Vinicio, 147 n.72
Chamorro, Violetta, 77, 99 n.27
Charismatics (in Nic.), 99 n.23
Chávez y González, Msgr. Luis, 20,
  104, 112, 118–19, 120
Chile, 2, 23, 59, 141 n.3, 293–94, 306
  Catholic action movement, 278–
    79
  Christians for Socialism movement,
    302, 314
Christian communities (Peru), 260,
  262, 264–68, 274 n.12. See also
  CEBs.
Christian Democratic parties (Chris-
  tian Democracy), 23, 278
  El Salvador's PDC. See PDC (El
    Salv.).
  Peru's PDC, 255, 277, 278–79. See
    COPEI.
Christian Federation of Salvadoran
  Peasants. See FECCAS.
Christians for Socialism movement,
  36 n.14, 280
  in Chile, 302, 314, 315
"Church in Solidarity" (Peru), 318
Church of the Poor. See Progressive
  Church.

Church schools in Nicaragua, 53, 62
  n.27
Church-state conflict, 13
CIMI (Indians' Missionary Council),
  155, 165, 166
Civil rights violations under Somoza,
  43, 44
Class, 6, 160, 212, 255–307
Class struggle, 124, 125, 181–82, 212,
  282, 293, 318
Clergy (Clerics; Priests), 18, 24, 60–61
  n.5, 155, 158–59, 291, 311. See
  also Bishops.
  in Brazil, 162, 167–68, 213, 230; in-
    volvement in CEBs, 156, 160,
    197, 227, 231–35; shortage of,
    158, 227–28
  in El Salvador, 108, 112, 117, 126,
    128; deportation of, 120–21, 122,
    123, 145 n.41; murders of, 120,
    122, 123, 126, 127–28, 129–30,
    133–34, 145 n.40
  in Nicaragua, 52, 55, 64, 73, 91–97,
    99 n.32; in Contra war zones,
    89–90; expulsion by Sandinista
    government, 48, 85–86; as office-
    holders, 44, 46–47, 60–61 n.5; re-
    moval by hierarchy, 93, 101 n.75;
    responses to revolutionary pro-
    cess, 68–79; under Somoza, 65–
    66
  in Peru, 271, 277, 285, 289, 304,
    318, 321; alliance with the elite,
    284, 285; in Christian communi-
    ties, 265–66; foreigners as, 281,
    314; under military governments,
    287–90; in ONIS, 262, 272–73,
    280–82, 312–14; political activi-
    ties, 301, 306, 316–17; scarcity of,
    286
Clericalism as trait of radical Catholic
  style, 294–96, 297–98
CNBB (Brazilian National Conference
  of Bishops), 11, 18–19, 155, 172,
  213–14
  and CEBs, 160, 161–62, 164, 171–72
  "Christian Requirements for a Polit-
    ical Order," 198, 217, 220–21 n.7
  criticism of military regime, 161–62
  on the poor, 226–29